The New Farmers' Market 2nd Edition:

Farm-Fresh Ideas for Producers, Managers & Communities

Vance Corum, Marcie Rosenzweig & Eric Gibson

New World Publishing
Auburn, California

The New Farmers' Market 2nd Edition:

Farm-Fresh Ideas for Producers, Managers & Communities

by Vance Corum, Marcie Rosenzweig & Eric Gibson

Supported in part by USDA's Sustainable Agriculture Research & Education (SARE).

Publisher's Cataloging-in-Publication
(Provided by Quality Books, Inc.)

Corum, Vance.
    The new farmers' market : farm-fresh ideas for producers, managers & communities / by Vance Corum, Marcie Rosenzweig & Eric Gibson. -- 2nd edition.
      pages cm
      Includes index.
      ISBN 978-0-9632814-7-0

    1. Farmers' markets--United States. 2. Farm produce --United States--Marketing.   I. Rosenzweig, Marcie A. II. Gibson, Eric (Eric L.) III. Title.

New World Publishing; 11543 Quartz Dr. #1; Auburn, California 95602. www.tableoftheearth.com

Preface and Acknowledgements

It's been nearly 15 years since the first edition of *The New Farmers' Market* came out in 2001. While we are enormously grateful for the enthusiastic reception this book has received, it's time for an update. The number of farmers' markets in the USA has multiplied threefold since that time, and likewise growers and markets are steadily evolving in the ways they start, sell at, manage, organize and promote farmers' markets and local agriculture.

As you can see, this book's second edition has been revised and expanded throughout. Some topics – such as using social media to promote vendors and markets – have had significant expansion. Also, there's a new chapter which Vance feels is vital for market success: Chapter 11, Adding to the Product Mix. Another change to note is that some of the material in the first edition has been moved online (freely available), such as the resources and appendices.

It takes a village to raise a market. So, too, with a farmers' market book. We are tremendously grateful to the many growers, market managers and others who have shared their stories and wisdom with us over the years. Their contributions have enriched this book immensely. A special thanks also to Sustainable Agriculture Research & Education (SARE) for their ongoing support for this book as part of their work in maintaining and promoting sustainable agriculture in this country.

My personal gratitude as well goes to Vance and Marcie, with whom I helped write the first edition. This second edition is predominantly Vance's effort; I think the farmers' market industry is lucky to have someone so knowledgeable and passionate about farmers' markets to write a book like this. Enjoy!

– Eric Gibson, New World Publishing

Contents

Introduction

Farmers' markets reassert our faith in the importance of learning about crops and soil, recipes and toil – about farming, food and right livelihood. As the mission statement of The Land Institute in Kansas says, "When people, land and community are as one, all three prosper; when they relate not as members but as competing interests, all three are exploited."

Consumers have lost touch with those who grow their food as sadly as farmers have lost contact with those who eat their food. When a customer says, "You grow the best sweet corn I've ever tasted," she reconnects to historical food roots and inspires a renewed sense of pride in the farmer.

With liberalized trade agreements, the global farm is at our market door. The concentration of food retailers has led to contracts with the largest farms. Millions of farmers have been forced out of business and the rest are receiving a smaller share of the retail food dollar. Growers feeling the price squeeze are tempted by the lure of development money as farmland values vault skyward.

Meanwhile the consumer is consumed with price savings. In 1956 Americans spent 18.6% of household income on food. By 1997 they spent only 9.2% on food. The clear priorities are cheap food – an artifice of a petrochemical subsidy – and wasteful personal spending choices.

In 2011, Americans spent $478 billion on groceries. They spent $165 billion on unwanted snacks and meals, $117 billion on fast food, $96 billion on beer, $65 billion on soft drinks, $40 billion on lawn care, $17 billion on video games, $16 billion on chocolate, $11 billion on bottled water and $6 billion on speeding tickets. And over $160 billion on gambling and a similar amount on illegal drugs for recreational use.

We've succumbed to the get-rich-quick-with-no-real-work mentality and enjoying unhealthy vices. As a nation we are paying the consequences, enduring vast debt and debilitating health. We spend vast billions on pleasing our bodies, yet are unwilling to commit to a Food Quality Protection Act that would cost the average consumer $6-8 per year to care for our food and the environment.

Farmers have suffered economically and consumers nutritionally. America is becoming obese, and leading the world toward lives increasingly filled with diet-related disease.

Two changes are essential to a solution. Farmers must be passionately committed to practicing their craft and consumers must be prepared to pay a higher price for good food. The expansion of farmers' markets is a hopeful reflection of both parties' willingness. From 1,755 markets in 1994 and 2,863 markets in 2000, USDA has recorded an explosion of growth to 8,526 farmers' markets by August 2015.

The farmers' market renaissance over the last 45 years has revived a rich tradition of vibrant entrepreneurship as it enriches local food culture, bringing a farm and quality food consciousness into the minds of millions of people. Market founders are part of a long line of historically critical socializers and civilizers. Indeed, civilization comes from cities that sprang up from marketplaces.

Markets are at the heart of great cities and small towns. They are the birthplace of democracy and politics, if we consider ancient Greece. Democracy and economic freedom are connected to the encouragement of markets by government in certain times.

When markets were banned and destroyed, during the Roman Era and the Mercantile Era in Europe, the result was monopoly, inefficiency, loss of quality and a decline in the quality of life.

The decline has recycled in our era along with the shift from localized businesses to a corporate chain culture, leaving most economic activity in the hands of a few hundred major retailers. We have largely lost our regional cultures in favor of a homogenized experience.

While traveling from market to market throughout Europe years ago, I visited the small city of Bourg-en-Bresse, France. I was overwhelmed by hundreds of market stalls overflowing the central plaza. Unbridled competition filled my senses. Residents brought foraged mushrooms for inspection by an expert mycologist. Every sight proved that this Wednesday market was the community center for food health, food education and social interaction.

The scene is much the same in Turin, Italy, or Munich, Germany or Chengdu, China or Cuzco, Peru. A clear commitment to community food security is most visible in Barcelona, where for 175 years the municipality has built and operated public food markets, each an architectural marvel that complements a church as the central elements of community life. In both design and function, markets reflect a community's depth of economic, food and cultural roots.

Across America our communities seek similar life. Strangled by highways and malls, downtowns are attracting visitors with markets full of quality – produce, activities, musicians and relationships.

They reinforce old varieties that prioritize flavor over shipping integrity. These markets teach independence for vendors and buyers. They preserve a place where an individual's food choice can make a difference in one more small grower maintaining his share of the market and a place in the community. They give meaningful life to all. As Oxnard farmer Jim Tamai said to me years ago, "I started in farmers' markets for the cash, but I stayed for the people."

In his essay on Conserving Communities, Wendell Berry states that "no food economy can be, or ought to be, only local. But the orientation of agriculture to local needs, local possibilities, and local limits is simply indispensable to the health of both land and people, and undoubtedly to the health of democratic liberties as well."

It is our hope that the practices and programs shared in this book will give people the tools to strengthen local farms and establish a new model for food security as we build healthy community-based economies. We need to assess resources and incorporate our entire community in strengthening our farmers' markets.

It's been said: "Luck is when preparation meets opportunity." A Louisiana citrus grower finally came to the Crescent City Farmers' Market after repeated calls from the manager. Selling out within an hour, he called his wife to bring more fruit, "Oh my God, I've been doing it all wrong!" Planning with integrity and implementing with enthusiasm, we wish you luck in doing it right.

– Vance Corum, October, 2015

Getting Ready for Market 1

"Our marketing plan called for us to diversify markets, increase income and decrease risk. Farmers' markets were the most fun and we couldn't beat them for instant customer surveys."
– Marcie Rosenzweig, Full Circle Organic Farm, Auburn, CA

DO FARMERS' MARKETS FIT INTO YOUR MARKETING PLAN?

Are farmers' markets a viable outlet for your produce or value-added product? Who should consider selling at a farmers' market?

+ Small-acreage farmers and market gardeners who grow high-value, low-volume crops and need high per-acre returns.
+ Those tired of being price-takers in the wholesale distribution system who want to take on the additional responsibilities to become price-makers.
+ CSA (Community Supported Agriculture) farmers who wish to supplement their marketing while gaining visibility for their CSA operation.
+ A rural farm with an under-performing farmstand – or none at all – that wants to do outreach for their farm in a nearby town or more distant city.
+ Any grower who wants to test their product line and get quick customer input.
+ Farmers who need cash flow while awaiting payouts from other accounts.
+ Farmers with an unusual specialty crop that may get little notice in wholesale channels because it needs a personalized promotion effort.

+ Those with ready-to-eat ripeness that won't tolerate the delays and rough handling of the traditional marketing system.
+ Anyone who likes to grow fruits and vegetables, wishes to supplement his or her income, and enjoys meeting people.
+ Conventional farmers who need cash flow to keep their farms afloat.
+ Urban micro-farmers who want to feed their neighbors as part of the local food movement.

The start-up

"A farmers' market is the only business I know where you can show up with a case of produce and you're in business."
– Frank Beckwith, Beckwith Gardens, Yarmouth, ME

For new or small-acreage farmers with little access to established marketing channels or with small amounts of produce to sell, farmers' markets are a great way to get started in farming. As one farmer said, "All you need is a vehicle, a table and insurance."

Another grower said: "I recommend that all beginning farmers start at the farmers' markets. It takes years and years to develop the uniformity you need to sell to wholesalers."

Farmers' markets offer:

+ Minimal marketing start-up costs – vehicle, canopy, table, sign, scale and cashbox;

- Exemption from standard size and pack regulations (at most markets);
- Little or no packaging, advertising and promotion costs – many farmers' markets are well established and centrally located;
- Better prices – substantially higher than wholesale;
- Immediate, direct feedback – customers are the best people to tell you about price, quality, variety preferences, and ideas for other crops to plant.

Farmers' markets are an instant market and they save the overhead of opening a retail outlet with on-farm buildings and high-cost liability insurance. While it's best to carry liability insurance for farmers' market participation, it's usually less than for an on-farm market.

Advertising and other marketing costs are generally borne by the market rather than by individual growers as are the costs of providing site amenities like parking and restrooms. Farmers should still use their marketing skills to present their own space in an attractive manner. The market sponsor usually works through local regulations and restrictions – zoning, health department, business license and site insurance – which take considerable time and effort comparable to those for a roadside stand.

The small-acreage farmer

Small volume and lack of uniformity often preclude wholesale trade for the small grower. While maintaining crop quality, small growers can market crops "field run" – picked directly into boxes to avoid further handling damage from repacking. Almost anyone with a little land and the ability to grow quality crops can sell through farmers' markets.

Carole Laity of Your Kitchen Garden did constant upkeep to her small display baskets as people followed instructions to "Taste the tomatoes!" at the Portland FM, OR.

Advantages of Selling at a Farmers' Market

Profits!

By eliminating or taking over mid-level marketing activities such as transportation, brokerage and handling, growers get better-than-wholesale prices by selling direct at farmers' markets. They also save money bypassing the standard containers, packing and labeling needed for wholesale accounts.

Jay Visser of J-N-A Produce near Manhattan, MT grows six acres of market vegetables, herbs and bedding plants. He usually takes in about $1,500 each day at the Bozeman Farmers' Market while also selling to restaurants, a few chain stores, one independent supermarket and a restaurant distributor. For Visser, the main advantage of the farmers' markets is price. One quarter of the farm's production is sold through farmers' market but it accounts for half the farm's gross income. Not surprisingly, Visser says, "We try to sell as much as we can at the farmers' market!"

One 80-acre California raisin grower found that he made more than 90% of his farm profit from just 5% of his crop, selling just four acres of grapes fresh while drying the rest for his raisin buyer.

Cash flow

Another advantage of farmers' markets is ready cash. As one grower said: "You get the highest dollar for your produce, often higher than grocery stores, and you get it today, not in 30 or 90 days." Immediate payment is especially helpful for small or startup growers whose capital is limited.

How much money are growers actually bringing home from markets? It depends on the farmer and the market. Many major city markets have vendor sales above $1,000 per market day on average, but that may mean $200 for one farmer and thirty times that for another. The average is often lower with new markets. For instance, the Austin Farmers' Market downtown had average farmer sales of $329 in 2004, its second year, which doubled to $679 in its tenth year.

The Neighborhood Farmers Market Alliance in Seattle had average vendor sales of $1,142 per market day at its University District market in 2012, its 20th season, while its other six newer markets averaged between $575 and $830. Their best market also averaged 58 vendors per day, well above the 23 to 38 vendor averages of its cousins. Larger markets with more vendors, variety and competition tend to attract larger crowds that generate higher sales.

Even relatively smaller markets can provide substantial income for an individual vendor who has just the right product mix. Since the largest markets often have lengthy waiting lists, a good grower need not be disappointed, but rather try selling at a modest local market. Build a reputation and put yourself in good standing for stronger markets in the future.

Colorado micro-farmers can gross $10,000-15,000/acre yearly, while some larger acreage producers (10-200 ac.) easily gross $2,000-5,000/market day. "It helps if you have a greenhouse to extend seasons or develop specific niches such as growing unique bedding plants, hanging baskets of flowers, or heirloom tomatoes," says Chris Burke. Tunnels or hoop houses can do the same with less investment.

Many farms across the country plan crops that will make $20,000 per acre at markets. Paul and Sandy Arnold of Pleasant Valley Farm in upstate NY live by that rule. Clover Creek Family Farms in Upper Lake, CA downsized from two acres of vegetables grossing $33,000 to less than one-half acre grossing $15,000. In the process of nearly doubling their gross sales per acre, they also nearly maintained the same profit. Their main goal was to eliminate hired labor to do it themselves, and free up time for off-farm jobs and vacations.

© Vance Corum

Capay Organic was a successful small organic farm when it started Farm Fresh To You. Three sons now farm 600 acres, selling through farmers' markets, wholesalers, restaurants, food service and America's largest CSA.

Advertise other outlets

Make every customer aware of other avenues for buying your products, whether it's a farmstand, CSA, local stores, restaurants or your website.

Doug Cross of Canter-Berry Farm, Auburn, WA, noted, "You get a crowd at the farmers' markets. Instead of 100 people a day coming by your roadside stand, there may be thousands coming by at the larger farmers' markets. We do a robust amount of business with 10,000 people on our mailing list for our pick-your-own, and most of our customers originated at the farmers' markets."

CSA farmers also do everything from marketing their concept to box delivery at the farmers' markets, often allowing customers to switch out a given product for something else at their farmers' market stand that day.

Sheldon and Carole Laity of Your Kitchen Garden in Canby, OR, began farming in 1991 just as the Portland Farmers Market opened. With a small crowd of 1,000 customers in the early years, they found restaurants keenly interested in their beyond organic produce. When their restaurant and retail sales supported their farm sufficiently, they discontinued the market, long before it moved and expanded to its current size and national reputation.

Customer feedback and test marketing

Customers can provide valuable feedback on new or old varieties, marketing ideas, packaging suggestions and immediate response to new products. Use the market as your research center; it's far cheaper than paying an agency to do a focus group. Start a conversation with an open mind. Ask about how they prepare something they are buying, or ask whether they have tried particular items, even if you're not growing them yet.

By giving unusual items a try at the markets, growers get in on the ground floor of coming trends. They create the latest produce trends as supermarkets incorporate products that are hot in the farmers' markets. Talk about your product, provide samples, share growing and cooking tips, tell your farm story – these are great ways to educate customers about new products, increase demand for unusual or high-quality items and build customer loyalty.

Watch and replicate the actions of other effective marketers. Check their websites as well. The header for www.missionarychocolates.com shows "Rx Missionary Chocolates, the prescription for your chocolate addiction." Make people smile.

According to Karen Durham, former manager of the Bellingham Farmers' Market, WA, "One grower used the market to test-market unusual, designer potatoes. He came in with gold and blue potatoes, and worked with the chef in the market to develop potato recipes. He also worked with the customers: 'Would you like to try this?' He asked them if they would buy them in the market and he kept records of their responses. Then he went to the wholesalers and told them: 'I think you can sell these in the supermarkets.'"

Farmers' markets allow you to talk with and educate people about your farm and your growing techniques. You get to pitch your product face-to-face with the buyer. One Southern California farmer was considering pulling out his exotic chocolate fuyu persimmon trees. When he tried selling them at the Santa Monica Farmers' Market, 80% of those who tried his samples bought a bag! Instead of ten flats a week on the Los Angeles wholesale market, he was moving a full truckload because of direct personal contact and aggressive sampling.

Farmers selling both wholesale and at farmers' markets, in fact, often find that new or exotic varieties sell well for them at the market. By test-marketing new products such as madarinquot, Indian eggplant, tatsoi or baby bok choy at the farmers' market, farmers have convinced consumers to add new items to their diet and larger buyers to try them in wholesale channels.

Personal satisfaction and social contact

Farmers' markets are fun! You enjoy talking to people about your products, production practices and even challenges. Growers who are used to wholesalers talking down their product in order to pay lower prices are especially grateful for the positive feedback they get from customers who enjoy their produce. As Sue McEvoy, Sue Mac Farm & Herbary in Washington, NJ, says, "I enjoy the people – this is necessary if you want to go to farmers' markets. Customers have known us for years, and we exchange Christmas cards and notes."

Many markets also report a special camaraderie among market vendors. Valerie Schooler, ex-manager of the Wenatchee Farmers' Market, WA: "We have a friendly bunch of guys here at the market. They work their butts off during the week and this is their social outing."

> "I enjoy getting off the farm. The farmers' markets keep me in touch and I don't feel so farmbound. Going to the farmers' market is like a one-day vacation both socially and physically!"
> – Gretchen Hoyt, Alm Hill Gardens, Everson, WA

Farmers' markets are also a great family activity. According to Paul Nelson, Untiedt's Vegetable, Waverly, MN: "The farmers' markets help keep our family together. Each family member has their own job at markets and the kids help out. Our grandparents sell with us on the weekends and it's a family get-together. We all grew up in the business. It teaches good family values and lets the kids learn to deal with people."

Farm continuity

Because farmers' markets are enabling farmers to achieve sustainability, a new generation of youth are taking over their family operations. Probably nothing is more satisfying than being able to hand over the reins of marketing to your kids – for you and them. It is the ultimate proof of worth when kids return – often after college or work sojourns at other farms or businesses. All the parents' work in building the farm is validated when young people recognize the ready-made successful business they can take over, and parents give them the authority to take it in new directions.

Laura Unger literally grew up on her family's farm – prepping for market, folding berry flats and doing market day set-up and sales. At 16, she began to manage their booth at five farmers' markets, make store deliveries and help mom Kathy in the office. A year away working in downtown Portland convinced her how much she liked the farm. In 2010 Laura at 23 took the reins over six employees for their new road-side stand, and 25 other employees for the 14 farmers' markets where they sell most of the family's 140 acres of berries and vegetables. In 2014 her brother Will returned to the farm to help dad Matt.

> "Mom and I do so much together. We're in on every hire and fire. I'm still her child, so it's difficult getting my voice heard. But we all respect each other, and Will and I bring new ideas. We started a 14-week Berry Box CSA, then a vegetable CSA, no-bake chocolate-covered strawberry mini-pies, and a newsletter and Farmer's Daughter blog to educate our customers. I've revamped the website to build traffic, and social media is becoming our main form of advertising. I do a Facebook post at least once a week (if not daily), Twitter, the newsletter monthly, Instagram three times a week and we're on SoilMate."
>
> – Laura Unger, Unger Farms, Cornelius, OR

Will has implemented new production increases, built high tunnels to extend their berry season and added 45 acres of berries including acreage specifically for New Seasons, a 15-store Portland food retailer.

With siblings Will and Laura positioned to take over in a couple years, parents Matt and Kathy couldn't be more proud, and the community couldn't be happier. In late 2014 these farm transition developments were recognized when they were awarded the Excellence in Family Business Award by the Oregon State University's Austin Family Business Program.

Disadvantages of Selling at a Farmers' Market

Limited sales volume

While farmers' markets may have many people coming through them, the farmer must be involved personally in each sale. These are one-to-one sales ratios rather than one-to-many. You'll spend greater time dealing with people and a higher proportion of time marketing for the volume achieved versus traditional methods of moving your product. Since produce is highly perishable and must be marketed quickly, farmers' market sales may be insufficient to absorb all of your production, and other marketing outlets may be necessary. Farmers' markets are most profitable for small volume, high-value crops.

Nevertheless, mid-sized farms have countered this limitation with family members or employees handling multiple farmers' markets. This is a good strategy if a grower prefers to concentrate on production rather than small, individual sales to the ultimate consumer. Honesty and trust are essential since large amounts of cash as well as the farm's reputation are at stake.

Time involved

Be prepared for long hours spent in loading, traveling to the market, setting up, unloading, and the reverse at the end of the day. A typical 4-hour market just 30 minutes away from the farm can easily take eight or more hours out of the day. All these hours and the value of your time should be taken into account when deciding whether a farmers' market is profitable for your farm.

Sue McEvoy picks on Friday for Saturday market. The produce goes into a big walk-in cooler and gets loaded in the truck at 5 a.m. for the market's opening at 9 a.m. The couple is home by 2:30 p.m. on Saturday and pick till 8 or 9 p.m. for the Sunday market. "We're often prepping and bunching cut-flowers in the dark," Sue says. "Then it's up at 5 a.m. for market and we're home Sunday by 4 p.m. And that's IT for Sunday night!"

For Gretchen Hoyt, a day in the life of a farmers' market seller is also not easy. She's up at 4 a.m., driving two hours to a Seattle farmers' market and making it pay double by delivering to two grocery stores en route.

Market access and free market competition

Every market has their own standards for how many sellers may sell a given product. Smaller markets tend to protect their vendors by only allowing one bee-keeper, one corn grower, etc. Unintentionally, this may limit their potential for growth because customers want choice. Farmers need to think of what products they can grow to fill an empty product niche, and then prove themselves valuable by serving a new crowd of customers.

You might start with some value-added products, specialty greens, mushrooms or heirloom peppers. If the manager says you're competing, point out that you have a chocolate pepper or a bi-color corn that no other farmer sells.

Larger markets may allow every valid farmer to participate, and there may be a dozen strawberry or tomato growers. This can be intimidating for a new farmer trying to gain a foothold with consumers. Try some innovative marketing ideas that no one else is using – your own unique blend of prices, samples, canopy, multi-tier display, daily specials, signage and service.

Much like New Seasons Market in Portland, OR touts themselves as "the friendliest store in town," you can be the friendliest vendor in your market, without saying so on your sign.

Special considerations

There may be waste unless you have secondary markets lined up. Cold, rainy days or even bright, sunny days may keep customers away. Marketing through farmers' markets is a seasonal business with fluctuations in labor requirements and cash flow.

Any individual market may have space or product limitations, irritating rules, bureaucratic policies and internal and/or external politics to contend with.

Special costs involved in farmers' markets include vehicle, travel, employees, display, canopy, your business sign, and liability insurance and health permit, if required.

A different skill set

Retailing skills. At farmers' markets the farmer becomes a retailer and needs to know about merchandising, display, quality control, pricing, packaging and so on.

People skills. Dealing with customers requires a friendly, outgoing personality, patience and product knowledge. You need to enjoy being around people and be okay working long hours, generally on weekends. If what you really enjoy about farming is the quiet solitude of growing your crop, selling at farmers' markets prob-

Three kids of Waterwheel Gardens in Emmett, ID represent the future, another generation of local growing who affirm their parents' farming passion.

Lady-Lane Farm caters to glass-loving milk drinkers in Oregon. You won't forget their name, with a 1' x 10' banner on the canopy front and a 3' x 6' backdrop.

ably won't work for you unless you find a marketer for your team.

Daily sales will likely reflect the person you send to market. An employee more interested in making cell calls or text messaging than serving customers should be let go quickly.

Production planning and management skills. Can you coordinate production with marketing? Estimating how much to pick for market takes planning and finesse. It helps to watch the blips caused by holidays.

If two people are part of your operation – one focused on production and the other on marketing – the marketer should be telling the producer what changes need to be made each season. Listening to the consumer is key in determining how a farm changes over time. This can be particularly challenging when the producer is an older sibling or parent of the marketer, especially when the decision involves grafting over trees to new varieties that have come into vogue.

Unless you have an impressive amount of a highly sought-after crop, like a truckload of sweet corn or specialty melons, you should have a variety of produce to sell and sufficient quantity to make the stall look full. The perception of choice and bounty are important; few customers will stop if there is limited volume of each product. This is true for the last customers at the market, just as with the early-birds. If you want to sell out every day, you won't have enough product to continue building the customer base along with all the other vendors in your market.

To optimize your investment of time and energy in the farmers' market, you'll want to be in the market as much of the season as possible. Learn and use season extension techniques like succession plantings of early and late season varieties. Use row crop covers, tunnels, greenhouses or cold frames and shade cloth to grow beyond the weather. Investigate short-season varieties for planting on either side of your main crop. Use timelines to plan when to plant so you don't have weeks in the middle of the market when you have nothing to sell. Customers are creatures of habit. If you help them break their habit of coming to you by not being in the market, you'll spend three times the energy getting them back.

However, even if you have a short-season crop – just three weeks of berries or 10 days of a special peach – you can still build a reputation. Ask the market manager to put out a sign or send a notice to the market e-mail list announcing boysenberries, donut peaches, fava beans or Brussels sprouts coming next week. Then reinforce with your customers that you only have two weeks at the market so that they make the impulse decision.

CHECKING OUT THE MARKETS

"Look at what the market will bear before you even grow the product."
– Gretchen Hoyt, Alm Hill Gardens, Everson, WA

The first question to ask about a new crop or product is: "Is there a market?" Ideally, as part of your business plan, you'll research all marketing possibilities before you put any seed in the ground. If you're already in business and looking to diversify your marketing outlets, your research is more product-specific. In either case, you're trying to identify the market, in the broad sense, for your product. Simply defined, a "market" is a group of people who are, or will be, your customers.

As you check out farmers' markets, look for whether your potential customers are there and whether they're already getting the product and service you want to provide. If your product is mainstream, are there mainstream shoppers in that market? If your product is up-scale or trendy, are those shoppers in the market? If you have or can generate volume to keep your prices low, are there price-conscious customers in the market?

Start with farmers' markets in your immediate area. To find them ask your county extension agent. Statewide listings may be available from your state department of agriculture, and some websites are maintained by industry groups, like the Washington State Farmers Market Association, and the Farmers Market Federation of New York at:

www.wafarmersmarkets.com

www.nyfarmersmarket.com

The USDA also has a website which allows you to click on the state of your choice:

http://search.ams.usda.gov/farmersmarkets

There are a growing number of websites nationally – and others more regionally – that promote farms and farmers' markets, including:

www.localharvest.org

www.soilmate.com

Size, seasonality & location

Each market is unique and there can be a big difference in the ambiance. Some markets are large, structured and more competitive. Others are small, loosely confederated and more laid back. Find the market that feels most comfortable to you and caters to your customer base.

Larger, more established markets often fill as early as October of the previous year, or have a waiting list. Smaller markets may not have any requirements at all. Either way, contact the manager in advance to learn the ground rules.

Many markets operate from May to October while others have a shorter season. An increasing number – over 12% – are year-round. By and large the earlier in the season you can start at market, the sooner you'll build a loyal clientele to carry you through the season. However, if the market does a "soft" opening without much fanfare, you may be wise to wait for their summer publicity campaign.

Other criteria necessary for a good market are a good location with sufficient customer parking and adequate population density nearby. Poorly located markets attract fewer consumers. While adequate density may be difficult to achieve in a small town, if done right the market may be the community's key social gathering spot.

Visit the markets

The best way to get to know a farmers' market is to shop it, talk with vendors and listen to patrons. Are shoppers enjoying the experience, meeting and greeting friends and still buying produce? Do they mutter about prices as they leave? Are vendors generally happy, greeting customers like old friends? Are they in their stalls selling or in their neighbor's stall complaining about the market or its management?

Go at different times of the season and the market day to get a feel for the market as a totality. Is this market a going proposition in the early season but a dud when other near-by markets open? Conversely, does this market pick up in the fall as other, shorter season markets close? Spend enough time to get a feel for the volume that growers are moving. Check the prices. Can you be competitive and still make a profit?

Is it a market with 500 customers or 5,000? Find out if the manager does regular or periodic customer counts. If s/he doesn't, make an estimate yourself with vendors' help. Noting the vendor count helps – a market with 10 vendors isn't likely to have as many as

Hot Products: Fresh and Value-Added

Fresh products

"Tree- or vine-ripened is the reason people come to the markets."

"Fresh-from-the-farm, inseason, mainstay fruits and vegetables."

"The strongest items consistently are 'early' sweet corn, cuc's, zucchini, tomatoes, peppers and melons."

"Staples are still the big item here. Specialties are just starting to emerge. Our market traditionally serves older customers – it's really a 'beans and 'taters' audience."

Specialty items not found in supermarkets.

"Anything unusual sells here."

"We offer eight different varieties of cherries here, not just a Bing!"

"Growing different varieties of sweet and hot peppers is a great niche, since they are an important ingredient in salsa, an expanding product line."

Heirloom varieties

"'Old' is 'in.' Old fashioned, heirloom varieties of roses, for example, like your grandmother grew. We have one grower who grows over 80 varieties of roses, with their names all on labels. We have other rose growers in the market, but there's always people in line for hers. Most of the other roses are bred for long stems and visual appearance, not smell. The old heirlooms look fantastic, and they also smell great."
– Mark Sheridan, Mgr., Santa Barbara FM, CA

"Some of the old apple varieties, like Winesap, Arkansas Black or Northern Spy that you won't find in the supermarkets."

Salad mix

"The mesclun craze just doesn't seem to bottom out. The more farmers are getting into it, the more customers, and each farmer seems to have a different mix with each one tasting different."

"One interesting variation on mesclun mixes is a farmer here selling mixed bunches of vegetables, rainbow mixes of radishes or chiogga beets."

"Due to the competition, we give our mixes names and we offer different 'flavors' with different ingredients."

"My salad mix has large leaves instead of baby leaves and I can sell my product for 50 percent cheaper. I found a niche of people willing to pay $3 a pound for salad mix instead of $6 a pound."

"We sell head lettuce with roots on (washed) as 'live.'"

Herbs

Herbs are a great niche item that also work in saches, pestos and herbal vinegars.

Ethnic

"It's a combination of more ethnic buyers coming to the market and other people liking the ethnic foods."

Organic items

"There's a trend toward organic here (New York) at the markets. People are still shopping primarily for price on the East Coast, though, and only a certain percentage of people will pay extra for organics."

"The consumers are more educated now. People are starting to take care of themselves a lot better and they're searching for organic."

Fresh flowers

"There's a lot of competition in the market for flowers. You have to stay ahead of the competition. This means reading a lot of flower and gardening magazines and being a member of the Association of Specialty Cut Flower Growers."

Also mentioned:

Products for canning, vegetable seedlings, bedding plants, maple syrup, nuts, baby vegetables and greenhouse tomatoes.

"We sell compost, which we make from leaves and grass clippings (green waste) from the city of Boulder, and sell it in 40 pound bags at the market to home gardeners. Another good draw is our tomato plants. We

grow 20 different varieties, which are purchased by home gardeners to plant themselves. With each plant, we hand out an information sheet on how to grow tomatoes."
– John Ellis, Farmer John's, Boulder, CO

Value-added products

"Garlic sells for $1 a bunch, but sell it with dried herb flowers and two cayenne peppers and it sells for $10 a bunch!"

"Make your product attractive! Dress up your product by tying it with ribbon, or bundling different items together. If you are selling items in jars, cover the lid with a small circle of fabric, etc."

"Value-added is little more work out on the farm but gets premium prices. A few years ago you could bring sunflowers and sell them, but now they have to be put in with other flowers in an arrangement. You can't just bring things, put them on the table and expect them to sell. It takes a better job of presentation."

"The market for dehydrated vegetables is really taking off. The 'country kitchen' look is really in. The key is to use down home, pretty packaging."

"Items for fast preparation. People are uneducated in cooking and in prepping food or produce."

Gingham-covered jams may suffice in some areas, but more and more people expect a sophisticated look, especially in urban markets.

Some of the many value-added items growers are selling in farmers' markets are:

- Baby food (organic)
- Bakery items – bagels, bread, cookies, cupcakes, scones, fruit cobblers, apple dumplings, fruit pies, fresh tortillas
- Baskets – fruit, jam, salsa, gift mix
- Braids – garlic, pepper, flower
- Canned items – roasted garlic, vegetables
- Corn shocks
- Crafts
- Cultivated mushrooms – buttons, crimini, enoki, morel, oyster, shiitake
- Dog biscuits (vegetarian)
- Dried beans – cranberry, fava, hominy kernels, posole (corn soaked in lime and dried) from colored corn
- Dried fruit – peach to persimmon, fruit squares
- Dried vegetables – mushrooms, tomatoes
- Flowers – cut flower arrangements, dried flowers
- Gourds
- Greenhouse items
- Grains and flours – stone ground corn, emmer, flax, wheat, pancake mix
- Herbal products – braids, crafts, lotions, balms, soaps, oils, teas, bath herbs, dried herbs, lip gloss, salve, massage oils
- Hickory chips
- Honey – flavored, from avocado to sourwood
- Jams, jellies and preserves – low- and no-sugar, cactus apple, fig, rhubarb
- Juices – apple, berry, carrot, pomegranate
- Lettuce – mixed 6-pack veggie starts
- Marinated fruits and vegetables and syrups (wild cherry)
- Molasses
- Nursery stock
- Nuts – salted, flavored
- Oils – almond, camelina, jojoba, olive, walnut, organic
- Pastas
- Pesto – all kinds
- Pickled items – kimchi, sauerkraut, vegetables
- Popcorn
- Potpourri
- Prepared foods – pizza relish, onion rhubarb salsa, tomato sauce, salsa verde mix with tomatillos, onion, garlic, chilies, cilantro
- Roasted peppers – on-site roasting
- Soaps – generally handmade
- Spices
- "Squirrel corn" (field corn put in packages with a feeder stand)
- Vinegars – gourmet, and special ingredients like meyer lemon, habanero pepper, pomegranate, cherry, berry or edible flowers
- Wild craft – fiddlehead ferns, huckleberries, seaweeds, etc.
- Wild mushrooms – chanterelle, hedgehog, lobster, matsutake, morel, truffles ❧

1,000 customers nor is a market with 60 vendors likely to have that few.

How well you do depends on the market's overall volume and the need for your product. Are many other growers offering the same product or variety as you have? You may do well by going to a small market where you have a relative monopoly. Yet at strong volume markets, you may do even better with six or seven competitors. Play the numbers game and go to a very large market if you have a specialty product unfamiliar to most consumers.

As you study the market's clientele, ask if they are right for your products? It may be worth traveling to a market farther away to maintain a premium price.

Does the market fit your schedule?

Consider whether the market's days and hours of operation meet your work schedule. Some farmers double up markets on a single day, dropping an employee with product at a second market and picking them up later in the day.

Look at whether the market attracts a food-buying crowd or is more of a festival market with crafts, pony rides, etc. which may distract customers from the fresh food focus. Evaluate your potential sales realistically – do you want sure sales from a smaller food crowd or lower profitability from a larger festival crowd? If you have a properly packaged value-added product, like flavored nuts, you may want to seek out the festival market much like your county fair.

According to Mary Lou Weiss, former manager of the farmers' market in Torrance, CA, the Tuesday market caters to seniors and mothers with strollers, and vendors average about $500. The Saturday market is a "family day," and vendors' sales average about $900. Both days are viable for those farmers.

Other things to look for. Remember that customers want quality, freshness, variety, restrooms, and easy parking. Also evaluate services

The Oregonian provides sponsorship through in-kind advertising for this festival promotion.

offered to vendors, such as stall size, shelter, restrooms, electricity and water for drinking or washing produce. Are these available at the market you're considering?

Market promotion

Is the market well promoted? Does the market attract enough customers? Are advertising and promotion controlled by the market?

Does the market's advertising and promotion timing coincide with the availability of your products? Look for signs of active promotion, like prominent signs and banners, flyers placed on windshields or posters on store windows. You may not want to waste your time and resources in a market that's not actively promoted.

Does the market have an event schedule? Does it host comparison tastings for tomatoes, potatoes, cheese or your product? You might donate product for a chef demo or cooking competition. [See other ideas in "Promoting the Market" chapter.]

Does the market allow sampling. Samples increase sales! Find what's necessary to do sampling, i.e., can you prepare greens at the table or do you need to have a food handler's permit? Must samples be cut in a certified kitchen and then covered at the market?

Does the market have EBT capability (Electronic Benefit Transfer) to accept SNAP (Supplemental

A recipe and literature table including promotional items for fundraising is one healthy sign of a well-run market.

Nutrition Assistance Program) debit cards, formerly known as food stamps? This helps increase sales, and it's essential in markets serving lower-income communities. Does the market have an ATM machine to process credit and debit cards?

Once you've narrowed down the choice to markets that fit the bill in terms of size, clientele, ambiance, timing and promotion, take a look at some of the less obvious qualifiers.

Market rules & regulations

Rules and regulations vary from state to state, and local rules may vary market to market, so check with the market manager before you apply to sell. There may be requirements for using only certified scales, labeling, sales tax reporting, vehicle permits, and provisions for SNAP and the Farmers Market Nutrition Program. Some markets prohibit processed foods. You may also need a health permit from each county in which you sell your product.

Check the market website first or request a written copy of the market rules and regulations from the manager to learn if they correspond with your plans. Make sure you can comply with them and that the market serves your needs.

Find out how much it will cost you – stall fees, association membership, promotion fees and insurance. Most markets charge a fee to participate; if they don't, that may be an indicator that there is little value to the market.

Fees may be collected daily, weekly, monthly or seasonally. The most common are space or percent based, usually about 5-10%. Markets tracking sales volume usually require that the vendor provide a "load list" for each day of sales. This list tracks what's brought into the market and what's taken back to the farm; fees may be calculated on sales per the load list.

What you are permitted to sell can vary based on the organization's rules. Some market rules define precisely how many people can sell particular products. Some define the geographic area, like a county or 75-mile radius. Other unstructured markets may require that you simply show up on Saturday morning.

Can you abide by a strict "farmer-grown" policy? Some markets require that you grow everything you sell. Other markets allow you to sell items from other growers or even out of state.

Look for a market that guarantees you the same stall site for the season rather than assigning stalls on a first-come, first-serve basis. Selling from the same spot every week helps develop loyal, repeat customers. As one grower said: "If I get there late and am down two spots, my regular customers think I'm not there." By the same token, make sure that the same person – family or employee – is selling for you and that their clothing, hat, signs and vehicle have a consistent look.

However, if you only want to sell for a short period, a full-season stall works against you and the market. Also, a manager may test a new spot for you to gain new customers.

Insurance. Check to see if you need to carry individual insurance for accidents at the market or for food product liability. Farmers' markets usually have insurance but it may not cover individual sellers. You can probably add a rider to your existing home or farm policy. [See Appendix]

Market organization

Is the market well-organized and professionally run? Have you seen or heard publicity about it? Are they open about finances, rules and problems? Is the market sponsored by an active, supportive farmers' market association including farmers and community mem-

Santa Barbara Pistachio has diversity with a crop by marketing many flavors of pistachios, in-shell and shelled. The vertical sign helps catch the eyes of customers at a distance.

bers or is it the work of one individual? Does it have a good website, promoting the vendors?

Can you reach the manager or organizer by cell phone or only during office hours? Does s/he live in or near the community? Does s/he know the area well enough to explain the ethnic and income mix of shoppers at the market? Does the manager/organizer admit to mistakes, or does s/he always say "not to worry" or "no problem" when asked specific, tough questions?

Do the organizers or manager have a positive community reputation or track record? Is the market working with other markets, especially regarding choice of day and hours; i.e., are the sponsors concerned about markets in general, not just theirs?

Becoming a Seller

Now that you've chosen a market, the first step is procuring a space before the season actually begins. Some established markets have waiting lists or on-farm inspections that must be done before you can sell. It is important not to plant until you know exactly where and how you will be selling. Know your markets first!

Ask the market manager if there's room for another grower and for your type of product. Show interest in meeting specific product needs of the market, especially if it looks like too much competition will keep you out.

What if there's a waiting list? Define your niche. If you are trying to get into a highly competitive market, set yourself apart – braid your garlic, make your basil into pesto, tie your colorful peppers into ristras or coronas (strings or crowns), or offer buttered sweet corn on the stick – as well as selling it as a fresh vegetable. Adding value to your product tells the manager that you know how to capture a different market segment that wants more than raw produce. You can also distinguish yourself by pricing differently than others.

The fundamentals of selling at market are pretty straightforward, but nuances can take years to learn. It is important for growers to select markets wisely.

If your farm or crop is quite small, consider alternatives. Could you consign your produce to a regular participant if market regulations permit that? Or sell through a market-operated stand that takes a commission, such as in Eugene, OR? Would you share a stall with another small-acreage grower?

Keep records. If you're going to 12 markets, but 85% of your income comes from eight of those, cut the bottom four! You'll do a better job and profit just as much. Don't forget the time and costs involved in traveling to a more distant market. Your prices there should reflect your greater costs. [See the chapter, "Running Your Farmers' Market Business."]

CHOOSING CROPS & PRODUCTS FOR FARMERS' MARKETS

Diversity vs. specialization

"I see at least two models for farmers' markets here: one for the large cities, where the small acreage producer can bring lots of different things to a varied market. Truck gardens can work in a large city market. In small town mid-America, however, it's hard to introduce new products like organic, or specialty fruits and vegetables. Bok choy or Swiss chard just sit there. Corn, lettuce, tomatoes, green beans and melons are the big tickets. Find out if the consumer demand is there in your particular market before committing yourself!"

– Charlie Springer, Mgr, Richmond FM, IN

Phil Smith of Westwind Gardens built this chili roaster for the 1998 Salsa Festival in Beaverton and used it to increase pepper sales at several Oregon markets. Roasted peppers are Phil's niche.

Should you specialize, or offer a wide choice of products? It depends on the market, your growing inclinations and your profit goals.

In a small rural market, you may want to offer one-stop shopping with a wide array of familiar produce. In larger, more competitive markets, you might specialize in fewer but higher value items like honey or berries. If you have only a few items, create diversity with a line of products. An almond grower might offer raw, roasted, smoked, blanched and slivered almonds, almond butter and almond oil in a variety of packages and sizes.

A kiwi grower might add the grape-size hardy kiwi, that may appeal to kids as snack food or adults as a light dessert. A peach grower will consistently test new peach varieties, and may add several varieties of dried peaches to boost her offerings in the late season when customers might be looking at snacks for hiking, skiing or ice fishing.

> "Consider the convenience of customers. We take a big variety of vegetables to market. Some people say they don't have to go anywhere else because they can get everything from me."
> – Eydie Ridder, Baraboo FM, WI

Having familiar traditional produce encourages one-stop shopping, but what differentiates your stall from the supermarket besides your pricing? Offer products supermarkets can't handle: in-season, tree- or vine-ripened, fresh-picked and organic. Bring at least one very unusual item. People will stop and ask: "What is it? How do you cook it?"

> "The key to farmers' market success is to offer both diversity and 'something special.' If you can establish a following by offering something special such as certified organic, you can develop a loyal clientele. If you sell lettuce that no one else does, your lettuce buyers will also buy your tomatoes. We offer 15-20 different items at the market at the height of the season, and several varieties of each item."
> – Lisa Bloodnick, Bloodnick Family Farm, Apalachin, NY

Carry a few colorful impulse items like cut flowers, herbs, or a specialty produce item. These attract people to your stand, and having something new each week encourages repeat visits by your "regulars." Don't try so many items that you only bring a little of each.

Avoid local crops in a glutted market; it's like "carrying coals to Newcastle" or selling ice to Eskimos. You're likely to have lots of competition selling strawberries or artichokes in Watsonville, CA or corn in Iowa. If you decide to join the fray, make sure you're ready with a spectacular display, quality, price and identity that set you apart from the rest.

Make your niche

> "I plant a couple rows of something new each year. Taste and appearance are what sells at the market, and farmers' market varieties are often completely different varieties of the same crop than you would sell on the wholesale market."
> – John Paul Barbagelata, Barbagelata Farms, Linden, CA

Successful farmers' market growers participate consistently, have a diverse mix of products within their stall that contribute to the overall product mix in the market, and have sufficient supplies throughout the season or year. Trends in farmers' markets are toward product diversification, unusual or organic products, and value-added items that can increase profit margins.

A Vermont maple syrup producer at New York City's Union Square Greenmarket has diversity with a crop, with various sizes and packages of syrup from utilitarian to gift as well as sugar and sugar candy. The sign is great, but if a crowd develops the sign won't be visible.

"Look for something unique and novel to bring to the market. Bring unusual varieties of peppers or heirloom tomatoes. Don't come in with a half acre of corn. Go through a seed catalog and if it's something you don't see in the grocery store, it might be a possibility."

– Dan Best, Mgr., Sacramento FMs, CA

The key to farmers' market success is to offer something customers can't find in supermarkets. Customers often perceive produce quality at farmers' markets to be superior to supermarkets. They look for varieties not found in the supermarkets and the greater availability of organics at the farmers' markets.

On the other hand, farmers' market varieties could be the same as their wholesale cousins – just picked later. As John Paul Barbagelata says, "A tomato picked vine-ripened for the farmers' market is a totally different tomato than one picked green for the wholesale market."

Find the missing link

"Stroll through the local supermarket. What doesn't travel well or is NOT on the shelf is a good item to grow and sell. Why sell what is cheap and in mass at the supermarket? Finding your niche means selling what is not available anywhere else."

– Diane Green, Greentree Naturals, Sandpoint, ID

Not every niche possibility is an opportunity. Do your homework and know what your farm can handle. Ask yourself if there is a market for this product. As Jane Desotelle, manager of the Adirondack Farmers' Market Co-op in upstate New York, relates, "We're in a remote rural area and the unusual veggies are a hard sell here."

If a market manager suggests that you grow a product, evaluate it relative to your growing conditions and market demand. Some products won't pay you enough, but others may be key in attracting customers to your stand.

"We've cut out things like sweet corn where we were competing with larger growers. It just wasn't practical on a small scale. Now we con-centrate on the items that the bigger growers don't grow, like heirlooms and specialty varieties, where the yields aren't as high but the flavor is outstanding."

– Lisa Bloodnick, Bloodnick Family Farm, Apalachin, NY

With the maturing of farmers' markets in some areas, it has become more difficult for the entry-level grower to find a market opening. Standard varieties and "the usual suspects" – tomatoes, sweet corn, watermelons, summer squash, bell peppers, etc. – are probably already spoken for. You may still be able to grow these mainstream items if you can differentiate your product – a Nantes carrot or a Raspberrry Jewel pluot – from what's already available. Grow what you love in all its splendor, package it for the market of today, and display it in a way that stops traffic in the marketplace – that's how you'll make your niche.

Diversify within a crop

"Chip and Susan Planck of Wheatland Vegetable Farms, Purcellville, PA, may grow only 18 categories of vegetables and small fruits, but they offer a lot of choices within those categories. For example, they grow 25 varieties of tomatoes, five of eggplant, six of beans and 15 kinds of greens. 'A new crop complicates your life,' Chip says. 'Diversity within a crop is easy to achieve.' At market, they promote the different varieties by name and offer samples of each. 'People aren't coming to buy tomatoes anymore,' Chip says. 'They're coming to buy Brandywine or Early Girl. They've discovered over the seasons which varieties they like best.'"

– *Growing for Market,* Dec. 1995

If your farm is set up for raspberries, grow early, midseason and late varieties. Grow some golden, purple and black as well as the red. Grow some that freeze well and promote that. Consider adding other cane berries like black, boysen, logan or ollalie.

Look at different packaging sizes for diversity or different forms of the product. Ask customers if they would like a 25-pound pail or box of IQF (Individually Quick Frozen) berries for summer smoothies and

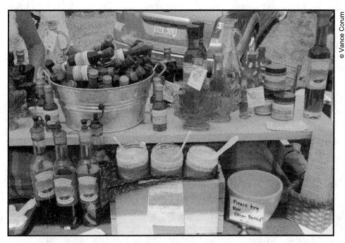

From a single product, Hillside Lane Farm in Stowe, VT now has a huge line of maple syrup with apple, blueberry, cranberry and more; cheese spreads; wasabi; chocolate mousse mix; and farm bread, using a variety of packaging styles that stop customers in their tracks.

homemade ice cream, or at season's end for cereal and fruit pies through the winter.

Sell to ethnic groups

Cater to neighborhood demographics. If you sell in a larger population center, consider tailoring your product line for the market's neighborhood by growing crops used by that culture, e.g., Asian, Hispanic, Italian, Jamaican, etc. As large supermarket chains and box stores have replaced mom-and-pop stores in many areas, their central purchasing provides a homogenized product mix aimed at the largest number of buyers. This means that items like fresh chilies, specialty eggplants, Asian vegetables and fresh herbs could provide an opportunity for the small-acreage farmer. People of some ethnic backgrounds are a "natural" for farmers' markets since they're used to purchasing in open-air, bulk-selling markets in their home countries.

Farmers of those same ethnic backgrounds have an obvious cultural and linguistic advantage in meeting the needs of their people. For instance, Hmong families have greater experience in production practices and kitchen preparation of bittermelon, gai choy and galangal, whether in Minneapolis, Sacramento or Anchorage.

Do your homework first. Talk to customers and scout the neighborhood to check specific food needs. Intent is important here. You must want to provide a service. If all you find interesting in this group of customers is their money, don't do it – you won't succeed. Don't just jump into this market. Some cultures value the process of bargaining for low prices. As a trial balloon, grow a couple of "ethnic" varieties of crops you already produce, say a Russian tomato or a Puerto Rican pepper.

Introduce new products again and again

"When Asian pears first came out, everyone saw the first ones who sold them make money, so the rest went out and planted them and lost money as the market got saturated. Now the same thing is happening with pluots!"
– Mary Lou Weiss, Former Mgr., Torrance FM, CA

Check seed and nursery catalogs for something new, and be the first one to present this product in a market. It doesn't work to walk through the market and copy others: be an innovator! When you are, you'll get the higher price if you educate the consumer with samples, recipes and background.

According to John Ellis, Farmer John's, Boulder, CO, "You need to be ahead of the curve. If you see a

Barbara Arnold's dried flower boxes are a colorful value-added item to extend the season at the Kootenai FM in Hayden, ID.

Adding Value To Your Crops

Examples of value-added products include: seasoned nuts, juice, peeled garlic, dried fruit, guacamole, jams, jellies, lettuce mixes, garlic braids, almond butter, pickled products, chocolate covered nuts and raisins.

Adding value by processing your product can involve simply cutting the stems off of broccoli. It can also involve a number of steps, as in preparing and packaging jams. Before embarking on a processing project, consider these factors:

♦ What are the possible ways to process your raw product? For example, if you grow stone fruit, some processed products might include jams, jellies or dried fruit.

♦ What is the consumer demand for the processed products you can produce? One of the great assets of farmers' markets is that you can talk to customers about their preferences. Also, talk to market managers to see what products they think will sell.

♦ What are the costs involved in processing? By developing a projected budget, you can get a good idea of what your costs will be. If you are considering making jams, some of your costs will be the additional ingredients (sugar, pectin), equipment (pots, etc.), jars, labels, and labor. Don't forget to add in labor as a cost — including your own. It could make the difference between pursuing and not pursuing a project.

♦ What is your estimated profit? Estimate conservatively how much money you anticipate making from the processed product. This includes developing a price for your product and projecting future sales.

♦ Test market your product. Solicit feedback from customers about each version of your product as it evolves, before continuing your investment in it. This allows you to tinker with the product until you get just what customers want.

Regulations AAAARGGHH!!!

Before you start work on a new project, ask your market manager or Extension Advisor whom to call to find out what regulations you will need to follow, whether they are from the health department, or county, city or state agencies.

Check with your local health department about what is considered a "processed product." The health department in Los Angeles, for example, defines processing as "changing the form, flavor or consistency" of a product. Once you cut a raw item, it is "processed" because its form has changed. If you are selling a processed product, you will need to prepare your product in a kitchen approved by the health department. Many growers rent space from restaurants or churches that have commercial kitchens.

– Mark Wall, *CFM News,* Aug. 1992, Southland Farmers Market Association. ❧

crop that's becoming more popular with the chefs, try to plant more of it. My restaurant distributor also keeps me informed about what leading edge chefs are looking for. I also make notes at the end of the year about the good sellers in the market for myself and for other vendors."

You're in the food business. Read about food. Listen about food. Watch the food channels. Read food blogs. If you don't subscribe to magazines like *Gourmet* or *Cooking Light,* at least read them at the library. Check the morning news shows, especially the day of the cooking segment. Talk to local chefs. Is there something they see on the horizon? Pay attention to trade shows for related industries like the deli and specialty foods. Try to get a feel for what's coming and what's waning.

This St. Petersburg, FL grower displays heirloom tomato starts on a 4-level rack, sprouting seeds on a rack in back, and other starts on a low stairway.

"Remember that most new products are short term advantages for only two to three years in the competitiveness of the farmers' markets. Their advantages usually disappear as fellow vendors turn on to your new product. Many of the growers have been doing the same thing for years and wonder why their sales are decreasing when the overall market sales are increasing."
– Rebecca Landis, Mgr., Corvallis, Albany FM, OR

"You can't grow for all people, so you have to learn what most of your customers want and grow for them."
– Kathy Rhoads, Rhoads Farm Market, Columbus, OH

Be sensitive to the economy. If people seem to be pulling back from eating out as much, maybe you can provide the extra something that makes their home-cooked meal special.

Extend the season with continuous supply

Make small frequent plantings so everything goes to market at peak maturity. One San Diego County farmer makes 60 plantings of corn, a few rows every other day. And that's just the corn!

To bring fresh-picked broccoli to the farmers' markets, Larry Thompson of Thompson Farms, Boring, OR, plants half an acre every two weeks. When he sold wholesale, Thompson planted broccoli in 5-acre blocks. Instead of the three crops he planted for the wholesale market, he's now planting 25 crops for the farmers' markets. He does a lot of transplanting so he can time the crops exactly. "Consistency is important in farmers' markets," Thompson says. "You can't run out of product or you will lose customers."

Unlike many farmers' market sellers who try to capture early or late season profits, Thompson feels it compromises crops by pushing them beyond their normal growing season. "Each crop seems to have an optimum time, and I feel they don't taste as good when they're pushed," he said.

Still, one of the challenges of farmers' market is to choose products to stretch the season from, say, June until November to maximize returns and keep your customer base.

"You need to have something to offer all that time. In summer, our main draw is our herbal plants. We sell about 80 varieties in 3-inch pots. This takes us 'til August. Our vegetables carry us through August and September, while October is big with mums, cornstalks, winter squash and gourds, and potatoes. Another way we stretch the season is with our homemade herbal soaps."
– Sue McEvoy, Sue Mac Farm & Herbary, NJ

Try to have crops available as early in the season as possible. If you consistently supply desired produce before other growers, consumers will learn to look for the products they want at your stall. According to Cheryl Boden, West Union Gardens, Hillsboro, OR, "One of the biggest windows of profit is early season crops. Look for early varieties, or get plants to come on early by using floating mulches, row covers, or transplants to capture the early markets. People are hungry for fresh produce when they come to the market in June, and early season customers often keep coming back throughout the season."

Adjunct products can keep you in the marketplace beyond your normal cropping period. Plant the "too small" cloves of your seed garlic in 4-inch pots and sell them for snipping. Make pesto using the greens from young spring garlic that won't make a decent head.

California, with its multiple and varied climates, has longer market seasons – often year-round – than most other parts of the country. This can be particularly challenging for the smaller-acreage, seasonal grower. At Full Circle Organic Farm in Auburn, CA (co-owned by author Marcie), we planted extra heirloom tomato, eggplant and pepper starts to make sure we had something to sell when the farmers' market opened in May. Sometimes we also had greens, peas, and potatoes, but the transplants gave us an early presence and cashflow in years when harsh spring weather had kept us out of the fields. On the flip side of the season, in late October and into November, we'd pick the remaining large-fruited tomatoes that wouldn't turn and sell them with recipes for Fried Green Tomatoes.

Sell everything

Non-food agricultural products may be a niche for you. Try gourds for crafters and/or to make into value-added products: curly willow branches for flower arrangers, dried chilies in various colors for wreath makers, or pumpkins and decorative gourds in fall. Cut flowers are often the biggest money maker in the market. A grower in Edmonton, Alberta, sells bunches of cedar boughs for $4 a piece. People love to decorate!

One October when the pumpkins from Dehn's Gardens, Andover, MN, came down with spotted little speckles from a hailstorm, Bonnie Dehn dressed up as a scarecrow to sell the pumpkins as freckled pumpkins! Some corn growers plant a small plot of multicolored decorative popcorn. They sell some in the husk with just a strip peeled back, some with the whole husk peeled back, and some tied to a paper bag with popping instructions. Around Halloween and to a lesser extent at Thanksgiving, they bundle up stalks and sell them for fall decorations.

At Full Circle Organic Farm we'd pull basil plants in fall, dry the wood, and bundle it to sell for smoking wood to barbecue enthusiasts the following year. Orchardists might consider making small bundles of fruit wood for barbecues or wood-fired ovens in upscale restaurants. Herb bunches that don't sell fresh can be hung to become dried bunches.

Flowers are another option. Growing annuals and perennials can be a profitable niche. Well-arranged bouquets will enhance the appearance of your display and attract impulse shopping. Sunflowers have become so popular that seed catalogs have special sections dedicated just to them.

One grower cuts and sells the blossoms from onions that have bolted in the field. Another lets the smaller, late artichokes bloom because the flowers sell for more than their smaller chokes would.

Grow organic

Organically grown produce is another market to consider. U.S. sales of organic food and beverages grew from $1 billion in 1990 to $26.7 billion in 2010. Organic fruits and vegetables in 2010 represented 11% of all U.S. fruit and vegetable sales. They are

The Shadboldts of Rickreall, OR have grown their cherry hobby into a thriving family business with dried cherries, chocolate covered cherries, jams, and gift packs at farmers' markets and www.thecherrycountry.com.

THE NEW FARMERS' MARKET

highly visible in many areas, with some farmers' markets being dominated by organic produce. Nevertheless, mass retailers in 2010 sold 54% and natural retailers sold 39% of total organic food sales.

Organic growing requires more than just a substitution of "approved inputs" for "restricted inputs." It's a major commitment to improving soil quality and fertility and working with the environment. If you're currently growing with conventional practices, it may be several years before you'll be able to use the "organic" label and your yields may be less during the transition years. If you're starting a farm on fallow ground and you can show a history, you may be able to work toward certification your first year. Consult with your local certification group and talk to other organic growers.

There is expense involved in being certified, which needs to be considered as any other farm expense. With the National Organic Standards in effect since 2002, you must be certified by an accredited third party. Growers with gross sales under $5,000 per year are exempt from the requirement of certification and submitting an organic systems plan. For more information contact an organic certification organization. [See Resources, Chapter 2, "USDA Organics Program."]

Business considerations

Beyond the potential of every new crop for the market lie the business considerations.

Does the crop grow well on your land and under your growing conditions? Forcing crops to grow in locations far from where they evolved or outside their normal season brings another set of problems. Stressed plants are more prone to insects and disease. Can you get enough of a mark-up to cover the cost of dealing with these challenges?

How much labor does the product entail? Having labor when and where it's needed is the perpetual problem in agriculture and especially so with non-commodity food crops. Berries, beans and peas spring to mind immediately. For each of these crops, every single fruit must be handled one at a time and it takes a lot of individual fruits to make a pound or a pint. Be sure you know that the labor you need will be available when you need it – and at what price – before you go into these crops.

Know the cost involved in growing, marketing and transporting for each particular crop you sell at the market. Start out by figuring what it costs you to grow the product. One way to do this is to grow a small test plot and track your costs. For some perennial crops, there may be enterprise budgets developed by your land grant college. Then you need to know your costs of marketing, going to town, taking it to marketplace – all your time and labor. Vendors who don't know their true costs often end up selling at a loss. [See the chapter, "Running Your Farmers' Market Business."]

Add value

"Adding value" to a product means doing some additional processing that increases the raw product's worth to the customer. This may include convenience-oriented processing such as pre-packaging or sorting for size as well as other forms of processing such as drying, canning, seasoning and flavoring, or incorporating the product into crafts.

Value-added items work well with farmers' markets. As one grower said: "You can bring fresh berries to the market on Wednesday and if they don't sell, you can come back and sell raspberry jam on Saturday."

Yet another grower said: "Farmers are finding they can make more money in the fall on corn shocks than on the corn. Consumers are willing to pay almost anything for something to decorate while they will quibble pennies over food."

Value-added products extend the season into winter months and provide customers with wonderful house and holiday gifts. Farmers' markets are a great place to test value-added products before launching them into bigger markets. Store buyers have been known to cruise farmers' markets looking for well-accepted locally produced jams, vinegars, oils, cheeses and more.

Since the requirement for having a certified kitchen to prepare processed foods is often prohibitively expensive for an individual grower, consider going in on a cooperative basis with other growers to make it affordable. Check with your market manager about the feasibility of the opening of a community kitchen that people can rent reasonably by the hour.

As we've said, farmers' markets are great as a test-market for new products, and especially so with value-added. As Doug Cross, Canter-Berry Farm, Auburn, WA, said: "Get customer feedback and find out what they want. We sold our blueberry jam, syrup and vinegar before we sold chutney, but people kept asking, 'Do you make a blueberry chutney?' and we looked it up, made a sample batch, and sampled it out for six months ('too sweet' or 'too sour' etc.) before we started selling it."

The possibilities are many and the demand for value-added products seems to be rising. Fifty-two percent of the managers questioned in the Farmers' Markets and Rural Development Project witnessed an increase in value-added products at the end of the 1990s.

> "Markets like the Crescent City Farmers' Market are an important retail outlet for folks who are not large enough or rich enough to get their products into grocery stores... which is increasingly hard to do without paying for shelf space. They're a place to start."
> – Economics Institute, *1999 Report to the Community*, Crescent City FM, LA

 ## BUSINESS INCUBATOR

Thousands of farmers have started their businesses through farmers' markets. Countless thousands of others have survived as farmers thanks to the higher income resulting from farmers' market sales. In fact, market success has lead even substantial operators to enter some of the more successful farmers' markets, often grossing thousands of dollars per day.

> "Farmers' market are a great place to incubate a small business. Where for $10 a day can you go and do your own market survey, meet customers, and get started selling? Judy Dempsey, in Perth,

Ontario, started in business by coming to the Perth Farmers' Market selling prepared foods, and her business grew so fast that she left to open her Feeding the Hungry Planet restaurant in Perth, which has been written up as one of the top 100 restaurants in Canada."
> – Bob Chorney, Exec. Dir., Farmers' Markets Ontario

Of all the valuable things they provide to the agricultural entrepreneur, farmers' markets excel at allowing them to develop value-added products, build a customer mailing list and pursue agritourism ventures.

In their report, Farmers' Markets and Rural Development Project, researchers Gail Feenstra and Chris Lewis said that about seven percent of vendors in each farmers' market were expanding their businesses each year. Managers reported that farmers' markets provide important contacts for other marketing venues such as restaurant or retail accounts and CSA start-ups. Farmers also are taking advantage of the Farmers' Market Nutrition Program (FMNP) and the National School Lunch Program to provide fresh produce to low-income families and children.

Karen Durham in Bellingham, WA, reflected, "We participated with other local ag groups in the county working on a farm map so people can buy direct from the grower on the days when the market isn't open. We did this to build the farmer-customer relationship and to help the farmer make a living from the farm. In the long run, if farmers are making a living from the farm, it will only help the market. The issue of competition between markets and CSAs or supermarkets or farmstands is often raised, but if each market does well, then all the farmer sales benefit because consumers get used to buying local and want to buy local."

Growers use farmers' markets in conjunction with just about any form of marketing:

Community supported agriculture

Various farmers' markets have combined the products of several vendors to provide weekly boxes for market customers. Many individual growers report happy marriages between CSA and farmers' market sales.

"Six farmers out of the 50 who regularly sell at our University District market every week also have CSAs. The amount of money attached to their CSA pick-ups is added to the total amount of sales for that day at the market. The market provides the CSA farmers a 7-8 hour pick-up site in the middle of the city one day a week during the growing season. This is a great benefit for the CSA grower. They can also sell additional produce to new customers and do outreach to new CSA subscribers at the FM. I surveyed the farmers at the end of the season to see what kinds of connections they were making at the market. A dozen of our vendors were selling at a high-end restaurant through connections they made at the market."

– Chris Curtis, Director, Neighborhood Farmers Market Alliance, Seattle, WA

"We do four different farmers' markets and also have a CSA, and we feel it goes hand in hand with selling at a farmers' market. All of our

One sign of a strong farmers' market is the presence of chefs. By providing convenient parking for large trucks, Santa Monica goes the extra mile to serve local chefs and purveyors who ship produce to restaurants worldwide the same day – the best that southern California has to offer.

pickups are at the farmers' markets. When CSA clients come to the farmers' market they pick up their boxes at our stand and they often buy something additional."

– Bob and Pat Meyer, Stoney Plains Farm, Tenino, WA

"Most of our CSA customers have signed up as CSA customers from having heard about it at our farmers' market booth. Many of our regular customers had expressed concern about getting to our booth and finding their favorite products gone. Signing up for the CSA ensures that their produce is held for them."

– Lisa Bloodnick, Bloodnick Family Farm, Apalachin, NY

Farm stands

Growers gain visibility using brochures and signage at farmers' markets to increase retail traffic at their roadside farm stands. Some growers also sell to roadside stand operators who buy for resale at their stands. The farmers' markets are a good central place for them to pick up the products that are picked fresh daily. The markets lead regular customers to local roadside stands.

"At the farmers' markets we hand out brochures about the farm and a lot of people come out to the farm after they've met us. The market gives us the selling opportunity to meet folks that don't come out to the farm. Since our farm is off the main highway, the markets help maintain our visibility."

– Ronald Smolowitz, Coonamessett Farm, East Falmouth, MA

Chrissie Manion Zaerpoor of Kookoolan Farms, Yamhill, OR, uses her alternate Sunday presence at the Hillsdale FM to build her CSA mailing list. She then offers cheese-making workshops, reinforcing their stature as the Northwest's largest and most complete inventory of home cheese-making supplies. During the winter they offer a variety of fresh and value-added products that keep their three workers employed year-round.

Farm stays and agritourism

Invite customers to the farm. Offer on-farm visits, demonstrations and workshops. Let them know their purchases support local open space. Use the farmers' market to distribute brochures and talk with customers, encouraging visits to the farm. In the process, you build a more lasting commitment from your customers.

A survey conducted in New York and Iowa showed that about 30% of farmers' market vendors in those states have engaged in agritourism activities. Agricultural homestay legislation was passed in California in 1999, allowing up to six rooms for overnight stays exempt from restaurant law. By 2008, California farms and ranches hosted 2.4 million visitors, according to a UC Davis Small Farm Center study by Penny Leff, including 3% foreigners and 8% from outside the state.

The Center now maintains a list of agritourism operators at:

www.calagtour.org.

Most are motivated by the desire to increase farm profitability, to educate the public and use a new marketing tool. They commonly use word of mouth, websites and feature stories to attract their clients.

For those offering farm stays, a useful site is:

www.farmstayus.org.

Mail order

"In addition to direct sales, tourists provide an opportunity for vendors to develop and expand mail order businesses. Consumers who purchased products from the farmers' market while traveling often later seek those same products through mail order to give as gifts or for their own consumption. Several vendors offer special packaging for gifts and provide brochures and order forms promoting this kind of trade. Furthermore, the market has a printed directory with a brief description of each vendor's products and services. The directory gives traveling consumers the opportunity to continue to pa-tronize the vendors' businesses even after they have returned home."

– *A Case Study of the Laytonville Farmers' Market,* by Christopher J. Lewis

Al and Becky Courchesne of Frog Hollow Farm in Brentwood, CA, make sure that their website at www.froghollow.com is visible at seven farmers' markets and their retail space within the Ferry Plaza Marketplace in San Francisco. Their homepage proudly notes mentions by the New York Times, Oprah and Martha Stewart, while the Los Angeles Times calls Farmer Al a "rock star" of good food. The website in turn reflects where they sell – through the markets, their Happy Child CSA with 60 drop-off locations, their Ferry café, and retail outlets in several states and British Columbia. It also reminds customers to request that their favorite retailer stock product from Frog Hollow.

Similarly, Rob Valicoff of Valicoff Family Farms in Washington's Yakima Valley provides mail order apples and peaches at:

www.applesonline.com.

Originally he developed many customers by handing out two pieces of free fruit to each customer at farmers' markets, even at Pike Place with huge crowds. Having tremendous confidence in his quality, he wanted to ensure that everyone tasted it, and with his laptop he was ready to take down their order. He has a second website oriented toward regular Seattle metro area customers, who have a half-hour window in which to pick up boxes of apples at a church, bowling alley, restaurant or shopping center.

Restaurant sales

"There are some 22 restaurants in L.A. that send chefs to shop in the market. Restaurants like Spago and Border Grill come to the market on a regular basis. They bring a pickup truck and about four helpers, and spend about four hours shopping the market. They sample everything, talk to the farmers, and establish relationships with farmers. L.A. chefs are very competitive and try to stay one step ahead of each other. The farmers kept saying we've got to do something for the chefs, so we started Chef Appreciation Day. Chefs are very loyal and come every week even when it's raining. A grower might say, 'My whole trip was worthwhile because one restaurant bought $200 worth of stuff from me today.' We had a catered breakfast reception for the chefs and gave them each a little market memento – a little framed work of art to put in the restaurant."

– Laura Avery, FM Supervisor, City of Santa Monica, CA

Retail outlets

Having a brochure, rack card or poster board proclaiming other outlets where farmers' market customers can get your products is simply good business practice. You gain credibility by having multiple outlets – it implies success.

"We're often asked: 'Where can we get them during the week?' and we tell them the stores where they can buy them. It makes a great sales pitch in selling to the stores, to tell them we promote their store at the markets."

– Matt Megrath & Walter Ross, Farmhouse Tomatoes, Inc., Lake Worth, FL

Even better is to have a list of your retail outlets visible on a sign at your farmers' market.

THE QUALITY HARVEST

The pick of the crop

For beginning farmers, we state the obvious: know when it's ripe. Know also what the market quality measures are for your crops. While most farmers' markets exempt produce sellers from standard pack and labeling regulations, they do require adherence to quality standards. Bringing only your finest quality product to the market is the best way to attract customers and sustain your price. This standard, of course, varies with the demographics of each community, but everyone wants good quality even if not all can pay top price.

By taking over the middle steps, reducing the handling and transit distances, and keeping control of the product, the direct marketer gains the profit advantage of getting vine- or tree-ripe produce to the consumer in good shape. This simply isn't possible in conventional channels where fruits and vegetables travel an average of 1,300 miles to their destination.

Quality starts in the field. It can be maintained or deteriorate from that point depending on how you handle the product, but no post-harvest measures – no matter how sophisticated – can improve quality. It only goes downhill, unless you arrest that process in some way. [See PostHarvest Handling tips in Appendix.]

Maturity vs. ripeness

There's a difference between maturity and ripeness. By USDA standards, a mature fruit or vegetable is one that can continue to progress to ripeness. Ripeness has definitions of color and softness. Marketing standards address size, shape, blemishes, wounds, scars, color and spoilage. They don't address taste or nutrition. To give the standards their due, if something has a totally funky shape, is bruised, rotten or beat-up, it's probably a clue about the nutritional content and taste, anyway. It's good to remember that market standards are a baseline, not an optimal standard. Standards can be found on the internet at:

www.ams.usda.gov/standards.com

or through your local USDA office or some state agriculture departments.

Sugars and complex acids only develop while the product is growing. Once it's harvested, the challenge is to maintain that sugar in the product. If your crop is picked too green, you may be able to get it to change color and soften but with a few exceptions the flavor probably won't improve. The longer you can leave it in the field while preserving keeping qualities, the higher the price you will be able to command.

There is such a thing as too ripe, not only in terms of the quality standards, but also in terms of consumer acceptance. Look for optimal ripeness – that blend of eating quality and keeping quality. Your produce is going from the field to the cooler, to the truck, to the farmers' market, to the customer's vehicle, and finally to the customer's kitchen. It's not good enough that produce looks great in the field and the market stall if it looks like compost fodder when it gets to the kitchen. Do your own quality control. Take some of your product from your market stall, bag it, take it home, and use it as your customer would.

Harvesting ripe produce takes finesse and a gentler touch than conventional picking allows. Packing as you pick is an art form requiring good spatial skills. Training helpers is important. Teach employees your quality standards and don't assume they know how to pick a tomato even if they've done it before.

> "With Full Circle, as I was setting up for market, I took a box of our Radiator Charlie's Mortgage Lifter tomatoes out of the van and put it on the table. As I removed the lid, I could see the imprint of five fingers in the flesh of each tomato. Because our helper had worked on two farms previously, I had foolishly assumed she could pick tomatoes without instruction, and I had not passed on what I'd learned several seasons before. You have to pick the heirloom, thin-skinned, tough-stemmed Charlies by supporting their shoulders or you will inevitably dent them trying to get them from the vine."
>
> – Marcie Rosenzweig, Full Circle Organic Farm, Auburn, CA

Many farmers pick into the same containers that will be on display at the market. Is there a higher standard? Art Lange of Reedley, CA, was ahead of his time in guarding supremely high quality. In the 1980s when he picked six peaches and placed them into foam-lined shoe boxes with a fold-up handle (which he sold for $5), he was one of the first to get fruit from tree to table with the touch of only one hand. It was fruit so deliciously ripe that few but farmers have ever tasted something so heavenly.

Field Packing

Once it's out of the field, produce quality deteriorates with every handling and with heat. Each transfer provides an additional opportunity for bumps and bruises, the primary cause of post-harvest disease. Therefore, insofar as possible, pick and pack at the same time. Bring the display container you will use into the field. Consider reusable plastic containers available in various colors that can complement your product display at market, such as from Rehrig Pacific, Flexcon or Intercrate Container. If you're packing for two different marketing venues, e.g., fancy quality for farmers' markets and baby vegetables for restaurants, take both boxes into the field and sort as you pick. Remember, "baby" veggies are more delicate than market size. Keep backup supplies of hand tools, bands and other picking items with you to avoid extra trips back to the shed.

For bunched root crops, i.e., carrots, radishes, beets, baby turnips, and green onions, bring banding materials into the field and bunch as you go.

> "At Full Circle, we used rubber bands because they conformed to the tops and held well when wet. If you put a pre-determined number on your wrist, you'll have an automatic count of the number of bunches dug. We piled bunches onto recycled nursery flats, unstacked the flats at the wash area, and hosed the dirt through the holes in the flat bottoms.
>
> – Marcie Rosenzweig, Full Circle Organic Farm, Auburn, CA

Some crops such as green beans, peas and summer squash require picking several times per week to maintain productivity and provide optimal product quality. If you make multiple pickings and don't have same-day market outlets, put the harvest date in a prominent place on the container so you move them in order of picking.

Whether you're large enough to have a flat-bed or trailer in the field or you are using a cart to move your harvest, provide shade for your product. Canopies work best for larger vehicles, but you have good versatility with Reflectix, a foil-sandwiched, double bubble insulating product available in rolls in a variety of widths at your local home center. Another option is Prodex, which has closed cell polyethylene foam within the foil sandwich, and an R-value of 16.

Reflectix is the same reflective material used for Blockade windshield sunshades. These can be laid across individual boxes as you go and moved up as you stack. Sunshades can sometimes be purchased in

Washable, shallow plastic totes effectively transport sensitive crops directly from field to market. Signage complements the product desirability in seducing the customer to sample and buy.

closeout stores and, properly taken care of, will last several seasons. Take produce to the shed as often as possible; cooling within an hour of harvest significantly improves your quality control.

Packing it in

Some crops simply don't lend themselves to field packing because of specific cooling requirements or the need for washing or grading. The goals of packing are to immobilize the product, to cushion impacts, to avoid compression, to minimize loss and to facilitate sale. Choose packing materials to help you meet these goals.

Set aside an area of a barn, pole shed or shade canopy with waist-high tables, packing supplies, non-slip surfaces under foot, and fresh, potable running water with good drainage. Consider work-flow when you set up this area. Bring the produce in on one side and take it to the cooler on the other. Have a dry place for boxes, labels, scissors, knives and the certified scale within easy reach and away from the washing station.

Washing stations can vary in size and complexity, as do farms. The simplest is probably wash basins or dedicated plastic muck buckets and a hose with a spray nozzle. Extra greenhouse-type benches work well for drip-drying. If you're doing volume, get some movable roller conveyors so you can reconfigure on the fly as different crops come in from the field. Be sure you have enough room to move about in your packing area. Between the sharp implements, the supplies and the water, the packing shed is a prime location for workers' compensation injuries.

Write a safety manual and train your employees. For California growers, this is a legal requirement for doing business. Train about sanitation, too. Remind people to wash their hands after using the restroom – consider having a sign in the restroom, too, as required in restaurants. It would also be useful to provide disposable gloves; they're cheap insurance. Wash basins, buckets, reflective shields, knives, scissors, and work surfaces – everything used from week to week – needs to be thoroughly washed and sterilized. Chlorine bleach is the most cost effective way to do this. If you have objections to chlorine, good, old-fashioned sunlight for a couple of days after washing with soap and water, and before reuse, works pretty well. Ask your Extension agent about an "HACCP list" and use it to critically review every potential step in your pick-and-pack process where safety problems may occur, everything from worker injury to pathogen entry.

An excellent resource on the use of chlorine bleach as a post-harvest disinfectant in wash water and on produce is Publication 8003 from the University of California called *Postharvest Chlorination*. Written by Trevor Suslow, this eight-page pamphlet has recommended dilutions and produce-specific recommendations. It also talks about non-chlorine alternatives and gives timely web references.

Cool it!

While you may read advice to pick produce the morning of the market for freshness, we recommend you pick 12 to 24 hours ahead, then clean and cool your produce. Doing this will dramatically improve the keeping quality of your product.

Proper post-harvest handling and temperature control are probably the biggest things missed by small-acreage growers. Vegetables are living things and have respiration after they're picked, i.e., they consume oxygen and give off carbon dioxide and heat. Baby lettuce or mesclun, for example, picked and bagged at dawn but not cooled will feel warm in the center of the pack within a couple of hours. This is metabolic heat. Another form of heat is "field heat." This is heat picked up by the produce from simply being in the field. Produce self-cools while it's attached to its roots. Once it's harvested, it no longer has that ability and starts gaining heat from the environment.

The keeping quality of your produce depends on your ability to remove the field heat and slow down the metabolic rate. How you do this depends on which crop you're handling. Water, or its solid form, ice, are the most efficient removers of heat. (Think of your body in a swimming pool.) Water does pretty well at getting the dirt off, too. Crops that cool well using water as a heat remover are greens, brassicas, lettuces, salad mixes, some herbs, and root crops. The challenge when using water is to remove as much of the water as possible before final packing. Sitting in dampness promotes decay.

For other more delicate crops like strawberries, fruit crops, peas, beans, and herbs with fuzzy leaves, cool air drawn across the produce works well. The University of California at Davis put out plans for a table-top, forced air cooler that could cool one or two strawberry boxes at a time. It may be possible to create a similar cooler using a room air conditioner, a box, and a fan.

There's a trade-off between packing in the field and getting produce cooled quickly. Packaging provides a block to free coolant flow and creates a modification of the atmosphere surrounding the product.

The packaging you use needs to be compatible with the cooling method required by the crop. Waxed boxes for greens and brassicas provide containers that can be ice- or hydro-cooled without deterioration. Paperboard boxes with large holes facilitate forced air cooling. Most other methods simply use the transfer of heat from the produce to the cold room or refrigerator air. This works but takes considerably more time

– which is why we recommend picking a day ahead if possible.

If you are going to market within a day and you can do so, pack in your market display container. This will save set-up time and eliminate one more transfer point.

Optimum storage conditions including temperatures for a wide variety of produce items can be found on the Post-Harvest Outreach website at:

http://postharvest.ucdavis.edu/Most_Useful_Post harvest_Websites/

Other good resources are *Knott's Handbook for Vegetable Growers,* and ATTRA's publication on post-harvest handling.

Cold rooms, walk-ins & fridges

Once you've removed some of the heat and slowed the metabolic rate of your crop, you'll want to maintain that crop in an appropriate temperature environment.

Jim Thompson, agricultural engineer with the Post-Harvest Outreach Program of U.C. Davis once said, "Don't try to control what you're unwilling to measure." Whether you have a commercial cold room, a farm-built walk-in box, or a recycled restaurant fridge, you will need an accurate thermometer to know when your temperature is right. Commercial cold rooms usually have a built-in thermometer with a face reading outside the door. You'll need to get some kind of thermometer for farm-builts and recycled. A good refrigerator thermometer will do. Place it at product height where it can be easily seen, and read it every morning and evening. Adjust your thermostat accordingly.

Consider getting a walk-in cooler to help keep products fresh.

"You can convert an air-conditioner to make a decent walk-in cooler. Ours paid for itself in the first year by helping keeping quality at the market throughout the day. It also helps to bring ice if it's really hot. We bought an old ice machine for $50 from a restaurant equipment supply company."

– Cheryl Boden, West Union Gardens, Hillsboro, OR

How much cooling space you need depends on two things: the size of your operation in general and the number of times per week you'll empty the space. Most direct marketers turn space quickly. Between our farmers' markets, restaurant and co-op sales, and our CSA, Full Circle Organic Farm turned cooler space every other day. The longer you hold produce, the more complex your system becomes.

If the price of a new, commercial cold room doesn't fit into your farm budget, there are less costly alternatives. Publication 21449 from the University of California is a nine-page booklet called *Small-Scale Cold Rooms for Perishable Commodities* that covers several options like marine containers and refrigerator trucks, and includes plans for owner-built cold rooms. Used restaurant equipment dealers may have walk-in boxes and/or large refrigerators available.

Here's what we at Full Circle learned over the years about different types of refrigeration.

- Used walk-ins: Check to see what's included. Generally flooring isn't, as these units are designed to install over a concrete pad with a drain. They may or may not come with the actual cooling system, and the cooling system may be based on somthing you're not familiar with, like ammonia or an out-of-date chloro-florocarbon such as freon that's expensive and difficult to replace.
- Most walk-ins run off three-phase industrial electrical standard wiring and require their own circuit, as conventional wiring is two-phase.

- Walk-ins are designed for indoor use, so they're not weathertight and need to be under shelter.
- Used refrigerators may have worn-out compressors and also use freon as a refrigerant. Watch for worn seals and latches.

None of this is meant to keep you from considering or using these alternatives; we have done so ourselves. Just know you'll probably need more than the original quote and allow some extra cash for repairs, pads and/or wiring.

If you use a room air conditioner, realize it will run hard almost continuously in a hot climate, and you will need to supplement the humidity in your cold room. [See Resources, Chapter 2] Room air conditioners are meant to move temperature only a few degrees and not into the 30s or 40s. For the most part, they are also designed to remove humidity, which produce needs to stay fresh. They will get you through the growing pains, though, and are more efficient in moderate climates. With tomatoes, peppers, eggplants and other chill-sensitive crops that need to be held just above 50°F, a swamp cooler and a walk-in cooler built from straw bales may fill the bill.

Humidity

Humidity and temperature are a balancing act. The warmer the air is, the more water it can hold. Water moves from a wetter environment to a drier one until both are equalized. Dry air will literally pull water from your product, but the colder the air, the less

Products: Lemons

"If it doesn't taste good and look good, leave it home."

"Don't bring fruit too early in season or unload overripe vegetables at season's end. If the product doesn't taste good, customers get a bad experience and it hurts future sales potential."

everyone else does."

"Talking down the product! Saying: 'I'm sorry, these beans aren't as good as they were last week.' Always speak of your product with pride!"

"Too little product on display!"

"Farmers here are afraid of tak-

ing product home. They'd rather bring in a little, sell out, and go home rather than bring extra and have to take any home. We have more public than product!"

"Not taking advantage of value-added."

water it can hold. If you can't decrease temperature enough, increase humidity around your produce to hold down moisture or water loss.

Water loss is cumulative – once you lose it, you never get it back, so prevention is the name of the game. Produce is 95% water – *that* is what you have to sell. Product water loss is lost quality and lost profits.

Using plastic liners or bags in boxes after the initial cooling will help prevent water loss. Damp – not wet – bath towels placed over roots, tomatoes, peppers and eggplant will work for small-scale farms. Misters – manual or automatic like you see in grocery stores – work on a larger scale. Again, complexity rises with the length of time you hold the product.

Other storage issues

If you're storing your produce more than 36 hours, other issues like ethylene compatible crops and geotropism come into play. Take a post-harvest class and get a good reference book that covers your crops.

Some crops like onions, potatoes, and winter squash need to sit and cure between harvest and distribution. These guys like a different environment than your cooler will provide. Keep some space reserved for them.

To market, to market

Now that you have your quality product in your cooler, it's time to take it out again and get it to your customers. Whether you take your produce to the local farmers' market 15 minutes up the road or to the urban market 150 miles away, the challenge remains the same – getting it there in good shape.

Taking your produce to market is another transfer point with the potential to degrade quality. If your vehicle is older and has a stiff ride, consider using egg crate foam pads under your boxes as cushion against bumps along the way. Pack your load tightly to reduce movement and stop shifting. If your truck doesn't have them, make load locks to keep your boxes from moving around as you go to market. A piece of 1x1-inch wood and two vice-grips will work in a pinch.

Larger growers with longer travel times will want a refrigerated truck. Mid-size growers can retrofit a panel van with a roof-top air conditioner. Smaller growers can build boxes with hinged lids from rigid foamboard insulation and duct tape. This and frozen one gallon jugs of water will keep produce cool on the way to market and throughout the day.

When you set up your market transportation, find a way to put your tables, display fixtures and other market paraphernalia in the vehicle so you can set them up before you move the produce. This saves set-up time and moving your product, plus it allows you to unload produce into space sheltered from the heat. Roof racks or side racks are an option.

> "At Full Circle Organic Farm, in both our original truck and our market van, we built a false floor. The tables, umbrellas, stands, pipe frame for the scale and product bags, etc., all went under that floor. We could pull into our market stall, set up and drape the table, ready our product slant display, and put down our mats before we touched a box of produce."
>
> – Marcie Rosenzweig, Full Circle Organic Farm, Auburn, CA

Think ahead when you pack your vehicle for market. Arrange your boxes in such a way that you can fill and refill your display without rearranging everything. Put more of your hot sellers toward the front so you don't have to reach very far to replenish them as they get low.

If you're dropping crews at multiple markets, pack the reverse of this for each market and pack and label each market separately. This will allow you to get your crew in the stall with the display bones ready to fill without having to rearrange boxes or missing a product.

It's a good idea to keep a checklist of what products and quantities to bring to each market and have someone other than the truck packer check it off again before you leave.

Another tip: fuel the vehicle on the way home from market or your last trip out. Having to stop on the way to market, or worse yet, running out of gas on the way, is not an experience you need to have.

PREPARING FOR MARKET

How much to bring

Especially in a market that's new to you, it's difficult to predict how much to bring. The first day isn't a good indicator because customers aren't yet familiar with you and your products. When you bring new products to market, you often hear, "Oh, I didn't know you had THAT. I just bought it at the grocery store. I'll buy it from you next week." You may have better quality than the vendor they usually buy from, but they bought out of habit before they saw yours.

Your market research can be of some help here. If you're one of only a couple of vendors with a given product or you have something that sells well for you in similar markets, bring a generous amount.

Try to bring enough produce to last throughout the day, so that there's enough left for your last few customers. Develop secondary uses or outlets for what doesn't sell. You can also donate unsold product to soup kitchens, or make compost. If you sell out early, increase what you bring by small amounts, or look at your prices – maybe you're under-pricing your product. The aim is not to sell out, but to keep repeat customers.

A good rule of thumb is: 5-10% of your load comes home. If you're bringing home more, you're either going to the wrong market, bringing too much, or not doing a good job of selling.

Don't get greedy. If you do well with 20 bushels of string beans the first year, you may not necessarily do better with 60. You may saturate the market and end up eating them.

In any case, you need to bring enough to have an abundant looking display. If you have smaller amounts, use a smaller table and baskets to keep the look luscious.

After the first two or three markets, it's time to fine-tune your product mix. Keep records. Start bringing products proportionate to sell-through, i.e., more of your hot items if you have them and less of the others. If you're doing multiple markets, shift products according to what the hot sellers are in each.

Insurance

Even if a market doesn't require it, it's a good idea to have liability insurance. It's not expensive when you consider the possibility of a lawsuit brought by someone tripping over a water jug next to your truck or cracking a tooth on a piece of peach pit in your homemade jam. Check with your insurance agent about adequate coverage. Farmers' markets have insurance, but individual sellers are generally not covered. [See Appendix]

Be prepared

To get ready for market, prepare a checklist of things you need in order to do business, such as scales, bags, change and so on.

"What we're really doing is taking a store out to a different parking lot 300 times a year. It's very important that we take everything we need. Some things are trivial like thumb tacks. But if you forget the thumbtacks, you can't put up the signs. Preparing for market also means stocking up on recipes and other printed pieces. Every item for sale has a sign identifying it, often by variety, and nearly everything has a half-sheet with recipes or cooking instructions. The informational material is the key to recruiting new customers. At any market, on any day, there's always somebody who is there for the first time."
– Chip and Susan Planck, Purcellville, PA (*Growing for Market*, Dec. 1995)

Over the years at Full Circle Organic Farm, we found that as the season wore on we became dumber, not smarter, so we started making checklists and using other memory devices to be sure everything we needed got to market. One useful tool was "the Big Blue Box." This was just a cheap plastic tote but it allowed consolidation of all small market aids that might otherwise get lost. Within it were other organizers – a plastic zippered bag for price signs, another for recipes, a bag of clothes pins, a box of push pins, a box of assorted pens and markers, rolls of produce bags, etc. We also kept our grower certification and our organic registration in plastic sheet protectors connected by a ring for easy hanging. The box stayed in the van, and the only things that left the box at home were the tablecloths for washing.

Your checklist might include:

- Shelter: patio umbrellas or a canvas patio (open-sided tent). This provides shelter for yourself and your produce and can contribute to a colorful display.
- Stall structure: tables, tablecloth.
- Containers suitable for your produce, as well as customer take-home containers.
- Cash and cash box.
- Signs: booth and product/price signs.
- Scale: If selling items by weight, you'll need a scale with valid seal from your local Weights and Measures Department.
- Sample station: anything from a special berry basket labeled for customers as "samples", to a full cart with splashboard roof to place out front.
- Rubber mat: Be kind to your feet and ensure you're still standing at age 80.
- Educational materials: recipes, pamphlets and flyers – especially helpful if you're selling anything new or unusual!
- Display items: sign-making materials like chalk and an eraser; tags (paper, plastic or cardboard), markers, scissors, tape and pens, bags, price tags, pocket knife, duct tape, markers, stakes.
- Business items: pencils, pens, calculator, a sales and tax record book, tax charts, and business cards, and a pad of note paper for jotting down new marketing ideas or special order requests from customers.
- Fresh, potable water in a spray bottle or pump sprayer to keep products fresh.
- Personal comfort items like a mid-morning snack and plenty of water to drink.

Bring a stool for the inevitable lull time but avoid it when customers are in view. If it's a chair, you'll be tempted to sit, and that's not what a customer wants to see.

If you use a pickup with a standard length bed, bring an old hoe or other item to snag goods from deep in the back. Your knees and back will thank you.

Find creative ways to deal with the inevitable environmental problems. A lot of markets prohibit side-draped shadecloth because it creates a visual block in the marketplace. We bought colorful Japanese paper umbrellas and repositioned them as the sun moved to keep our greens in good shape. They attracted customer attention, and gave us a unique presence.

At the beginning of the season, after the cropping was planned, we created 4x5-inch price signs for each variety using computer clip art for appeal, and leaving a large space for the price. These were laminated at the local copy shop so we could use dry erase markers to make pricing changes as necessary. No more making signs while trying to set up the stall!

Farm identification

"Have your name and telephone number on your bags and labels so people can call you midweek, so they can come to the farm and pick up something extra. Over the years I've had

Samples are essential but the personal touch make them even more powerful for Achadinha Cheese of Petaluma, CA.

This Stowe, VT farm is easily found at any market because of their unique paint job. Every farm needs to set themselves apart.

Bring yourself! Farmers' market customers want to meet the farmer!

A note about personal appearance. Take a shower and put on clean clothes for market. This is a daily job interview and performance review. You represent your farm and your product. Be the picture of health, cleanliness and vitality. A funky farmer will overshadow great fruit in short order. Clean your fingernails – trust us, it matters. You can go "in costume" if it's not too outrageous. Overalls and a straw hat are fine, if you're into it. Matching t-shirts and aprons give a unified and service-oriented feel to the stall.

The Pacheco family gave their employees the ability to do creative branding. Occasionally they wear a tie-dye T-shirt and matching tablecloth to proclaim that Achadinha Cheese has a true "counter culture."

Be ready for the opening bell! You'll lose a lot of sales if you're not. As much as one-third to one-half of your daily sales can be made during the first thirty minutes of the market day. Do as much bunching, bagging and pricing as you can beforehand to prepare for that initial rush of buyers. The more you do in advance, the smoother your day will be. ❧

several vendors stop coming to the market, because their customers started coming to the farm."
– Charlie Springer, Mgr., Richmond FM, IN

Bring business cards as well as brochures about your farm and what you offer there so you can use the market to increase on-farm sales for your CSA, pick-your-own or roadside stand. For example, customers may purchase small amounts of blueberries at the farmers' market but come to the farm to pick large amounts for freezing, canning or drying if they know doing so is an option.

Running Your Farmers' Market Business

2

"Manage your business and don't let it manage you! Don't try to grow everything, just what you love to grow and what makes money."
— Don Rogers, First Pioneer Farm Credit

KEEPING RECORDS

"Keep good records. Because of this I know what each vegetable grosses in dollars per foot of space. This allows me to adjust my planting each year, and continually increase my income."
– Chris "Marketman" Labeots, Baraboo, WI

OK, let's face it. Keeping records falls right behind root canals on the popular-things-to-do list. If you look at it as a battle plan to get and keep the most dollars on your farm, however, you might see it in a whole new light.

Especially with a perishable product, meticulous recordkeeping is essential to controlling risk and waste. Good records enable you to place your crops in the markets where you'll get the highest return. This year's records become the basis for decisions about next year's cropping patterns and marketing outlets.

Art Lange has reduced the risk that a major portion of his crop will go unsold by using multiple outlets and keeping records, not only of pricing but of quality considerations for each market outlet. By selling into his best markets when demand is high and supply low, he maintains his best prices.

"Some restaurants order from us at the farm for pickup at the market. They don't get a special price if we're in low supply. The price depends on supply and demand and quality. For us, selling to both farmers' markets and restaurants is a balancing act. We've tried to sell to one or the other but it doesn't work. If the fruit is a little too ripe the customers love it, but if it's a little too green the wholesalers will accept it because they're used to a lot greener. So we can pick the fruit a little greener for the wholesalers. Let's say we have a bumper crop of Babcock peaches, a fantastic peach but it has such a short shelf life that you can't sell very much of it to the jobbers. The jobbers try to bring you down on your price, but if you're getting $2 a pound for the fruit at the farmers' markets, you don't have to sell it for $1 a pound to the wholesalers. Most of our fruit sells for about $2 a pound and up at the farmers' markets and about $1.75 to the jobbers."
– Art Lange, Honey Crisp Farm, Reedley, CA

Create a list for each market you attend and every other outlet you use – an extended copy of your load list works well for this. Keep records of volume brought to market, volume sold, unit price, amount brought home and notes about special circumstances affecting sales. Events going on at the market – cooking demonstrations or tastings, or a ball game or fair – can impact sales in one direction or another. Make a note of holidays. Sales may greatly increase the week of a feast like Thanksgiving or be slow the week when folks traditionally eat out or travel, like Mother's Day or the 4th of July. Looking back at previous years' records for the same market can be really helpful here.

How much to pack for an individual market is part recordkeeping and part intuition. Look to your records to determine previous sales at that market.

Plan to bring 10-25% above what sold last time, adjusting for weather and any special event at the market, and calculating for desired growth in sales.

If you sell out well before the end of the market day, you probably didn't bring enough. Consider 'sell-out' to be having only a couple of any item left, because the last of anything always sells more slowly. It's better to have a small amount of leftovers at the day's end. If you bring in one truckload of produce and sell out within an hour, either you should have brought more or your price was too low. If loyal customers come to see you and you're out of product, they may go to someone else!

When you do multiple markets, it's useful to look at the differences in what is selling at each market. This allows you to tailor your load to the local tastes and get the best return. You also see if you're selling enough at any given market to cover your costs of attending.

According to a 1995 *Growing for Market* newsletter, Chip and Susan Planck of Wheatland Vegetable Farms in Purcellville, VA, are meticulous record keepers. With as many as 14 farmers' markets in the Washington, D.C., area each week, including four Saturday markets, the Plancks have developed a system to maximize their revenue.

They created a form that is used at every market, every market day. The form tracks how much of each item is taken to market, the unit price, the time it sold out, or the amount left at the end of the day. All these forms are kept in a big binder, organized by market, and consulted at the beginning of the week. This allows the Plancks to plan where to slot their produce each week, sending the most of any given crop to the market where it sells the best at the highest price.

There is considerable variation among the markets the Plancks frequent. For example, they can sell 100 bushels of cooking greens a day at the Washington, D.C., market, where 95% of the customers are African-American, but only 35 bushels at a market in a predominantly Anglo suburb. Even among the suburban markets, there are nuances in sales patterns caused by a combination of customer preference and competition. Chip says, "The significance of that is crucial.

It means we can make the most of everything we send to market. It's worth the coordinating time."

To see if a market is paying for itself, you need to know all your direct costs of marketing. Include stall fees, association dues, vehicle overhead, maintenance, insurance (vehicle and liability) and payroll. Pay yourself, at least as much as you would pay someone else to do the work – harvesting, loading and unloading, travel and market time, preparing point-of-sale materials and packaging supplies. If a market isn't pulling its weight and a price adjustment is out of the question, you need to pull the plug and find a market that will.

Along with direct marketing costs, you need to calculate your overhead and costs of production. Overhead includes everything from office supplies to interest on loans and equipment, and the cost of land and buildings. Production costs include actual cropping costs like seeds/transplants, fertilizer, water, fuel and labor.

Don Rogers, a farm business consultant with First Pioneer Farm Credit, suggests setting up a winner/loser sheet as a simpler alternative to traditional cost accounting for deciding which crops to grow and which to drop.

1) Rank the crops you grow by looking at things like:

  ♦ Customers' favorites and what you're known for. Calculate sales minus variable costs for each crop, e.g., write down seed, labor and other costs in the strawberry category based on inventory of product taken from the field. Know how much you produced and how much of this was actually sold – what is your percent sell-through?

  ♦ Ease on timing of crop, i.e., is it a crop you're always late on? By the time you get it to the market are other vendors also selling it?

  ♦ Hand labor required in producing and harvesting the crop.

  ♦ Price you are getting for the product at the market.

2) After each season, adjust the acreage and mix of your crops using this ranking.

3) Try something new each year to put on the list and stay ahead of the competition.

4) Check competitors to see how they have changed.

Recordkeeping can be a tedious task, but doing it often can make the difference between staying in business and failing. While a pencil and paper still work, using a computer can dramatically cut the time it takes to find and analyze critical differences.

There are several easy-to-use, small business accounting packages on the market; all have some cost accounting capability. Perhaps the best known of these is QuickBooks by Intuit. It even lets you run payroll, helpful if you have employees.

If you grow vegetables, melons and the like, the book *Market Farm Forms* [see "Marcie's page" at the back of this book] comes with a diskette of templates that work with a spreadsheet program to allow you to track your predicted versus actual harvest and sales in several markets per week, and it calculates the percent sell-through by item. It lets you compare markets, or markets versus other outlets.

If the "business" of business is new to you or you need to fine-tune your operation, your local Small Business Development Center offers classes for minimal fees.

Chong Choi presents the roots of her Korean heritage. A great attitude, superior product, straight-forward pricing and clean image help create success for Choi's Kimchi in Portland, OR.

STAFFING THE BOOTH

"If you hire someone who is friendly, cordial and nice you're going to make more. We evaluated returns at the end of the summer and noticed a big difference in whom we had sent to the market."

– Dan Haakenson, *The Small Commercial Gardener*

What draws people to your booth at the farmers' market is your merchandising skills. What induces people to buy your produce is interest, quality and perceived value. What keeps people coming back is your customer service. There's a business rule-of-thumb that it takes five times as much effort and resources to get a new customer as it does to retain one you already have, so customer service is critical to your bottom line.

Customer service means friendly, knowledgeable staff, a convenient layout and minimal wait time. It can get hectic when you have more than one customer. Make sure you have sufficient help to meet demands, especially when popular products such as strawberries, sweet corn, and tomatoes first come into the market.

Gathering Together Farm in Philomath, OR keeps a vegetable encyclopedia at their booth so staff can look up varietal details if they don't know the answer to a customer question. That's service!

"Our marketing guy advised us to try ShiftPlanning.com. With up to 40 people to manage – since we sell at 75 markets – it saves a tremendous amount of time. We post the shift changes, and employees know it's their responsibility to check it. We avoid lengthy conversations explaining the changes. We've also found that we rotate employees to different markets periodically since customers are asking for more discounts. We may let employees cover their own neighborhood markets, but only if they maintain sales."

– Donna Pacheco, Achadinha Cheese, Petaluma, CA

A minimum of two people in the booth makes it easier to wait on customers, allowing one person to take a break or restock your display. With only one person at the booth, as you wait on customers the displays will get low. Poor displays signal lack of choice to customers who then look elsewhere. This potential loss of sales might be prevented if one person is regularly restocking.

Use the same selling crew at each market visit, if possible. Like your permanent sign, familiar faces will help build a "known quantity" comfort level for your customers.

Spring Hill Organic Farm of Albany, OR posted a picture on Facebook of owner Jamie Kitzrow and an employee staging a mock booth layout using kids action figures. They showed their positive work attitude with smiles and a question for their customers: "Is it really work when you use ball players in the setup?"

Hiring & Training Market Employees

"Fifty-seven percent of farmers already selling at markets indicated that a shortage of labor has been problematic for them, although not enough to prevent them from participating in farmers' markets. In addition, 38% of respondents said concern about having enough help to grow produce for a farmers' market affected why they had never, or no longer, sold at farmers' markets."

– *Barriers & Opportunities,* Farmers' Market Trust

Finding, hiring and training the right employees are critical to the success of your business. Luckily, these skills can be learned. In most areas the local branch of the state employment office fosters employer associations. These groups offer free seminars and workshops during the year on such subjects as interviewing skills, writing employee manuals, safety training and the like. The local Small Business Development Center works with entrepreneurs to help businesses grow and succeed. They, too, offer low-cost and no-cost training for business owners.

Stu Leonard, a successful Massachusetts retailer, has noted, "You can't train 'nice;' you have to hire 'nice.'" Other employers have been known to tell employees, "If you're not fired with enthusiasm, you will be fired, with enthusiasm." You can't have a bad day when you're selling – you're in show business.

Hire employees legally. Most of us remember a Presidential appointee or two caught in a "nanny-gate": they didn't confirm that a potential employee was legally able to work in this country, and/or they weren't paying social security and unemployment taxes properly. These folks not only lost the opportunity for a great position, they had to pay back taxes with fines and penalties. In some cases they lost the employee and had to pay stiff fines for not checking their paperwork.

Again, your state employment office will have forms for you and your employee, and will sit down with you and show you how to complete them. Office phone numbers can be found through an online search ("state employment office" "your state") or in the "Government" section of your phone book.

Local high schools and colleges, ATTRA and the website Good Food Jobs are good places to post jobs. The cost is minor, and you will want to refresh your ad at least monthly to ensure that your post pops up on the first page of listings.

Requiring a resume guarantees the candidate's desire, avoids you wasting time and gives you background so you can explore their skill set more fully.

"Interviews should have three key components: selling the job, interviewing the candidate, and taking questions... a good interview should be a two-way street. It is a chance for you to evaluate an applicant and for him or her to evaluate you. Strong candidates will have multiple places they can work, so it's important to take the interview as an opportunity to really sell yourself and your farm as a prime place to work."

– Ariel Pressman, WI talent recruiter, in *Growing for Market*

Your history and farming experience give a candidate some idea of what they will do and learn with you. Strong candidates have choices, so you need to sell yourself and discern compatibility much as the potential employee is doing.

Before you can look for an employee, you have to know what it is you want someone to do. Write a list of tasks. "Sell at the farmers' market" is pretty general. Make it specific:

- Meet truck at the market space 75 minutes before opening.
- Erect shade structure.
- Help set out produce.
- Place price signs and recipes next to appropriate product.
- Greet customers with a smile.
- Correctly weigh produce and make correct change for customers.
- Restock product as needed.
- Consolidate product to keep a full display during market.
- Other tasks as assigned.

This list of tasks is the basis for a job description. It also lets you think about the skills you need in an employee, and whether someone else could do some of these things. With two people in the booth, you could have someone good at display, stocking and working with customers, and another who's a good customer person with strong math skills who can weigh produce and make change quickly. If you're one of the people in the booth, think about what skills might complement your own.

> "When hiring help for the farmers' markets, look for a good salesperson. This is number one, even over having an interest in the produce, because selling is their number one job. Look for salespeople who are friendly and who like people."
> – Gretchen Hoyt, Alm Hill Gardens, Everson, WA

For some good tips on being an effective employer, check out the online article, "Be the Boss You Always Wanted to Have" – there is a plethora of online advice on this subject.

Develop a manual on how to handle sampling, cash, customers, security concerns and product information, such as what products are upcoming and ways to cook and store the products.

While a manual is a great reference and learning tool, it's no substitute for one-on-one training. Here are the four basic steps in any training process:

- *Tell* them how to do it. Verbally explain the task at hand, one step at a time.
- *Show* them how to do it. Physically do the task. Do this separately from step one.
- *Watch* them do it. Observe carefully the entire process without interrupting or coaching.
- *Fine-tune* the teaching. Praise what went right. Re-tell and re-show what didn't quite work.

SETTING PRICES

"We all lose at the farmers' markets by trying to compete on low price. Rather than lowering prices, look for ways to make your food look better by washing it or improving the way you grow it, or by getting it more quickly to market."
– Gretchen Hoyt, Alm Hill Gardens, Everson, WA

"Sell top quality consistently and customers will keep coming back. I've seen time and time again that customers are extremely loyal if you bring only the best quality to market. People sell geraniums at several stalls at our market, but at one stall they have geraniums that last all summer and into the fall, and people line up at that booth to buy them."
– Teresa White, Mgr., Cedar Rapids, IA

Most customers seek quality first, then price. Farmers' market customers want freshness, ripeness and flavor above all else. Many are willing to pay a premium price for fine quality. So offer only top quality produce. Accommodate your customers. Guarantee your product. THEN, get as high a price as the market will bear!

Gail Hayden, executive director of the California Certified Farmers' Market Association, tells the story of how five growers brought peaches to the market, creating an oversupply. The growers were trying to sell their peaches for $1.00 a pound. "Although the growers wanted to lower prices, I advised them to raise prices," says Gail. She explained that farmers' market shoppers were looking for varieties of peaches they can't find in supermarkets. Some growers lowered their price to 80¢ a pound and still took product home; others raised the price to $1.20 a pound and sold out.

Hayden's point is well taken. Consumers often perceive diversity and choice at the market differently than farmers do. Farmers like the ones above tend to look at diversity in terms of individual crops, i.e., how many vendors are selling the same items they have – peaches, melons, tomatoes, lettuce. Consumers tend to look at diversity in terms of types of crops – white freestone peaches versus yellow cling peaches, cherry tomatoes versus slicing or sauce tomatoes. They also assess types of growing methods – organic, biodynamic, IPM; types of display and merchandising skills; and individual farmers' personalities.

The sweet corn that Gary Pahl of Pahl Farms in Apple Valley, MN sells at the farmers' markets goes for about 40-50% over supermarket prices –

While people are used to paying by the pound, a $3 purple cauliflower is not only a good price but it motivates the impulse buyer to test something new.

a cost customers are willing to pay because the products are guaranteed fresh, not more than one day old and often picked the same day. "You're selling freshness," Pahl states. "You pick on Saturday morning and sell it that day while chain store produce is usually at least four days old. As soon as corn is picked the sugar starts converting to starch and the corn loses flavor. With some of the new varieties this is a slower process, but it still doesn't beat that same-day freshness."

Be honest about the value of what you are offering. Don't be afraid to charge more if your customers agree that it is of superior quality. If an item is selling very fast, and you will soon sell out, you may have priced it too low for that situation. Learn to judge the market by how things are selling and adjust your prices accordingly. Rather than establish a lower price perception by lowering a sign price, make a SALE sign for the remainder of market. Note, however, that a day of slow sales usually indicates few customers at market and this may not be improved by lower prices.

No matter what your products are worth, some people will be glad to pay what you are asking and some will tell you the price is too high. There is a mix of these customer types in any location and you need to determine what the ratio for each product you are selling is in order to maximize your day's sales. Listen if there are too many complaining about price. Some customer grumbling is to be expected: "Your competitor is cheaper." If only one customer in twenty complains, so what? Smile, and repeat the classic line, "He knows the value of his produce; I know mine," and use the opportunity to educate – explain your growing methods, uniqueness, freshness and so on.

Charging What the Market Will Bear

Be a "price setter" and have a great crop to back it up! What is the maximum amount you can get for a product? Go off-season to a good supermarket and see what they're getting. Try to get at least this price in-season and do not lower prices if you can help it.

Farmers' markets are an alternative to cost-plus pricing, so going for top price is a valid way to make high profits in times of high demand and limited supplies. Unless the quality and uniqueness of your product justifies your premium price, however, customers will soon go elsewhere.

Going Rate

Know what's going on in the market! Get someone to watch your booth for half an hour and walk the market. See who's selling what. If you say you're selling the best tomatoes in the market, you'd better make sure you are. Do a taste comparison. While it is good to know competitors' prices in order to see if yours are out of line, don't set your prices solely by what others are charging. Perhaps you're offering products and services that justify a higher price.

> *"The greatest fine art of the future will be the making of a comfortable living from a small piece of land."*
> – Abraham Lincoln

See if your state department of agriculture publishes a price report or an ag report that gives farmers some idea of what farmers' markets, supermarkets and wholesalers are getting for produce. Other guides are local supermarket prices and other sellers at market. On the internet you can find that USDA provides regular national and regional price reports for fruits and vegetables, including organic, at:

www.ams.usda.gov/mnreports/fvwretail.pdf

If you subscribe to Rodale's New Farm magazine, you can check for organic prices nationally by crop and market at:

www.rodaleinstitute.org/Organic-Price-Report

Also, do a web search for "USDA cut flower price reports" and you will find Boston and Miami price reports as well as import shipment reports to stay aware of your biggest competition.

Gretel and Steve Adams consistently charge retailers more for their flowers than the wholesale florists charge because they are fresher with no shipping damage or shrink. Knowing the typical mark-up is 100%, they gain farmers' market customers with a price lower than the retailers can match.

"We sell our bouquets to grocery stores for $7.50, where they retail at $14.99. We want to give people an incentive to buy directly from us, so we sell those same bouquets (minus the sleeve and UPC) at farmers' markets for $13…"
– Gretel Adams, Sunny Meadows Flower Farm, Columbus, OH and *Growing for Market*, June 2014

Since seasonal bunches require less labor – zinnia, dahlia, ranunculus, anemone, broom corn, millet, marigold – they fetch $4-5/bunch when retail is about $7.99. High-dollar large blooms may be made into bunches of 5 to 10 stems, dependent on head size, making sure the customer is getting value.

Be careful about the perception of price fixing. Walking the market to note what other members are charging and even asking them about their pricing is not price collusion, it is simply trading information. Getting together with other members to "set" prices, however, is illegal.

"For the folks who believe broccoli is broccoli and don't see any difference in supermarket produce and ours, we feel it's not worth trying to compete with the supermarket. Our customers are those who can appreciate that our produce is thousands of miles fresher than supermarket produce."
– Tom Roberts and Lois Labbe, Snakeroot Organic Farm, Pittsfield, ME

Break-Even & Even Make a Profit!

"Unlike many growers who yo-yo prices up and down following the supermarkets' lead, we believe in keeping prices steady throughout the year. By figuring our cost to produce it and adding a profit, we are able to keep our lettuce at $1 a head through the season, while grocery store prices go from $.60 to $1.50. Last year, when prices of lettuce went up to $2.50 a head in the supermarkets, most vendors also raised their prices. There were angry letters in the paper about the high prices at the farmers' markets. We kept ours at a dollar a head because we knew what it cost us to produce it. Our consistent price policy has brought a loyal following, with 80% of sales from repeat customers. They know our prices are fair and they know the quality is there."

– Bob Meyer, Stoney Plains Farm, Tenino, WA

In the report *Barriers & Opportunities* by Farmers' Market Trust, 67% of farmers surveyed indicated they needed daily sales between $500 and $1,200 in order to sell at a Philadelphia farmers' market. This sales level is achievable at existing markets in Philadelphia where the average first year sales reported by farmers at markets operated by the Farmers' Market Trust are approximately $500 per day. About 16% of respondents were looking for sales above $1,200, a level that can be attained at well-established markets in many communities. *In terms of profits, a surprising 70% of those now selling at farmers' markets did not know if profits were too low* (emphasis ours). However, 68% reported that sales met expectations and 17% stated that sales exceeded their expectations.

What sales do you need to make any particular market worthwhile? Know your costs of production and sales, so you'll know what you need to charge to make a profit. Keep detailed records and calculate profits per acre per crop. To do this, you need to keep track of costs and income as best you can for each crop. Calculate your break-even point per volume (quart, etc.) of product, and then add a profit percentage.

To find your actual costs for each crop and your margins according to various marketing channels, try a tool from the University of Wisconsin-Madison:

www.veggiecompass.com.

On the other hand you may want to follow some sage advice offered in a June 2012 *Growing for Market* article:

"A long time ago, a farmer I worked for passed down some really basic pricing advice that he had received from an old Italian farmer at the Minneapolis farmers' market: the cost to harvest and pack your produce shouldn't be more than one-quarter of the price you charge at market. So, if you pay your harvest labor $10 per hour,

$$4 \times \left(\frac{\$10}{1\ \text{hour}} \times \frac{4\ \text{hours}}{100} \right) = \frac{\$1.60}{\text{bunch}}$$

and it takes four labor hours to harvest and pack 100 bunches of beets, you would charge a minimum of $1.60 per bunch.

— Chris Blanchard, Rock Spring Farm, Decorah, IA

Market Considerations

While setting prices at cost plus mark-up is useful in setting the least amount you can charge to cover costs and make a profit, other factors should also be taken into account when determining price point:

Quality and selection of produce. A premium price requires a quality product. Customers may be willing to pay a higher price for an item if they feel the quality difference justifies it.

Competition. Regardless of cost and desired mark-ups, prices must be competitive with other sellers for similar products.

Uniqueness of product. How many other products like yours are in the market? The more unique your product is, the more you can set your own price as long as the price is fair in the customer's eyes. The more common your product is, the less leeway you will have in setting prices.

Time of the year. The first fruit or vegetable of the season may be able to command a premium price while end-of-season products may have to be priced low in order to sell. For instance, the first summer squash in the market may command as much as double the "main season" price. In the fall, however, when the winter squash starts to come in, and most customers have eaten their fill of summer squash, the price to get sell-through may have to be 30-50% less. Obviously, this begs the decision of whether you can pick and bring end-season squash to market profitably – maybe it's time to turn it under.

Market clientele. You may price your product differently in each market. Look at the volume you can move at various prices based on the area demographics, whether lower or higher income.

Be a Price Leader!

"Do not undercharge. Farmers have hurt themselves by undercharging. Be proud of your livelihood and charge what you need to make your livelihood. Don't try to compete with the supermarkets. Offer something different and bring your finest produce. It hurts business to bring day-old products."

– Chris Burke, Burke Organic Farm, Boulder, CO

"Rather than lowering prices towards the end of the day, find secondary outlets such as soup kitchens or non-profit organizations like AIDS hospices, McDonald houses, or food kitchens to whom to donate produce that doesn't sell at the market. Talk to church people to find these secondary outlets. There's usually a kitchen that feeds underprivileged children in your area. Don't sell it cheap and don't throw it away. It gives you a real satisfied feeling to donate it to people who need it. I'm not able to donate a lot of money to these organizations, but donating food gives the feeling of contributing."

– Bonnie Dehn, President, Central Minnesota Vegetable Growers

You also can move excess produce by finding other ways to use it. If you have too many apples, don't drop price; make pies, cider, or cider vinegar instead. Seek secondary market outlets such as sales to restaurants, grocery stores or roadside marketers who don't have enough of their own produce.

One of the biggest mistakes many vendors make is selling too cheap, competing with supermarket prices. Supermarkets, however, frequently sell things below cost as a loss-leader to get the customers in to spend money on other items. Don't get caught in the "I can do it cheaper" syndrome. As a small company, you don't have the means, volume or experience to market products more cheaply than the supermarkets. Homegrown and organic are worth more.

Under-selling is bad not only for you but for the market. Popular items that sell in great quantity may be sold at a wide range of pricing. Keep good feelings in the market by not creating an over-supply of any item or undercutting competitors' prices on a regular basis.

You cannot win a war against the big guns, especially the box stores. We're seeking quality buyers, not quantity buyers. Here's a general rule: a five percent increase in price gives you even net sales with a 14% drop in customers while a five percent decrease in prices requires a 20% increase in sales to stay even.

Cutting prices often results in only marginally more sales since it generates in many buyers a distrust of the product being offered at "fire sale" pricing. Being known as the cheapest or always having a sale attracts the bargain hunters – customers who will go down the aisle when they find someone selling for one cent cheaper – rather than the quality-conscious customer who will pay appropriate prices. Don't reduce your price just as the market ends to avoid taking product home. You "train" folks that, if they wait until the end of market, they'll get a bargain, and they'll be back every week looking for a discount.

It's actually less costly to do better marketing and promotion than to cut prices. Train your sales force to be friendly, hand out recipe sheets to stimulate sales, spiff up the appearance of your booth, and change the style or location of your displays rather than cut prices.

Lower-Price Markets

Having said all the above about getting the highest price, there is a place for moderate prices to build your market. Ask yourself if you are hurting your sales (and the market) with $4.99/lb. peaches.

In many areas of the country, customers expect and get lower prices because the farmers' market has positioned itself as a place for both quality and price. Some markets have certain farmers with high quality and other farmers with somewhat lower quality, each with appropriate pricing structures. Having lower price farmers can be very helpful in building the market customer base that, in turn, supports necessarily higher price vendors.

Most areas of the United States include lower and middle-income communities where price is a critical factor in consumers' selection of where to shop. If a farmers' market is to be successful, farmers' prices need to be realistic from the buyers' perspective.

Farmers at Heart of the City Farmers' Market at San Francisco City Hall processed $230,000 in electronic benefits from SNAP recipients alone in 2013, more than total annual sales for most markets. To reinforce low-income shopper loyalty, it's not uncommon to find markets in the Bay Area or any part of rural America where vendors drop prices dramatically during the last 30 minutes or hour. Low prices attract bargain shoppers who readily accept the declining variety at the end of market day.

The artistic signs of Hillebrecht Farm of Escondido, CA show which grapes and raspberries should be sampled. Their quality reflected the quality of the 1980s.

PRICING TECHNIQUES

Price for convenience. Hit even numbers in spite of psychological barriers. Your high quality will overcome it and this makes it faster and easier to move products. Today's consumer is sophisticated enough to see through the 99 cent ruse. If items are priced at $1, $2, $3, etc., no coins are necessary. If you're selling flowers and you want to pass sales tax onto the customer, have your price include the tax – as the Adams family does with their $13 bouquets – so they come out on the even dollar as above.

Multiple pricing. "$2 per pound, 5 pounds for $8." Encourage multiple or higher-volume purchases by offering savings for multiple purchases over the single item price. Four kiwi for a dollar pushes more purchases than 25 cents each.

Volume discounts. If you sell in an area where people still process their own produce, encourage large purchases by offering volume discounts. Marketers selling large volumes of produce for home canning and freezing may encourage the customer to buy in larger units such as flats of berries, boxes of tree fruits, or 20- and 25-pound units of vegetables, including carrots or oranges for juicing. Think IQF berries (Individually Quick Frozen) from your freezer to theirs.

Appropriate unit of pricing. Give some thought to the appropriate quantity or unit of sale for each item.

Sweet corn by the dozen may not be appropriate if most of your customers are couples or single-parent families who will not consume this quantity within several days. Encourage smaller purchases so the corn will still be fresh when they eat it. Then they will likely return for more.

Reward loyalty. For repeat and faithful customers, give extra produce rather than lowering prices, e.g., give a free flower bouquet to loyal customers who make purchases of $10 or more. Santa Barbara Pistachio Company gave a FREE canvas tote bag – $3 value – to customers purchasing $30 of product. It was much more effective than a 10% discount, and it created countless free mini-billboards on people's shoulders.

A sale item each week. Selecting a different "special" keeps your booth looking like there's something new happening all the time.

Quality Prices, Quality Products

Stress quality and uniqueness. Perhaps your sweet corn is raised without chemicals or spray, for example, or you grow unique varieties like "Wonderful," "Sweet Sue" or "Gold Cup." The fact that people are coming to the farmers' markets means that they're looking for a reason not to go to the supermarket, so give it to them!

"Best ideas for getting top prices at the market? Signs on tables that say 'FARM FRESH' or

'PICKED LAST NIGHT.' Folks are usually willing to pay a little more for fresh."

    – Diane Green, Greentree Naturals Farm, Sandpoint, ID

"You just can't get cheaper than the supermarkets. You can't compete on prices, so consumer trust becomes all important. Consumers are looking for fewer pesticides, for example. It's expensive to get certified organic in New York, so the growers bring photos to market to show customers their growing methods."

    – Jane Desotelle, Mgr., Adirondack FM Co-op, NY

Guarantee satisfaction. Guarantee that your crop is better than what customers will find in the supermarket: "I guarantee every melon I sell. If you don't like it, bring it back!" Better yet, guarantee 100% satisfaction. Imagine a market where every farm met that standard!

As Ronald Smolowitz of Coonamessett Farm, East Falmouth, MA, says: "If products are not top quality, toss it; take only your best to the market. I give my customers my best quality products, and those customers are there no matter what my prices are, and they bring their friends and relatives. They tell me: 'I know your berries are really good; I don't find any mold in them. So I keep buying from you even though I know your prices are higher.'"

Use small-unit pricing. For expensive specialty items, price in small units. Instead of $5 a pound, make it $3 a half-pound or even $2 a quarter pound! Smaller-unit pricing makes it easier for the customer to buy and try out a new or expensive product. Similarly, try selling expensive items like strawberries, blueberries and raspberries by the pint rather than the quart. Snow peas at $4 per pound may find some customer price resistance, so try selling one-quarter pound for $1. Customers will pay more for two individual pints than they will for one quart.

The strawberries Smolowitz sells at the markets are prepackaged in pints, not quarts, and raspberries likewise come in a one-half pint size rather than pints. "People tend to buy in smaller quantities," Smolowitz says. "We get a lot of retired couples or single households and people don't can like they used to."

Susan Planck tells her employees that when an item isn't selling well in bulk, they should repackage it into quart boxes. "The quart box is the most amazing phenomenon," Plancks exclaims. "Visually, it looks like a lot. Little tomatoes amidst a bunch of big tomatoes won't sell, but little tomatoes in a quart box sell well."

Sell smaller packages for more. Diane Green of Greentree Naturals Farm explains this strategy, "If I ask $2.50 for a pint of raspberries, people think I'm nuts and refuse to buy at that price when they can buy them for a $1.00 at the next stand. I package them in 1/2 pint containers, and sell them for $1.25 and sell out EVERY TIME. I have no idea why a smaller package for more money will sell better, but it works!"

Price hard-to-find items above the market. Do this for unusual products like garlic scapes or where competition is less intense, especially where there are quality differences. Even when yields are great, main-

Create action. *Two burners on an island table and the reassuring voice of John Eveland of Gathering Together Farm give people confidence in cooking kale for the first time.*

tain your price. You will not stimulate additional purchases with a lower price. People will only buy what they need.

Give samples. Let customers taste your quality! Cut slices: "These brown turkey figs are fabulous!" Especially with a new or unusual product, give out educational literature or recipes to show how to use it. Any specialty mushroom – chanterelle, lobster, matsutake – will gain new followers if you cook up some samples in olive oil or butter.

"Showcase" your product with great merchandising. Why do you think expensive jewelry is back-dropped by velvet or other fancy fabric? Make dynamic displays using attractive packaging. Market manager Dana Plummer of the Downtown Waterloo Farmers' Market says, "Consumers will pay twice as much if they're at a good-looking stall that's pleasing to the eye, where samples are provided, and where the vendors are customer-friendly."

Provide service. This is what customers don't get in the supermarkets or "big box" stores. Start interactions with a smile. Ask your market to provide carry-out service for large purchases or for seniors, or do it yourself. Provide nutrition information and storage tips, and suggest ways to use the product (recipes, etc.) to increase demand.

Maintain your base pricing. Try not to lower your prices even when your competitors are dropping theirs. If competing farmers drop prices, keep your original price even late in season, but give something extra. As one grower said: "If special sales and lower prices are appropriate due to overabundance of supply or promotional activities, we find that retaining the base price and then adding extra value is much better than simply getting a lower price. For example, when corn is over-supplied and other farmers are down around $2.75 per dozen, we keep our base price of 35¢ an ear, 6 ears for $2.00, and $3.75 per dozen. To attract the customer we offer 6 for $2.00 and then get a 7th ear free, or buy a dozen at $3.75 and get 2 ears free. We find people often buy a dozen at $3.75 to get two free. We get 27¢ per ear and keep our base price for future marketing. Our competition gets 23¢ an ear and will have difficulty raising the price in the future should the corn supply change. Again, quality is critical."

Finally, if and when you do make upward price adjustments, make them as little as needed rather than all at once.

Bottom Line

Does it pay? Check the bottom line.

Some farmers go to farmers' markets for the pleasure of talking to customers and getting feedback on their products but they fail to keep tabs on costs. They may be losing money without knowing it. Keep track of how much you take to the farmers' market and your costs of producing, transporting and selling your products. Be sure to include labor costs (your own as well as hired labor) and personal expenses for lodging and food. Subtract the value of unsold food at the end of the day.

Compare your costs with revenues to determine your net farmers' market income; compare this with what you might have made selling through other marketing outlets. Are the farmers' markets profitable for you? Don't forget to consider non-immediate returns, like the benefits of using the farmers' market as a test market for new crops, building your personal e-mail contact list, creating restaurant or CSA sales, establishing connections with wholesale buyers or meeting customers who want to visit your farm, etc. Watch your bottom line! ☙

Your Farmers' Market Retail Storefront

3

"You're driving in with a truck and setting up a retail store. Think like a retailer because that's what you are."
– Eric Gibson, *Sell What You Sow!*

Once you start setting up to sell at a farmers' market, you're no longer a farmer; you're a retailer, and you need to think like one. As a retailer, an entirely new set of questions and challenges arise.

BUILDING THE STORE

If you take your show on the road to weekly markets, you'll generally have about 30 to 90 minutes to build your store, erect displays, and merchandise them before the market opens. Whatever you use to create your storefront, you will need to be able to put it up and take it down easily and quickly. Even if your space is permanent, you still need to be able to clean and stock it quickly so your energy can be used to make sales.

Make sure people remember the name of your business. Try to create a unique look that is connected to your business name. Repeat your name coming from various angles.

Shelter

Shelter has three main functions: first, to protect product quality and incidentally customer comfort; second, to provide your farm with recognition; and third, in some cases to define your sales floor.

Some growers who live in a mild or even cold climate may feel little need for tents or canopies for protecting product quality. Nevertheless, canopies help define space and create business credibility. Some growers have the benefit of historic market buildings or shelter spaces and thus have no need to erect one of their own.

Consider where your market is located. Is it under the trees or in the open parking lot? If you are outdoors rain or shine, investing in a canopy may be essential to protect your products. Be sure your structure has a minimum height of seven feet for adequate head room.

If you do feel shelter is necessary or desirable, here are some things to consider:

Three Twins Ice Cream captivates the customer's visual field so thoroughly that they are forced to stop, read about and consider the options.

- Produce and flowers are visual sells. It is necessary to balance the need for shelter with the need for light on the product. Weather permitting, it may be fine not to use a canopy at all because more light brings out the color and natural light is best.

- Color contrast helps attract customers' attention. Choose the color of your awning carefully. Colors affect the appearance of food. A blue or green covering can make produce look green; a yellow shade, however, can make it pop. Darker colors attract heat. White reflects sun and doesn't change product colors, but shows dirt.

Viridian Farms of Dayton, OR understands the power of repetition, and their "growing for gastronomes" tagline affirms a keen attention to quality.

- Bring along extra lighting for an indoors, evening or winter market. Use halogen spotlights or track lights indoors rather than incandescent lighting. Fluorescent is a "no-no," as it makes everything look dead. Outdoors, hang 12-volt spotlights using a marine battery.

- Tarp and pole structures are cheaper than canopies but screws and bungie cords can get lost or damaged, and require more set-up time.

- Pop-up tents create a more intimate setting with the four vertical posts defining the space. Customers must come into your space to buy. Depending on the area of the country, the newness of the market or your presence there, and what other vendors are using, this may be an advantage or a hindrance. Decide whether you want to fit in with how other growers are setting up, or stand out.

- Umbrellas may be market- or patio-style but can be trouble in the wind. Market umbrellas are actually designed to mitigate this by having a separate vent piece on top to prevent the wind from making it a flying projectile. Umbrellas give a more open feeling to the stand than tents or canopies and allow more light to the product. However, they offer less protection from the elements.

- Use hanging weights to keep any covering from moving in the wind. With stronger wind gusts possible, cans or buckets of cement may be necessary; use them for merchandising or hide them under tables to avoid a customer tripping hazard. You also might tie them down with bungie cords using the weight of your vehicle or display table.

- Anchor umbrellas at two different points and use only the vented type. If your umbrella can tilt, be sure it is high enough to be well above eye-level at its lowest point.

- Whatever you use, think safety first. Ask yourself what would happen if a 50 m.p.h. wind lifts your canopy ten feet up in the air and then it comes back down, weights pulling sharp poles toward people's heads. More than one person has been hospitalized from an incident.

- Canopies are most dangerous during set-up and tear-down, when weights are not attached. Even a minor gust can wreak havoc.

- Keep any displays in front of the space at least waist high so they are visible and less likely to cause a customer to trip.

[See Resources, Chapter 3 for more information on shelters]

Bigger is not necessarily better: If you have little produce, take a smaller space so you can fill it easily. The look of abundance is more important than the

*A Hong Kong fruit display shows the power of an artistic 8'
waterfall. A nearly vertical display does not slide.*

size of the stall. When we first started Full Circle
Organic Farm, we didn't grow enough to fill an entire
market stall, so we sold off the back of our 1953
Chevy pickup truck. We built stake sides to fit into
the side-rail holes. Internal rails allowed us to use tiers.
We set L.A. lugs (wooden-ended, paper-wrapped containers used for shipping fruit) on end, slanted from
one tier to another. We had two tiers, three boxes
wide, then tailgate space. It looked full and fabulous!

If you have a choice, try to get a stall where your
customers face away from the sun and utilize shade
caps or hats or umbrellas to protect yourself and your
product.

Many retailing terms are used interchangeably
outside the retail environment. This can be somewhat
confusing to the novice retailer. To make things easier
to understand, here are the terms used in this section
of the book and what they mean.

- Sales floor – the space accessed by the customer to
  view, select and purchase your product.
- Backroom – space you use to store extra product,
  display fixtures, signs, bags and other sales tools. If
  you're in a weekly market, this is generally the back
  of your truck.
- Display – the general layout and physical structures
  used to hold your product.
- Waterfall Display or Fall – a mass display that
  seems to flow from a case.
- Tie-In Promotion – a promotion in which two
  products are displayed together and one item is

given away or sold at a lower price with the purchase of the other.

- Merchandising – the creative handling and presentation of products on the sales floor to maximize
  their sales appeal.
- Selling – the art of serving the customer and exchanging your products for their money.
- Suggestive Selling – a marketing technique in
  which tie-in or complementary products are recommended, such as basil with your roma tomatoes.

SALES FLOOR

"We've learned over the years that
the better things are displayed, the
better they sell. You've got to attract people to your booth."
– Judy Medicus, Cat's Paw Organic
Farm, Union Bridge, MD

Sketch out your plan on paper first. This can save a lot
of time when you are setting up your stall space. The
drawing should show the layout of the sales area, the
location of tables or display fixtures, a list of the fresh
items you are going to display, and the location and
amount of space allocated to each one. Some farmers
do this for each market day. Done on chalk board and
taken to market, this helps employees to create great
visuals.

Another idea is to do a dry run before your first
market. Lay out rope or chalk the sales floor. Erect
your shelter or umbrellas, put up your tables, and set
empty boxes or baskets where you think they will go.
Use some of your kids' colored construction paper for
color blocks. Stand back and look at the space. What
needs a pickup? Is it visually interesting? If you walked
by it, would you be able to tell, literally at a glance,
what was there? Is the entire sales floor visible from
the front or does one display block another?

Become the customer. Walk around in the space.
Turn around in the space. Do it again with one hand
holding a full shopping bag. Are you comfortable?
Did you run into tables, floor stacks, or displays?

Two thoughts on U-shaped arrangements:

"Have the produce displayed where people can see it. Get it out front as close as to the people as you can. An inverted U makes a pathway into your stand so people can get close to your produce."

– Charlie Springer, Mgr., Richmond FM, IN

"We need to move away from flat displays. Lots of growers try to create more space with a U-shape but we found that a lot of people are not comfortable walking into a display. They feel you've got them there and that they have to talk to you or buy something. The answer is to go vertical or U-Shape outwards."

– Randii MacNear, Mgr., Davis FM, CA

There are other choices, of course. Use a V-shape or a W. This creates an indent to draw shoppers to the product, but not such a deep place that they feel

Using buckets on steps, Thomas Farm of Corralitos, CA creates a tulip waterfall to pull customers into their booth.

surrounded. Shallow U shapes with side tables or wings less deep than the main area is long would be another solution. Randii's solution keeps the display space for larger vendors without the "cave" feeling. Again, this is a regional influence.

Give Your Customer Plenty of Room

Vendors often have a small area, 20-27 feet deep and 10 feet wide, a typical pull-in parking spot including their vehicle display. Stacking baskets in the front and trying to draw in the customer may not leave enough room for more than one customer to stand on the sales floor. Don't try to pack too much in. It looks great but the stall gets crowded very easily. If your space is too small, it might be best to park elsewhere – get there early and unload to create a more open space. If you have a pickup, use vertical space and bring vertical cement blocks and boards to construct an on-site structure.

There is a retail term – "the butt brush." Researchers watched customers in several department stores. They determined that when a female shopper was brushed from behind more than twice, she moved on to a different area even if she desired the product she was originally looking at! This strong sense of space among Americans flies in the face of the "pack more in" display design.

Give the customers extra space on the stand to assemble their veggies. The bigger the space, the more they buy. The bigger the bag, the more they buy (within reason).

Riverdog Farm of Guinda, CA builds risers on five table set-ups that will pull people into their market store.

Plan Traffic Flow

"Put as much product between the customers and the checkout as you can, so that they will have an additional opportunity to buy more on their way to the scales. We make people walk 30 feet past islands of produce. They're standing in line and looking at the display."

– Mark Phillips, vendor, NYC Greenmarket, in *Growing for Market*, May 1996

"One grower has plastic baskets you can pick up at the beginning of their booth, not to keep but to shop within the booth. It's a 30-foot booth, and at check-out at the back of their booth, you hand in the basket and they bag it and tell you what the price is. This is more convenient than having people put it all in bags and then have to carry a bunch of bags around, and it saves them money on bags, too!"

– Mary Lou Weiss, Former Mgr., Torrance FM, CA

Let the customer flow in your booth lead to the checkout. Try to prevent long lines – customers may just leave. Give them a taste of something while waiting, which may lead to an additional sale.

If you anticipate considerable demand for a product, locate it in two or three places.

Designate a "pay here" line to speed up the process and minimize confusion.

Get enough help so lines don't get too long.

Have one person handling the cash box, and one assisting customers and forming a line, rather than having customers throng around trying to pay.

It's OK to have a small line, however. In fact, it's a big plus. It makes your stall look like something's happening! It's like a shopping mall – crowds attract crowds. The trick is to have a line, but not long enough to get customers discouraged. You can regulate the line length by talking to people a little longer or hustling them through. For example (if the line is too short), you can slow things down by explaining how to cook something or the best variety for a particular use. If line is too long, have product litera-

A colorful, artistic fabric sign covers the back of a pickup at Angel's Garden in Santa Barbara, CA.

ture or attractive signs about your farm within eyeshot to attract their attention while waiting. Or refer them to the product literature rather than taking much time to talk to them. As always, smile!

Use All Available Space

One way to make better use of the space is to utilize corners. Corners are vital eye-catchers as well as selling points. Yet too many growers leave their corners unused while supermarkets have long recognized the importance of corners.

"A dozen buckets of flowers on the corner of a stand will attract customers like a magnet. Yellow is a real eye-catcher. Farmers use it on the corner of a display even if they have only a little bit."

– Tony Manetta, former Director, Greenmarket, New York, NY

As the markets get more crowded, growers are learning to do more with less space. Learn to use vertical space, or "cubic footage" instead of square footage, and display an area instead of "setting a

Two-tiered round fixture at the center of a U-shaped stall space entices shoppers to circle it and brings them into the stall of Gathering Together Farm of Philomath, OR.

table." Going vertical in the back corners can fill and soften an otherwise square space.

"I even saw an onion grower using the tops of the onions to hang them from his canopy. People could just reach up and take what they need. Of course, it smelled like onion everywhere, too, and that was great."

The "Back Room"

Too frequently, the market vehicle is your back room. You have quicker access using the space underneath your display tables or even additional tables in the back of your store, the sides covered with floor-length curtains. This is where your extra stock, display fixtures, bags and packaging supplies, sign making supplies, and cleaning equipment should be – easily accessible to you but out of the customer's view.

Trucks. Be careful about the appearance of trucks behind your stand. You want customers to notice your product first, not the truck. Unless you have a vintage vehicle outfitted to look like the classic "farm truck," get the focus away from your truck. Strategies can include placing a sign with the farm name in front of your vehicle to make a backdrop for your display.

Make the back wall of your sales floor complement the rest of your display. Compare yours to other farmers to ensure you're doing your best to stand out as a quality retail environment.

Cleanliness/Neatness

Today's consumer is critically aware of food safety and anything involving the food they eat needs to project cleanliness. Even as customers have become more aware of production methods, they are still concerned with marketing as well. So, make sure your booth is immaculate.

Keep things tidy throughout the market day. Restock and rearrange your product continuously to keep the stall looking attractive. Go out front and check it from the consumer perspective. Empty boxes can be stacked neatly at the back of your space, reinforcing the volume you've already sold. Haphazard, loose boxes are a safety hazard to you and your customers. Growers often fall over their own boxes!

Keep a trash basket out front for customers, even if only for samples from other farmers. Put another trash

Gathering Together Farm employees can easily access a 3-tier display from front or rear while customers have a wall of greens from 2' to 6' high.

box behind your booth to help you keep a clean and uncluttered stall.

 ## LOGISTICS

Cashier Space and Cash Drawer

Bring enough change to the market so that you don't run out! Most other sellers at market will be glad to help out if you run short of change and you should be happy to do the same for them, but don't become a pest by relying on your neighbors to bring enough change for your operation!

Don't run out when the first two customers each hand you a $20 bill. Remember, if YOU are the farmer breaking the big bills, it means shoppers are coming to your stand first! Sometimes a seller leaving the market early or the person collecting the stall fees are good sources of small bills in an emergency.

At Full Circle Organic Farm, we ran a $100 cash drawer, or till, broken this way: 17 dollar bills, 5 fives, 4 tens, a roll each of quarters, dimes, nickels and pennies plus 2 more quarters. About twice a season, we'd have a change problem when we got hit by a bunch of $20 bills at the beginning of market, but for the most part the $100 till worked for us.

At a minimum you want to have $100 in your till to start the day, broken in various denominations including rolls of each coin. Some farms may have $500 in small bills, ready to be hit by a bunch of $20 bills at the beginning of market.

If you're in a tourist area and are selling value-added products, you may need more change or you may need a check-cashing policy. Know the pay cycles of the dominant local employer, generally the 1st and 15th of the month, when you will need more change.

Cash Handling and Drawer Etiquette

Set up your cashier area facing your sales floor. Turning your back to make change is impolite and leaves you vulnerable to shoplifting. Also, plan to merchandise smaller, higher-value items, such as fancy jams, herbs and spices, etc., at the checkout area.

While you must decide how you will handle your cash at market, having a cash box keeps everything centralized and facilitates making change. Keep the cash box on a table where you can see it at all times. To conceal the box, place it inside a fruit box sitting on its side. Or drill a hole through your table and cash box, and bolt it down each day. Need we tell you how often cash boxes are lifted each year by fleet-footed individuals? If you're in a permanent space, you may get a cash register and scale combination with a cash drawer that opens only at the completion of a sale.

Another alternative, one we used at Full Circle Organic Farm, is an old-fashioned maple cash drawer with a lock and a bell – ka-chinggg. You know every time the drawer is opened, and it is too big and heavy to pick up and stuff under one arm. Lock it if you need to move away to help a customer or to restock. Lean a box or basket on the cash box to create an incline for display space.

Some sellers prefer a market or carpenter's apron with at least three deep pockets for holding bills and coins. If you keep change in apron pockets, keep bills larger than $10 in your jeans or a deep pocket or lock them in the glove box of your vehicle. If you're going to use an apron, consider changing your pricing scheme to accommodate even-change transactions, i.e., even dollar amounts or change in quarters. Anything else will leave you fumbling or potentially chasing errant bills in the wind. If you're particularly adept at it, a metal change dispenser that straps to the waist may be another way to go.

Train your cashiers to handle cash properly. If two or more employees are working in the stand at one time, designate only one as the cash handler. The more hands in the till, the more chance that the till won't balance or a customer won't get the correct change. Tips for your cash drawer follow:

Bills should be face up with the top of the portrait's head to the right. This makes it easier to keep the bills straight so you won't accidentally put a $5 in the $1 slot and you make change faster.

Try to find a cash drawer with clips to hold the bills down. They're slightly more expensive but will pay for themselves in saved time. When you make change, simply pull the bill you want from under the clip. If you can't get a box with clips, use a large paper clip or lead weight on each denomination to keep the till neat and easy to use.

Of course, if you have complete trust, it's easier to have several employees or family members handling questions and making the transactions, rather than sending them over to a cashier.

Change

Take the customer's money politely and place it above the cash drawer or on the lid of the till while making change. This lets you see at a glance what money the customer gave you and prevents misunderstandings.

State the item price or sale total and what amount the customer gave you ("$6.27 out of $10"); then count out the change. Count aloud the coins to the nearest dollar and then the bills from the smallest to the total amount given to you by the customer. "That's six twenty-seven, 28, 29, 30, 40, 50, 75, seven, eight, nine, ten dollars." Give the customer the change, with a thank you, and then put the money in your cash drawer. You can't imagine how many customers comment with pleasure that you know how to make change!

Market Crime Watch

On the whole our customers are very honest. There are, however, a few bad apples. We can all help out by keeping our eyes open and being smart.

Over the last twelve years there have only been a couple of instances of cash boxes being stolen. Odds are it won't happen to you but why take a chance? We recommend that cash boxes be used only for loose coins. Aprons are your safest bet for your bills. Even cash boxes that are nailed to the tables are at risk of being robbed. How often do you let customers shop from inside your stand? Even the most unlikely person can grab a handful of money in the blink of an eye. Keep shoppers out from behind your stand.

It might seem like small potatoes to steal fruit and vegetables, but everything adds up over time. Again this is only a small problem involving a few shoplifters.

Last Thursday a vendor alerted me to a woman shopper. He thought he had seen her put some vegetables in her bag without paying. He pointed the woman out to me. She looked like anybody's grandmother, nicely dressed with a big designer shopping bag. So I watched her from a distance. She walked in front of another farmer's stand and kind of hesitated for a moment. At the time the sellers were all behind the stand, and the lady walked on. The farmer left his stand. His wife and her mom were busy with customers. The little old lady circled back. Quick as a wink she dropped a small orange juice in her bag and kept on walking! I couldn't believe it! I had to bust a grandma.

Shoplifters seem to work in many different ways. Sometimes they will quickly fill a bag, set it down on the ground, fill another bag for you to weigh and only pay for one. Other times they will fill a bag, put it behind their back, then an accomplice will walk by and take it away. More often a shoplifter will just walk away and you think someone else behind the stand waited on him or her. If in doubt, ask your partner: "Hey! Did you get that guy's money?"

Most shoplifting occurs during the busiest time of the morning. What can you do about it? Be aware. The more eyes on your side the better. When you are slow at your stand and someone across the way is real busy keep an eye open for him. Report anyone suspicious to the manager immediately. Hire one of your small children to keep an eye out for thieves. They can easily see under the table for the two bag trick.

Together we can keep these small problems from becoming big ones.

– Reprinted with permission from *Renae's Rutabaga Newsletter*, Feb. 1996, Renae Best, Sacramento Certified FMs, Elk Grove, CA ✿

With baskets and bags, Happy Boy Farms of Watsonville, CA invites people to load up in their 20x20 store protected by canopies and umbrellas.

You'll save time and money – and show respect – if you drop the price to the nearest nickel ("Let's call it $6.25") and avoid counting pennies.

Some farmers find it useful to write down every sale. A calculator can be a blessing when things get busy. Battery-operated printing calculators assure customers they're being charged correctly. If you can't do math in your head and you don't use an electronic scale, get a calculator and use it.

Keep pens and a paper pad around for quick calculations, notes, and recipes on the fly. Pens will also allow folks to write checks, sign up for the mailing list and counter-sign travelers' checks and coupons.

Security

Farmers' markets by their nature are joyous, chaotic places, and in the huzzah, it can be easy to lose your focus. Keeping the cab of your truck locked and putting the till in when you're restocking can save the day's receipts. If you have two people working the stall, one can restock in front while the other tidies up the cashier area.

While you should be able to make change early in the market, be wary of people trying to break large bills for very small purchases, say a $100 bill for $1.50 worth of goods. This is one way unscrupulous people

decide whether you're a good "mark" – by getting some idea of how much money you have in the till. Also, protect yourself by periodically pulling some of the larger bills from the till. Lock them in the glove box or drop them into a "lockbox" attached to the chassis that can only be opened back at the farm. If you get so many ones, or any other denomination, that you can't pull them individually from under the clip, count off 20, put a rubberband around them, and lock them away. Your till should never look full to the casual glance. Stash it, don't flash it!

Taking checks is an individual decision. There is no law compelling you to do so, but make sure your policies are clear and uniform. Maybe you only take checks from locals or only with a picture ID. From a security standpoint, it's a good idea to take only checks pre-printed with the writer's name and address. Ask for the customer's phone number if it's not already on the check.

Travelers' checks are about as good as cash but only if they are counter-signed in front of you and the signatures match. Don't be afraid to ask for a picture ID. You're looking for the picture and description to match the person in front of you and the signature on the ID to match the one on the check. Honest people will appreciate your thoroughness.

Train all staff in handling credit/debit cards, federal coupon programs and checks. At 2.75% per transaction, a smart phone Square can be helpful in sealing the deal on a high-value sale.

Con Artists

Good customer service skills will go a long way toward preventing problems. Greet every customer coming into your booth and make eye contact. Theft is a crime of opportunity. Friendly merchants who recognize their customers are not an easy mark and potential thieves will find someone else who is.

Vance has watched as a fast-talking charlatan bamboozled a farmer into handing over a $20 bill along with the "purchased" item. The thief convinced the farmer he had wronged his "customer." When the true wrong was uncovered, the charlatan fled empty-handed. Be ready, especially well into a long, hot market day, to think clearly and control the situation when someone suggests they gave you a large bill. Remember: There are people who practice the arts of heist and smooth talking and often leave the victim feeling positive or unaware of the wool pulled over their eyes. Place the bill above the drawer and carefully make only one transaction at a time; that will go a long way toward protecting yourself from such confidence artists. Avoid becoming a victim of the skillfully practiced deception.

Markets can be visited by theft rings – groups of three or four individuals who hoist wallets from customers walking from stall to stall with their handbags open. The "mark" or "chicken" is easy prey for a professional who lifts the wallet, passing it to another team member and walking away innocuously. This scene is usually played out in a more crowded market where even undercover police have a nearly impossible job noticing the theft in progress. Farmers can help their customers by encouraging them to close their handbags and keep them close to the body.

One farmer sheepishly admitted he'd been taken by three well-dressed women. As he packed up the rear of his truck, they pressed close around and reached across him to inspect his fruit. Of course, they didn't buy anything. As he pulled into his farmyard three hours later, he reached for the money roll in his apron pocket. It was $1,600 lighter.

Counterfeits

Brian Moyer at Penn State Extension heard from a market hit for $600 in counterfeit $100 dollar bills. When he spread the word, he was shocked to get manager and farmer responses that the same had occurred at markets throughout the mid-Atlantic and Northeast. It can happen anywhere, even to you.

The counterfeit $100 bills were actually bleached and reprinted five dollar bills with intact watermarks. They passed the pen test. The fake bill can just as easily be a $10, $20 or a $50.

Know your money. Study American currency. Make sure all staff know Lincoln is on a $5 (not $100), Hamilton on $10 and Jackson on $20. Check the paper characteristics and the print quality to find the differences.

- A President's portrait is lifelike, clearly jumping off the paper in 3-D, while a counterfeit appears more lifeless and flat, the details merging into a darker background.
- The Federal Reserve and Treasury seals have sharp, distinct saw-tooth points. Counterfeits may have uneven or blunt points.
- The fine lines in the border should be clear and unbroken. Counterfeits may have scrollwork lines that are blurred and indistinct.
- Genuine serial numbers are evenly spaced and the same color as the Treasury Seal. You may notice differing ink shade or poor spacing or alignment of counterfeit numbers.
- Genuine currency has tiny red and blue fibers embedded in the paper. Find the colored lines on the surface, and you're holding a fake.

A scale is almost essential. A Senior Farmers Market Nutrition Program sign covers the box here where the cash drawer is hidden.

As much as you're tempted to accept a $20, $50 or $100 (there are no $500 bills), don't get taken too easily. When you sense a ruse, spend the time to compare the bill with a genuine one of the same denomination and series.

The U.S. Secret Service investigates counterfeit currency. Study their website:

www.secretservice.gov/money_detect.shtml

which includes a more thorough description and images comparing genuine and fraudulent bills.

If you are taken by a thief, don't let the learning experience stop with you. It will probably happen again and again until all farmers learn how to be more aware. Immediately share your story with other farmers and your market manager to help prevent others from being victimized.

Choosing Scales

For the items you sell by weight, a simple spring scale hung from a bracket will suffice. It needs to be certified by the County Sealer of Weights and Measures, possibly for a small charge. Check with the market manager and town clerk's office to be sure you comply. A legal scale is helpful but not necessary, however, if you sell produce by the piece or volume to eliminate the time and hassle of weighing.

Hanging spring scales may add authenticity and "market appearance" for both the seller and customer. If yours is single-faced, place it within easy reach and make sure the scale shows weight visible to both you and the customer. Double-faced hanging scales do this seamlessly. Electronic scales, likewise, have displays on both sides.

"A battery-operated scale saved us a lot of money this year. We don't have to figure prices in our

Bounty attracts bounty as an employee of Phillips Farms hands change to a customer in the Vallejo FM.

heads and round figures off as with a hanging scale. If you're serious about selling at the farmers' markets, get an electronic scale."
– Edie Barker, grower, Portsmouth, NH

As your business grows, consider purchasing an electronic scale. Manufacturer's Suggested Retail Prices (MRSP) for battery-operated, price-computing scales are around $500, but online prices run 20-50% less. [See Resources, Chapter 3.] A price-calculating scale's greater accuracy will pay for itself quickly if you do large volume. At times you can purchase reconditioned electronic scales for the same price as spring scales.

Battery-operated, electronic scales that beep out the prices really speed up customer sales and avoid the tendency to round-down price, common with hanging scales. Every bounce on a spring scale costs you money in time. If you have intense activity in your booth or you want to be paid fully based on more accurate weight, it pays to invest in an electronic scale. ❧

Display 4

"Study what the supermarkets do. They spend a lot of money to research things like the distance the average customer will lean in to select an item."
– Lisa Bloodnick, Bloodnick Family Farm, Apalachin, NY

"One of the maxims of selling anything in a retail setting is that you have about three seconds to catch the customer's eye. At a farmers' market the window of opportunity may be even smaller with so much color, fragrance and activity calling out to shoppers from every direction. With so little time to make your sale, you need a display that will stop shoppers in their tracks and pull them to your market stand. And how do you do it? First, learn the tricks of the trade, merchandising strategies that work for supermarkets and that will work for you, too. Go to the supermarket and survey the produce section. Notice what catches your attention as you scan the displays and figure out why that particular display appeals to you."

– Tony Manetta, former Director, Greenmarket, New York, NY, in *Growing for Market,* May 1996

Earlier we defined display as the general layout and fixtures used to hold your product. The term is also used broadly by many market managers to refer to your entire stall as in "your display." Think of display a bit like stage-craft, like dressing a set for a play. What you do needs to provide a backdrop for the action without detracting from the product itself. Display sets the tone and is still an integral part of the market experience for the consumer. Display also distinguishes your farm, and you, from the other farms and farmers in the market.

Once you've defined your sales floor, decide what to use as your central display

fixture or fixtures. This is the backbone from which the rest of your display will be built. Tables, platforms, or even truck tailgates may be used to display produce. You can use boards on sawhorses or milk boxes – whatever keeps the food off the ground and moves it toward eye level.

The most important feature of your central display fixture must be SAFETY. Your structure must be sturdy enough to support your product and be jostled by customers without collapsing.

"Elbow to eye level lets customers see and evaluate the produce. Keep all food off the ground. Use a focal point or centerpiece to bring the eye to your booth. A salad bowl, made with your produce, highlights your offerings."
– *How To Improve Your Sales,* Southland FM Assoc.

A friendly employee stops people with a sample outside the "store" while vertical displays on either side and a 6'x9' photographic banner invite customers into Freddy Guys Hazelnuts grove.

In baseball the strike zone is over the plate and between the knees and the middle of the chest. In display the buy zone is between the knees and the top of the head. Product placed below knee level or above the top of the head falls outside the normal visual field and goes unnoticed. Even the zone between the knees and the navel is less obvious to most people than that between the navel and the forehead. Retailers have studied this for years. A classic example is found in the cereal aisle. "Adult cereals" are at about the 5 foot level and above, the prime visual awareness zone for adults. Notice the height placement of cereals like CocoPuffs and Lucky Charms. It's much closer to your navel, pretty much the eye zone of a 4-year-old child.

With a 45-degree wagon pepper display at the Olympia FM, WA, Bob Sullivan gets the product to customer eye level.

What does this mean for your display? Try to build the backbone of your display at the 3-foot level and go up and down from there. Thirty-six inches is the height of most kitchen counters, and pretty much the belt height of average American adults today. The more available your product is to the consciousness of your customer, the better your chance for a sale. With displays lower than three feet, however, you may be tapping into little people and kids. Don't forget to appeal to kids who pull an adult in your direction. A staircase of boxes will do.

"Place high ticket or new items like an exotic product right by your work area, so when people look at you, they see the product. If you're selling flowers, hold some of them right next to your face. Something about holding a product personalizes it or makes people notice it more. The product you're holding is the one people will buy! If there's something you have only a small quantity of, such as basil or green beans, hold it up and say 'Would you like some basil today?'"

– Gretchen Hoyt, Alm Hill Gardens, Everson, WA

When you hold a product you bring it more into the visual awareness of your customer, because of both the higher position and the movement of the product itself.

Once you have the backbone of your display in place, it's time to start working the vertical lines.

VERTICAL DISPLAYS

Create a vertical emphasis both to increase space and to improve the visual look of your display. Tiered display shelves are very inviting and help make all products visible. Many growers and managers also feel "going vertical" is a better solution than a U-shape.

"Stack your produce to create an appearance of plenty and to make it more visible from a distance. Start stacking from a few feet above the ground (never put food on the ground) and make tiers that reach above your waist on the table. Every item should be tilted to give the customer a better view and make your supply look larger. On the table top, don't settle for just one level of produce. Stack boxes at the ends and

Farmers and employees create waterfall displays during set-up time at the Davis FM. Notice the display goes from knees to eye level.

stretch a board across them to create a second tier for smaller items."

– *Growing for Market,* May 1996

If you're attending weekly markets without a permanent space, you must build your display on the fly each time. Folding tables or plywood across sawhorses will realistically be your choice for the backbone of your display, though they are less stable than tables when slanted displays are built on them. Keep in mind the need to balance the weight across the display. Too much weight may be a bad idea at almost any height. A customer in California once tried to pull a watermelon from the bottom of the pile and the entire table fell over, fracturing her ankle.

The simplest way to create a display slanted to the consumer's eye is to use a 2x4 or a set of boxes as a riser, and set the back of your display containers on the riser.

To create a vertical from your table down, use something like wooden blocks to support a board in front of the table, then stand the product boxes resting between the board and the tabletop. Two-step ladders will also do the trick here.

Now go even higher. Hang dried flowers, bunches of herbs, ristras, onion or garlic braids from your canopy using S-hooks made from coat hangers. Be

A stair-step and a smile show these bonsai trees to best advantage in Santa Monica.

careful not to put so much weight on one side you unbalance the canopy. If you don't use a canopy, consider making a pipe arch from which to hang product, your banner, your scale or other items. Use two ten-foot lengths of 1/2-inch, EZ-pull conduit bent at right angles with a pipe bender, and varying lengths of straight conduit coupled between them. Hang your scale from this along with seasonally changing products.

"Our table is hinged at the front so the back can be elevated. This creates an attractive, comfortable display. We copied the height, width and angle from the local supermarket chain tables."

– Lisa Bloodnick, Bloodnick Family Farm, Apalachin, NY

"Our display tables are built with a 15-degree slope, with all of the bagged items like potatoes, carrots and peas out on the front three-quarters of the table. On the back we prop up Styrofoam grape boxes for cucumbers, summer squash, zucchini, cabbage, onions, etc. By tipping the tables we've really made our display stand out. It's different than any other at the market."

– Jay Visser, J-N-A Produce, Manhattan, MT

If you have a more permanent location or are talented with a skill saw, consider doing what Lisa and Jay have done and build the slope into your display.

Vance created a sea of apples for Kiyokawa Family Orchards of Parkdale, OR by filling two boxes deep on tables to overflowing, and using empty boxes to create stairways and a low apple bed behind employees. It facilitated an 80-box sell-out in late April.

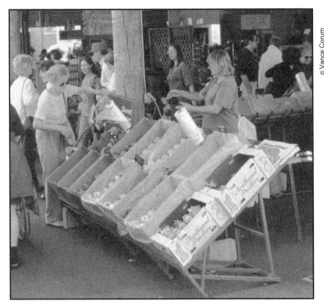

Sullivan's Homestead sports an adjustable custom iron display in Olympia WA. Note the bag rolls on mounted posts.

Any crop can benefit from a little height. For perennials and nursery stock, use an empty 2- or 3-gallon container upside down to raise the plants off the ground where customers can see them better. Don't force your customer to lean over to check a variety tag or grab their selection.

DISPLAY FIXTURES

For value-added products, consider purchasing some easily moved tabletop fixtures [see Resources, Chapter 5]. Stair-stepped displays create an array of depth, color and texture, and work especially well with vinegar and bottled products stacked row on row, for example. The height difference makes the product label more visible to the customer as well as adding interest.

"To display our produce at the markets, we use apple boxes as well as grape lugs that we get from supermarkets. The grape lugs are cardboard but they have wooden edges. We repaint them and put handles on them."
– Tom & Lois Roberts, Snakeroot Organic Farm, Pittsfield, ME

Look for used crates, baskets, or grape lugs ("L.A. lugs") from your local supermarket, and sanitize them thoroughly before using. Again, prop boxes or baskets at a slant toward the customers for easy viewing. Organic caution: If you are growing organically, be aware that organic certification rules may forbid using crates and boxes with chemical fungicide residues from commercial packers. Check with your certifying organization.

"Baskets are 'in' as display containers, along with stacked produce wooden crates, placed at an angle, with pretty tablecloths and lots of flowers."
– Diane Green, Greentree Naturals, Sandpoint, ID

Baskets are beautiful, but they need to be full. Crumpled newspaper or an inverted berry basket in the bottom can raise the remaining produce to the top. Baskets can be purchased in bushel, half-bushel, peck and half-peck sizes. New baskets, while attractive, may be expensive. Stopping by garage sales on the way home from market, or the flea market in the off-season, is a good way to pick up inexpensive

A small custom-built wooden stairway serves to display cherry tomatoes at the Ferry Plaza FM in San Francisco.

Tone-on-tone color scheme of natural colored soaps in older wooden boxes provides a sophisticated look that supports the price of this value-added product.

display items. Bring all sizes of baskets and containers to redistribute your product as you sell down – this helps keep your display looking full.

Display containers should blend well with and enhance the appearance of your produce, not steal attention from it. Browns, brick reds, dark greens, dark blues and natural wood colors will contrast well with the many different colors of produce in your display.

> "Cut-flower bouquets in cut-off coke bottles, 12 inside wooden crates, then slightly tilted toward customer side, and kept full at all times, gives an effective visual splash of color."
>
> – Anneli Johnson, Ex-mgr., Copley Square FM, Boston, MA

Plastic bottles, cut off gallon water jugs, pitchers and other water- and ice-holding vessels can be concealed inside baskets and boxes, leaving a strong display while still preserving the product.

Wood is good

> "People are looking for that natural feeling and wood brings home that message."
>
> – *Growing for Market,* May 1996

Using wooden flats or crates to display vegetable and produce gives a more "country" or "earthy" feel instead of using plastic. Old-fashioned containers also give a farm atmosphere to your booth: try a kitchen cabinet drawer, wicker or bushel baskets to highlight fruit or vegetables. Or put burlap bags over cardboard.

Unpainted wood stays wet and cool longer when watered than painted wood or plastic [see Resources, Chapter 5].

Light to highlight

Let your product drive the fixture. Honey, jam, jelly and juice are most appealing when light can shine through to highlight their color. Plexiglas stair-step, table-top fixtures can do this for you. Place "warmer" fixtures around a modern look like clear plastic: a woven bee skep or hive for the honey; a couple of pecks with fresh fruit next to value-added items; and flowers for anything and everything, just to give a colorful look and prompt a smile.

Sometimes changing the orientation of a fixture can increase sales. One grower had dried fruit in clear plastic tubs with hinged tops. By tipping the table in back by 10% he increased sales 50%! This made the products more inviting and accessible.

Creating falls

Lyle Davis, owner of Pastures of Plenty near Longmont, CO, says: "My background in retailing helps a lot. We use a lot of tier-stepping and waterfalls that make customers feel like they're reveling in 'abudanza' (Italian for 'abundance') when they visit the booth. The waterfalls create high displays of flowers or produce that spill out." The waterfall structures are supported underneath with boxes and crates.

Terhune Orchards of Princeton, NJ effectively uses wooden boxes for a down-home, farmstand atmosphere.

Falls, or waterfalls as they are also called, give the feeling that the pile of produce is endlessly deep. This isn't a haphazard dumping of a lot of produce; it's a purposeful construction. The displays of apples, pears, and oranges in the supermarket are really only two fruit deep. (End caps, at the end of aisles, are sometimes deeper.) They are built on platforms that create the height. You can do the same thing; just make the center platform box the same height as one to three times the average diameter of what you are displaying so it will hide behind the layer. For an even more dramatic look, build an extension off the table and continue the fall onto that.

Make it easy to buy

"Have plenty of plastic bags handy and accessible. Customers are accustomed to that convenience. Have some in your pockets to offer customers. 'I have a bag here if you would like.' As soon as they accept your offer, you have made a sale."

    – Dan Haakenson, *The Small Commercial Gardener*

Hilario and Soledad Alvarez of Mabton, WA draw extra curiosity for their extensive organic vegetable line with a wall of chili ristras (strings) on one side and coronas (crowns) on another at the Yakima Farmers' Market.

Natural light adds a sparkle to this already-sweet product. Marshall Farm's honey bear and honey sticks slow down kids at the Ferry Plaza FM in San Francisco.

Everything you do for display is worth nothing if your customers are unable to reach your product. Make it easy for them. Leave a space at the edge of the table where customers can set their parcels while getting out their money or bagging their produce. If they feel awkward in your stall, they will go elsewhere.

Keep your display no more than an arm's reach in depth, and between knee- or waist-level and eye-level in height. Studies show that 75% of products purchased are displayed between elbow and shoulder height. The more you bring product close to people's senses, the better your chance to effect their touch-and-buy response.

Take-home containers

Take home containers can become part of your display, make the customers' purchases easier, and add value to your product. Common types of containers designed to be sold with the produce include kraft (brown) paper bags, colorful shopping bags, plastic bags, boxes with handles, pulp board trays, and plastic or wooden berry boxes. Wooden baskets, cardboard boxes, and mesh bags also can be used.

Line selling containers with carry-out plastic bags so that when a customer selects an item it may be picked up immediately – no waiting for sacking.

You can use "lunch" type bags to sell by the bagful, or berry boxes to sell by the unit. If it's appropriate in your market, ask the customer if they need the berry basket. If not, transfer the berries into a bag allowing you to re-use the berry container. But don't look cheap over a basket, especially if your berries may get squashed on the way home.

While paper bags are more environmentally friendly, plastic bags for moist items are a necessity.

A stairway of heaping sacks of grains, beans and potatoes and a welcoming smile ensure success for this market vendor in Ica, Peru.

Use paper sacks for small, individual items, and have large grocery bags for customers who buy a substantial amount of products. There may be regional differences here, too. If your customers are accustomed to plastic produce bags in the grocery store, chances are they will feel more comfortable using the same thing at your stall. See-through mesh bags are good, too, letting customers see the quality of your product while allowing air circulation – great for hot days. Make sure they reinforce the color of your product.

Barrel bags (paper grocery store bags) can be purchased at many larger "wholesale-type" stores [see Resources]. Generally flat-bottomed ones are better for produce needs; they are usually made of stronger material than the "card store" type of bag. Seedling flats may be bagged two to a shopping bag, but trays made from cardboard soda boxes/flats (2" high) from a local retailer are more efficient at transporting large numbers of seedlings. Boxes from your local liquor store protect taller plants.

Market By Market

Jan Fellenz was setting up her stand in Geneva, NY one Thursday morning when she heard another vendor remark, "It's looking a lot like Wegmans over there." Referencing the #1 supermarket in Western New York, it may have been meant as a dig, but she was proud of it. Like her, you need to learn the "personality" of your markets, and how to tweak your display and pricing to improve sales.

Her loyal Geneva customers want a "just the facts ma'am" approach, whereas Canandaigua's Saturday more upscale customer base demand samples and fun items with an agri-tourist twist.

"The spots in our markets are small, only 10' – 12' wide so we need to make every inch count. Our market niche is nice produce at a fair price. We sell mainly staples: tomatoes, peppers, lettuce, sweet corn, melons, potatoes, squash, a few herbs, some eggs and raspberries. We have a fair amount of competition from the other vendors. Since we try not to compete on price, we need to ensure that our stand is welcoming and encourages people to buy.

"Before every market, Jan drew up a stand plan showing where everything would go in the display. The plan changed week to week depending upon what we had for sale. If we had lots of something like sweet corn or melons, they would go in a separate display in front of our table with signs to draw attention to them. We also featured samples of items like raspberries, cherry tomatoes, tomatoes and melons. When we had lots of tomatoes, we displayed multiple package sizes – singles, quarts, 4 quarts, 8 quarts and half-bushel to ensure that we had a package size to satisfy everyone from snackers to canners."

– Andy Fellenz, Fellenz Family Farm, Phelps, NY, in *Growing for Market,* Jan. 1, 2004

No one wants a hole in the market. If another farmer is a no-show, be ready to fill in 5-10' of space with a stairway or waterfall wing off your main display to colorfully draw eyes toward you.

Linda Chapman and Deryl Dale gradually found that their 5-acre farm in Ottawa, KS depended on diversifying their crop of flowers and their markets so that bad weather in one market would be redeemed on another day or through a different market avenue. They primarily sell flowers in three weekly markets: in a college town, a downtown urban setting and an upscale urban neighborhood. They change their product mix to meet the distinct customer bases of each market and season.

THEMES

"Generally the types of special selling displays can be broken down into five areas: production equipment, printed materials, actual crop material, kitchen help, and 'bits of country.'"

– Mark Wall, *Certified FM News,* Southland FM Association, June 1992

Displays can be built around a theme or suggestive of the farm name. This narrows the type of fixtures used for display and focuses the message. Sub-themes can revolve around seasonally appropriate displays – Spring / Easter, Summer / 4th of July, Fall / Halloween / Thanksgiving, and Winter / Christmas / Hanukkah.

Drop your stake sides and set up your display on your truck. One of the first organic strawberry growers in California markets, Jim Cochran used a quality Swanton Berry Farm sign and colorful, voluminous displays slanted on his truck to attract buyers.

Production equipment can include something as simple and different as an orchard ladder (taller is better) or a cider press. Interesting hand tools, power pruners, pumps, drip irrigation bits or a small tractor will all bring customers over to your table. Antique equipment attracts attention.

Crop materials can be something as simple as a flowering or fruited branch of your crop, some leaves, or unusually shaped fruits and vegetables. If you don't have the actual branch, enlarge a color photograph and hang it as a backdrop.

"Kitchen items such as appliances and/or utensils for cooking, ripening, preserving, juicing, and cutting can increase sales by planting ideas for more uses in customers' minds. Examples of commercial or home-made items can also spur sales, such as salsa ingredients (with an example of salsa), samples of your crop pickled, or any item that uses your products."

– Mark Wall, *Certified FM News,* Southland FM Assoc., June 1992

Filling a mesh bag with all the ingredients for someone's fresh, homemade salsa can also spark sales. Or why not add that value-added item to your product list?

Spicy pickled carrots, preserved cherries, pickles, lemon curd and more from Zoe's Favorites in Yacolt, WA help extend the market season. Baskets and canning equipment raise product for easy customer viewing.

THE NEW FARMERS' MARKET

The country or farm look

The niche for Lyle Davis at the Boulder and Denver markets is very high quality flowers combined with specialty vegetables. With twenty years experience as a produce manager at an Alfalfa's Whole Foods Market, Davis constructs stunning farmers' market displays. Farm antiques like old picnic baskets and old toys like little red wagons or goat carts are used as props to help create the "country look." Such items can be found at flea markets or antique markets.

Make displays that look like they came from the farm by using actual farm items. Wooden crates or boxes work well. Bales of straw are a great substitute for a table, particularly with fall crops, and sometimes you can even sell the bales, too. Even an attractive, "country look" tablecloth can add to your sales.

Even items that are NOT directly connected to your specific crop can entice shoppers. A wasp's nest or your hat or tin sign collection are examples of items that – although perhaps not unusual for farmers — would stand out for your customers.

Country boutique

When you have an expensive product, you need to have an elegant-looking booth. A high-end olive-oil or herbal vinegar seller, for example, might sport the "country/European look" with a rustic apron and

An internal L-shaped display with a table island allows more room for customers to see products, and protects them while the customers shop.

tablecloths. White painted kitchen tables or other wooden pieces and floral tablecloths and painted baskets can give a boutique look. This style lends itself to gift-giving as additional sales potential.

> "Display your products in similar basket-style containers with colorful cloth liners, and provide gift bags and tissue paper that customers can make an instant gift with."
> – Georgia Paulsen, Mgr., Topeka FM, KS

Farm name themes

Kicke the Bucket Farm is a diversified market farm built on a converted dairy by the Kicke family. They use old milk cans in their stall to support boards for a display shelf. Glass bottles hold single sunflowers for sale. Standing buckets hold a variety of potatoes, onions, and roots. Buckets laid on their side "spill" varieties of eggplant, peppers and tomatoes across a slant table. Plastic bags are pulled from rolls strung on the handle of an old hoe suspended above the display. The cashier stand is set up on three haybales set on end.

Seasonal themes

Seasonal themes work well such as fall squash and yam displays or summertime berries, figs and soft fruits. Do a complete rearrangement of your stall when the produce seasons change. Do not imitate supermarkets by trying to provide out-of-season

A small wheelbarrow lifts squash blossoms closer to the customer's senses for Rick Steffen Farm of Silverton, OR.

products such as tomatoes in January. Produce has its best flavor, holding qualities and overall value in season, when it is available at its greatest volume and lowest price.

Spruce up your stand with seasonal items such as corn stalks and pumpkins after Labor Day to get your customers in a Halloween mood. This will pay off as the holiday nears. Think of interesting ways to display pumpkins such as bringing a step ladder and putting them on each step of the ladder.

An 11-pound kohlrabi makes people stop to ask "What is that?" at the Astoria Sunday Market, OR.

Mobile displays

High-value or heavy products, especially those needing refrigeration, can justify the expense of a full trailer display. Bakers do breads and pizzas in trailer-mounted brick ovens. A Hillsboro, OR beekeeper built a roller system to slide his honey display out the back of his covered pickup truck. Wayne and Lee James of Windsor, CA carved their name, Tierra Vegetables, onto a banana squash that grew into a centerpiece sign amidst a trailer load of winter squash at the Marin Farmers' Market.

Color in display materials

Keep color in mind also when you are selecting display materials. A bright, but not gaudy, cloth, for example, will dress up your display. Use simple but effective color and background behind a beautiful natural product. Green is great beneath fresh fruit, for instance, but not over it.

Go easy on bright plastics. Baskets are a perfect display medium and even cardboard boxes can be wrapped in burlap sacks to look "warmer." Their natural look is a nice, neutral backdrop which helps accentuate the bright colors of produce.

Grab their attention

Remember that for all your display efforts directed toward capturing the passing customer, it may be a single item that stops people in their tracks…a 50 lb. cabbage in Anchorage, a 500 lb. pumpkin on the back of your truck, a $300 flower arrangement or an 8-ft. diameter chile ristra ready for a Nordstrom entrance. That one item turns people's heads, brings them closer, makes them stare, inspires photographs and provokes dinner-time conversation. You don't want to sell it. It is as important to your business as your sign. It gives people a reason to remember you. What will your head-turner be?

> "You will fail 100% of the time if you don't throw up the shot. Go ahead, put together a display of beauty every day and see if people stop in their tracks. That's the silent 'thank you.' Then do it a bit differently next time."
> – Vance Corum, farmers' market consultant ❧

THE NEW FARMERS' MARKET

Merchandising 5

"A farmers' market is 'theater.' Display, layout, containers, signage, composition, color, contrast, structures and lighting, as well as the products and service you offer customers and how you talk to them, all come together to tell your story. What makes you unique?"
    – Leon Sugarman, architect and urban designer, San Francisco, CA

"Whenever possible, try to appeal to as many senses as you can manage. Mixtures of colors and different sizes can be attractive. Fragrance is a powerful draw. Cut some strongly scented samples just for the aroma. Noise also can be attention getting, such as country music wafting from your pickup (not too loud). Give customers the opportunity to touch something with an unusual texture. All these things can bring them right up to your table."

– Mark Wall, *Certified FM News*, Southland FM Assoc. June 1992

If storefront layout is the foundation and display is the structure, then merchandising is the paint on the building, the icing on the cake, the clothes on the model, the... well, you get the idea.

Over and over we hear feedback from both successful growers and managers that professional presentation is vital to successful sales. Americans have been trained to buy with their eyes first. Are your products displayed on nice tablecloths and your piles of fruit or vegetables kept full? As one manager said, "Growers are going to a more upscale, polished look. It's not just a few boards thrown across some crates anymore."

Earlier, we defined merchandising as the creative handling and presentation of products on the sales floor so as to maximize their sales appeal. Merchandising is a blatant appeal to the emotions and the senses. Think of yourself as an artist with several palettes of colors to choose from: visual palette – color, contrast, shapes, sizes, scale; scent palette – herbs, flowers, fruits, spices; and touch palette – soft, firm, crisp, rough, fuzzy, cold.

APPEALING TO THE SENSES

Visual Palette – Color Me Sold!

"It's the attention to color and detail that makes people want to come over to your booth and see what's going on. Doing beautiful geometric shapes with items like corn and carrots and tomatoes, and beautiful lines of color like beets followed by radishes, followed by white radishes, followed by black radishes."

– Tony Manetta, former Director, Greenmarket, New York, NY

Selling 3-packs of mixed berries is a quiet suggestive sell. People are naturally attracted to explosions of color. Hanging diverse colored peppers on a ristra or chain accomplishes the same goal.

Use color and texture to enhance eye appeal. In a big market, you have only a few seconds to get peoples' attention, so use strong color contrast.

Capitalize on the rich color palate of your fresh produce. People enjoy food with their senses, so displays must be eye- and sense-appealing. Bright, vibrant color contrasts within produce groupings also lead to tie-in sales. When considering what to plant, use color as one of your criteria.

A good deal of what we perceive is based on color. Color and movement, in fact, are the primary differentiators in the visual world. This may be a good time for a review of light and the color spectrum.

Sometime along about the sixth grade, you probably were introduced to the wonders of a prism. A prism bends light causing it to display the separate colors of the visible spectrum. The visible spectrum runs from red at one end to blue at the other end with all other colors in between. At the center of the spectrum is yellow. Red, yellow and blue are called primary colors. All other colors are a mix of the three primary colors and are called secondary colors – the most common being orange, green and purple.

When you put the primary and secondary on a color wheel, they line up like this: red, orange, yellow, green, blue and purple. Colors next to each other on the color wheel are called complementary colors, meaning they sit pleasantly next to each other, possibly because the secondary color contains the primary color next to it. Red and purple are an example of this. Colors across the color wheel from each other are called contrasting colors, meaning they provide counterpoint to each other, possibly because the secondary color in this case contains none of the primary color opposite it. Red and green are a good example of this.

White is the presence of all colors of the visible spectrum and black is their absence. Colored objects reflect their own color and absorb all others. White reflects all colors and black absorbs all colors. Clear and translucent colored objects, like colored glass and plant cell walls, transmit their own color and reflect all others. In photography, you'd call these filters.

Why is this important? Knowing something about color allows you to select colors for your canopies, umbrellas, fixtures and labels that complement and highlight your products. It also helps you avoid combinations that may be perceived as irritating.

"One farmer has all white tables and tent, lavender boxes, and white signs with lavender writing."

– Nancy Caster, ex-Mgr., Irvine Center FM, CA

The grower above probably had berries or greens rather than tomatoes, colored peppers, oranges or peaches. The lavender and white color scheme would complement boysenberries and contrast with oranges or tomatoes.

"A friend of mine, a K-Mart manager, explained that supermarkets use either green or yellow to accent the produce. So we changed our boxes to bright yellow boxes to show off the green and red vegetables, and made the stand mauve. It was great advice and the bright yellow boxes have become our trademark."

– Dan Haakenson, *The Small Commercial Gardener*

Both men here have discovered what many commercial merchandisers have known for years – the eye is drawn to the color yellow, in the middle of the spectrum, first. Full Circle Organic Farm selected yellow aprons and a yellow background table covering. Simply by the force of color, they drew the attention of consumers as they walked through the marketplace. Wearing yellow, they had the added benefit of movement. Yellow also complemented the mixed vegetable offering.

If you don't have a lot of variety in your produce, create a color mixture with packaging by arranging cut flowers or plants among the produce, or by using bright shade awnings or signs. Be careful that the reflection from surrounding colors does not cast an unwanted hue on the natural color of your produce.

The brush strokes of Pelindaba Lavender's logo invite people to 10 acres of fields and their spired retail store.

Canopies act as a filter, transmitting the color of the awning itself onto the produce. Because your reds and yellows have only reflected light from outside your canopy to reflect their colors, they look duller and less ripe.

A few examples of crowd-capturing, profit-making, creative merchandising ideas include a "waterfall" of potatoes created by an inclined board covered with spuds of all shapes and colors; wicker flower-gathering baskets used to display a colorful collection of peppers, eggplants and squash; or buckets of flowers lined up according to the colors of the spectrum, creating a rainbow effect from a distance.

You can backlight jars of maple syrup, honey and vinegar, or use an indiscernible source of lighting (hidden behind a small panel) to heighten the appearance of various grade or varietal colors.

Try hanging a light chain from the side or corner of your canopy. Position hooks down the chain to hold bunches of beets, basil, carrots, cilantro or other items forming a vertical line of color.

Color Psychology

Study the psychology of color manipulation and use before designing your stand. Consider how color affects customer response. Even hospitals and prisons now use color to effectively modify behavior. Here are a few thoughts for starters:

White represents purity, calm, cleanliness and goodness. It puts customers at ease making decisions, especially reinforcing for value-added products.

Black beckons with boldness, elegance, formality, power and authority. One Olympia, WA vegetable grower covers his tables with black sheets to allow his product colors to stand out.

Red is fire, passion, action, excitement, desire, energy, speed and impulsivity. It dynamically pushes the customer to act now. Coca Cola and Tiny's Organic in East Wenatchee, WA know that red stimulates the appetite, and is full of energy and excitement. It might be perfect for your honey products or energy bar.

Blue exudes confidence, security, calm, optimism and trust – learned from gazing at a blue sky or ocean. Blue signage is easy to read and leads to confident purchasing. You can use it to reinforce loyalty, reliability and open communication.

Orange is the color for jovial, creative, playful, enthusiastic and affordable products and services. Kids wear orange aprons every month as they do building projects at Home Depot. How can you create that kind of brand loyalty for your farm's future success?

Yellow will enhance feel-good products because sunshine translates to warmth, excitement, inspiration and happiness. You're tracking with Chiquita bananas or Sidewalk Farms at the Liberty Lake FM in Washington.

Green connotes life, freshness, health, nature, tranquility. It aligns with organic, green or eco friendly products.

Brown is another Mother Earth color that represents stability, age, comfort, and relaxation, and fits with eco products. Connect with the reliability of UPS.

Purple has long represented royalty and spirituality, combining red strength and blue stability. Often associated with luxury and relaxation, your soaps and body care products will benefit.

Pink is fun, energetic and youthful, and generally associated with products for women and girls. Pink is perfect for strawberry lemonade for you lemon growers.

You are aware that red means "stop" and green means "go," but reactions to color are not universal. People from northern countries respond to cooler colors but those from the tropics favor warm colors. White aligns with marriage in the West but in China it is the color of death (purple in Brazil). Yellow is sacred to the Chinese, but indicates jealousy in France and sadness in Greece.

Your retail business success within the farmers' market isn't influenced by your color scheme as much as by how your target customers respond to color, your products and the entire environment. Much as there are cultural variations, age influences abound. Children respond best to the bold primary colors while seniors react well to more subtlety. Know your target market, then fix your colors.

Grouping Color vs. Mixing Color

"With colors the key is similar to landscaping where the trend is to have large, full blocks of contrasting color rather than scattered and patchy color blocks. We might have a huge tier display with 10 varieties of sunflowers of all similar colors, for example, and next to sunflowers are the beans – Romano and purple and yellow-waxed beans in huge lines of parallel spilling colors – green, purple and yellow. Like items are grouped together, like summer vegetables and scallions and all the beans grouped with peppers and eggplants, and all the bouquets together. Common, like items are grouped together using large blocks of contrasting color."
– Lyle Davis, Pastures of Plenty, Longmont, CO

You can use large blocks of color to create the image of bounty, then group produce of a contrasting color beside it. For example, red beets, golden beets, radishes and turnips might be contrasted next to green broccoli, spinach, mustard and kale. This is a color

Organic Pastures of Fresno, CA uses blue and white with the cow motif to convey the trust consumers can have in the purity of their 100% raw and organic milk products sold in Los Angeles and San Luis Obispo markets.

block merchandising scheme. Try different schemes to see what works best in any given market.

"Make checkerboards of black and red raspberries or yellow and red tomatoes in quart boxes, tiered on red plastic crates."
– Mark Phillips, NYC Greenmarket vendor, *Growing for Market,* May 1996

The above example is a contrast or pattern merchandising scheme and it can work well even with smaller quantities of product to create interest.

Sometimes what you think will work isn't as effective as theory would indicate. I'm personally fond of color block merchandising, so I filled my wooden boxes with bell peppers in four different colors and placed them on a slant in nice color blocks. For some reason, they weren't moving as we thought they should. My husband took an immense flat basket, 4-feet across, from the van and dumped my beautiful, well-planned display into the basket, mixing the colors. The peppers started selling like hotcakes! The contrasting colors and overabundance called to consumers from across the market.

"Draw a map of your table on Friday night when you know what you've got to sell and color in with colored pencils to see how color arrangement will look."
– Cheryl Boden, West Union Gardens, Hillsboro, OR

If you have product of all one color or muted colors, try for a sophisticated look by going for tone-on-tone. Use all the same colors, i.e., signs, tablecloth, etc., in a shade lighter or darker than your product. A four-color, high-end label can help your product stand out in a crowd.

Table Coverings

Tablecloths can create an elegant look for a high-end product but they make any stand neater and more attractive. They should be long enough in front to hide back-stock and clutter under the table. Make sure your tablecloths are washable and keep them clean. Solid colors create a more uniform look, while a small pattern hides the dirt better. Be careful with large patterns, however, as they might compete with the product.

Table coverings of bright fabric with fruits and vegetables are eye catchers but may overly distract the customer's eye from your product. Checkered table-cloths, aprons, and crocks help create the "country look," but may not work as well with urban Gen Xers (born 1966-76) or Millenniums (Gen Y, born 1976-94). Even aging Baby Boomers are probably ready for a more upscale look. No matter what your look is, avoid shabby! Replace worn banners and tablecloths.

"Growers are going to colorful table coverings; a shaded shopping area for customers to linger around; products displayed in similar basket style containers with colorful cloth liners; providing gift bags and tissue paper so customers can make an instant gift; and having products carded with significant information about the product history, contents, growing and eating information."

– Georgia Paulsen, ex-Mgr., Topeka FM, KS

The Scent Palette: It Makes Scents

"Growers here are doing a better job of getting all the senses going. One of our basil growers keeps a little basil on the side to crush, so that people are smelling it all the time! Another example is the tuberose, a Mexican variety of lily, which has a fantastic scent. When they come into the markets, the growers can't keep them in stock.

"Tomatoes are another example of catching customers by smell. Some growers are picking the tomatoes with a bit of the green stem and the calax left at the top. The tomato itself doesn't have a smell; it's the green stem that gives the tomato its aroma! So when people pick this up, it smells like a homegrown tomato. They come in with their eyes, and then you've got their nose and you've made the sale."

– Mark Sheridan, ex-Mgr., Santa Barbara FM, CA

Scent is a powerful invoker of memory and can enhance mood. In the 1990s, department stores started using scent to improve the moods of shoppers and increase sales. Think aromatherapy. Scent, or more correctly the sense of smell, is also a major component of taste, which makes sampling of fragrant new and seasonal items a good sales technique. Consider planting something fragrant if your normal crops don't lend themselves to this sense.

Don't overlook the power of the sense of smell, especially when your customers are hungry. Squash a couple of strawberries on the hot pavement, and the smell will waft through the air! The fragrance of apples, ripe cantaloupes and nectarines, or the tangy aroma of a freshly sliced, sweet onion can stimulate sales.

Touch Palette – Oh What a Feeling!

Texture is perceived visually as well as physically. Think of those salad greens. The pebbly skin of an avocado or the soft down of a peach are noticed visually well before they are touched. The play of light and shadow over the surface emphasizes the feel of that surface.

Dimension and form are also perceived by vision before touch. Consider the many varieties of summer squash: dark green, green striped, or yellow cylinders; flattened, scalloped, pale green or bright yellow orbs; pale green teardrops; and bumpy, pastel yellow crooks.

While the visual impact comes first, the allure should build toward touch. More than anything, your goal is to have the customer touch your product. It's the first step in buying, whether it's motivated by the desire to satisfy their curiosity about the spiny kiwano (trade name for a horned melon), to confirm the ripeness of a pear, or to check that a tomato hasn't passed its prime. People want to check the quality of the product.

Certainly you want them to pick up the bottle of vinegar, the box of chocolates, the bag of hazelnuts, and the jar of jam, honey, pickles or kimchi. They may be checking the ingredient label or the production site, given the growing awareness of food sensitivities and allergies. Weigh the risk of potential breakage versus the extra sales created by people being able to handle your product.

Samples

The key to a sale is getting your product into people's mouths, and every part of your display and market presence should be directed to that end. When customers touch your product, they are being stimulated with the prospect of a given taste. This is why a sample can be so powerful, because it gives a hint of the full pleasure to come, whether from a luscious cherry, a flavorful hazelnut, a titillating chocolate, a ripe cheese or a warm baguette.

Let shoppers pick up the bag of bread to smell and imagine ripping off a hunk to dip into their soup or jambalaya. Or see the smile on the face of a child or grandparent. Customers are envisioning the memories of the future, and you are providing that experience.

If you absolutely don't want shoppers to touch your product, put it in a tight display case, behind a sneezeguard, or labeled "Please don't touch my tomatoes." And be ready to provide an ironclad guarantee of satisfaction that demonstrates your confidence in having the best quality they've ever tasted.

Merchandising for Interest & the Suggestive Sell

Using a combination of colors, textures and fragrances will create interest and excitement in your booth. These variations will keep the customer's eye moving throughout your space. You can use these merchandising schemes to suggest the uses of different products you sell.

Place compatible products together – farm salad dressing with greens, popcorn with apple cider. Put impulse items (jams, jellies, flowers, honey sticks, crafts and gifts) for convenient sale near the cash register.

Organize products in related groupings, perhaps from the beginning of the meal to the end – salad items, cooking vegetables, herbs, citrus, soft fruits, apples and pears, melons, tropical fruits, and luxury items such as flowers and decorations.

Merchandise exotic specialty crops together as a group. Displaying them side by side with ordinary varieties makes customers wonder why they should spend the additional money for them, while placing them in a separate section helps emphasize the products' premium or exotic quality and makes them look different and interesting.

Contrasting textures and sizes of produce is also an effective merchandising tool. Zucchini, gold cukes, cucumbers and other cylindrical veggies can be stocked in different directions if next to each other.

Arrange in terms of color and texture – a mountain of radishes or carrots bracketing greens. For a fancy look with a small quantity of green beans (especially haricots verts), arrange them in a sunburst pattern shooting out from a single, central tomato.

Creative touches enliven a produce display, e.g., carrot wheels, fresh flower bouquets, edible flower arrangements, garden-like groupings of lettuce and greens, baskets within the displays, or hand-stacked potatoes and yams.

Change your display at least with every change of season, if not with every new crop. Use some straw bales to announce the coming of fall, and circle your canopy legs with corn stalks.

Create some garlic braids:

http://www.bloomingfieldsfarm.com/garbrdhow.html

and provide directions to encourage customers to buy more.

Touch can replace taste. The wool spinning at SuDan Farm of Canby, OR beckons people to feel wool hats, socks, mittens and more.

Spruce up your display and avoid monotony by using tilted tables, barrels, produce baskets, buckets, paper sacks, burlap, pallets and bulk bins. Vary heights with extra pop-up boxes on your display table to lift certain items.

As one market manager related: "We had a vendor that had such a beautiful arrangement of veggies, placed in and around and on top of apple crates that the most common comment from customers was, 'I can't buy anything – it would put a gap in the display.'"

Have fun and remember your display should not be so picture-perfect that it makes people afraid to touch or take items. Make your display inviting! Removing one or two packages from a full display may even help customers start buying. It shows that customers are coming so fast that there isn't enough time to restock.

A pyramid of melons – several rows of 4,3,2,1 – satisfies the visual palette, but you should have a plentiful supply of melons in front for the touch palette.

Happy Boy Farms of coastal Soquel, CA presents an island of heirloom tomatoes accented by basil and peppers.

ABUNDANCE

"People are attracted to large displays. They like to think they have a choice. Get as much out in front of the customer as you can, even more than you expect to sell."
– Tony Manetta, former Director, Greenmarket, New York, NY in *Growing for Market*

"We have found that the bigger the display the more you sell. Some farmers have a tendency to put a few baskets on display and leave the rest on the truck. This person will NOT sell as much of the product as the one that brings it all off the truck for a huge display, even though they both brought the same amount to market."
– Butch Hollister, President, Connecticut Farmers Association for Retail Marketing (ConnFARM)

"Pile it high and watch it fly!" Abundant displays attract attention. At a New York City Greenmarket one grower displayed green beans in a small bowl which she refilled from a basket in her truck. The effect was that few people saw her green beans. In contrast, another grower made a mountain of radishes and the splash of color drew people from across the street.

Well-stocked displays make customers want to come and get it! They don't want the last of something from a bare, picked-over display; they want the best. A cornucopia of produce conveys abundance, prosperity and quality. Look at your booth from the shopper's perspective. A constantly restocked overflowing crate will often outsell five half-full crates. Don't put two flats of berries on the table with 50 flats sitting on the truck. Show people volume!

"Sometimes it's the little things. Everyone's selling tomatoes this time of year, for example, and we sell tomatoes by the quart in plastic baskets. So we add a tomato or two to make it look overfull."
– Judy Medicus, Cat's Paw Organic Farm, Union Bridge, MD

Creating the Bountiful Look

Display in full baskets. Small amounts in any container can look "picked over." As you run out of product, put the remainder in a smaller basket, making it look full. Reduce the size of your display, or delete a table.

You Are Part of the Display!
A Market Tour

Abundance

Abundance is what brings people to the market. In our technological society, people-to-people abundance is vanishing. Most market managers and farmers/vendors know the "pile it high and kiss it goodbye" principle about product abundance in a booth, but the same applies to the people in the booth.

Think abundance! Can we make our markets and our booths welcoming and bountiful and one that customers will enjoy? Unless you enjoy being with people at the market you should find someone else to sell your products, because what you're selling is yourself. You are part of the display! Of course you grow the best products. It is you who are behind the stand that counts!

Walk around the marketplace and look at other displays. Ask yourself: What is it behind this display that I like? Most of the time, the person behind that booth is really happy and loves to be there. Have people take pictures of you – are you smiling and do you look happy to be there?

I can walk around the market and tell who's having a great day and who's having a terrible day. Here is a sweet pea grower. He is a joy to have at the market. He puts a sweet pea in everyone's hair and they also buy his sweet peas. Here is an organic nursery seller who does a tremendous amount of one-on-one with customers. He also does well week after week.

Here are some organic farmers who have a warm and fuzzy feeling to their booth. Bring kids to the market – it adds vibrancy. Look at her big smile! Her farm is mortgaged to the max but you'd never know it from her smile!

This is crucial: Don't let anyone or anything take those four hours at the market away from you. Don't let any problems with other sellers, or any problems with your children or your spouse, interfere with your hours at the market. Commit yourself to that market for four hours. On the way to the market take a deep breath and clear your consciousness.

Booth

If a vendor asks the manager, "What's wrong with the market?" Ask them, "What's wrong with your stand?"

Make sure your booth is immaculately clean. People are thinking about food safety nowadays and anything involving the food they eat needs to be immaculately clean.

When you have an expensive product, you need to have an elegant looking booth. We have an olive oil seller who has the country European look with a rustic apron. Market umbrellas are a nice way to make your booth look nice, especially in green and white and maroon.

Improving displays

We work with our sellers with suggestions about color, height and so on, and we invite experts such as people from the landscape or architect design department at the local college or students in these classes. Also look at other stands or in retail stores to find people selling similar products to what you are selling and see what they're doing with their products.

We take slides of our sellers' displays and we ask design experts to come to our annual meetings to critique them. It is a courageous act on the part of the vendors to have their displays critiqued publicly. However, there is no shame, no blame – it's only a question of finding how we can do it better. There are no mistakes, only lessons. How can we improve our display and our stands?

Pretty soon the whole market buys into the idea of improving their stands, and the vendors even start coaching each other. The key in dealing with vendors is to coach, not criticize.

– Randii MacNear, Mgr., Davis FM, CA ✿

"Even if you have only one kind of product such as berries, put it in several sizes of boxes and use up your whole area, even if it's for just one item!"

– Gretchen Hoyt, Alm Hill Gardens, Everson, WA

Peter Jankay of the San Luis Obispo County Farmers' Market Association, CA, believes the merchandising of a display makes a huge difference. "A person can have a mountain of peaches in one display and it looks junky, while another grower's mound of peaches may look great." The second grower may have been more meticulous. Often the difference comes down to a farmer's care of each individual fruit so people don't feel they have to go through the whole pile to find quality. "It not only has to taste good; it has to look good."

Stock fully, but don't pile products so high that it makes a customer fear an avalanche. For most products eight inches is the maximum height. Some quality-conscious growers stack fruit no more than two layers high. You don't want to crush tender items on the bottom or block airflow.

Other excellent merchandising ideas:

- Intersperse product with leaves, herbs or flowers;
- Add a flower bouquet on a table corner for color;
- String balloons or chili peppers around the canopy or entryway;
- Interweave garlic braids with roses;
- Hang dried flowers, peppers or braided garlic from the latticework above your stall;
- Create a mini-florist shop, with flowers on the edge of the stall, wreathes and swags hanging from your canopy.

The Paradox of Choice

Our society has gotten carried away with having an ever larger selection of products to choose from. Scientists have been studying the effect of too much choice for decades.

Sheena Iyengar, a Columbia University business professor and author of *The Art of Choosing*, con-

Roger Konka of Springwater Farm uses a heaping display and prebagged mushrooms ready for Portland customers who are in a hurry.

ducted a classic experiment in 1995 where shoppers were faced with an array of jams in a California gourmet market.

With a display of 24 jams, 60% of customers stopped. When six jams were displayed, only 40% of shoppers responded. In both cases, customers tasted two jams, on average, and they were given a $1 coupon. However, only 3% of those at the large display made a purchase while 30% bought jam from the more limited display.

Iyengar suggests that "the presence of choice might be appealing as a theory, but in reality, people might find more and more choice to actually be debilitating." [See her TEDTalk "How to Make Choosing Easier"]

Compared to other pistachio growers, Santa Barbara Pistachio has always had substantially higher prices, but they do not offer a simple choice of unshelled, shelled and salted. They offer five distinctive flavors reinforced by full-color artwork on a convenient zip lock bag. They outsell the competition.

If they had 15 flavors instead of five, would people be more satisfied or more confused? Too many samples slows the consumer's decision-making. One answer is to sample two or three and let them decide. They can try others next week and satisfy a different member of their household.

"We arranged our (garlic) varieties in a consistent and logical order to facilitate customer interaction. Our hot varieties ran across the top of the display rack, with general purpose varieties in the middle, and mild varieties at the bottom. Customers were less overwhelmed by the choices presented when they could easily understand the organization of the options."

 – Eric and Joanna Reuter, Chert Hollow Farm, Boone County, MO in *Growing for Market*, August, 2014

Tahiti Joe's in FL has a substantial line of hot sauces, and a separate line of sweet sauces. Taking a different tack, they allow the customer to sample all three dozen sauces, much as fruit growers frequently have samples of every variety available. Names and descriptions are sassy. Joe has admitted that after re-naming one of his best-selling sauces, sales went up 50-fold!

A Swiss scientist, Benjamin Scheibehenne, has examined dozens of choice studies. He says that it may be too simple to conclude that too many choices are bad, just as to assume that more choices are always better. It may depend on the information we're given, the expertise we rely on and the importance we ascribe to the choice.

Does the paradox of choice affect your products? Whether selling jam, pasta sauce, pesto, vinegar or salad mix, there may be a limit to the number of different flavors you should offer. If too many choices can paralyze the decision-maker, don't indulge them with unlimited options. Give them a more targeted choice.

PACKAGING

"A lady at our market sells flavored vinegars. She hand-dips the top of every bottle of vinegar in wax to seal it, and ties a bow around each bottle. The products are tiered, so the back products are as visible as the front products and she always has a fresh bouquet of flowers on her table."

 – Patty Brand, Exec. Dir., Friends of the St. Paul FM, MN

Clear plastic cartons or plastic tubs work well for many value-added products like cobblers. Netting over berry containers allows air circulation but keeps berries in place. But remember, you can get too slick. Fancy packaging that works well in an air-conditioned store may not work in a farmers' market. People want to touch and smell the product. When packaging makes an item less visible to customers, display an open sample, e.g., if salad mix is packaged, display a salad in a bowl as well.

Get Rid of Rotten Stuff

"Always get those few rotten pieces of fruit out of sight. Nothing turns a shopper off more than a big moldy peach sitting in the middle of a box of perfectly good fruit."
 – Renae Best, Certified FMs of Sacramento, CA

It is painful but necessary to throw out perfectly good, but slightly damaged produce. Many customers are bothered by damaged produce. They will remember where they bought it and be reluctant to return. Tomatoes squeezed to mush have no appeal but to canners. Set aside seconds or culls for the food bank or an unemployed customer.

Tahiti Joe's fills your visual field with great branding from top to bottom at the West Palm Beach Greenmarket.

© Vance Corum

Bulk vs. Prepackaged

"We have tubs of beans for customers who want to pick them out individually, and we leave bags ready-made for customers who know what they want."

– Cheryl Boden, West Union Gardens, Hillsboro, OR

"We bag up the peaches into 2-pound bags at about $4. With pre-bagged, people tend to buy more. We have an area for people who want to pick their own. Close to 80% of people just take a bag. After the first couple of weeks they get to know me and know there are no bad peaches at the bottom."

– John Ellis, Farmer John's, Boulder, CO

Honey Mama's in Portland, OR has a nectar fudge bar which is packaged in colored paper with a bow, and samples vigorously which easily gets new customers.

The decision to display and sell your produce prepackaged or in bulk depends largely on your clientele, the produce item, and where you are selling. If your customers are commuters who want in-and-out convenience, selling by the count or by prepackaged units makes sense, whether it's fresh herbs, a salad mix or a shoebox of ripe fruit. Home canners or ethnic groups accustomed to open-air markets may prefer buying in bulk.

"People's experience at the supermarket is that there may be some bruised product in the bag, so many vendors let the customers bag products themselves."

– Randii MacNear, Mgr., Davis FM, CA

The customer's perception of choice is everything. Employees on a lunch break want the quick checkout offered by pre-packaged goods. Weekend shoppers are more likely to prefer selecting their own fresh produce from the farm. Give your customers the choice.

Where you sell can be an important factor in whether or not you choose to prepackage. California law requires that all fresh fruits, nuts and vegetables sold in closed, consumer containers shall be labeled with the name, address, and ZIP code of the producer, and the identity and net quantity of the commodity in the package. This means pre-printed or hand written labels on each package – a requirement that may offset the speed of the sale from prepackaging. You can avoid these "closed" container requirements by putting a tie on the bag after the sale. Research the requirements in your area before making this decision.

Selling in bulk, by weight, is still popular because people are used to buying by the pound and feel they are getting full value for the price. It also avoids the controversy in pick-your-own sales of over-filling the containers, or customers adding more to the container. Selling by weight requires the use of accurate scales. In most jurisdictions scales must be "legal for trade" and certified by a county authority before they can be used in a market setting.

Here are some comparisons:

Packaging advantages

- Helps maintain freshness;
- Can enhance product and market appearance;
- Provides customer convenience – eliminates bagging and weighing;
- Provides seller convenience – easier to move items around, less work at checkout;
- Gives a way to list price, seller's name and address, recipes and other information; and
- Protects product from damage.

Bulk advantages

+ Consumer can choose quantity;
+ May appear fresher to consumer;
+ Consumers tend to buy more of certain items, e.g., nuts and dried fruits (but less of others);
+ Enhances market's "home-grown image";
+ Less refrigeration needed for bulk produce;
+ Reduced labor involved with packing, weighing and labeling;
+ Reduced cost for packaging supplies; and
+ Appeal for ethnic groups who may be used to buying in bulk.

Which way you go may vary by the time of year or point in the season. Do your homework first to make sure you get what you need to stay in business [see Pricing, Chapter 2]. Tom Roberts and Lois Labbe of Snakeroot Organic Farm in Pittsfield, ME, change their units of sale depending on where they are in the season. Some items such as carrots and beets sell by the bunch early in the season when they first come in and are smaller; later when they become larger, the tops are cut off and the roots sell by the pound or are packaged in three-pound bags. Carrots, for example, sell for $2.50 in a 3-pound bag. Roberts explains, "We usually do better putting them in 3-pound poly bags. It's so convenient for customers to just pick up a bag. Sold by the pound, people may just pick up a few for that evening's meal. Very few people buy very much (quantity) by the pound, yet they don't seem to hesitate to pick up a several-pound bag."

Tiny's Organic of East Wenatchee, WA sells their donut peaches in a donut box emblazoned with their mascot elephant, Tiny.

The chief advantage to prepackaging is convenience – easy sales at the market and fast checkout. However, you will spend time weighing, packaging, labeling, and packing the packages for market. Certified scales must be used in establishing the weight of the pre-pack. Leftovers must be dealt with. Are you giving them to a soup kitchen or other hunger program? If you compost your leftovers, you must spend additional time to unbag them, then recycle the bags – a cost probably not accurately assessed or passed on to customers.

Unit Pricing

Selling by volume, piece, or unit rather than by weight generally saves time on the sales floor, both for the customer and salesperson. Unit pricing makes the checkout move more quickly and allows the vendor more time to talk to customers.

"Most of our produce is sold pre-bagged at the market except for the large items like zucchini, summer squash, cucumbers and cabbage. It takes a lot of time to weigh the products. Also people pick through products and we end up with a lot of damaged product. Weighing with a scale takes time and tends to form lines. People also tend to buy more with a pre-bagged product, where they have to take at least a bag. The farm's potatoes are sold in three different size bags – 2, 5 and 10-pound – and are graded with the smallest baby reds in the 2-pound."
– Jay Visser, J-N-A Produce, Manhattan, MT

"Everything is pre-packaged at my stand. I weigh it in one-pound bags. Other vendors have scales and let the customer weigh it, but you have to give up space for them to do this. I also price to include tax for minimal money handling. We have a 5% tax, so I sell an item for 95 cents, $1.00 with tax. It moves faster this way."
– Diane Green, Greentree Naturals Farm, Sandpoint, ID

Products sold by the unit, such as pumpkins, larger winter squash, melons or watermelons, work best grouped by size and priced accordingly. The customer readily sees the correlation between price and size. Price in $1 or 25 cent increments for easy-move pricing or sell by the bunch or bag. Not having to weigh things means faster transactions. Lining display containers with carry-out plastic bags enables the customer to select items with no wait for bagging.

For units containing more than one item, e.g., "Sweet, white corn 5 for $1," the layout can allow for some pre-bagged and some bulk so customer preference is accommodated. Other examples of unit pricing are berries sold by the quart, pint and 1/2 pint, or fruit sold in peck, 1/2 peck and 1/4 peck baskets.

Packaging for Today's Consumer

In the summer of 2000, the Farmers' Market Federation of New York ran several surveys and focus groups to get a better idea of what consumers' wants and needs were within the context of farmers' markets. One panelist in a two-person household on a fixed income craves the fresh fruits and vegetables he gets at farmers' markets and appreciates vendors who sell small quantities and various quality grades at reduced prices. As boomers become empty-nesters, smaller households and today's rapid-paced lifestyle dictate a different type of packaging than was done previously.

> "We're finding that people don't cook. Ten years ago people would stop at our roadstand and take a dozen ears of corn and not even blink an eye. We have people stop today and take two ears of corn... 'Oh, can I take 2 ears of corn for my microwave?'"
> – *Barriers & Opportunities*, Farmers' Market Trust

"Grocery stores have switched over in the last several years to take-home, throw-it-in-the-mi-crowave, put-it-on-the-table items like vegetable trays or salad mixes. We're living in a two-worker family society. People don't spend a lot of time cooking and they typically purchase for one or two meals. Instead of 20 pounds of garden peas, they'll take a 2-pound bag or they'll take six ears of corn. So we display in pre-packed and smaller quantities as much as we can, in addition to offering our bulk pack."

– Allen Shoemaker, Shoemaker's Home Place, Blackfoot, ID

SAY IT WITH SIGNS

Signage is a merchandising feature often overlooked in the planning process. Well-conceived signs can add color to your stand, provide information to support a sale and create "brand" for your farm. Signs can be divided into three basic categories: price signs, information signs, and brand signs.

Price Signs

Generally, prices should be clearly marked on or near the products. Consumers are used to shopping at retail stores where they don't have to ask. If people have to ask, they'll assume it's too expensive. A large, attractive chalkboard or white board rather than individual price tags for each container of produce can work if you have just a few items. With a long list of items, put the price on or near each item and a reader board or chalkboard to highlight your offerings. Be careful how you write prices: "$.10" can look like "$10" at a glance – better to use "10 cents" or the cents (¢) sign.

With sales of higher value crops, it's better to show the pricing of quantities normally bought and consumed within the week. For example, snow peas commonly used in Asian dishes are usually purchased in 1/4- to 1/2-pound quantities. Because they are labor intensive, snow peas sell for about $4 to $6 per pound. Consider pricing yours in 1/2-pound increments instead. Your sign now reads "Snow Peas $2.50 / half pound" – a perceptible difference.

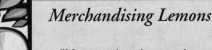

Merchandising Lemons

"Not posting item prices. Vendors often think they need to hide this information from other competitive vendors. You're not selling to competitors; you're selling to customers who are used to seeing prices posted in supermarkets."

"No signage!"

"Not posting farm name; people want to know who you are."

Some markets have rules that individual items must have prices posted with them rather than on a board. Check your market's rules before deciding how to display your prices.

"We hired an artist to make signs with borders. The basic sign can be used over and over. Felt tip markers are used to put the prices on the signs and the signs are laminated so that we can use fingernail polish remover to change prices. The signs are placed next to or on top of the produce. Plastic sticks purchased from a garden or floral supply store with three prongs hold the signs in place. They can also be stuck into a potato or a flower vase. An alternative is to put prices on a chalkboard off to the side or in the back."

– Gretchen Hoyt, Alm Hill Gardens, Everson, WA

"We use 5x7 inch cards with each type of product, laminated so they can withstand the weather. To change prices, computer print labels are pasted on the cards, which can be tricky in wet weather. In addition to prices, the cards carry the name and description of the product."

– Rudd Douglass, Blueberry Ledge Farm, Gardiner, ME

Making price signs ahead of time, in a way that allows you the flexibility to change price as market conditions change, will save you time and make you money.

Laminate your product signs, so they can be reused. Use dry markers, grease pens or dry erase markers so prices and other information can be updated easily.

A green chalkboard along with several colors of chalk works well for posting a price list. Poster board and felt tip pens (green, red and blue are good colors) are also convenient. Print as neatly as possible.

Fail Better Farm of Unity, ME uses colored chalk on pieces of roof slate as price signs for cucumbers to cookies, squash to scones at the Downtown Waterville FM.

Department store metal sign-holders with slots allow you to replace the signs as needed for product or price changes.

There are two schools of thought on the merchandising impact of pricing signs. One is to use consistent labeling in your display so it doesn't overpower the product. This can also help with branding. Signs are the same size, background color and style. They may include the farm name on the sign.

The other school of thought is to use card stock that contrasts pleasantly with the product, such as yellow for blueberries, or buff for other products. Use red or orange markers to do the lettering. Avoid stark black on white; white card stock shows dirt, and is glaring in bright sunlight. Use lots of signs! Blue, green or red markers are preferable to black. Color-code your signs, i.e., use neon red for tangelos, green for avocados, etc.

Information Signs

"Product signs at the booths are giving more information. There are more signs saying 'Organic' or 'No Chemicals' than there used to be. The signs are also including cooking and storage tips, and there's more identification than just a price tag. People are asking more questions than they used to ask. The population is getting more generations removed from the farm now and they're not as familiar with what things are at the market in their raw state. Market customers don't know how to prepare products so were getting a lot of questions like: 'What is it?' and 'What can I do with it?'"

– Diane Eggert, Exec. Dir., FM Fed. of New York

Label everything. Research shows that market customers want to know where their food comes from. Post significant information about the product history, contents or growing/eating information. Gathering Together Farm in Oregon has a produce encyclopedia at their stand so that employees can research a customer question on the spot. That's a great way to ensure ongoing, on-the-job training while serving the customer.

The more information your signs can convey, the better: Can this be eaten raw? How do you cook it? What are its nutritional strong points (e.g., "It's high in vitamin C.")? Is it a nutriceutical? What is its nutrient density? What can it be compared to? Details like these help breed customers' trust in you and your products.

Information labels add value to your product and differentiate you from your neighbor. Again, you can create a uniform look by using the same color and style for these signs. It's possible to combine these signs with price signs by leaving a space in which to write price. As you do this, remember people read from left to right and top to bottom. By putting your price in the bottom right corner of an information sign, you have a better chance your customer will actually read the sign.

A Seattle vendor uses a crosscut of wood to educate people about the sweet cinnamon scent of the Matsutake mushroom, the most prized in Japan.

> "Right now we have a lot of Aconcagua peppers coming on, which is a very unusual variety, and we're making a sign saying they're very sweet and don't have bitter taste. The sign is a foot and a half tall, and we place it behind the display of vegetables with tear-off recipe sheets at the bottom of the sign. This works great with unusual vegetables. You need to let customers know how to use anything new."
>
> – Judy Medicus, Cat's Paw Organic Farm, Union Bridge, MD

If you are offering a new or unusual variety, label it and consider having a handout on how to prepare or store it. Especially label specialty items not readily identifiable: "Arugula adds zest to your salad!"

Be creative in your product signs. "Sweet, Ripe Kiwis," "Savoy Cabbage, Crisp & Crunchy," "Walnuts: Crack 'Em Yourself," etc. Don't just sell apple cider; sell "Icy Cold Apple Cider" to motivate customers on a hot day.

Little, erasable, slate boards placed in baskets make attractive, point-of-sale signs.

> "Labels are easily made using stick-on labels designed for putting on computer disks. These are available at business supply stores along with a computer program to design the labels. Several hundred labels and (computer) program sell for under $10."
>
> – Robert I. (Bob) Neier, Extension agent, Wichita, KS

Here are more tips on what to say on signs:

Product description: Let people know that your product is crunchy, tangy, tart or sweet. Use colorful language to describe your crop: "Slender and Tender Green Beans," "Crisp cabbage straight from the field," etc.

Educate on nutritional benefits: "Nutrient-dense kale – ANDI score of 1000." Post another general sign "Aggregate Nutrient Density Index (ANDI) scores show the nutrient density of foods on a scale of 1 to 1000."

Give USDA nutritional information with vitamin and mineral content.

Provide useful information: "Good for soups" or "2 lbs. of these apples make an 8-inch pie," etc.

Guarantee product: "100% Happiness Guaranteed! Tell us next week what you think."

Highlight what you are offering that day, or note "Today's Special – Delicata Squash."

Give a brief history of the product, i.e., where it originated, how it came to this country, what traditional dishes use it.

The pamphlet, *Helpful Hints to Be Successful at the Kitchener Farmers' Market!* (Kitchener, Ontario) puts it this way, "Promote your positives! Make sure your signs promote the positive things about your product: home-grown, organic, hand-crafted, Grade 'A', additive-free, MSG free... Let people know if your product was picked fresh this morning by the headlights of your truck! It makes your product much more desirable than what's available in stores!" Again, your personal relationship with the customer is a prime opportunity to educate.

One note of caution: Read your market rules before working on signs. Some markets discourage or ban certain phrases perceived as misleading.

One grower lists the transplants he sells each spring on a sheet of paper with color, size, name and days to harvest, so customers don't have to ask what it is. It frees him up to check out what they want and collect money. The sheet changes from week to week as one variety sells through and another becomes available. Because it's done on the computer, the changes are easy.

"Since other vendors at the markets may be selling out-of-state products, we are careful to have 'Locally Grown' or 'Minneapolis Grown' signs prominently displayed. Locally-grown is definitely a big pull at our markets."

– Jim Beulke, Beulke Farms, Wanamingo, MN

Doug Cross of Canter-Berry Farms in Auburn, WA, uses signs to educate his customers. "What can you do with blueberry vinegar?" one sign reads and then gives the answer. "People will still ask," says Cross, "so you need to speak to them as well. Talking is just another way to get it across to them."

Use varietal names with your product. People want to know what they're buying; they want to tell friends or teach kids to distinguish. It helps separate

Hand Farmed Organics proudly tells Queen Anne customers in Seattle that they are local, certified naturally grown and handle WIC and Senior Farmers Market Nutrition Program checks.

farmers' markets from supermarkets that don't distinguish varieties. Putting a picture or hand-painted representation of the product on your price sign helps make the connection in an eye-catching manner.

These ideas are really about one thing: differentiation. What makes your product different from others in the market? What makes your farm different? Why should the customer buy from you?

Directive signs. Directive signs. Instead of "Please do not squeeze the peaches," try a more positive, educational approach, "Unlike supermarket tomatoes, these are picked ripe and bruise easily. Please don't squeeze." Use a cartoon of the fruit or veggie with a face and legs and a speech balloon that says, "Please don't squeeze me, I bruise easily."

"Tree-ripe tastes so much better than brown bag-ripened fruit. Customers come back again and again! They really like it soft but not too soft; it's a challenge! Since some customers poke something and take the one next to it, however, our booth has signs: 'Very ripe, soft fruit,' 'Do not squeeze fruit!' or 'Squeeze my fruit and you get no fruit!'"

– Art Lange, Honey Crisp Farm, Reedley, CA

A former extension advisor, Art was known for picking his orchard at least six times to harvest only the premium ripened fruit. He ultimately avoided customer squeezing by putting six peaches in a white box with a fold-up handle. It was his signature marketing technique that stood out from any pre-packaged bag. He wasn't afraid to charge appropriately, and 6 for $5 was a standout price in the 1980s.

"Display your Farmers Market Nutrition Program sign prominently. We posted three FMNP signs: one up high at each end of the booth and a third in the center of the booth in front of our table. The signs were very effective in drawing

A Business Without a Sign Is a Sign of "No Business!"

Think about it. Everyone from the lumber yard to the laundromat has a sign in the front window that lets people know about his or her products and services. It would be pretty foolish to go to the trouble of setting up shop without one.

Perhaps you're saying, "Yeah, that's crucial for a retail storefront, but we're just a small farm selling berries and vegetables at a Saturday market. Why hang a sign when folks walking by can easily see what we have to offer by looking at our table or the back end of the pickup? It's an added expense that's not really necessary."

Erik and Kay Dee Cole of Cole Garden Farms in Corvallis, OR, have a different outlook on the subject.

"People seemed to gravitate to our booth after we had a sign made," Kay Dee said. "I think they see us as a real business and that we're serious about what we do.

"We'd been selling herb plants and annuals for three years and just recently decided a sign would help make our booth look more professional. At first we thought it would be expensive, but the fellows at Van Dykes Signs in Tangent, OR, designed and created just what we wanted for only $30.

"We wanted something that looked fresh, green and living with just our farm name and location on it. Since we sell a variety of plants, it had to be fairly generic. Their artist drew up a few examples for us to look at, and we fell in love with the one with an ivy border. It's perfect. I just wish we had done this sooner."

Signage does more than send people in your direction – it gives you credibility and name recognition. It completes the package like the ribbon on a birthday gift and the icing on the cake.

Jeff and Annie Main of Good Humus Produce, Capay Valley, CA emphasize the personal nature of their business by using first names on a laminated, hand-colored sign.

It's a snap to get just what you want nowadays because modern technology has developed snazzy computers that churn out a wide variety of type styles and colors in vinyl that adhere to canvas and other materials.

Katherine Ankeny and Kellie Green from Out of the Blue Organics in Sweet Home have also gone the extra mile by creating their own artwork on their canvas sign.

"We wanted something whimsical, inviting and fun, so we plunged right in and designed it ourselves," Ankeny said. "Neither of us is an artist, but we gathered ideas and came up with a plan using bright, clean colors such as blue, white and yellow along with a farm scene painted in the corner."

These two women, new vendors at the Corvallis Saturday Farmers' Market, have already made a name for themselves in just a few weeks selling fresh salad greens and vegetables. Folks flocked to their charming booth filled with bouquets of purple lilacs tucked between baskets of produce lined up on sturdy cedar-slatted tables. Everything was snapped up in record time along with their "recipe of the week" cards featuring a zesty salad dressing. "People kept asking us what we'd be bringing the following week, and many asked for more salad dressing ideas. They said they'd look for our farm sign."

So, next time you're at Saturday Market in Corvallis, check out Cole Garden Farms and Out of the Blue Organics. You can't miss them – just look for the signs!

– Fresh New Ideas, marketing column by Cappy Tosetti for the *Capital Press Agriculture Weekly*, Salem, OR ๏

Signs of Success

If you could generate 25 cents more with each customer, how much would that mean in sales? Signage is an effort that guarantees results!

Focus on features and benefits. There are three questions that most customers have: What is it? (Features). What is it good for? (Benefits). How much does it cost? (Price).

Let people know what the product is good for and how it's used. This is a service that the employees at Walmart or Safeway often don't match.

Focus on the sizzle! Sell the romance, the story, the benefits. What is it about this product that will make the customer want it? Do creative listening with your customers to find what it is about this product that makes it special and unique. Is it a hard-to-find variety? Make it special, but still fact, not fiction.

Be truthful. Don't overwork superlatives such as "new" or "fresh". Instead of saying "fresh," say "fresh picked this morning" (if it's true).

What should your signs say to clinch the sale? Look for benefits such as superlative taste (and give samples to prove it), or a savings in time, money or stress.

Vicki and Charlie Hertel, Vicki's Flowers and Produce, Cornelius, OR, are known for good corn. They promote it at Portland area markets with a sign that proclaims: "Picked fresh this morning!" ❧

The Nutty Vermonter invites customers to sample with spoons in their jars and checkerboard borders on all signs and labels.

FMNP customers to our booth. Make your prices FMNP/WIC friendly. Almost 20% of our sales were to FMNP customers and their preference was to purchase exclusively with their coupons. For us this meant that we had to set our prices so that it was easy for people to make their purchases in $2 increments."

– Andy Fellenz, Fellenz Family Farm, Phelps, NY, in *Growing for Market,* Jan. 1, 2004

Farm Name or Brand Signs

Branding is the art of connecting your name, farm name or product name with a value held by your customer base. For fresh produce it's freshness, health, wholesomeness and the "farm." For value-added products it can be taste, comfort, gourmet treat or many other things. You want folks to think of these values when they think of you and to think of you when these values spring to mind – this takes repetition of your name many times over.

"Develop name recognition. A customer arrives at the farmers' market for the first time. What are they looking for? Something familiar! If they have heard your name or seen your sign before, they are more likely to visit your stand first. Use a large sign to identify yourself. We purchased a custom-made sign that mounts on the back of the pickup. As customers approach our stand, they can see our name in large letters behind the stand."

– Dan Haakenson, *The Small Commercial Gardener*

Display your farm name prominently so customers can find you and remember you easily. An attractive booth banner or wooden sign with your farm name, location and logo painted on it helps keep your customers coming back to you week after week and makes it easier for them to refer friends to you. Add a booth flag with cherries or tomatoes.

For the same reason insist on setting up in the same location throughout the year. Make sure your farm sign is well above your display, either on the canopy front or making a back wall for your stand – just a few customers can totally block a sign hanging from your table.

Bags. Having your farm name and logo printed on bags is an excellent low-cost way to keep your image in the customers' eyes. Your state department of agriculture or farmers' market association may have a program for cooperative purchases of printed shopping bags.

Providing customers a free hat, shirt or bag that costs $5 is much more cost-effective than giving a 20% discount on a $25 bulk purchase. You habituate a customer to large purchases, maintain your price rather than teach them to look for discounts, and make customers part of your farm promotion team.

Printed materials. Nutritional information, books on production, marketing order pamphlets, recipes and clipped articles (you might want to copy them for interested customers) all make your customers value your participation in the market.

Mailing lists. Building a customer mailing list, (snail-mail and/or email) is essential to give you additional opportunities to contact your customers and reinforce your brand. You can notify local customers

Little Organic Farm of Marin County, CA, proclaims its water-wise approach with dry-farmed produce.

of your season or a particular crop. You also can capitalize on tourist traffic and infrequent or seasonal customers, even introduce your CSA concept or encourage visits to your farmstand.

A gift pack on your table or a CSA descriptive sign is more likely to spark interest in your mailing list. Have a clipboard sign-up sheet or provide slips of paper with lines for name, address, city, zip, phone and e-mail. Hold a drawing periodically for a small gift if you want to build a list quickly.

Valicoff Fruit Company of Wapato, WA has signed up customers on their computer at the Pike Place Market and allowed them to select gift packs to be sent on a specific date. They hand out free apples to "buy" customer time so that they can describe their website to a good number of the market's nine million annual visitors:

www.applesonline.com.

Order product from other farms to see how you compare as far as quality, packaging, price, speed of delivery, customer service and complaint resolution.

Pulling It All Together

Encourage customers to remember you by having something unique in your stand! Make sure your stall has its own personality which will make it easier for shoppers to remember you and buy from you again next week.

Get out in front of your display and look at it critically from a customer's point-of-view. Everything should be clearly visible, alive and enticing. If it doesn't command attention, change it. Then come in and review your display close-up. Sort through each box and throw out the ugliest products that detract from the in-close visual impact.

Develop a focus

If your focus is herbs, fill up your space with fresh herbs, dried herbs, herb plants in various size containers, potpourri and sachets.

"One of the biggest draws to any one stand at a farmers' market is YOU! Those of you who come to the market neatly dressed with smiles and ready to greet your customers with helpfulness are going to have a great day! Others who won't make the effort to shave or comb their hair or even get up off the tailgate of their truck when a customer approaches are going to have a lousy day! The choice is yours. Remember the way you look and your attitude should add to the beauty of your stand!"

– Renae Best, Certified FMs
of Sacramento, CA

Attire

"It's important to have not only the farm name, but your personal name displayed on your apron. People I don't even know come up to me in the markets and say 'Hi Donna!' They like to feel they're not buying from a stranger."

– Donna Sherrill, Sherrill
Orchard, Arvin, CA

Incorporate yourself into your display. Customers are coming to see you, too – you are part of the show! For years everyone with Peacock Farms in Dinuba, CA wore a blue T-shirt with a gold peacock emblem. Wear a hat or bib apron with your farm name, and have a nametag so people can say hello. Personal items can reinforce your products, from cherry aprons to apple or pumpkin earrings.

"Some of our vendors wear costumes representing what they sell. The egg guy wears a chicken hat, the honey person wears a beehive shirt, and the plant lady wears a shirt covered with leaves."

– Larry Johnson, Mgr., Dane County FM, Madison, WI
in *Growing for Market,* April, 2007

"Summer Squash" by Anthony Holdsworth

Personalize with photos and bulletin boards

Display a picture album or a display board on a tripod with photos of your farm and family, the gardens and greenhouses, or even a bird's eye farm view to help personalize your business. Customers love to see where the products you sell come from. Have albums of your farm and products as well as any articles that have been written about you and your product for customers to look though. While customers wait in line at your booth, you can talk with them about your farm and farming practices. This helps customers feel part of your operation! ✍

Sales & Promotion 6

"These markets I go to, people just love you. It is a very gratifying experience. You're making money, performing a good service, and they love you for it."
– Greenmarket vendor, New York City

In the smallest farmers' market you may feel like Spaulding Gray presenting a quietly manic monologue in a one-man play. In a large market you'll feel more like a cast member of a full Broadway production of Andrew Lloyd Webber's "Cats." Either way, you are a central figure in a play on the set of your local farmers' market.

Marketers start their learning around the Four Ps of Marketing: Product, Place, Price and Promotion. The goal is to put the right product in the right place, at the right price and at the right time. You provide a critical fifth P: Personality. Like it or not, customers' decision to buy product from you rather than another farmer may be based on how much they like you, perceive you to be helpful, want to support you and other factors aside from your actual product.

Yes brand Ladybugs makes a positive statement from canopy to banner to table at the Beverly Hills FM. If your brand is tastier, be excited with it.

A lot of folks recoil at the concept of "selling." We've been trained as a culture to view sales as an arm-twisting, high-pressure, slick, less-than-truthful occupation, whose practitioners get you to purchase things you neither need nor want – think selling iceboxes to Eskimos. No wonder we often hear, "I want to be a farmer, not a salesman!" Most farmers would rather do anything but something called sales.

Actually, sales is none of the above. Certainly today's consumers are far too sophisticated and, frankly, far too tired of sales pitches to have any of this stuff "work" on them. In its simplest form, retail selling is the art of serving the customer and exchanging your product for their money.

Farmers across the continent have come to recognize the benefit of being a producer and a seller. The good ones have learned to enjoy the sales role. Farmers' markets are all about relationship marketing. When you approach a new customer, think of building a lasting friendship rather than simply making a sale.

Having that attitude will cause you to go the extra mile – giving an extra plum, apple or tomato, or a free introductory kale, quince or pok choi and a quick cooking lesson – that causes the customer to remember you…because people don't care how much you know unless they know how much you care.

From the start of any interaction, try to avoid having the customer say "No." Instead of saying "Would you like a taste?" you might say, "We have the sweetest carrots you can imagine. Our samples are right over there." The customer is more likely to try them, and less likely to say "No thanks" than if you ask a direct question.

It all starts with attitude. If you don't have positive energy to sell, you probably won't do well. Send a family member or employee who has a "Yes!" attitude.

IT'S A PEOPLE BUSINESS

 "The most important tip I would give a farmer is to treat your customers as if they were the most important people on earth."
– Butch Hollister, President, Connecticut Farmers' Association for Retail Marketing

Butch says it all. Your customers ARE the most important people on earth when you're in front of them. You can grow the best produce in the world or have the best chutney recipe, but if no one buys it, you're out of business. Your farm and business exist only because of your customers.

The friendly interchange between farmer and customer is the heart and soul of a farmers' market. People come to markets seeking a more personal shopping experience than grocery stores offer. Getting to know the farmer who grows the food will bring them back again and again.

"People today are looking for a connection, not just a quick change-maker. Have a nice comment for everyone. You don't have to be a used-car salesperson, just be real. People are looking for a 'real' experience at the farmers' market; they're not looking for another cashier at the grocery store."
– Gretchen Hoyt, Alm Hill Gardens, Everson, WA

The most popular growers are those who provide entertaining conversation, a bit of education about their produce and some indication of interest in their customers, without getting too familiar. "You have to like selling to people," explains former Greenmarket director Barry Benepe. "You have to like to chat. You can't be a wallflower."

Greet customers. Say, "Good morning" or "hello." If someone is looking at your beets, say: "I just packed those this morning. If you have any ques-

tions, let me know." Don't be a pest but be available to help them. Each customer is an individual; some customers appreciate additional information, while others consider suggestions too "sales-y" and just want to shop.

Project an image of wanting the customer's business. Eye-contact is also important. Don't wear sunglasses unless you absolutely have to. It helps to remember you're not just providing a head of lettuce; you're providing the farmers' market experience and yourself, a real-life farmer.

"Don't just do farmers' markets for a living. If you don't enjoy it, and you're tired, it'll show and customers will walk away."
– Cheryl Boden, West Union Gardens, Hillsboro, OR

Farmers who are not "people persons" may find they are not good in the market. Assign the job of working with customers to the most outgoing family members. One farmer says, "I always take my mom – she's friendly and she loves to chat with customers."

Don't let shyness prevent you from becoming a topnotch customer service person. Simple human warmth, and the sincere desire to serve the customer are more valuable selling traits than having an extroverted personality. According to Vallejo, CA, market manager Brooks Kleim, "Two growers can have markedly different styles, yet be equally effective. The desire to serve the public seems most important."

"We have one farmer who sells hard-neck garlic, which doesn't have a lot of shelf life but has a great taste and comes off the stalk easily. He's convinced customers that it's a great product. He's a good sales person, engages every customer, and speaks to each customer as they come in: 'Hi, I'm farmer so-and-so and I want you to taste my product.' Then he'll give them a fact sheet about his product. These are not new things but not everybody does them. If he's not in the market I'll have people asking where he is."
– Karen Durham, former Mgr., Bellingham FM, WA

Putting on a Show vs. Hawking

"The farmers' market is an event, not just a place to buy food. Most customers are there not just for the vegetables but for the atmosphere and entertainment. When I sell pumpkins I dress up as a scarecrow and call it the 'Kodak moment.' People climb up on the giant pumpkin and have their picture taken with me as the scarecrow. I started this 21 years ago and now the children of the children are coming, so now it's a tradition. I'm not out to sell pumpkins, but to entertain, so the children and their parents have a favorable experience and want to come back."

– Bonnie Dehn, President, Central Minnesota Vegetable Growers

In a Greenmarket a sprout seller says, "What would you like?" Then he repeats the response: "One-half alfalfa, one-quarter sunflower, one-quarter clover" as he scoops it up, boom! boom! boom! and puts a lid on the container. He's a great showman. Put theater in your farmers' market!

Yet whether to "hawk" or not is a delicate question. It depends on how you do it. Shouts of "Delicious and nutritious!" "Come and get your kohlrabi!" "Give peas a chance!" or (in the case of a farmer selling honey) "Pure and sweet, just like the ladies!"– at best, lend a festive, joyous mood to the market. At its worst, hawking creates a low-vibe, carnival atmosphere and makes customers feel uncomfortable. It can be especially irritating to vendors if loud and

Protecting Your Body

Your personal body temperature is critical to your happiness and sales. You won't think if you're too hot or care if you're too cold. Make sure you and your employees know the essentials about body comfort while selling. The first rule is: don't let your body get over-heated or cold in the first place; recovery can take longer than you think. Body heat loss depends on how much skin is exposed, not which part of the body. If your core gets cold, your extremities are probably even colder. Try an arm windmill exercise to throw blood to your fingertips, and create some core body heat at the same time.

Body: Protect your core body temperature with layered clothing. Rather than cotton, try to wear a synthetic, wicking first layer of clothing that pulls moisture off the skin; follow with an insulating layer. In summer a light long sleeve can protect your arms from direct sunlight. A neck wrap, periodically dipped in cool water, can help reduce excess heat.

Hat: Your head is about 7% of your body's surface and loses or gains heat proportionally. In cold weather wear a hat for basic warmth; in hot, a light hat is good protection from direct sunlight.

Footwear: Keep your feet warm with wool socks and waterproof boots. Footwear should be breathable or feet get sweaty, which could mean cold in rubberized boots.

Rubber mat: This is essential for your back, knees and general comfort while standing, and is also good insulation against cold. A mat is a great investment in your body's future.

Water: As water evaporates naturally from our skin, getting rid of extra absorbed heat, we need to drink water regularly to replenish it. Drink several quarts of water during market to keep hydrated – this is all too easy to forget when we get busy. In cold weather, water is still important to maintain your core body heat. With more in your system, it's easier to stay warm.

Gloves: Try thin, inexpensive sport gloves with a "tech" index-finger tip (for use with cell phones). They are thin enough to handle money and better than bare hands, though not real warm. Warmer gloves with exposed finger tips can also allow for money handling.

Canopy: Especially with severe heat, having your body protected from direct sun through most of the day is a good goal. ✨

constant all day. Use discretion if hawking is permitted at your market.

Serving a Crowd

"Quick service is a fine art. Customers are usually in a hurry and appreciate fast service, but you don't want to be too quick as to be rude. You could also lose add-on sales if you don't give the customers enough time."
– Chris "Marketman" Labeots, Baraboo, WI

Serve your customers quickly and give them your undivided attention. Try to develop a system for serving customers in the order they arrive. If you show your eagerness to serve the customer, they will forgive having to wait for a good product because they feel you're doing your best to serve them. Make eye contact with the next person in line to let them know you see them there.

Even making a connection with the newest person at the end of a long line can be essential in assuring that they'll wait. Asking them to come grab a berry, or a sample of peach or carrot, makes their wait more delicious, giving them time to contemplate buying more than they imagined. Or they might read your farm brochure or a recipe.

Once you serve them, acknowledge with a quick: "Thanks for waiting." If long lines are chronic, hire more help during peak hours and consider other ways to speed up the checkout process.

"Be prepared for the rush. Sales during our first hour are often 1/2 -2/3 of the total sales for the day. We use up to six people, three cash boxes and three scales to keep customers flowing smoothly through our stand. Four people are selling while the other two are refilling boxes and providing customers with plastic bags."
– Dan Haakenson, *The Small Commercial Gardener*

Having a separate scale and cash box for every courteous salesperson is the fastest method. Pre-packaged items save weighing time when people are especially harried on their lunch hour.

Keep busy

"Stay busy! Even if your stand is perfect, fiddle with something. Make customers feel like you're not waiting to pounce on them. Keeping busy also conveys prosperity and abundance and makes customers feel comfortable."
– Gretchen Hoyt, Alm Hill Gardens, Everson, WA

Don't just sit behind your booth and wait for people to come to you. If you appear disinterested, customers will be disinterested in you. Polish your apples, offer samples, replenish your display, use your spray bottle, bag more produce, clean up around the table, move big bills to your safebox, sweep up out front, restock your bag supply, cut more samples…

Make sure your employees are "on board" with your policy of enthusiasm! Every employee needs to be fired with enthusiasm, or if he is sitting doing Sudoku when he should be attending to customers, he needs to be fired, with enthusiasm. Don't make customers wait for help.

IMPROVING YOUR SERVICE

"The best 'advertising' for the market is the simple, age-old, farmer-customer, one-to-one contact. The customers ask the farmers questions like: 'I'm growing such and such potatoes and having trouble with scab. What should I do for it?' And the grower might answer: 'We're organic and we do this and this and this,' and the person may walk away satisfied, even though there may not be an immediate sale. They'll be back to the market and probably to that individual vendor."
– Mary Carpenter, former Mgr., Dane County FM, Madison, WI

Learn to listen to your customers. If a customer is looking at the cabbage, you might ask, "When did you last put up sauerkraut?" After the ensuing discussion about canning, the customer may go home with 20 pounds of cabbage to make canned sauerkraut.

Take impromptu customer service polls. Ask questions like: "What new variety could we grow for

Selling What the Customers Want

Jerry Rutiz, a grower of mixed vegetables near Arroyo Grande, CA, became one of the top salesmen at the Santa Monica Certified Farmers' Market by following the oldest principle known to marketers: giving the customers what they want. "If a customer is looking at my basil," says Rutiz, "I ask, 'Is there a variety you'd rather have?'… and they might answer, 'Yes, cinnamon basil,' or 'Yes, purple basil.'"

Rutiz looks for specialized varieties that the supermarkets don't carry, such as Chantnay carrots ("a sweeter, crispier carrot than you get in the grocery stores"), and Blue Lake greenbeans ("better tasting, more tender").

"I try to find out what the customers want and no one else in the market is growing," Rutiz continues. "I also ask the manager what is lacking in the market. Once she told me no one was growing brussels sprouts, so I grew that. This usually works for a few years, until other growers catch on and start growing it – then I try something else."

At least a third of Rutiz' products are unusual crops, for which little growing literature is available. "Experimentation gives me a challenge. If I planted lettuce year after year, I'd get bored. I'm trying new things all the time and it keeps me interested.

"Most of my varieties are not available in the supermarkets, so I don't have to follow their prices," adds Rutiz. "I figure what it costs me to grow and market a product, and then I set my price. If I can't get the price it takes to make a profit, I stop growing it." &

---

you?" "How can we serve you better?" Find out what customers like about you, what isn't working for them, and what else they wish you would offer. Your customers' wish lists are the key to new income opportunities.

Listen to yourself. Consider buying a tape recorder; turn it on during a busy hour to record your conversations with customers and play it back. Is your presentation repetitive? If so, vary it; look for other ways to communicate the same idea. Are you pleasant with customers? Are you honest and sincere? Listening to your conversations with customers helps you improve these things. Watch other vendors in your market and at other markets.

Try to remember what each customer has purchased previously and ask them how they liked the product. Point customers to other vendors if you cannot provide a service for them.

Satisfy special requests if you have time. Carry large purchases out to the customer's car, especially for elderly customers. To encourage large sales, let customers know that you will hold their purchases for them if they pay now.

"Always try to get a bag in the customer's hands. If they have a bag they will buy something."
– Chris "Marketman" Labeots, Baraboo, WI

Be Reliable

"One of our most successful growers is certified organic, which is a big draw for him and establishes a niche. He's been a long-time grower with the market and is very knowledgeable. He tells his customers all kinds of information about his products, how to use it, cook it, and his farming methods. He shares all this with the customers and they really like this – they like to know what they're getting. Another of our most successful growers has massive amounts and a great variety of fruits and vegetables throughout the season. He rents two spaces and sets up in an L-shape with two canopies with row after row of fruits and vegetables. He sells it by the bunch and by weight depending on what it is. Both of these growers are very picky about what they bring to market. The customers know the carrots will be sweet and that they'll always get great quality produce from them. The customers know they can trust them. In the six years I've been here, they've never missed a Saturday – customers rely on them."

– Barb Klimstra, former Mgr., Redmond FM, WA

Selling your produce yourself is ideal – no one sells it like the farmer who grew it. But if you'd rather grow than sell, hire enthusiastic employees and have the same people represent you at the market. Be consistent and dependable.

Keep regular hours at the market. Bring enough product to stay the entire market. If people come to find you and you're not there, or certain products are sold out, they go home disappointed. Part of keeping good relations with customers, as well as other vendors and market management, is not leaving the market before the posted time.

Product Guarantees

"Guarantee your produce. We bag all of our produce and include a written money-back guarantee. If a customer is dissatisfied in any way, they do not need to return the merchandise; they just mention what was wrong, and we replace it with fresh vegetables or return their money."

– Dan Haakenson, *The Small Commercial Gardener*

Have a "Satisfaction Guaranteed" policy for everything you sell. If there is a complaint, simply return the money or replace the purchase. Your object at the market is to sell, not to win debates. Arguing will only lose you additional sales. It's a matter of establishing trust with the customers. If they know your product is quality they'll return week after week.

Bob Sullivan makes known his goal with straightforward instructions on his sign at the Olympia FM: "Our one aim is to please. If you are pleased, tell your friends. If you are not, tell Sullivan's Homestead."

Alternately, ask the complaining customer how you can win back their trust. They may be satisfied with simply having the chance to lodge their complaint and be heard. Or they may ask for two peaches to replace those that were squashed at the bottom of their bag. Giving them a bit more than they ask should help regain their faith in your farm.

"Take breaks during the day. This is necessary to keep you cheerful and fresh with customers. One woman was furious; the market manager had told her I had berries but I had run out. She was yelling and very upset. I said, 'Oh, you must feel bad having come all this way,' and she smoothed right out. I turned her onto a neighboring vendor who had berries and she's been my customer ever since."

– Gretchen Hoyt, Alm Hill Gardens, Everson, WA

Allow customers to blow off steam. Show empathy and concern; show that you value their business. Ask questions to obtain details and solicit solutions. The fault may be the customer's; perhaps he neglected to cool the produce properly. Give him another dozen ears of corn anyway, saying, "Try to get it into the refrigerator right away, and if you eat it within a day, I think you'll be more satisfied."

Keep Customers Coming Back

"Find out what the customer wants and give it to them. Customers want different things. Some want mild onions, some strong. Some want low prices, others want to make a purchase as quickly as possible, regardless of price. We do our best to get to know our customers and cater to their individual needs. This policy goes beyond friendliness and courtesy. If a customer comes to our stand with vegetables from other vendors, we offer them a large bag with handles to carry it all to their car. We try to give them a reason to come back."

– Dan Haakenson, *The Small Commercial Gardener*

Better customer service is the key to repeat business. Serving your customer comes ahead of everything else. Straightening displays, talking on the telephone, or socializing with other farmers takes a back seat to serving customers.

Third-generation Glashoff Farms of Fairfield, CA uses old boxes to raise their jars, which include 3 oz. "carry on size" jams ready to fly.

It takes five times more energy and resources to get a first time customer than to keep one you already have. Your main goal is to keep customers returning to your stall week after week. Try to remember customers' names or at least something about them if you can. Be nice – give something extra, especially your long time customers. In any market five other sellers may be selling what you're selling and you need to give customers a reason to return to you.

> "I'm a stickler on customer service – even if a person is walking by my booth, I teach my kids to say, 'Good morning! How are you today? Are you looking for anything special?'"
> – Sue Goetz, Goetz Farms, Idaho Falls, ID

Helping the Customer Buy

> "Every salesperson hears a prospect say, 'Your price is too high.' What the prospect is really saying is that their desire is too low. The key is to increase the prospect's desire rather than argue about price. Establish the benefits, create more desire for them, and minimize the price compared to the benefits."
> – Adapted from the *Master Salesmanship Newsletter*

Relationships are built on satisfaction that a fair deal is being reached. When a sale is made, it should be a win/win for the farmer and the customer.

Educate your customers about your products. The more the customers know about your product, how it is used, and what goes into producing it, the more they are willing to pay a premium for top quality.

Look for the benefits in your product. Produce fresh from the field has a higher nutritional value. It keeps in the customers' homes longer. They know who grows it – you! They know how it's grown and they can ask you questions. Maybe you don't use preservatives in your product. Maybe your cider is fresh pressed yesterday and ozone-preserved, rather than flash pasteurized. Explain the difference between your American, Japanese and Indian eggplant.

Chert Hollow Farm in Missouri presented a garlic tasting challenge, which intrigued new customers who had always seen garlic as a monolithic item. Anyone buying multiple labeled heads went home with a tasting data sheet. Upon returning it, they were invited to a farm event where the drawing price was one each of all their varieties. It worked for garlic; why not try it with peppers or peaches?

Credit Cards

"Why would I ever need to take credit cards?"

You are the straight-forward, super-average farmer who does all his business by cash. No one ever has a problem with cash, or so you think.

But remember when the first person asked if you take personal checks? Maybe you resisted until the fifth or tenth person asked, and you changed your policy and began getting some checks. That expanded your business a bit. Or you didn't change, because you wanted to avoid the risk.

The same thing happened with the first person asking if you accept credit cards. Either you did a little homework and decided to change, or you rejected the idea as unnecessary and never knew what benefit might have come to you.

Consider the out-of-town visitor who doesn't have cash, or the man who has used up his allotted $40 market cash but suddenly wants a flat of berries or a bouquet of flowers, or the woman who forgot that her partner raided her wallet last night – and all of them only have a credit card.

Credit cards may be the single biggest boon to your business of any change that you can imagine. Don't look at credit cards as a troublesome addition to your "to do" list. View it as one more opportunity

Selling To Ethnic Groups

Q: Aren't ethnic groups generally a lower-priced market compared to the Anglo-American customer? Aren't they used to buying at open-air markets at comparatively low prices?

Salts: Yes and no. It's certainly not a top dollar market like selling to trendy yuppies, but it's definitely not bottom either. You've just got to be prepared to haggle. Most American farmers don't like haggling – it runs against most Americans' grain. Yet most ethnic groups just don't like having a set price. I usually set a price at high-middle, and I'm willing to dicker down to middle or low-middle.

I tried an experiment at a farmers' market once. I set a price ridiculously low on some cucumbers and yard-long beans, almost giving them away. Some ethnic customers still wouldn't buy it, because I wouldn't dicker! The next week I set the price high, and they dickered down and ended up paying twice what they would have gotten it for the week before! It's not so much the price they get it for, it just runs against their cultural grain to pay the asking price.

Q: What are some of the advantages of selling to ethnic customers?

Salts: Customer loyalty, volume, and consistency. Once ethnic customers find that you've got what they want, and that you are nice to them and cater to their culture, they will come back week after week, and year after year. Selling to ethnic folks may not be for everyone. You have to enjoy dealing with peoples from other cultures.

I've found ethnic groups to be a great niche market for me because there's very little competition. I may not be getting the price that some other sellers are getting selling to the yuppies, but my ethnic customers are a lot more stable. Yuppies can be very trendy, but the Chinese, the Indians, the Arabs and the Vietnamese have been buying the same vegetables for thousands of years. Ethnic customers aren't so much into food preservation, like canning – but many do make preserves such as kimchee or pesto or chutneys or pickles that take large quantities of produce and herbs. They also eat a lot more fruits and vegetables and they're a lot more accustomed to cooking from scratch. Even college students from other countries cook from scratch, believe it or not – it's not all phoned-in pizza. And then there are traditional banquets for holidays and weddings and the like that take LOTS of traditional veggies. The tradition in their countries is shopping at open-air markets. They don't want their produce all wrapped up in plastic.

Q: What's most important in selling to ethnic groups?

Salts: You not only need to grow the crops the peoples are used to, but to cater to their cultures. The social part is VERY important. You're selling a service and experience – not just veggies. It's the ultimate relationship marketing. We try to offer a social experience to our ethnic customers – greeting them in their native languages, asking their advice on ethnic cuisine, learning something of the geography and customs of their homelands, etc. I try to find out what their holidays are and have special items in stock when their holidays are coming.

Basically, just talk with them: "Are you from India? What part of India?" They're usually surprised anyone is asking them such a question, but they might say, "Andhra Pradesh." And I say, "Hyderabad?" And they just about fall on the ground: "Oh, you used to live in India?" Well no … but it all boils down to showing an interest in their culture.

A supermarket COULD try to compete with us on the product front – but can you see them doing it better on the social front? We have such an advantage! Small market grower-marketers can stop griping about unfair competition from factory farms. We just have to connect with customers who want to buy the "goods" in which we have a great comparative advantage. And those goods are not only great products but service and relationships.

Q: Yuppies are getting to be a difficult market to sell to. They purchase small amounts, and they want everything prepared. I've heard that ethnic peoples are the future of farmers' markets.

Salts: Well, we do sell to so-called yuppies also, and value their patronage, though it's true that they rarely buy much quantity. They like exotic produce but usually buy one of this and can you give me just a pinch of that. We find that so-called ethnic customers buy and use fresh veggies greatly in excess of their percentage of the total farmers' market customers – and patronize farmers' markets more than do Anglo-Americans. Perhaps 50-60% of our current farmers' market customers are ethnic, and the proportion of ethnics in the population is growing rapidly. If present trends continue, the Census Bureau projects that nonHispanic European Americans will be a minority by the year 2050, with the nation 25% Hispanic, 10-12% Asian-Pacific Islander and 16% black.

Q: So your book gets into some of the basic ethnic languages a farmers' market seller might learn?

Salts: Yes. I will have a glossary in about 20 languages for elementary farmers' market terms such as greetings, "yes," "no," numbers, etc. It doesn't include all 2500 languages of the world, but some of the basic ones like Arabic, Spanish, Portuguese, Korean, Chinese and Vietnamese.

Customers are 80% Asian and 10% Indian in Milpitas, CA.

Q: Could you tell us a little about your own market mix?

Salts: Our marketing is approximately 50-60% farmers' markets, 20-25% ethnic and vegetarian restaurants, 15-20% CSA, 5-10% on-farm sales, booths at festivals, etc. Our product mix is perhaps 25-30% "standard" veggies (even Chinese like sweet corn); 25-35% "heirloom" old-fashioned varieties (tomatoes, sweet sorghum, wild blackberries, etc.), and 50% ethnic veggies, mostly Oriental but with generous and increasing dashes of Middle Eastern, Italian, East European, Asian Indian, Southeast Asian, Mexican, etc.

We try to offer both products and services that the Super Mega-markets and Fast Food International can't. We offer very fresh, carefully harvested, great-tasting, old-fashioned or ethnic produce, often with "weird" appearance or short shelf lives, served up with a generous side-dish of advice, multicultural socializing, and just plain old personal friendship.

Our heirloom veggies tend to draw a lot of vegetarians, gourmet hobby cooks, older people ("Why my grandma used to grow that in her garden! I haven't seen that in years!"), and curious passers-by ("What IS that!?"). Actually, heirloom veggies could be considered just another sort of "ethnic" veggies – the veggies of our own fast-vanishing traditional American culture.

People are often loathe to buy "weird" veggies at first, so we give away a lot of free samples, plus recipes or suggestions for use. We are building a steadily growing clientele of "addicts." "Why you WERE right! That crazy fuzzy tomato / red okra / guinea bean / (or whatever!) tasted great! Can I get three pounds this week?"

– An interview with Steve Salts, truck farmer and author of *Around the World at Farmers' Market: A Handbook for Small-scale Grower-Marketers of Ethnic and Heirloom Vegetables, Fruits, and Herbs.* ✷

for you to give great customer service, the way they want it.

If you don't accept cards, you're turning over business to someone that does, or letting it escape to outside the market. Credit cards will increase your overall business because you are capturing customers who wouldn't have bought from you. Even your dedicated cash customers occasionally forget that they have to buy extra products for a party that night; either they pay you by card, or stop at the supermarket on the way home.

> "When I first started at the farmers' market, I had a beautiful line of bottled products with colorful and sophisticated labels, and I was ready to handle cash and checks. When I realized I was losing tourists and even local customers, I signed up with a credit card company and my business jumped by 40% immediately."
>
> – Connie Rawlings-Dritsas, Blossom Vinegars, Portland, OR

Picking the right credit card processor is critical if you want to avoid considerable annual fees. Compare at least these factors:

* Where you accept payments: Since you're accepting payments in person, pick the credit card processor that fits you. That may be different if you also want to accept payments at your roadside stand, on your website or at a Fancy Food Show.

With higher price items such as nursery stock – or a gift pack of infused vinegars from Vermont's Hillside Lane Farm – credit card transactions are a necessity.

* Frequency of payments – Some providers better serve low-volume businesses while others give lower rates for volume processing.

* Amount of payments – Find the right credit card processor whose rates fit your average transaction amount. You will pay a higher percentage if your average transaction is low.

* Interface functionality – Make sure your processor has a mobile application compatible with your smartphone. Check that your processor's payment gateway syncs well with your website.

* Customer service – You want quick and easy solutions to any glitch that develops, fast payment of your funds and few chargebacks. Ask about dispute resolution to stop chargebacks before they happen. Check the company's customer service track record, and look out for glaring problems such as a frozen account where they hold your money for months. Your goal is service without frustration.

Credit cards aren't for everyone. They do take time to process, and that can take away from your ability to handle the next customer quickly. They may be unnecessary for a vegetable grower who has only local customers.

When you choose a processor, you will project a certain number of payments each month and the average amount. Once you're in business, the reality may be different. You may decide to expand your gift product line to take advantage of tourists, or you may suddenly recognize the potential for more sales with higher ticket items like nursery stock or new CSA memberships. Your new circumstances may cause you to reassess the processing company that is appropriate for your evolving business. Keep this in mind during your initial investigation of the right credit card company for you. Hold onto your notes because a year or two later you may be a sizably different company with a new set of needs from your card processor.

Perhaps you want to skip credit cards. With 7+ billion cell phones worldwide, the Square - plugged into your phone - is the fastest way to consumer cash.

Providing Product Information

Add value and service by helping customers choose the best produce for their needs. Suggest good ways of using produce and keeping it fresh. Give out simple recipes. Put together a mesh bag of all the ingredients customers need for a great salsa, with a recipe sheet enclosed. Encourage feedback from customers.

People are busy and not used to cooking and prepping food, so offer tips on what you grow. Answer questions concerning varieties, growing methods, storage, cooking, serving and nutrition to help sell your produce. The personal touch at farmers' markets is one of your crucial "edges" over the supermarkets.

"Customers really respond to our presentation of garlic as a diverse ingredient that could be targeted to specific culinary uses. This allows us to charge higher prices than for garlic presented as a bulk commodity crop, and attracts a loyal following of customers who seek out our garlic and then buy other items as well.

"We designed and printed basic information cards for each variety, presenting its name and culinary qualities/uses. We also set up a white board with a comparative grid of garlic virtues, for easy customer reference. Customers were very interested in the ability to choose among a variety of specific uses and target their garlic to their culinary needs for the week."
– Eric & Joanna Reuter, Chert Hollow Farm, Boone County, MO in *Growing for Market,* August, 2014

Prepare to answer questions about your products such as when peak supplies are available or what quantities to buy for canning and freezing. Make sure employees and family members are well-informed.

Convey your enthusiasm about your products to your customers – it's catching. Instead of saying, "Lettuce, $1/head," you need to get into the ambiance of the product, giving the varietal name like "Winter Red Romaine," and describe how it's fresh that day and how its premium quality will hold up for two weeks.

Storing produce at home

"Customers' changing eating and shopping habits are a constant challenge for farmers' market sellers. People under 35 don't can (put food up for later) so much – very little – and they aren't familiar with a lot of our products. We hand out flyers and recipes so they know how to prepare our products. Garden beets or rhubarb, for example, are items they don't see in the store, so we have to educate them how to make a rhubarb pie and how to prepare and store it."
– Allen Shoemaker, Shoemaker's Home Place, Blackfoot, ID

Talk to customers about storage tips as you serve them: "Put these peaches in a brown paper bag and they'll be ready to eat in three days. Check that they give a bit on the shoulder." People waiting in line will also appreciate the information. Give suggestions: "Use this in two days; this will last all week; don't wash until ready to eat; place in water vertically in refrigerator." If you don't know, call your Cooperative Extension office and find out. They may even have handouts you can use.

"Canning and freezing is quickly becoming a lost art. Because of the availability of fresh, frozen, and canned vegetables, young families have quit storing produce for themselves. Some of that is due to the hectic lifestyles we live, where canning might be too complicated or time consuming. However, much of the lack of interest is because of ignorance on exactly how to get the job done. If we take the time to educate our customers we will have the opportunity to provide the produce to them. We would recommend starting with salsa because of increased interest in this product."
– Dan Haakenson, *The Small Commercial Gardener*

Suggest fermentation so people can stretch a product's season and remember you all winter. Mention the benefits of probiotics, how to make them and resources they can use. Sandor Katz, author of *Wild Fermentation*, recommends not just cabbage and salt for sauerkraut, but also grated carrots, onions, garlic, seaweed, greens, Brussels sprouts, turnips, beets, and burdock roots. [See Resources, Chapter 6]

Check Mark Frauenfelder's YouTube video or recipe at:

http://boingboing.net/2009/01/12/making-sauerkraut-is.html

Educate Customers About Healthy Food

If you are going to educate customers about healthy food, you might want to be fairly educated about what to avoid as well. The war on carbonated soda has spread its message effectively, but many other so-called foods are equally responsible for degrading the American diet.

Food blogger Andrew Wilder has led the way with Unprocessed October, an experiment in avoiding sugar, fat, preservatives, flavoring and artificial colors. Starting in 2010, he has inspired thousands of people to take the challenge of avoiding all processed foods for an entire month. See:

www.eatingrules.com

Look up other great online resources on health food with searches such as "healthiest fresh foods," "chemical offenders in food", "unhealthy food additives," "health benefits of organic foods," etc.

Nutrition information

Farmers need to take the lead in teaching consumers about food benefits. While the number of practicing primary care physicians in the U.S. was estimated to be 209,000 in 2010, they are treating the sick. More than 140,000 farmers across the U.S. have regular weekly contact with people; they need to treat the healthy...to a healthy dose of education.

"Eat your Colors" (a 5-A-Day program mantra) is a reflection of the exciting and on-going research revealing the tremendous health benefits derived from consuming a diet rich in fruits and vegetables. Much of this research has seemed to indicate that the benefits are due not only to vitamin, mineral and fiber content but also to the phytochemicals and anti-oxidants found in fruits and vegetables."

– Dr. Claudia Ferrell, family practice doctor and Berry Patch Farm, Brighton, CO in *Growing for Market,* August, 2004

Studies show that strokes in women are reduced by 5-8 servings of fruit and vegetables per day, especially crucifers, and greater vegetable consumption is linked to reduced risk of cardiovascular disease and certain cancers.

Ferrell urges farmers to take their role seriously, provide nutritional information and recipes with as many colors as possible. Gear them to working moms, not just foodies. Keep it simple: "Add sautéed zucchini and peppers to spaghetti sauce for increased nutrition."

Let nutrition influence your seed selection. "Grow a dark green zucchini instead of a lighter green – the darker is associated with higher lutein levels to help preserve eyesight – and tell your customers. Consider growing multiple colors of beans, zucchini, peppers, onions, cauliflower and cabbage," Ferrell advises. Make sure your value-added products truly add value for people's health.

Stay up-to-date on your product research. Most diseases result from many factors; nutrition is only one. It's tempting for organic growers to believe that healthier soils produce healthier crops, but many factors including climate may come into play. It is fair to state that organic production seems safer for the environment.

Nutritional knowledge is basic to produce retail selling. Know vitamin content and each product's

Gee Creek Farm of Ridgefield, WA notes that its organic chickweed at $8/lb. is "good for lungs."

health benefits and inform your customers, either through product literature, verbally, or with signs. Gee Creek Farm of Ridgefield, WA, takes it seriously with "good for lungs" organic chickweed and many probiotic, fermented vegetables.

Cherries combat osteoarthritis. Carrots and winter squash are excellent sources of beta-carotene, the precursor of Vitamin A. Potatoes are an excellent source of potassium. [See Resources, Chapter 6]

Be ready to answer customer questions concerning food or direct them to appropriate resources. Check the web, produce associations and your Cooperative Extension office for information, studies and handouts. Encourage your market manager to ask for Master Gardeners and Master Food Preservers to staff a booth at your market on a regular schedule.

We can rebuild the health of Americans. If we don't, we will have more people suffering ill health and the economy will slow under the burden of insufferable health care costs.

Gardening information

Some of the most successful farmers we know are willing to share their "secrets" with their customers. This helps establish a relationship with customers. Let's face it: someone who has tried to grow any food crop at all is more appreciative of the time and effort it takes to bring food from the soil. These folks will no doubt be your most loyal and supportive customers.

"The idea is to get people to think about what they're buying in food. They can go to Wal-Mart and get a 6-pack of tomatoes and have no idea what they're getting. That tomato might do well in Indiana but can't grow in Maine. We sell seedlings at the market and we sell the customer a variety that will work for them locally, because those are the varieties we grow ourselves.

"We ask them what they want. If they want a tomato for canning, we sell them a heavy producer rather than an early-season variety. By asking them very specific questions about what they want in a tomato, we are providing a service the big supermarkets can't provide. They might want an oddball tomato like a red pear-shaped cherry tomato.

"We also answer their gardening questions like, 'My cucumber plants died – why?' I'll query them about their growing conditions and tell them why, so I'm their plant doctor. This kind of consumer education has to be done on a one-to-one basis with a local producer rather than mass-marketing, and when the whole farmers' market has this attitude, it makes a great impact on the customers so they want to keep coming back."

– Tom Roberts, Snakeroot Organic Farm, Pittsfield, ME

Recipes

"To promote new or unusual varieties, we hand out recipes at the market. The ones that work usually have only a few ingredients. No more than five or six ingredients max. Concentrate mostly on the few items you're trying to push that day, whatever you're trying to move – don't clutter the stand. And it's also best if all the ingredients are available at the market. People shopping at the market are looking for something they can fix that night. With our pesto recipe mix, if we put out a pesto recipe with our basil plants, I will triple sales. We put a pile on the table, and they read it right there on the spot and pick up some basil."

– Lisa Bloodnick, Bloodnick Family Farm, Apalachin, NY

One of the most productive ways to educate buyers and promote your products is with recipes. Especially for oversupply, in-season crops, print recipes. You can use recipes to teach inexperienced cooks how to use farm-fresh fruits and vegetables. Shoppers especially need suggestions on what to do with new or unusual items. Use fairly simple but unique recipes that use at least one or two of your products. Offer a variety of recipes and include your farm name and phone number on each one.

Format and print your recipes in the off-season so they'll be ready when the crop is. Consider having the printer pad up the recipes so that you can put them on a special display and customers can help themselves. Use the reverse side of the recipes for promotional information about your farm.

Growing for Market has done most of the recipe work for you. Their book, *Farm-Fresh Recipes* by Janet Majure, has about 300 recipes, set up three to a page. It covers the major crops, from high-value herbs to apples and tomatoes, and less familiar veggies like greens, fennel and rhubarb. With spiral binding, it's perfect for copying (with permission granted) and has trim marks for accurate cutting.

> "Make sure recipes are available when there is something new. With pickling cucumbers, for example, which the farm generally sells three tons a week over a three-week period, we give out our own recipes and get others from Extension Service. The internet is another source for recipes. We found over 2000 recipes for fava beans by searching the web."
> – Bob & Pat Meyer, Stoney Plains Farm, Tenino, WA

Everyone becomes stagnant with meal repetition and new ideas are exciting. If customers don't know how to use delicata or spaghetti squash, give them recipes and they're hooked. They may not necessarily buy this week, but if they go home with a recipe, they probably will buy next week.

Looking for innovative ways to use your product in recipes? Have customers join a recipe contest. Or work with a chef to develop new uses for your products and to find out what other products the chefs or consumers can use. The mesclun mix craze got started because California farmer Warren Weber worked with Bay Area chefs to find innovative ways to use the new salad greens available.

Consider the time of the year. Concentrate on quick and easy recipes – nothing too complex that keeps customers in hot kitchens in July. Better yet, use recipes that call for grilling or roasting over coals.

Sampling

> "I consider sampling to be the most effective marketing method available."
> – Jay Conrad Levinson, Guerrilla Marketing

If your produce is suitable, offer samples. A taste is worth a thousand words, and many of those who try will buy.

> "People tend to graze through the market before they buy and they make decisions based on what tastes good. Farmers are selling themselves short if they don't give out samples."
> – Mary Lou Weiss, Ex-Mgr., Torrance FM, CA

Product sampling is especially important for introducing new products or varieties, especially ones that taste great but are sometimes hard to sell. People don't often buy unfamiliar products. Above her sugar snap peas, one grower had a sign that read: "Free sample – taste one. Edible pods – crisp, sweet. Eat the whole pea!" Because they were the size of green beans, customers expected them to be tough but after sampling them were surprised to find they were tender and stringless.

Over a display of apples with nine different varieties, for example, you might set out a sign, "Please Sample." This makes it easy for customers to find out which one they want. Busy farmers may have one or two helpers simply cutting samples and refilling plates. One Vermont farmer explains the soil conditions and challenges of each melon variety as he samples.

Sampling is not only the best advertising you can do; it's also inexpensive. Hand a customer a small paper cup of cider, and they'll probably want to purchase a gallon – that's cheap advertising! Lots of growers hesitate to give away free products, but if giving away $50 in samples makes the difference between a $300 day and a $900 day, it's worth it.

In traditional food merchandising there is an adage that for every 10% of oversupply, prices need to be lowered 30% to move the product. Rather than seeing an oversupply in the market, give away your excess 10% as free samples, and hold your price.

> "We slice up tomatoes and put out tasters, and start hawking our slogans: 'When was the last time you had a really great tomato?,' 'Taste the Farmhouse difference,' and so on. We put on a show!"
>
> – Walter Ross, Farmhouse Tomatoes, Inc., Lake Worth, FL

Sampling slows shoppers down, giving you time to talk with them, which usually results in a sale.

Sampling to sustain a price

> "A lot of fruit looks alike and most people can't tell how it tastes just by looking at it. Most customers don't want to pay $2 or $3 a pound for tree-ripe fruit, but once they taste it they can't resist."
>
> – Art Lange, Honey Crisp Farm, Reedley, CA

> "Sampling is critical, not just for new items, but for items which taste great but are expensive or may not look good. Let's say you've got really sweet carrots, for instance, that you have to charge a high price for because they have less yield, expensive seeds or they're harder to grow. Without sampling these great carrots, the customers won't know it's worth paying the extra money. Some of the really ugly products can taste delicious. Calico corn, for example, has a white and yellow appearance and it looks like there's something wrong with it, yet it's the most delicious corn."
>
> – Donna Sherrill, Sherrill Farms, Arvin, CA

Full Circle Organic Farm in CA was one of the first to bring heirloom tomatoes to market. Radiator Charlie's Mortgage Lifter was one of their signature tomatoes. Charlie's are a huge, pink-red slicer, but they aren't perfectly round, and they have a tendency to shoulder crack. It's a funny-looking tomato to a public used to perfectly round, red orbs designed for long-distance shipping. After sampling the Charlie's for a couple of months, they sold out weekly. Sponsoring and setting up an heirloom tomato tasting for the entire market, everyone's tomato sales went up.

Kashiwase Farms displays their samples on a cart covered by a sneeze guard at the Marin FM, CA.

Heirloom tomatoes sold for double the conventional tomato price.

Sampling How-to

Provide sliced vegetables, fruit, melons, or fresh berries in clean, covered dishes and provide toothpicks, napkins and spoons or wooden ice cream sticks. Don't cut up too much at one time so as to keep them fresh. Keep a bucket of sanitizing water to rinse your knife and to wipe fruit before you cut it. Have a trash can available.

Invite customers to sample; people are far more inclined to try it if it is offered to them. If you are going to sell a lot of product, you'll need some extra helpers. Get them out in the crowds to encourage samples; that will really bring them in: "Free taste!"

Check with the market manager and/or your county health department for health regulations concerning sampling. The most common regulations are that samples be prepared in a health department certified kitchen, that they remain covered, and that perishables be kept iced. You are usually required, for example, to give samples on a disposable utensil without anyone's hands touching the sample, and you may be required to wear food service gloves and cover your hair. All this may seem like extra trouble but samples make sales!

Up the Sale

Have tie-in merchandise next to your produce. If someone buys salad mix or lettuce, ask what they are serving for the meal and suggest several dressings they might like. With a carrot sale, let them know your tomatoes or cucumbers are perfect this week.

Show your support of other farmers – if you're selling a salty cheese similar to Manchego, tell them a nearby farmer has membrillo (quince paste) that would be a nice complement.

Have introductory offers for new products: "Free arugula with purchase of zucchini." "Buy five avocados, get free cilantro."

Joe Smith in Denton, MD, looks to see what will be ripe for market the next day. He might find just one pea that's ready. He'll pick it and post it prominently on a sign: "Ready Next Week!" This tantalizes customers who flock to his booth next week to purchase the fresh-picked peas.

> "Our tote is a wonderful way to upsell in farmers' markets, and it's great in cities where plastic bags have been outlawed. If we give away 10 canvas totes in a market, we've sold an extra 80 bags of nuts, which may add 50% to our sales that day. People wouldn't buy eight bags at once without that incentive. People know the value of getting something free that they'll use. It hangs in the kitchen ready to come to market, or carry shoes to the beach or the shoe repair. Over the last 15 years we've given away more than 15,000 totes. These people are doing our marketing for us."
> – Gail Zannon, Santa Barbara Pistachio Co., CA

Plan ahead and help your customers do likewise. Let them know what items are coming, and which varieties are best for home canning or freezing. Post a harvest schedule in your stall.

Finally, as customers leave, express your sincere thanks.

PROMOTION

Everything you do is part of your promotional effort to sell your products: from your business card and smile to support of your local school or chamber of commerce.

A 12-acre coffee grower in northern Nicaragua funds his local baseball team – uniforms, equipment, umpire pay and baseballs. He is able to do this because of the 10-cent and 5-cent premiums he receives for fair trade and organic, respectively.

Consider what you can do in your community: sponsor your local library's food lecture series, support a local bicycle racer or a race, or cover the cost of a chef showdown using your product at the market.

Become a guerrilla marketer, beginning with an attitude that anything is possible, and the more ideas you implement over the years, the more successful you are likely to be. Start with a business card; that is as basic as your handshake. Put them together when you meet someone.

Product Literature

> "Customers will not buy a new product if they don't know what to do with it!"
> – Frieda Caplan, Frieda's, Los Alamitos, CA

Frieda Caplan, a legend in the produce industry for promoting many little-known products like kiwifruit into the mainstream, stated that part of her success formula was to supply grocery store produce managers with recipes and storage tip-sheets for the new products.

> "We give customers a handout sheet with every bunch of flowers we sell that includes tips for handling and care of the flowers. Our flowers are fresh, carefully wrapped and guaranteed to last a week – a rose from the florist can be eight days old."
> – Chet Anderson, The Fresh Herb Company, Longmont, CO

Learn to use desktop publishing software and techniques. In the slow season you can make up educational brochures and flyers on your computer. Contents for such hand-outs might include:

• An explanation of product history and nutritional values of assorted produce;
• Special recipes for low salt, low fat, low sugar, low cholesterol, or high fiber foods;

- Your farm story to get the consumer more in touch with what you and your farm are "all about;"
- Advantages of buying locally-produced food; and
- A "position paper" if you're using special farm practices you want to advertise. Such an information sheet could save your vocal chords, considering the oft-repeated refrain of: "Is this sprayed?" heard at a typical urban market.

"The farmers' markets hold great potential for people to learn about farming," Gretchen Hoyt says. CBS' 60 Minutes Alar-on-apples story kicked off a media frenzy which stimulated greater consumer interest in potential food carcinogens.

Thousands of farmers now know their individual and collective power to respond to public concerns. Hoyt advises: "You can tell the consumer exactly what you're doing with your product. We at the farmers'

markets are the only farmers they might meet, so we are the representatives for agriculture. The farmers' markets give us a chance to talk face-to-face with customers and let them know the issues we're dealing with. Let them know we provide 40 jobs for every person on the farm, we keep the land open for future generations, and that we produce good, healthy, high-quality food. Family farms are in trouble, and we need to show the people that agriculture is not the bad guy, that without agriculture around the cities we will lose all the beautiful scenery. Get involved in your market politically. In many markets we're finding that spaces formerly reserved for farmers have been given to dumpsters or produce broker coolers."

Newsletters

Publish a weekly one-page newsletter to let customers know what's in season, recipe contests, and other events. Perhaps quarterly you can do a more substantial one with pieces on the farm and your environmental efforts, growing conditions, industry updates, kids' games, an invitation to a barn dance, etc.

"Newsletters provide a different service to your customer, providing current information and ideas. Write the majority of the copy prior to the beginning of the season. Then, during "crazy season," supplement the prepared material with current information. Each season is unique and brings new challenges. A timely article will help bring credibility to your newsletter. Keep the copy light. Try to entertain as well as inform your customers."
– Dan Haakenson, *The Small Commercial Gardener*

Local Media

Newspapers. Submit educational articles to your local newspaper food editor. A well-written, factual article is frequently welcomed by short-staffed local papers, and may be picked up from there by larger regional papers.

Chert Hollow Farm in Missouri invited their food editor to a garlic-tasting event on the farm, including taste tests for raw, roasted, and garlic butter. Participants clearly enjoyed filling data sheets with feedback

Brochures

Brochures can accomplish many things for you. Here are some guidelines:

Differentiate yourself and your operation. Capitalize on who you are, because customers like to know something about the farmer that grows their food. Many have lost contact with rural life and this is one small way to bring it back. Explain any special things you do to enhance the quality of your operation, how you are different from other growers.

Personalize your operation. Include a picture of your family and a short biographical sketch.

Provide your market schedule. If you have a complicated schedule, reference it in a brochure or on your website.

Introduce prices. If your pricing will be fairly stable, include base prices for all major vegetables with a short discussion on pricing policies.

Establish a guarantee with a strongly worded promise to replace any produce your customers find unacceptable. ∞

Websites & Social Media
How Growers At One Farmers' Market Do It

According to Brie Mazurek, Online Education Manager for CUESA (Center for Urban Education about Sustainable Agriculture), the nonprofit organization that runs the Ferry Plaza Farmers' Market in San Francisco, "Social media is another way to enhance conversation between growers and customers. Small farms are not impersonal brands. They have real people behind them. Farmers can use social media to deepen connections with customers and take them behind the scenes.

"Having a web presence is becoming crucial in our tech-centric age," Brie says. "The key is to start small. Posting once or twice a week to your Facebook page is enough to keep that connection with your customers. Remind them when you'll be at the farmers' market and what products you're bringing. If you've been out of the market for the winter, let them know when you'll be back with a truckload of strawberries. Getting the word out through online channels can make a difference in your farmers' market sales."

Full Belly Farm is a 450-acre farm which markets a diverse array of produce directly to customers through farmers' markets and a 1200-member CSA in the Bay Area. According to Hallie Muller, Full Belly's marketing director, the main social media tools utilized by the farm, in addition to its website, are Facebook, Twitter and Instagram.

The farm uses social media as a tool to connect with consumers on a personal level and tell the farm's story rather than promote products. In a Facebook post, for instance, Hallie might say "Check out this week's newsletter," and include a link to the farm's website, where website visitors can read a copy of the latest CSA newsletter. For selling produce, the farm tries to steer traffic to its website.

Another social media star in the Ferry Plaza Farmers' Market is Frog Hollow Farm, a 133-acre farm near Brentwood California, which specializes in unusual varieties of stone fruit. According Pearl Driver, the farm's Director of Marketing, "Remember that with whatever social media tool you use, such as Facebook or Twitter, it's all about being social, not just business. We like to limit our sales push to once a week, if that."

Social Media

Photos are a great format for telling your farm story (often used in conjunction with a brief text narrative). You can post photos (taken with a mobile phone) to show customers what's happening on the farm from day to day, educate them about products, and share your challenges and successes.

Photos help create a sense of attachment to the farm and in turn, help customers understand where their food comes from. Just using Instagram and a smartphone, you can upload your images to your Facebook page.

Facebook is convenient for conversation-starters or updates that require a bit of explanation, while Twitter is a more condensed format – most appropriate for headlines and quick updates. Use Facebook to engage customers with topics like: "what's going on at the farm," industry trends, recipes and photos of composting, food and new products. Ask questions of your audience on your Facebook page, and encourage dialogue, such as "What's your favorite way to cook leeks?" or ask customers to post their favorite recipes. Share links that are educational, not just links to your own page or business, with stories and articles that you feel would be of value or interest to your audience.

Finally, Facebook is just plain fun and fulfilling. "It's not just business," Hallie Muller says, "you're telling your story and what is meaningful to you."

Twitter can be used to let customers know what you're bringing to the farmers' markets, or to offer special deals to farmers' market customers, etc. Invite customers to send twitter messages to the farm and then find orders pre-bagged and waiting for them at the market. This saves them from having to come early to purchase items that usually sell out. Customers can also send special requests via twitter.

Pinterest, a pin-board style, photo-sharing website, can be used to share your farm's best photos in scrapbook fashion. Full Belly Farm has separate boards for fruity recipes, "best farm photos" or "what's happening on the farm," etc.

Videos & YouTube. Videos can be used to introduce new products, show people how a particular crop is grown, or demonstrate how to cook a produce item. Keep the video short – under two minutes – and make sure that it's on a specific topic. You might produce a video to explain the flavors and culinary uses of an unusual product on your farm, like radicchio, a variety of chicory. You can make perfectly acceptable YouTube videos with a digital camera or an iPhone or iPad.

Website

Should farmers attempt to set up their own website? Some farmers are making nice do-it-yourself websites, while others find a tech-savvy friend, family member, or customer, with whom they can barter farm product in exchange for website services. Others seek professional help, while others grab the nearest web-savvy 14-

Facebook pages of CUESA & The Ferry Plaza Farmers Market; Frog Hollow Farm; Full Belly Farm.

year old! If resources are tight, a basic web page or Facebook page can serve as your web presence – include your contact info, products, and what markets you're at.

Full Belly Farm's Hallie Muller feels that many farmers neglect giving proper attention to their website. "A lot of farmers feel that a social media website is sufficient and tend to slack off on making a great website. But a professionally designed and maintained website can be a huge asset – you need to invest a little time and money, as the return is well worth it! For many years, we had a rather funky website, but we began to see what a great marketing tool a professional website can be."

Google Analytics and Facebook's Insights are valuable tools you can use to find out valuable information about your audience. You can use it to find out what search terms people are using when they come to your farm's website; demographics such as what geographical region website visitors are from; and if they are new or returning visitors.

What About the Time?

Once you get a Facebook page and a website set up, expect to spend anywhere from 10 to 30 minutes each day – at least several days a week – maintaining your internet presence. This involves taking several pictures from your mobile phone, uploading via Instagram and writing a few sentences or a short story to go with each one, and uploading them as posts to your website or Facebook page.

Also, you may need to spend a few minutes responding to customer comments. Try to keep up active dialogs with your audience as best as possible. ∞

which further refined their marketing descriptions. And the newspaper article boosted the farm's profile.

Magazines. Provide a press packet to your local Edible magazine editor – there are 80 regional versions (and counting) – or at least a business card with an invitation to visit your farm. Tell her why your farm is worth some attention, where you sell, what chefs are buying from you, how you grow, and anything else noteworthy for a farm story.

Be ready to connect with photographers and writers who show up at your booth unannounced. Smile for picture-takers because they may be writing a story...or they may simply be showing photos to friends of a trip where they met a really happy farmer.

Public speaking. Present educational slide shows at local service and garden clubs. As an expert in your field, you will be consulted by all kinds of people, and perhaps even be invited to speak at the local junior college or high school on your chosen topic. These contacts will bring some of your best customers, and maybe your best employees, whether teachers or gung ho students.

Television. Many local morning and noon news shows are looking for local color to highlight the seasons. Let them know you are available to demonstrate a recipe on television or answer questions about fruits and vegetables. Local-access cable channels are another video venue. If you make yourself known and available, you are more likely to be interviewed on TV in relation to weather or other farm-related issues in your local area.

Paid advertising. While most promotion can be done better with effort than dollars, it may be worthwhile to place paid advertising in a popular, local publication.

"A change that has been very effective for us is the format of our ad in our weekly Pennysaver. Instead of laying out an ad, I write a letter addressing it 'Dear Friends.' We have never had as good a response to a written ad as we have this type."
– Peggy Frederick, Strawberry Valley Farm, Whitney Point, NY

E-mail

Put your e-mail address on your business cards, flyers, recipes, and newsletters. E-mail is great for answering customers' questions such as if you will be at the market next week, what you will be bringing, or to request a specific item or quantity like a bushel of pickles for canning. E-mail is an easy, inexpensive and convenient alternative to the telephone. Make sure your e-mail address is listed on your market's vendor contact list.

Encourage customers to e-mail orders before coming to the market. You can pre-bag their orders so they don't have to worry about getting to the market early to find products they want. This is important for caterers, restaurants, purveyors or anyone who needs larger quantities for special occasions. Pre-orders build your sales and customer loyalty. These larger sales can make the critical difference that justifies some farmers coming to market.

Along with e-mail, build your snail-mail list by copying addresses from checks you receive and inviting customers to sign your guest book. Send flyers before next season to remind faithful customers when and where you'll be.

Social Media

The 20th century has brought radical changes to the marketing realm. Most of the public is enthralled with social media, forcing farmers to stay current.

Farmers can sponsor a chef demo or provide product that the chef promotes during their demonstration.

"Amazing and true!! Just for buying your Spring Hill Organic Farm Market Bucks card before May 10th, 2014 we will throw in another $10 value Early Bird card AND a super swell cloth tote! Your $100 gets you $120 in fresh, organic produce and a tote to boot!

  - Spring Hill Organic Farm, North Albany, OR facebook

With prominent mention on its food truck, *Oaxacan Kitchen Mobile* encourages market customers to follow them on Facebook and Twitter. They build followers at markets and constantly remind their contacts to come see them at farmers' markets and elsewhere.

Food trucks are the social media mavericks of the food world. Because their survival depends on constantly updating potential customers on their location, they use Facebook, Twitter and Pinterest heavily. Their increased presence at farmers' markets is giving farmers a more detailed look at a playbook with payback.

Make sure employees are ready to tweet your followers with a picture of your market display, a daily special or a selfie to remind people who they should be looking for today.

Websites

While many farmers are shifting their focus to social media with good gains, a farm website can still play a valuable role in attracting and reinforcing customers. It can provide a fuller picture of your farm's products, location, markets, other marketing avenues, and philosophical approach. A brochure, pictures or sign at market can drive traffic toward your website where you may also want to sell products.

You also can display your eccentric side. Along with the description of hoop house production, well water, passive solar and sustainable wages in growing salad mix and vegetables year-round, TinyFarm.com shows its fun North Carolina humor. There is Carla's Corner with a post about "Beets Audio," with a photograph: "Chase has perfected the first organic and edible headphones for vegans, chefs, and locavores, may require more frequent ear cleaning,

but fully compostable. Will include a free set in one of our weekly vegetable boxes."

Tell Your Story

"What's the story you want to tell? If you stand for something, relate that to the customer. Write down in 25 words and positive terms how your farm is different from your competitors.

"Make some flyers describing your farm and produce to put on windshields and in store windows a day or so before the market opens. This will spread your name around and encourage customers to come to your booth. Develop weekly flyers to put in each bag of produce with recipes and news about your upcoming crops.

"Put the days and hours of your market on your business card and get in the habit of handing it out, 'Here take a card.'

"Make your product available to customers on off-market days as well. Provide customers with a phone number and address so they can contact you and arrange for pick-up at your farm or business."

  – *FM Forum,* FM Federation of New York, Summer 2000

Ask your market manager to put your farm description or a link to your website on the market website. Work with management to encourage the best possible presentation of the market. Offer specials that can be included in the market's weekly e-newsletter. If your best efforts at selling are being scuttled by poor market management, do a reassessment of your strategic plan and its implementation. Perhaps it's time to find a new market. Better yet, get on your market board and make the positive changes you want to see. ∾

Starting a Market

7

"The market serves as the 'front porch of Hollywood,' where people can relax and visit with neighbors."
    – Customer, Hollywood Certified Farmers' Market, CA

Experienced farmers' market organizers understand that their job is to design a set of events resulting in a certain degree of planned chaos. They are involved in the complex craft of coordinating an intricate web of people who are really the heart and soul of the market. The web includes farmers, consumers, board, volunteers, musicians, special event coordinators, community activists, nonprofits, sponsors, partners…the list can be never-ending.

The Farmers Market Federation of New York developed a list of ten principles underpinning successful markets that distill down to:

The side of a truck promotes local food heroes, promoted in part through Oregon SNAP funds to Gorge Grown Food Network.

* Time, location and season good for farmers, consumers and community.
* Central, visible, permanent location with good traffic, parking, amenities and growth potential.
* Wide diversity of products within competitive producer environment.
* Clear rules fairly enforced, with penalties.
* Strong, passionate manager paid fairly.
* Management which allows regular vendor input.
* Marketing plan for target audience includes advertising, promotions, entertainment and education.
* Adequate funding.

* Community involvement includes city, organizations and volunteers.
* Continuous self-evaluation.

The best markets have implemented these principles fully and regularly seek to make improvements in every aspect of their operations.

"The success of the Crescent City FM (New Orleans) owes much to excellent behind-the-sscenes organization without which other markets have failed. As manager Richard McCarthy noted, 'It's not as simple as finding a parking lot and notifying farmers.' In addition to securing a space, a successful market requires: staffing and security; parking; week-in, week-out continuity (rain or shine); garbage collection; safe food handling guidelines; knowledge of and compliance with local regulations; a name, logo, signage, phone number, and other elements that identify the market as a professional, stable retail operation; a governing board for resolving problems and complaints, accepting new vendors, and enforcing the market's own rules."
    – Economics Institute, Report to the Community

The Organizer

Let's define "you" here. You may be an individual. You may be a business organization – a chamber of commerce, a downtown redevelopment committee, a Main Street program. You may be a religious, social, educational or philanthropic organization – a church or ministerial association, a Lions or Optimist Club, a school or an American Association of University Women chapter, a neighborhood association or any group of people who believe the time for a farmers' market is ripe in your community.

Some of the best markets are organized by a single individual who is able to get others involved in creating a true community project. More people mean more challenges. As you compound the challenges you get larger results, if you stay focused on the goal. Thus, even an individual "you" usually results in a collective "you."

WHY START A FARMERS' MARKET?

Do you want a farmers' market to build community cohesion? Do downtown businesses need a promotional shot in the arm? Is the obesity epidemic making people consider local food over fast food? Is farmland disappearing and climate change affecting production regionally so that people are recognizing new value in local food? Are your inner city residents faced with little or no shopping choices? (For a free PDF of "The Public Health Effects of Food Deserts" and other articles, browse National Academies Press at www.nap.edu.)

Create an organizing committee that clearly establishes a primary goal of providing a viable marketplace for farmers and consumers. A secondary goal may be to improve downtown, but do not lose your reason for being a farmers' market organization. Make the market work on its own; if you let development issues run the market, they can run it out of business.

Be responsive to other organizational agendas in the community, always keeping your eyes on the prize as you make sure those agendas contribute to your primary goal, sustaining a farmers' market.

A Hmong crafts vendor adds to market culture and customer selection. Farmers' markets are a key entry point into the economy for small and new farmers and immigrants. Determine what vendors are desired and available before setting vendor limitations and product mix.

Certain markets have been organized specifically to provide access to fresh produce for low-income residents in urban areas abandoned by supermarkets. This may push you to address a different set of issues. An ethnically distinct neighborhood will allow you to bring in minority farmers to meet specific consumers' needs.

In some markets this has resulted in taking on the predominant characteristics of the people's home country, as in an eastside Vietnamese neighborhood of New Orleans. In an Oakland market it resulted in an incredibly rich mix of ethnicities reflecting Oakland's status as the most integrated city in America.

Many markets are developed with the goal of providing a community meeting place to celebrate the diversity of local produce, educate people about better nutrition and increase awareness of the difficulties facing farmers in the global marketplace. Communities want to make a difference. A local market is the best way to take action, redirecting weekly shopping dollars to the local economy.

Some communities want to generate more pedestrian traffic or promote evening events in the downtown or at a park. While this may lead to a focus on entertainment over produce, it may be the best way to build numbers to sustain the market.

Your goal may be multi-faceted because the organizing committee represents various community

Market Watch: Exotic melons a sweet success in high desert

An Armenian farmer begins to bring his Uzbek and Persian fruits to area farmers markets.

Reporting from Onyx – Thirteen years ago, when Ruben Mkrtchyan told his wife and four children that they were going to move from Glendale to a high desert valley in the middle of nowhere to grow the world's tastiest melons, they thought he had lost his mind.

"My mom and I looked at each other and said, 'What is he talking about?'" recalls his daughter Tatevik. "When we went up there, the land was completely empty, just Joshua trees and scrub."

But Mkrtchyan had a vision of fields and orchards blooming in the wilderness, one that he has realized to a remarkable extent. He now grows 15 acres of legendary melon varieties from Uzbekistan and Iran, and he has just started showing up at farmers markets in Los Angeles.

Mkrtchyan, born on a collective farm in the Ararat Valley, the fruit bowl of Armenia, earned the equivalent of a master's in mathematics just before the Soviet Union fell apart. In 1989, he immigrated to California, and since he didn't speak any English, he took a job in construction to support his young family. Eighteen months later, he went into business for himself as a general contractor, and in time he prospered.

Mkrtchyan started taking his family camping and particularly loved Lake Isabella, at the southern end of the Sierra Nevada. He looked to buy a ranch in the area, and when a real estate agent showed him a property in a remote valley seven miles east of the tiny community of Onyx, halfway between Lake Isabella and Ridgecrest, he was smitten by the stark beauty of the arid land, rimmed by mountains.

"I thought, this is unbelievable, because more than the mountains I love only God," he said last Sunday, in the house that he built on the property, which is now covered with melon fields and fruit trees.

The site is at the bottom of the valley, so it has a good well and is so isolated from other farms that there is little pressure from pests and diseases. That's a crucial consideration for growing Central Asian melons, which are intensely sweet and flavorful but much more susceptible than standard American varieties to fungal diseases such as powdery mildew.

Uzbekistan is to melons as France is to wine, a center of excellence and diversity. The most extraordinary of Mkrtchyan's melons is the variety that he calls Mirza, a Farsi and Russian name meaning "prince" or "high nobleman." The fruits are huge and elongated – 18 inches to 2 feet long, weighing 10 to 25 pounds – with beige netting and golden stripes over a cream background. The flesh is creamy white, slightly granular, much softer than that of conven-

interests. A market may state their goals as: to provide a marketing alternative for farmers, a vehicle for downtown revitalization, support for local business-people and a friendly, community-oriented market-place. Form a cohesive image of what you want to create and then outline the various elements that support that vision.

Feasibility

Whatever your key reason(s), first analyze whether your goal is desired and achievable. You may survey residents to determine their enthusiasm, or meet with the business community to ask for their support. Ask local chefs and caterers whether, what items and how much they might buy.

Assess the local retail competition and determine whether a sufficient number of farmers will partici-

tional melons, and intensely sweet and flavorful.

"It's like drinking from the river of the garden of paradise," said Amanda Broder-Hahn, pastry chef at Food restaurant, after tasting a sample.

Obinovot (the name means "father of sugar," says Mkrtchyan) tastes similar, if slightly less rich, but may be the world's most spectacularly beautiful melon, its rind an abstract artwork of canary yellow, orange, green and brown, accented by cracks and scratches that give it the allure of antique Chinese ceramics. Mkrtchyan also grows Sharlyn (one of the few Central Asian types that has been available here), which has tender, orange flesh, and Mashhad, a large, elongated Persian variety.

Ruben and Sonya Mkrtchyan sell Uzbek melons grown in Onyx. (David Karp)

Mkrtchyan's melons ripen from the end of July to the first frost, typically in late October or early November. He and his wife, Sonya, started to sell two weeks ago at the new Hollywood & Highland farmers market, which runs 8 a.m. to 2 p.m. Saturdays, off Orange Drive. This weekend they will start at the Calabasas and Brentwood farmers markets, and they have also been selling some of their melons to the Jons Marketplace chain.

Mkrtchyan has used his property as his own experiment station to try cultivating many crops, not all of which have succeeded. Walking through the orchards, he pointed to a pile of chainsawed, blackened cherry trees and to a grove of pears, susceptible to fire blight, that would be taken out next. Like many high desert growers (he's at an elevation of 3,200 feet), he lost most of his stone fruit this year to a late freeze. But his apricot trees — some of them grown from seeds from Armenia, the supposed homeland of the species, Prunus armeniaca — are flourishing, along with his mulberries. And he's excited about his Armenian quince, which he says bears fruit that is sweet and edible fresh like an apple. He also produces pristine, delicious honey from his beehives.

Two years ago, Tatevik, who initially looked askance at her father's proposed move to Onyx, gave up the stress of working as a real estate agent to form a partnership with a beekeeper in Camarillo. She named the venture Isabell's Honey Farm after her daughter and sells orange blossom, buckwheat and sage honeys at seven farmers markets.

September 23, 2011|By David Karp | Special to the Los Angeles Times ɞ

pate. If farmers cannot compete on price with imported produce, is a more quality-focused market feasible?

Study your community demographics, up to a 10-mile radius (or more). A survey in the newspaper – it never hurts to ask for free help – can lead to new observations about your likely customers, among newspaper readers. Compare those characteristics with the general populace from statistics available at

city hall or through the U.S. Census. Plan how you will reach every different segment of the population. Consider whether you need to modify the message according to the population segment.

Ask many feasibility questions as you develop a vision. Through a series of public meetings, allow plenty of time for the answers to evolve. A formal feasibility analysis may be valuable, but most markets put limited financial resources into actual develop-

What's In A Name?

Four states have a Springfield Farmers' Market – Illinois, Massachusetts, Minnesota and Vermont. Three communities have an Original Farmers' Market, two of them in Pennsylvania.

Aside from the event, place is usually the most common descriptor in a name, like the Villa Parke Farmers' Market in Pasadena, CA. Some name the host, like the Duck Soup Co-op Farmers' Market in DeKalb, IL. Some reinforce place and day, like the Hillsboro Tuesday Marketplace. Some include place, host and day, like the Park Slope's Sunday Down to Earth Farmers' Market in Brooklyn, NY.

People usually shorten a name over four words, with the exception of Heart of the City Farmers' Market in San Francisco. With a big heart logo in all its advertisements, the name is descriptive and memorable. It rolls off the tongue.

What, where and when is helpful, as with the Astoria Sunday Market in Oregon. Because this market replaced a "farmers' market" without any farmers, we needed to distance ourselves and create credibility. The Napa Chef's Market on a Friday evening needed to separate itself from the established Napa Farmers' Market on Tuesday.

However, the public awareness and acceptance of "farmers' market" makes it a pretty good term for getting some customer momentum. People remember it easily. There are billions of dollars in customer spending behind that name across the country.

Do a brainstorming session to list all the possible words that relate in some way to your planned market: community, downtown, park, square, plaza, fairgrounds, courthouse, open air, village, harvest, night, county name, Thursday, green, old town... If it doesn't fit in your name, it may be helpful to include in advertising or press releases.

Think of the best known farmers' markets: Hilo, University District, Ballard, Portland, Ferry Plaza, Marin, Santa Monica, Santa Fe, Boulder, Dane County, St. Paul, Topeka, Des Moines, Lancaster, Carrboro, Waitsfield, Union Square or... Maybe it's good media coverage. Still, keep your name simple. ✌

ment. Nevertheless, do not avoid the challenging issues of who should benefit from the market, how that is possible and what roadblocks stand in the way.

Scope of the Market

Along with your general goals, you want to define all your potential sellers. Is your market for producers only? Will you allow prepared foods, crafts and other non-agricultural items? Will you limit it to independent entrepreneurs? (Your state association may disallow franchisees.) These questions should spark a unique set of answers for you.

In California the scope was established by regulations of the California Department of Food and Agriculture in 1977, followed by legislation in 2000. "Certified producers" can sell exempt from standard pack in a "certified farmers' market." Both producers and markets are issued certificates by county agricultural commissioners. Naturally, other types of producers (and non-producers) have wanted to get in on the act. This leads to market growth and the need for market rules and enforcement.

Certain markets have more narrow guidelines, such as allowing only organic produce or producers only from within a given distance or specific counties. Other markets have more open standards, allowing "high-stallers" or peddlers, or defining an impact area of two or more states. Not only are state lines rather arbitrary, but they may constrict your desired mix of products. The onus is on the markets to create and implement a procedure to guarantee to their customers that your farmers are actually farming.

With support from USDA, Gorge Grown Food Network has a van which carries local products to supplement other farms at several of its Columbia River markets.

[See Managing the Market chapter for a more in-depth discussion of these as well as other issues your rules and bylaws might address.]

ATTRACTING FARMERS

Once you have your standard, set out on a path which has many branches. Don't depend on just one avenue for contacting farmers and other producers. Be ready for new outreach ideas to develop as you follow several of these steps:

- Visit established nearby farmers' markets, especially those on different days of the week.
- Drive country roads and make impromptu visits with farmers you find.
- Ask farmers for names of others with specific products you lack.
- Set up a booth at farm and direct marketing conferences in your state.
- Send press releases with specific story ideas to encourage newspaper stories.
- Write stories for rural and produce publications including details about an informational meeting.
- Host meetings around your state with a power point on effective display, and packets outlining your plans.

- Ask crafts organizations (potters, weavers, general) for their mailing list or a newsletter article.
- Look for a local farm trail map.
- Check the web for farm listings in your area and beyond. Check websites like Local Harvest and Naturally Grown.

Direct Mail

Another method is a direct mailing to a large base of potential farmers and gardeners announcing the market opening and a meeting to outline your plans. Include the time, place, speakers, topics to be covered, and an address and phone number for growers who cannot attend. Your local Cooperative Extension Service and Farm Bureau offices will likely help with the mailing and a meeting site. Check the mail piece carefully for impact and follow up with a personal call or visit.

Use resources where farmers are listed such as agricultural commodity groups, Farm Bureau, Extension Service, state grower associations and your state department of agriculture. For instance, the Indiana Farmers' Market, U-Pick and Agritourism Directory lists farms and markets by county, complete with address, phone, crops, e-mail and website. Search for the list of participants at farm conferences.

For the first mailing throw as wide a net as possible. Farmers will drive a distance, especially if they can combine loads for two markets. Growers will help spread word to others.

Hold a Meeting

In 1986, responding to a mailing, 140 producers attended a market informational meeting in Oklahoma City. They came from as far as 240 miles one way. Depending on contacts and the wholesale climate, a farmer may be desperate to match his/her dream with yours.

A market starting in New York invited potential vendors to a dinner, introduced them to local businesses and showed them downtown. Any gathering will answer questions and build confidence as growers see others who are committed.

At your organizational meeting quantify the interested growers, production volume and season by product. Clarify your reasoning behind the market location and organizational structure. Be ready to answer a challenging mix of questions candidly, especially about policies and costs. You may want to sign farmers up immediately and collect their membership fee.

Provide farmers with all your plans and solicit theirs. To match supply and demand, you want to know the volume of every item coming to market. This also will enable you to write more compelling press releases and ad copy. It may spark ideas for special events like a tomato or watermelon tasting.

Can the farmers help find other farmers with additional variety to ensure a good product mix from early until late in the season? Have you covered your bases with specialty products including breads, pastries, chocolates, processed nuts, pickled vegetables, pies, jams, mustards and vinegars? Have you talked to the best bakers and most well-known organic farmers delivering to local restaurants?

Challenge yourself with a checklist of the foods that you eat, and do the same with friends. To avoid heavy duplication, tell growers how much head-to-head competition they will have. Give farmers a sense of how many customers you expect, based on your promotional campaign. If you supply information so farmers can make good decisions, they will more likely help your market to succeed.

Market Size

When recruiting growers, consider the customer perspective. The rule of thumb is that one grower of a certain product is a monopoly, two amounts to collusion and three is competition. Customers expect variety and choices. Without a good selection of vendors and a certain amount of duplication, customers won't be fully satisfied. What distinguishes farmers' markets from supermarkets is the choice among vendors with the same product.

You certainly need to consider the farmer perspective as well. They need to make money to continue. The challenge is to be sensitive to both groups, farmers and consumers, without letting either side demand too much. Some farmers want monopolies but customer numbers will suffer generally if you listen. At least two vendors selling the same item in numerous produce categories is a good idea to start.

Flower growers are an important part of most markets, often giving immigrants a start in their new country, a centuries-old tradition.

© Vance Corum

"Findings consistently show successful urban markets have a strong integrated farmer component. Farmers benefit from clustering – the critical mass of producers with complementary products. A market with fewer than 12 growers will struggle – the more growers the more successful the market."

– *American Vegetable Grower*, "Community is Key to Market Success," 1995

Small communities may find 8-10 growers sufficient to meet expectations, but even a small market in a rural community may leave many potential customers less than enamored with the selection. Organizers need to take steps before opening to ensure that the best mix is possible; the average consumer is not as patient as a farmer in waiting for the market to grow.

Meeting customer desires and making the site seem full, you can sustain a market even at a small site without as much internal competition as you would hope.

The Santa Monica market now has nearly 100 vendors every Wednesday. When it began in 1981 with only 23 farmers on opening day, it was the largest Los Angeles market opening to date. Customer response was strong, due to an excellent publicity plan. Thus, the number of growers participating grew rapidly.

Customer expectations have changed dramatically. By 2000 most Americans knew what a farmers' market is. Much stronger openings were common.

Farmers realized that they have to risk crops just as market organizers risk time and money. When Yakima, WA, opened in 1999, there were 53 vendors and more than 4,000 customers. The right balance was achieved for a good start, and more vendors came quickly.

In metro areas where people may have become accustomed to markets with 80+ vendors, people's expectations are high. An opening with fewer than 30 may be difficult to sustain. Keeping as many as 30 may be difficult if your population base is small or you can't promise strong numbers on opening day.

Solicit new farmers who want to join your early success. Acknowledge that the market isn't for every-

Marin County: A Start-up Success Story

The Marin County Farmers' Market opened with 30 growers in July, 1983. Within two months more than 60 farmers were selling their produce there. According to the market's founder Lynn Bagley, the reason behind the market's start-up success was the work that went into the market prior to opening day.

"In our research into other markets, Bagley says, "I had heard of one market that managed to attract a lot of customers for opening day, but no farmers showed up. So I determined to get a strong commitment and then keep regular contact with the producers. We held pre-opening meetings, built a solid mailing list and kept everyone in touch."

"Everything goes into opening day. You've got to make it big and important so as to have patrons to support the farmers and vice versa. If you have two or three farmers there, how many people will keep coming? If you start out successful, it builds."

Bagley also did everything possible to let the public know about the event, such as holding a series of public meetings and organizing volunteers to call every other household in the zip code area. Volunteers put signs on major highways and two TV stations did features on the event. Front-page stories and features ran in the local papers as well as continuing stories throughout the season. This set the tone for the market's importance and on opening day most of the 30 farmers sold out within two hours.

"There's no town in the world that doesn't want a market," Bagley claims, "and people will come if you do your publicity."

The key to fund-raising, Bagley feels, is to hold special events and turn them into fund-raisers at the same time. Through media attention, a special event draws more people to the market.

Some growers would like to eliminate competition by limiting the number of sellers. "I feel there is definitely a limit," says Bagley, "but the more farmers you have, the more significant the event becomes, and therefore more people come. Diversity is imperative – the more variety, the more patrons you can attract."

Make sure that the people selling are the real growers. Once you allow non-producers to sell, the quality drops, and it hurts the reputation of the whole market. People want to buy direct from the farmer. ଧ

body, but even when there is an apparent failure for a farmer, keep the door open for the future. Many farmers will try a market at a later date when it is more established; with a solid customer base, they succeed on the second attempt.

The "See-Saw"

Start as strong as possible. For every hour spent recruiting farmers and every dollar spent attracting customers, you will save at least double that later on. The most crucial element of development is strong recruitment of farmers. However, the concept of "build the market and they will come" should not be taken as an excuse to ride the coattails – or tailgates – of the farmers. An equally strong outreach should be planned to draw consumers because without them, farmers will drop away or bring less product in succeeding weeks. Thus, organizers need to have a keen sense that they are balancing the see-saw of supply and demand on the opening day of the market.

Will you be a market of 10 farmers and 200 customers (20:1 ratio), or 70 farmers and 7,000 customers (100:1)? The former is much more common; the latter requires daring, and planning.

It usually takes about four weeks for the market to balance, that is, for the see-saw to find its right size. Your goal should be to build the biggest see-saw possible. Some farmers may fall away because of stiff competition, or poor quality, sampling or staffing, among other reasons. Some customers will not return because of a lack of convenience, atmosphere, product mix, parking, price, quality or other reasons. However, if you have done a good job building the see-saw, most of our customers and farmers are going to build relationships, have a good time, want to return and help spread the word.

Captivate the Consumer

In the spirit of guerilla marketing, be aware that there is really no limit to the creative ideas that help announce your new market to the public. With everything you do there should be a consciousness about publicity. Every speaking engagement and every chance encounter at a restaurant, church, social club

In order to have the product that customers want, leaders study the demographics of the area. In 2008 minorities were one-third of the U.S. population. By 2042 they are expected to be the majority.

or school event provides an opportunity to publicize the market and get others joined in that fun process. Simultaneously, it gives you a chance to ask if anyone knows potential vendors.

In Hayward, California, Lynn Bagley organized a mini-tasting to which the public was invited via a newspaper article. Farmers came with their products to a community building downtown and gave people a taste of what was to come. Those attending became part of the publicity octopus.

Experienced market organizers know that a good market doesn't just happen. Vendors ultimately judge a market and their participation in it by the profits they take home. You can hope that they will appreciate the friendly atmosphere in your town, but if the customer count is low and profits insufficient, a farmer will go to a more profitable market. One by one, vendors will leave and customers with them.

For a market to succeed, the organizer must supply enough enticements for both vendor and customer to view this farmers' market as the preferred alternative. This situation is particularly difficult for new markets because customers have built their expectations around produce departments in larger supermarkets, box stores, specialty stores or even at other successful farmers' markets. A new market must offer comparable customer satisfaction around quality and price, or replace it with a combination of friendly atmosphere, knowledgeable farmers and unique events.

The balancing act never ends. It may seem that everything is going along just fine, but if you lose 15% of your farmers, you may notice a drop-off in customers. Inevitably, some customers will have lost their favorite flower grower, organic tomatoes or specialty cheese. Never be so comfortable as to think that you have the see-saw perfectly balanced. That's when you'll fall off and the community will suffer.

LOCATION

A highly visible location with a landmark identity will make it more likely for your market to succeed. A hidden, poorly known location is more difficult for customers to find and more expensive to promote. Choose a central, landmark location in the community with easy access for customers, plenty of parking, visibility from main roads including freeways if possible, shade trees, seating, public restrooms, flat and smooth surface, water and electricity. Almost any site can work as long as you do your homework. For a Site Evaluation Tool, see:

www.farmersmarketsamerica.org.

The most critical factor that has limited markets' growth is a lack of parking. It can be overcome if the market has everything that people want, but inadequate parking will certainly dissuade many would-be shoppers, especially during inclement weather.

Look at population figures for a one-mile, three-mile and ten-mile radius from the site. Ask your local newspaper for their circulation numbers by zip code. Know where most of your customers will come from. Being on a heavily traveled road outside the main core of town may be better than a side street in the downtown.

Ensure that your vendors have enough space to operate. A site with under 5,000 square feet may be suitable for a small market where farmers with trucks use 270 s.f. each (10'x27') with an 8' wide pedestrian aisle. Medium to large markets will usually take up

An architectural rendering helped in planning the visual impact and inspired vendor confidence in the Chef's Market situated in a winding, outdoor mall in downtown Napa, CA.

10,000 s.f. to more than an acre, with 15-25' aisles, even without trucks allowed on site.

Consider whether you can fill the space from an aesthetic perspective and still have room to expand without needing to move to a new location. Moves frequently hurt a market's credibility, especially if you end up at a less visible and trafficked spot. Loyal customers – those 30% of customers who come every week – will follow your move, but irregular shoppers may lack the dedication to seek you out if they aren't well informed of your move.

Private Property

Countless businesses have recognized the benefits of hosting farmers' markets. Banks open their parking lots in St. Cloud, MN, Oconomowoc, WI, Tilton, NH and West Seattle. Markets borrow the parking lots of doctors in Kennett, MO; an insurance company in Tacoma, WA; a bowling alley in Rushford, MN; a locally owned supermarket in Morro Bay, CA; the Ace Hardware in Columbia, IL; the Agway in Ballston Spa, NY; a tea house in Salisbury, CT; and Yamashiro Restaurant overlooking Los Angeles.

Train stations are known for underutilized parking, perfect for markets from Saranac Lake, NY, to Newark, NJ, and on to Ypsilanti, MI, and Santa Fe. While at times they are outside the immediate town core, the consequent advantage may be superior parking. The station building itself may lend old-world charm and landmark status to the market. The depot plaza hosts the market in Cheyenne, WY.

Communities of faith were among the first to open their arms and parking lots – Baptists in Shaker Heights, OH; Episcopalians in Broomfield, CO; Methodists in Sparks, NV; Presbyterians in Charleston, SC; and churches all over Tennessee (thanks to the late John Vlcek). The Louisville market is at The Temple.

Shopping centers from Connellsville, PA, to Minneapolis, MN, have welcomed the extra traffic. They are not likely to charge the market when it guarantees their mall merchants a regular supply of customers. Many a mall has paid thousands of dollars to attract a market. In Sacramento, CA, they compete with each other to have market manager and attorney Dan Best place a farmers' market on their property. They know the day of operation will be decided according to farmer availability.

Some open-air malls have welcomed farmers – with trucks or without – into their inner courtyards in Corte Madera and El Cerrito, CA, and into their multi-story parking lot in Oklahoma City's Penn Square.

Farmers also realize that opening their property to other farmers can help build their own market brand while building new supply channels for their farmstand. Although most have only a handful of active farmers, Parker's Historic Clapdaddle Farm hosts 15 vendors in Ilion, NY; Nisqually Springs Farm hosts 16 in Yelm, WA, Archwood Green Barns has 30 in The Plains, VA; Crystal Spring Farm has 40 in Brunswick, ME.

Land trusts are a natural match in saving farms, e.g., Hunterdon Land Trust in Flemington, NJ. The Mount Hope Trust in Bristol, CT hosts a market in their south pasture, and on rainy days and in winter it moves into their large converted barn.

Collectively, farmers have organized much larger projects. Following the inspiration of Green Dragon Market (PA), farmers purchased 26 acres and built two buildings in 1987 to develop a rural destination, The Windmill Farm and Craft Market in Penn Yan, NY. With phenomenal initial success, they built another building and an open shed the next year, with later additions of buildings, concrete floors, restrooms and sidewalks.

Similarly in Alberta, vendors invested $1 million to restore an airplane hangar as the Calgary Farmers' Market in 2004. Within several years they lost the property, but their scale was enough to take their customers to a new site where they operate 9-5 on Thursday to Sunday year-round.

Public Space

Public properties are appropriate for public markets. Many organizers prefer the philosophical and practical alignment with public sites rather than malls. If our markets are each a collection of small farming businesses, it seems more appropriate to connect with and support other small, independent businesses rather than further the concentration of wealth in the few national and international corporations that dominate malls.

Everyone in Charleston, SC knows historic Marion Square where 125 vendors gather on Saturdays from 8 to

The website homepage of Vallco Shopping Mall promotes the Friday farmers' market held on a distant parking lot that almost feels like a forest in the heart of Silicon Valley.

© Vance Corum

THE NEW FARMERS' MARKET

Mad River Green in Waitsfield, VT fills with 16 farms, 21 prepared foods and 28 crafts from mid-May to mid-October, encouraging lively and leisurely intercourse among locals and tourists.

2. It's the municipal lot in Kent, WA and the state park in Warwick, RI. Library parking lots host markets in Beaverton, OR and Worland, WY as well as McAllen, TX at the largest single-floor library in America, site of a defunct Walmart. The Center for the Arts is just right in Bloomington, MN.

Markets operate at a park & ride lot in Cincinnati and at several Pennsylvania Turnpike service plazas including Allentown and Valley Forge. Markets are located at an elementary school in Holyoke, MA, a middle school in Menomonee Falls, WI, a high school in Providence, RI, and one has graduated to Oklahoma State University in Oklahoma City.

County properties are useful – administration parking and restrooms in Anniston, AL, health department in Hickory, NC, and fairgrounds in Alamagordo, NM and Longview, WA.

Federal properties are also available, as with the Palo Alto Post Office, or a street adjacent to a federal courthouse in Yakima, WA. While USDA was promoting farmers' markets in the 1990s, it organized markets on property at twelve different federal agencies, and published "How to Establish a Farmers' Market on Federal Property" (search that title on the web).

There is really no limit to where a market can be located. In Bourg-en-Bresse, France, it sets up in a large open plaza in the center of the city and winds its way into an abandoned gym where one

wall was blasted out years ago. In Edmonton, Alberta, the outdoor market moved indoor one rainy day because the manager had the keys to the bus barn. Years later the city wrote a lease so that the Old Strathcona Farmers' Market assumed responsibility for building maintenance. Having an indoor home allows the market to run year-round and allows many more independent farmers and craftspeople to depend on the market for their livelihood.

Downtown

For many communities, downtown is the obvious choice. It is the center of all civic and business activities and the farmers' market is both civic and business. With business leaving so many downtowns, farmers' markets offer some hope of resuscitating the economic engine. The National Main Street Program has seen the impact and urged many downtown leaders to consider how to put farmers' markets at the core of community and business life, much as they have been historically.

Ruth Yanatta Goldway was such a leader as the new mayor of Santa Monica, CA, in 1981. She put her vision and commitment behind a farmers' market, blocking off a key street with 60,000 vehicles per day. Over the objection of some businesses like the copy shop that depended on easy parking, the city persisted in favor of numerous businesses that weren't getting

Many independent stores benefit from the pedestrian street traffic generated by the Ballard Farmers Market, Seattle's largest market.

desirable pedestrian traffic counts. Six years earlier a state attempt to start the market had failed miserably, but with new timing and an inspired leader one of California's largest markets was created. The market sparked a downtown renaissance and major economic development plan leading to many new businesses servicing the area.

> "The market should be in a neighborhood business district which promotes the area as a cohesive whole. Area businesses and retail establishments surrounding the market play an important role in defining the market. This 'spirit of place' is an important part of successful markets."
>
> – *American Vegetable Grower,* "Community is Key to Market Success," 1995

Many a Chamber of Commerce has started or supported a downtown market. Feeling the resultant parking pressure, merchants may nudge their market to leave – as happened in Petaluma, CA – only to see downtown suffer while the market expands. The Chamber would have been wise to survey market customers about their downtown motivation and spending patterns before kicking the golden goose. "Hell hath no fury like a woman scorned" … or a farmers' market.

Any site is possible, so look for the characteristics you most desire and prepare to meet the property owner, which may be the City. Sell them on the market's community benefits before you address the specific location request.

In the Park

City parks are a great option for markets from New York City, to Chicago, Las Vegas and even little Sandpoint, ID. While they are often gems such as along the Deschutes River in Bend, OR, they may be hidden gems, tucked away from the eyes of visitors and even locals shopping Main Street, all of whom can benefit from a visual reminder.

Parks have many advantages, especially aesthetics. Shade trees and grass increase produce longevity. People love a quiet park or even one with a youth area

Four multi-story parking garages with 1200 spaces surround this Arizona Avenue location in Santa Monica, CA. Initially selling to people on the sidewalks, the market later reconfigured so farmers face each other with a central customer-friendly aisle.

or exercise stations. These add to family-oriented and people-watching opportunities. Parks are known in many communities as a safe haven, a place to be refreshed, so a farmers' market fits well with this identity.

Some advantages can also be disadvantages. Lush grass can become a mudhole in bad weather. If you can move the market a few feet each week, the damaging impact of shuffling customers' feet may be minimized. Farmers need to watch out for sprinkler heads when driving trucks across the grass.

Being next to the park may be sufficient. Having the nearby amenities of restrooms, a water feature, playground and grass to picnic on may be all you need. Keeping the farmers' trucks on the perimeter may be the perfect solution if the ground isn't solidly compacted. This is the answer in Vancouver, WA, where the market runs for two blocks along Esther Short Park, the oldest city park in the state. This new location as of 2000 followed the redevelopment of the park with a new playground and a covered performance stage that brings major events in market proximity.

Pasadena's first market in 1980 was sited on a park known mainly to its nearby residents. With great publicity it succeeded in setting a safe, friendly tone for the neighborhood, at least on Tuesdays. However,

THE NEW FARMERS' MARKET

Jack London Square was built to draw people back to Oakland's waterfront on San Francisco Bay. It asked Pacific Coast Farmers Market Association to operate a farmers' market as part of their massive publicity effort. It survives even with several other strong markets in the city.

while it has a reliable customer base, it is overshadowed by newer farmers' markets on more heavily traveled corridors, proving that high visibility and better parking can save many publicity dollars.

On the Water

Being associated with a large body of water has brought success to many public food markets such as Pike Place Market in Seattle and Granville Island Market in Vancouver, British Columbia. Water is no less important to the setting of farmers' markets from Ferry Plaza on San Francisco Bay to Ithaca on Cayuga Lake or Ft. Pierce or West Palm Beach along the Intracoastal Waterway.

Even a river helps make a destination market, as in Wilmington (DE) along the Cape Fear River, or Eau Claire (WI) near the confluence of the Eau Claire and Chippewa rivers. However, the market site should have more than simply water. For seven years the Portland FM (OR) struggled with 35 farmers and 1,000 customers on a parking lot between the Willamette River and the train tracks, hidden from any other activity center. Finally moving just a mile into downtown onto PSU and City property, it blossomed into one of the nation's best markets.

Without a convenient river, your next best option may be a local water feature. After a successful pilot in October, 2010, Houston City Hall hosts a market around its reflection pool. Portland (ME) operates along the natural, curving waters of Deering Oaks Park.

Ultimately, every location should make a community proud. At the least, location is a reflection even when it's the Walmart lot in Green Bay, WI. When your market is at Market Square in Sturgeon Bay, WI, your landmark imparts a sense of history and hopefully a more auspicious future.

Access

Thinking of our potential customer, what will attract him or her? We need to find a site which "feels" safe, convenient and accessible. Well-known landmark locations generally fit the bill, but they may not be available. Whatever our ultimate choice, we need to describe the location so people can easily find it and park.

No matter how many people are coming to our market, we may feel we have done a great job. A smarter reaction is to ask: "Why aren't others coming?" A phone survey of non-customers may reveal frustration over access. What might make the market easier to find? Put a sign at a freeway ramp or a key turn, give a reference landmark such as a well-known restaurant, or add a key directional phrase to your promotional campaign. Think of visitors and what they don't know.

The concept of service should be built into your market from the beginning. Parking attendants directing traffic off a highway give an extra sense of safety and good organization, so people have confidence in the rest of your operation.

The Portland Farmers Market runs six satellite markets including Pioneer Courthouse Square on Mondays. This iconic, colonnaded, brick event center with water feature serves as the living room in downtown's core.

Wheelchair customers prefer hard-surfaced markets because maneuvering on grass is difficult. Curb cuts or ramps facilitate wheelchair accessibility. For many lower-income customers, proximity to a bus stop is essential. Special busing from senior housing centers may be necessary to serve that clientele. The senior center may pay for their own shuttle or you might share the expense.

Parking

When researching a location, parking may be overlooked. Of all location elements, parking is probably the key limiting factor in market growth.

If you struggle to hold onto 500 customers for 20 farmers, compare yourself to a supermarket. You have 20 checkout counters to their 10. All your checkers want to be busy. You probably need twice the parking space of the supermarket. They are open much longer hours for business; you want to squeeze customers into a tight timeframe to make farmers' marketing time valuable. If you aren't seeing the pedestrian counts you want and need, analyze your parking.

If most customers compare you to a supermarket, you had better have parking every bit as convenient. If your market stands out head and shoulders from the competition – quality, competition, value, product diversity, exotic items, freshness, farmer friendliness – you may be able to get away with a less-than-stellar parking situation.

When you have parking challenges, find out how customers and ex-customers feel and experiment with solutions. Try a pick-up zone staffed by Scouts who hand over the ticketed bag of produce to a customer who drives up from a distant parking spot. Or pay the first 20 minutes of parking at a nearby lot where you have worked out a compromise price. Many cities have waived the meter fees on streets or in garages during market hours.

"Market complaints are highest among small-town markets. The most common complaint, by far, is insufficient parking. The fact that small-town markets are younger and less well established in a particular location may explain why

After members of the Ithaca Farmers Market built their clerestory, wooden floor building, they built bermed parking for 350 cars, and living passageways to warmly welcome their customers.

THE NEW FARMERS' MARKET

parking problems have not been resolved. Some solutions mentioned by managers included scheduling the market on off days, shuttle services and providing drive-up tables for customers to pick up their purchases."

– Farmers' Markets and Rural Development Project

According to former Bellingham Farmers' Market manager Karen Durham, parking is the first word for downtown merchants. Their study showed people who come by car want to walk less than a block and a third, so they organized a deal with a local transit service to run a shuttle every 20 or 30 minutes from downtown. In California, Santa Barbara's attempt to improve market access with a shuttle from downtown parking structures proved futile – both expensive and used by only a handful of customers. The Davis market has struggled with parking, trying shuttles from various points in town and the UCD campus without success.

> "We purchased tokens from the community-owned parking lots nearby good for one hour of parking and distributed several hundred for free last year. This costs the market between $400-800 per season."
> – Chris Curtis, University District FM, Seattle, WA

Think through the parking demands of your market. Consider average customer stay, sales per customer, market hours and farmer income needs in estimating necessary parking. If you plan to operate four hours, you will probably turn over each parking spot five to six times. If you want 2000 customers spending $20 each to provide 50 farmers an average of $800 daily sales, you will need about 350 parking spaces. Every market will vary. If you have limited selection, customer turnover may average 20 minutes or less. If you provide more selection and activities, such as entertainment or hot food concessions, that figure may approach an hour and will create extra strain on your parking. While that may be desirable in creating a community meeting place, you need to have a site with substantially more parking.

Safety

People in a buying mode should not have to watch out for bikes, skateboarders or an impromptu dogfight! While it's nice to have dogs around, if someone is bitten or steps in an unauthorized deposit, you won't gain points in the customer service department.

The health department also will respect you a little more if you separate animals and food by at least 20 feet. (In California, it's health law.) That goes for what's being sold as well. It's also a good idea to require farmers to keep food at least 6" off the ground.

Avoid customers mixing with vendors as they unload and prepare for market. Insurance companies reward with lower rates your safety precautions such as keeping customers safely away from moving vehicles and canopies during set-up and break-down, when weights are not attached.

Ringing a bell to open and close the market reinforces posted market hours, and lowers the risk of customer injury.

Restrooms and Other Amenities

The need for restrooms is not absolute, just practical. Markets with short hours may find them unnecessary. On the whole, however, restrooms are essential and have a determining impact on selection of the market location.

Markets like Lake Oswego, OR and Mar Vista, CA have dog-sitting services so that customers with dogs don't feel uninvited. Here at Inner Sunset FM, CA, they call it Valet Barking.

If a port-a-potty is the only solution, local companies frequently make a donation for the first season if you explain your financial need for community support to get your project off the ground. If you have to pay rent, you may want to look into full purchase of a unit as long as you estimate the cost of periodic cleaning and have a plan for transportation and storage. Hand-washing units also are a wise investment given the handling of fresh produce.

Local retailers have gained sales for themselves by demonstrating an open-door restroom policy for market vendors and patrons. Many public sites have restrooms along with other amenities including electricity, water and public seating.

TIMING

Beginning a new market is like starting any other business – first impressions are critical. Hopefully, the media will spread a positive image of the opening. Certainly, your first customers will have a great influence on whether other residents come out to successive market days. So, prepare for your opening as if your business depends on it. You will get grassroots reviews comparable to a Broadway show opening. Indeed, market is theater, so make sure you have every aspect of the show wired. Do a talk-through dress rehearsal with your committee. Write a letter to your farmers to make sure they recognize the importance of getting off to a strong start. Then get ready for a bit of improvisation.

Seasonal or Year-round?

To set the stage, discuss when you will make the most memorable impression that will lead to a strong word-of-mouth campaign within the local populace. Will it be in April with bedding plants and nursery stock or in July once your growers have a full variety of produce at good prices? At least for the first season, consider the later date. Your market will bring many more dollars to your growers in the long run if you start on the right foot. That long-term perspective honors all the selfless efforts of

your committee and the commitment of your producers.

Similarly, you want to close the market season on a high note. Don't wait for four weeks of rain to dampen the enthusiasm of 70% of your customers. Hold a harvest festival and leave people with a sense of anticipation of the second season to come – a bit earlier next year.

If you intend to close at the end of October (April if you are on a reverse schedule in a southern climate like South Florida), you can extend the season if you have sufficient commitment from farmers and customers. Market season is largely dependent upon growing season but considerably improved by hothouse vegetables, value-added products, crafts, prepared foods and other items you may include. Determine in advance what numbers you will need to avoid embarrassment as you publicly announce a season extension.

When we opened the Gardena Farmers' Market in 1979, we said it was seasonal. It was the first market in Los Angeles County, opening with five farmers and growing into the teens during the summer. As farmers met regularly at the end of market day in September, six of them committed to continuing through an

A simple water stand is a thoughtful gesture for customers at the Portland Farmers Market, OR.

THE NEW FARMERS' MARKET

uncertain winter. With an extra outreach push for Groundhog Day in February, we grew to nine farmers and managed to survive. It has served the community year-round ever since.

Most markets take a slower path to year-round operation. University District Farmers' Market opened in 1993 and gradually expanded its season while opening additional markets in Seattle. After 20 years, three of seven markets run by Neighborhood Farmers Market Alliance were year-round.

The length of your season, even up to year-round operation, may depend upon having a building. Even an open-air structure provides enough protection generally to extend a season by two or three months, possibly more if farmers have greenhouses on the farm and heaters in the market. [See Winter Markets in Chapter 12.]

Day and Hours

What days and hours are best for the market? None are best absolutely. Yet selection of day and hours are critical in maximizing the customer flow into your market. What works in your community may be a function of other markets already in existence more than what your fifteen-person committee thinks is the best time. Saturday is the most popular day but large metropolitan areas and even rural areas can have markets running every day of the week.

Analyze the habits and needs of your potential customers but take equal care in assessing the needs of potential farmers. If most of the farmers you want are going to a strong Saturday market, ask the public to prioritize the other six days. You need to help farmers and serve customers simultaneously.

Starting in 1979, five markets were developed over a two-year period in the Los Angeles basin. Then in 1981, the mayor of Santa Monica was ready. Instead of competing with two Saturday markets, the city decided to start on a Wednesday, July 15. With 23 farmers and $11,000 in sales, the market was an instant success. The following two weeks farmer numbers increased and sales grew to $13,000, then $15,000. Now with around 100 farmers on average,

Santa Monica's Wednesday mid-day market is still one of the West's highest grossing markets.

Weekday markets often do well extending over the lunch hour. In a heavily trafficked, urban area, hours from 10 a.m. to 2 p.m. allow farmers to avoid rush hour in both directions, serve business people able to double-task during lunchtime, and provide seniors the chance to finish shopping early.

Saturday markets often run from 8 a.m. to 1 p.m., although it's not uncommon to open at 7 a.m. or earlier, especially where heat is a factor. Larger markets may stay open until 3 p.m. or later. Anything over six hours makes a long day for farmers when time for packing, travel, set-up and break-down is added.

A Sunday market may be preferable for parking if your downtown gets heavy use on Saturday. Sunday may be the best market day with a more relaxed, family focus. Some farmers may not participate on Sunday but they may already be busy on Saturday. Churches can be sensitive to the perceived impact of Sunday markets, but markets seem to open at 8, 9 or 10 a.m. with little problem. Ask the faith community if a 1 or 3 p.m. closing better allows their followers to come after service.

If you have an evening market in a business locale, work with retailers to change window displays weekly and do cross promotions with the market to increase pedestrian traffic. Each activity helps the other.

On the West Coast at least, the grandmother of all evening markets is San Luis Obispo. "Thursday Night" attracts up to 10,000 people into the downtown core from 6:30 to 9:00 p.m. every Thursday year-round. Along with dozens of farmers and numerous crafts sellers, you may find 10 restaurants doing BBQ, local retailers open for the occasion, a volleyball game, non-profits raising funds, a flatbed truck for campaigning politicians, a car show and who knows what else. Every Friday morning a group of committed leaders including the farmers' market manager meets to review the previous evening and deal with issues before they become problems.

Oregon City Farmers Market
Power Of Produce Club

The Power Of Produce (POP) Club is a nationally recognized kids' program started at the Oregon City Farmers Market in May 2011 to empower kids to make healthy food choices by introducing them to where their food comes from.

It started with an $8,000 Healthy Eating Active Living (HEAL) grant secured from Kaiser Permanente by manager Jackie Hammond-Williams. The kids, age 5-12, sign their own Passport to Health for free, and receive a POP button, POP reusable shopping bag and $2 of tokens each week that they attend the market. The market tracks their participation on a calendar on the back side of the passport. Kids each decide whether to buy produce, grow a garden, or save tokens until they can buy such things as a blueberry bush or an apple tree. With volunteer supervisors in the POP Kids Cook! program, they also learn to prepare salsa, zucchini fritters and more at the market.

The POP Club was an immediate success. The Clackamas Soil and Water Conservation District quickly became intrigued because they saw that it presented a unique opportunity to connect kids and food. By supporting the market, they hope that it will help keep farmers viable.

Bob's Red Mill joined in as an education and nutrition sponsor of the POP Club. They provide whole grains for a bicycle-powered, grain grinding mill. Another partner is the Lions Club which coordinates physical activities in chalked squares, so POP Club kids can win a wooden dollar to spend. Both sponsors are reinforcing that diet and exercise help prevent diabetes.

The POP Club prints thousands of colorful bookmarks each year which schools willingly dis-

tribute to all children. In 2014, there were 1,434 kids in the Power Of Produce Club and 5,474 kid shopping trips to the Market. It continues at the bi-weekly Downtown Winter Market during the November to April off-season.

Weekly activities include seed planting (beans, sunflowers, let-tuce), salad-making, flour-grinding and pancake-making, jam-making, wormy fun with worm bins, crawly critters and fun bugs, cider-pressing and make your-own-favorite-farmer-a-button.

Plant a Carrot for the Market allows customers to purchase wooden Market Carrots for $5 each – all proceeds going to POP Club – to "plant" by their driveway, showing support for the Oregon City Farmers Market and the POP Club.

The POP Club was soon noticed by the Farmers Market Coalition which has helped to spread the word. USDA also posted it on their August 8, 2013 blog. Many farmers' markets across the US and Canada are now helping to build the next generation of market shoppers and good food eaters! [To be inspired, search for Power of Produce Club on YouTube.] ❧

Concentrated Selling Time

Hours need not be lengthy. If people can come within an eight-hour period, most can come within four or five hours. People generally will plan their day around a market visit so hours can be compact. Shorter hours keep farmers busy and customers shop in a more vibrant atmosphere, not feeling like every farmer needs to capture their attention.

Start with a shorter market timeframe unless you are appealing strongly to local artisans. If and when you need more time to serve a growing customer base and your farmers agree, announce that you are extending your hours by popular demand. Condensing hours is to admit that your planning did not create the anticipated customer response.

In smaller communities, two hours is plenty to serve most customers. Double to four hours would bring marginal additional sales, waste farmers' time and lessen the buzz. You can never satisfy everyone with your hours, so make the best decision possible and revisit your decision when you have more information.

Establish market day and hours with the buyers in mind. If your market is located near open businesses, try to complement their busiest hours. If the market is located on a commuter road, stay open to capture customers on their way home, if farmers are willing. It's a good idea to avoid opening and closing times that coincide with rush hour.

Multi-Day Potential

Many markets have experience going from one day of operation to two per week. The second day fails relatively more often than not. There seem to be several explanations. Markets don't do their homework to determine if existing or potential customer counts are sufficient; they don't invest the necessary

---

Farmers' Markets Through the Eyes of the Consumer

Be customer-focused. Keep your business abreast of what the consumer wants, when they want it and how they want it.

During this past winter, the Federation held several regional workshops and conferences. Consumer panels gave presentations on what they are looking for at a farmers' market, and here is what they wanted, or wanted more of:

- Product diversity – as large a selection of produce and other farm products as possible, including more organic products;
- Homemade baked goods – many people are too busy to bake for themselves and enjoy the sweets they can get at market;
- Plants and nursery stock – many customers enjoy gardening and being able to get their garden plants at market is important;
- Dried beans, and a wide variety of hot peppers, both fresh and dried;

- Special events – they give the market a fun atmosphere and encourage community spirit among patrons.

Consumer panelists also wanted more children's activities like petting zoos, as well as fun ways to educate children about farming and nutrition, whether it's at the market or by making school visits. Individual vendors may want to plant a special flower or vegetable in a large pot at the beginning of the season. Bring it to market each week for the kids to follow the growth of the plant and the development of the vegetable and then give them a treat made from that particular vegetable at the end of the season. Talk to the children about the plant each week. Pique their interest and their curiosity so they look forward to seeing its growth and progress.

– *Farmers' Market Forum*, Farmers' Market Federation of New York, Summer 2000 ∞

resources; they assume if one is good, two is better; and they fail to calculate the total effort invested in their initial effort and duplicate it.

Even California's model market in Davis encountered problems when it decided to replicate its Saturday market. No matter what their hours, the Wednesday market has struggled to get 10 percent of Saturday's sales volume. While they now operate 2-6 p.m., since 1993 they have hosted Picnic in the Park, positioning the market as summer evening entertainment from 4:30 to 8:30 p.m. During picnic months their sales grow to half those of Saturday.

Similarly, we developed the Hillsboro Tuesday Marketplace for a dinner and music crowd, knowing that the Hillsboro Farmers' Market on Saturday was doing a fantastic job of selling produce. Tuesday has a separate identity, an overlapping board and a larger group of community stakeholders.

In considering multiple days, clarify your goals. Are you trying to expand hours for your existing clientele or do you think you can double your sales with twice the hours? Consider what's best for farmer sales, not just customer convenience. You may dilute the impact of your good market as farmer sales decrease on an average daily basis. It may be wiser to use limited farmer availability at different locales over several days of the week as the St. Paul market has done in neighboring communities.

If you have a major site investment, a multiple-day market may make sense. Obviously, some markets want to appeal to customers' desire for convenience, and customer traffic justifies the expansion.

However, farmers' markets shouldn't pretend to be all things to all people. Part of what makes farmers' markets special is limited hours, forcing people to come on farmer time and find a sense of community in the process.

The Olympia Farmers' Market is a good, multiple-day model. It has tested varying hours, days and months over the decades. Now it operates Thursday-Sunday from April to October, weekends in November and December, and Saturday only in January to March. It has paid off an $800,000 construction bond issued by the city in the early 1990s. The new struc-

ture is situated at a prominent location, a turn-around at the bottom of four lanes of traffic on Capitol Way. The market is a major tourist draw generating far more traffic than the state capital itself.

"Start slow with Saturdays only and build into a regular three-day-per-week market as produce becomes available and customer demand increases. Make sure your options for future days are outlined in your contract. Mornings are preferable due to the cooler weather which enhances the freshness and longevity of the produce, and six hours is ample time to remain in the marketplace."

– Sara Pollard, *Do's and Don'ts of a Successful Farmers' Market*

Experience in Torrance on Tuesday and Santa Monica on Wednesday has shown a better total result when opening first with a mid-week market. Each had a large population base to add a Saturday market years later. In other markets where a weekday has been the later addition, customers seem less likely to compare it favorably to the weekend market they're accustomed to.

A major part of the decision about multiple-day operation must be left to a full assessment of what your market farmers and customers want. Even San Francisco's premier Alemany Farmers' Market, a large open-air concrete set of shelters built in 1947, had to keep cutting back from five days to just Saturday as other markets developed in the 90s. Now to keep the property in use, the City has added a Sunday flea market.

Rain or Shine

Building loyal customers and farmers is dependent upon each knowing the other will come consistently rain or shine. Especially from a distance, farmers in sun may be unaware of rain across the hills. Conversely, a lengthy downpour may prevent farmers from harvesting while the market is sunny. With all but a very small market, it would be impossible to notify farmers and customers that a market day is canceled.

Build customers' faith that farmers are depending on them to come, and you'll probably have about two-thirds of your normal balance. Everyone will do okay and you will maintain the continuity.

MANAGEMENT STRUCTURE

There are three basic models of organizational structure, and many other variants. One of your early steps is to determine who will sponsor the market: the city, county or chamber; a grower association or co-op; or a community organization created to pull all the stakeholders together. Each type has its benefits. Under any structure you will need to identify the chain of command, give authority to the manager, define the separation of powers and clarify enforcement procedures. [Look at the Dane County Farmers' Market story in the next chapter for a considered reflection on sponsorship, product limitations, space allotment and rule enforcement.]

Government-run

A city may appoint a municipal staffperson to oversee the market and hire managers to tend to it on-site. Farmer space fees go into the market and the city's general fund. This structure works well in the City of Chicago markets as well as Ann Arbor, MI. The City of Santa Monica established markets under its Economic Development Department and now has four market days at three different locations. As market supervisor for decades, Laura Avery coordinates staff and manages the oldest market while three part-time staffers run the others.

This model gives decision-making responsibility to one key individual with oversight by city leaders, or the chamber or downtown business association board. The liability is that boards may not have the time and background to make good decisions regarding market operation when they have their own separate organizational concerns.

Success results from a resourceful manager who gets input from farmers and makes recommendations that are approved by the supervising authority. Government finances and politics come into play when council members interfere. If managers use a sense of fair play in their decisions, council is best kept out of the process. The city-led market manager needs to know the political ropes and have the trust of his/her bosses. Any type of governing board should hire and fire, and make policy, but not usurp the manager's decision-making role.

The Council on the Environment in New York City runs the 60-site Greenmarket program. It operates almost like a nonprofit but with oversight by a city board.

Especially in the southeastern states, the state departments of agriculture operate a number of large wholesale-retail markets. For instance, Georgia's nine state-run farmers' markets form a network for more than $1 billion in sales of fruits and vegetables annually throughout the Southeast. Florida has 13 such markets, North Carolina five and South Carolina three. Retail customers in Asheville, Raleigh or Columbia generally shop in retail buildings or sheds separate from the wholesale activities. The markets have been capitalized by the states, and are supported by fees to cover ongoing operation and management by state professionals.

Grower-run

Growers often band together to form a co-op or association – or are organized into one by a founding dynamo organizer – and pay a nominal fee to join. The hired manager represents them in developing and managing the market. Many farmers believe that as producers, their board better understands what they need and how the market(s) should run. Certainly, they understand the farmer side better than a city staffer, but do they understand their urban customers, a necessary marketing strategy and the political scene as well as the city staffer?

Farm Bureau operates various markets in Orange and San Diego counties, using their well-established links with local farmers as an advantage over urban organizers.

"I suggest that farmers' market startups go the co-op way instead of having one person in charge. I've heard of other markets where one person has the power to make all the decisions of when and where to set up. It's better to have a board to take everyone's point of view into consideration."

– Jane Desotelle, Mgr., Adirondack FM Cooperative, NY

The Adirondack co-op works for several upstate farmers' markets west of Lake Champlain. The F.A.R.M. (Farm Association for Retail Marketing) organizations created in the 1970s and 1980s throughout the southeastern states give farmers similar control over their marketing in numerous towns and cities.

If an association runs the market, the city will be more inclined to insist on good business practices leading to more professional managers. Good managers understand how to convey farmer concerns to city authorities without estranging them. Their greater challenge is incorporating customers' views when the farmer board may slant the view on many decisions. Having several non-farmers on the board may compensate and lead to productive discussions.

The Pacific Coast Farmers Market Association (PCFMA), founded in 1988, operates more than 60 certified farmers' markets in the Bay Area, governed by a 10-person board of mainly farmers. Though not a member organization, PCFMA allows their farmers to elect one director each year. While they recruit community leaders from fields such as law, finance and health care, PCFMA is primarily a grower-run organization.

Community-run

The third model is a hybrid comprised of community stakeholders. The steering committee or board of directors – generally with about 5 to 15 members – may include farmers, artisans, business, chamber, visitors' bureau, city, Cooperative Extension, residents, media, faith community, civic and arts organizations, and others. Seek out a healthy balance of vendors and non-vendors. Some individuals may prefer to serve on a non-voting advisory committee.

"Growers alone cannot establish a farmers' market in a city. There must be a commitment and coordination between city officials and growers to get it done. A commitment on the part of the community is an essential partnership that must happen to make the place successful and sustainable."

– *American Vegetable Grower,* "Community is Key to Market Success," 1995

While the community model may have a larger, time-consuming board, it often has a better read on the community's pulse and what new directions to take. It also may have better access to political leaders. The board diversity provokes discussion, confronts issues before they become problems and leads to more connections that help fulfill goals.

The goal with any management structure is a complementary balance of a strong manager and strong board (or supervisors). If either side is weak, the organization suffers. The major duties of the board include market rules and guidelines, policy and goal setting, annual budget, staff review, and advertising program approval.

No one structure or size fits all market organizations. We continue to imagine the best structures to fit our communities. At times the structure becomes unhealthy and needs to be reappraised. An outside

Saturday Morning Market invites all of St. Petersburg to celebrate their seasonal opening every year with a dance at 1st Ave and 1st Street on the waterfront.

assessment can help redirect community energies to rebuild a healthier market.

Stakeholder Assistance

Who can help with the development and outreach for potential and fledgling markets? They will be stakeholders, whether formally on the board or not.

If you have enough volunteers involved, you may have a committee for every aspect of market development. Find an accountant and chamber member for the finance or budget committee, a farmer and Extension staff for farmer outreach, a good retailer and a newspaper staffer for publicity, city and business improvement association staff for location, an attorney and farmer for rules and bylaws, and a civic organization and city volunteer coordinator for special events.

Ask your city for specific resources even if they are not the sponsor. Work with city planners to locate a city street or park where bathrooms, barricades and storage are made available. Police and fire departments frequently want to sign off on safety questions. Economic development staff can connect you to key chamber staff and promoters, refer you to helpful promoters and assist with street banner placement. The mayor can cut the ribbon at your opening, helping attract major media attention.

Your state department of agriculture, Cooperative Extension, Farm Bureau, conservation commission and grower organizations can help with farm and political contacts, perhaps lining up a speaking tour in key agricultural areas. Ask for lists they may share or assistance with mailings.

A local farmers' market association may give you help including farm contacts, introductions, special event contacts and combined meetings and promotional campaigns. They may want a marriage of the old and the new, strengthening their organization and avoiding a duplication of efforts.

Your local business organization may be a major contributor through financial support, board members, insurance, publicity, printing, and contacts for free or reduced-fee services. Most businesses recognize the benefits the market will bring through heavier pedestrian traffic so they are eager to distribute handbills and put posters in their windows.

Residents' associations, neighborhood centers, senior citizen organizations, development corporations, churches, social organizations and charities all have something to contribute to this community effort. Take the time to reach out to staff and boards to see how they want to help. The list is unlimited. Virtually everyone in your community has an interest in seeing the market established. Your goal is to help them see how their interest group will be served through the market.

Developing Community Support

The satisfaction achieved in creating a farmers' market often directly relates to the effort expended in building a cohesive community group that actualizes the market's goals. We can meet diverse needs by joining representatives from city government, local merchants, nonprofit organizations and farmers in the planning process, and allowing different nonprofit groups to set up informational tables at the market.

Reach out to all elements of the population. Include farmers who cater to a mix of ethnic groups, income levels and lifestyles. Each of these groups has different buying habits. Unusual vegetables and "seconds," labeled as such, create a more diverse buying group and make the market more intriguing.

Businesses unfamiliar with the benefits may be reluctant to bring in a farmers' market because they fear it will be a distraction or exacerbate limited parking. Statistics and anecdotal evidence show farmers' markets are a boon to adjacent businesses. [see Appendix]

Be open to the community. In 2014 the Neighborhood Farmers Market Alliance (NFMA) gave away 322 booth spaces in its seven markets to 83 distinct nonprofit organizations. Such organizations help propel markets to greater success, and also make a positive impact on the health of their communities.

Educate townsfolk about the benefit of nutritious, lower-priced fresh produce being more readily available, especially important in low-income areas where families often skimp on purchases of life-sustaining fresh fruits and vegetables. NFMA facilitated $300,000 of food access in 2014 through SNAP, Fresh Bucks and food bank donations.

Set up a booth to give free samples, nutrient information on various products and general information about healthy eating habits. Ask your state agriculture or health department if your market can be approved to accept food coupons under the Women, Infants and Children (WIC) Farmers Market Nutrition Program. Obtain promotional material and recipes from various commodity groups as well as the 5-A-Day campaign. [See Resources, Chapter 6 and General]

"Know your elected officials! What they do affects your market! Know who your planners are, your mayor and city council. Space is critical with city planning. Otherwise you get shlepped all over the place and each time you move it costs you a lot of customers. Bring the mayor to the market for a Cabbage Toss to open the market season. Each time the city council does something good for the market, invite them to the market and do a photofest. We have a photographer who is a volunteer at the market."

– Karen Durham, former Mgr., Bellingham Farmers'
    Market , WA

ORGANIZER & MARKET MANAGER

"A good farmers' market has a good Market Master. You can count on it."
– Jeff Ishee, *Dynamic Farmers' Marketing*

In most instances there is one driving force behind the market, a person who is compelled to create a success. Sometimes it's a small group of people. Either way, this individual or group does the outreach to form a larger committee and to supervise all the necessary activities. Someone has to make things happen, meeting deadlines on the timeline for start-up.

This innovator often becomes the founding market manager. He or she will oversee on-site operations during the market day, including assigning spaces to growers, enforcing market rules, and collecting fees.

Manager Laura Avery, second from right, and assistant do weekly, live, public radio updates so listeners learn about the day's market picks in Santa Monica.

If this person hasn't created the initial committee, find a dynamo through a press release, a job announcement and word-of-mouth within your circle of influence. More important than being knowledgeable about produce, the market manager needs to be creative, self-motivated, organized, flexible and a people person. A marketing background is helpful in working with publicity as well as with community leaders and customers.

As Randii MacNear, manager of the Davis Farmers' Market, says, "The best manager is someone who likes constant problem solving, is a good listener and enjoys the swarm – the people coming, sellers, hearing community desires and resolving issues. It's both the fun and the tough part. It's the magic."

Some staff are hired as contractors, but if the market is the majority source of income, he/she must be made an employee by law. Check with an attorney or certified public accountant. To avoid a conflict of interest, hire someone who will not be selling at the market. The manager must be above reproach in all vendor relations, including space assignments.

Dependent upon your budget, pay should be commensurate with ability and responsibility. Given many start-up budgets, that leaves a lot of latitude for the organizing committee or board to pay much less than the manager is worth. Since the manager is likely to age considerably in a matter of months(!), you might establish a bonus related to several measurable goals, not just getting more farmers involved.

The responsibilities of a market manager may encompass a full-time position with support staff in a large urban setting. In a small community even a part-time salaried position conveys the message that the manager is a fair arbiter of any dispute.

Treat the manager with respect right from the start, and hopefully you will have a solid partner for years to come. Many governing bodies fail to appreciate the broad expertise and market history that becomes embedded in their manager; it is rarely transferred successfully to new managers. It doesn't take long for vendors to start calling the shots if they know the players and issues better than their hired staff.

Nothing is more important to many consumers than source integrity. This Alexandria, VA market vendor leaves no doubt.

Market Rules & Regulations

Rules generally define the type of market, governance, who may sell, permitted products, seller guidelines, standards of conduct, reservation and cancellation policy, and penalties for non-compliance. Every vendor should sign a copy of the rules so they acknowledge their responsibilities. The manager should maintain those copies in case any legal question arises.

Probably the issue most central to your market identity relates to the integrity and enforcement around who can sell what. Neil Hamilton points out in *The Legal Guide for Direct Farm Marketing* that few states control the use of the term "farmers' market" by law. Maine is one that specifically establishes it as a place where two or more farmers offer for sale farm and food products at least 75% of which they produce. Other product must be purchased directly from another farmer.

"Rules are essential to good market management. Rules help to control the chaos, ensure everyone knows their rights and responsibilities, and maintain the integrity of the market. For example, some markets will allow a certain level of re-selling from other local farms. But when this is set as a percentage, it can be ambiguous and, therefore, unenforceable. What does the percentage mean? Is it a percentage of what is on the table at any given time, a percentage of the number of products or the value of the products? Is it a percentage of the sales over the course of the season? Farmers are unclear on what the rule means and will find it difficult to comply. Likewise, the manager is put in a position of interpreting the rule and then tracking the farmers' product lines week after week to determine compliance based on their own interpretation. Always set rules that can be clearly understood by everyone and the manager can reasonably investigate."

– Diane Eggert, Exec. Dir., FM Federation of New York

The pure form of a farmers' market is one where all farmers may sell only what they produce. The huge success of the Dane County Farmers' Market in Madison, WI, reflects public support for this model where customers can get answers to any question directly from the farmer. The market's rules clearly state its broad range of goals:

- To give growers and producers of Wisconsin agricultural commodities and other farm-related products alternative marketing opportunities;
- To promote the sale of Wisconsin-grown farm products;
- To improve the variety, freshness, taste and nutritional value of produce available in the Madison area;
- To provide an opportunity for farmers and people from urban communities to deal directly with each other rather than through third parties and to thereby get to know and learn from one another;
- To provide an educational forum for consumers to learn the uses and benefits of quality, locally grown or prepared food products;

- To provide educational opportunities for producers to test and refine their products and marketing skills;
- To enhance the quality of life in the Greater Madison Area by providing a community activity which fosters social gathering and interaction; and
- To preserve Wisconsin's unique agricultural heritage and the historical role which farmers' markets have played in it.

Hamilton notes what we can learn from the only recent court case regarding a farmers' market rule, Bowen v. Dane County Farmers' Market in 1996. The vendor had been suspended for not producing what he was selling according to market rules. The Wisconsin Court of Appeals upheld the district court's summary judgment for the market and fees related to their defense against a frivolous lawsuit.

"First, courts will probably enforce the markets' rules as long as they are clear and are applied in a fair manner. Second, a market may need to be prepared to expend time and money to defend its actions in court. Third, while the case is unusual, because findings of frivolous lawsuits are not that common, it shows that a producer who sues a market when the facts are clear, may risk having to pay the market's court costs and attorneys fees."

– Neil Hamilton, *The Legal Guide for Direct Farm Marketing*

Assure safety and high standards by requiring members to obtain any applicable city, county, state or federal licenses. Food processors should have a certified kitchen or be legal under state cottage law. If organic they must use certified organic products. Rules may also cover stall appearance and safety requirements. You don't need to reinvent the wheel – get copies of other markets' rules and decide what works best for you. Change your rules if needed.

Local and state government often waive registration, tax and business license requirements for small producers. For instance, nurseries offering less than $5,000 of value during the course of the year may not need a nursery license; check your state agriculture department code.

Set a policy to discourage dumping of large quantities of produce at low prices. You might require farmers to stay within 20% of local retail prices, or to not go below wholesale prices, and to keep the quality and uniqueness of their products in mind when determining prices. The goal is to prevent price wars and undercutting by hobbyists unconcerned with making a profit. The Davis market faced such a situation with a dentist selling tomatoes and donating his profits to a local church.

Get legal counsel to review all your written rules and procedures, especially around quality and minimum pricing standards. A legal marketing cooperative allows you to establish an acceptable range of prices. Members of the market sign an agreement to abide by the pricing policies. These policies might only apply until a certain time each market day and until a fixed point in the season.

Establish standards for produce quality, cleanliness, display and marketing procedures. Do not allow dirty or distressed produce – the exception: a processing grade for home canners. A "replace-or-refund" guarantee will reinforce customer loyalty and serve as your best form of advertisement.

"The fewer the rules, the better. Too many rules bog down progress and discourage participation. Second, rules should be written to keep the customer happy. If there aren't too many rules, and they are written with a positive spin, and are aimed to make the customers' experience a happy one, then everyone wins. Goals for the market need to be established. Only after the goals are clearly defined should a set of rules be written. And then the rules should be used more as a guideline than as a strict enforcement tool. If a problem arises, use a market committee to handle them. Never reprimand a vendor in front of a customer. Instead, do it privately and in a way that will keep the vendor smiling through it!"

– *Farmers' Market Forum,* Farmers' Market Federation of New York

The point is really not how long or short the rules are, but whether they provide a fair process for resolution of inevitable questions and give authority to the manager when those issues are not addressed.

Neil Hamilton's analysis of 30 sets of market rules across the country led to a list of 20 provisions common to farmers' market rules:

- Organizer or sponsor – identifies who runs the market and sets out the philosophy and purpose of the market.
- Market manager - identifies who makes the decisions on day-to-day operation.
- Statement of the rules – makes the rules part of the agreement between the vendor and the market.
- Defining key terms – explains what key phrases, such as vendor, allowable goods, categories of products, etc., will mean in context.
- Approval of vendors and products - defines who can sell (farmer/non-farmer distinction), and what can be sold (produce-craft-food distinctions).
- Criteria for selecting vendors – establishes any priorities or preferences, and the basis for them, and allocates market spaces.

- Categories of products – rules for items such as baked goods, nursery plants, eggs, cheeses, meat, and processed foods, commonly related to inspections and handling.
- Changes in ownership and vendors' rights – addresses issues such as transfer or change of business and seniority for market spaces.
- Carrying rules – may allow farm vendors to sell products raised by other farmers.
- Application process and fees – provides for the timing of application, selection and notification of vendors, sets the amount and payment of fees, and allocates market spaces and locations.
- Types of vendors and length of market – creates categories of seasonal and daily vendors and may include the actual contract or application to participate.
- Membership and market organization – creates operational structure for market and may require a separate payment for membership in sponsoring organization.
- Necessary documents and permits – lists the various documents and licenses required to participate, including proof of insurance, tax permits, health inspection and other licenses. A market may re-

---

Managing Risk at your Market

Good risk management is the first step in "insuring" your market. Are your market aisles clear and unobstructed? Do boxes and baskets stick out into the aisle causing a trip hazard? Are produce and plants in vendor spaces kept up off the ground level? Is the floor clear of easy-to-slip-on garbage or produce trimmings?

Are the grounds properly maintained – pavement in good repair, and any crumbling curbing patched or painted? Is your electrical wiring in proper order? Do you have properly-charged fire extinguishers located throughout the market? Consider asking a fire marshal to walk through your market and offer safety suggestions. Keep cars from the market's selling area – cars and people walking and shopping are a dangerous mix.

Spread the risk. Require your sellers to provide the market with liability insurance so that if someone is hurt as a result of a vendor's negligence, the market is not left solely defending and possibly paying on a lawsuit. More and more insurance companies are looking to this as a means of controlling their risks. It's just a matter of time before this becomes mandatory.

– Condensed from *Farmers' Market Forum,* Farmers' Market Federation of New York, Summer 1998

---

quire information such as farm plan, load lists for products raised, and organic certification.

- Market operation – detailed guidelines on issues such as set-up, clean-up, selling times, notification for non-attendance, pets, parking, samples, sanitation, signage, hawking, smoking, food safety and food handling. Many provisions may be very detailed, making the operational rules the main part of a market's regulations.

- Enforcement process – sets the procedures for rule enforcement, including reporting violations, notice, penalties, suspension or removal, and appeals.

- Rule and law compliance - incorporates applicable state and local requirements into market rules, with agreement that it is vendor's responsibility to comply.

- Hold harmless and indemnification – vendor agrees to protect market organizers from any legal or financial liability in case of accidents or incidents at market.

- Food safety and sampling – specific rules for handling and storing different types of foods, with guidelines for sampling if allowed.

- Other provisions – labeling, posting farm name, using legal scales, accepting nutrition checks and food stamps, pricing guidelines, farm visits, and gleaning excess food.

- Signature line – creates a binding agreement between vendor and market.

Many other rules can be individually found depending on the market.

One market learned the hard way, via a lawsuit, that it could not restrict its selling to vendors from within state or political boundaries. It could, however, specify that growers be within a certain mileage radius.

Licenses

California law requires that all farmers must have a certified producer certificate ensuring that they grow within the state. The market also must be certified by the county agricultural commissioner who will periodically inspect the market to assure compliance with legal statutes about who can sell. Markets in other states do not have this enforcement support.

Familiarize yourselves with city, county, state and federal guidelines, especially agricultural and health regulations. Raw produce is generally not a problem, but concerns about sprouts, sampling and value added processing will draw health inspectors. Usually a county health permit is required for the market, as well as separate permits for any producers selling a product which should be processed in a health-approved facility, e.g. jams, chutneys, baked goods.

City staff are usually involved with site approval and conditional use permits. You may need to go before the planning commission and/or city council, so prepare a group of market supporters to reinforce all the community benefits of your project. Insist that the entire market operate under one umbrella business license; as one entity, every vendor should not be required to have their own.

In some localities any producer can sell their own agricultural product exempt from any business license requirement. Various states also have codified protections for farmers' right to sell their own products free of municipal license requirements, including Arizona, Florida, Pennsylvania and Washington.

Bylaws and Articles of Incorporation

Bylaws outline the name of the corporation, mission, membership, board number and terms, officer responsibilities, meeting times and conditions, committee structure, executive committee, insurance and indemnification, fiscal year term and amendment process.

Consider getting 501(c)(3) status for your market, a non-profit, tax-exempt designation assigned by the Internal Revenue Service to educational and charitable organizations. Having 501(c)(3) status allows you to raise money for non-profit projects, and gives the donor a tax write-off.

Most markets have some 501(c) designation, still non-profit but not necessarily tax-exempt. They usually fall under (c)(4) civic leagues and social welfare organizations, (c)(5) agricultural co-ops and (c)(6) chambers of commerce designations.

"Because of the space we provide master gardeners, master composters, P-Patch (a community garden program) and Seattle Tilth, we are providing the public education and advice on food production, organic methods of growing and composting. We also staff and maintain our own information table with local ag news and information. Our chef demos and produce tastings are also effective public education events. It's these events and outreach that are the education component of our 501(c)(3) status. Our charitable component is realized through our donations to local food banks."

– Chris Curtis, Exec. Dir., Neighborhood Farmers Market Alliance, Seattle, WA

Establish your mission, your purpose for being. Nancy Ricketts lists the goals of the Oak Park Farmers' Market, located in a Chicago suburb: "to enhance the quality of life in Oak Park by providing fresh, high-quality produce, a community meeting place, and consumer education."

The mission of the Yakima Farmers' Market, WA, is "to engage in activity to support Yakima Valley and other small and family-run farms and other independent businesses, and to create a vibrant, educational marketplace for the community benefit."

Articles of incorporation are filed alongside the bylaws with your secretary of state. These articles establish your incorporation by defining the corporate name and type, duration (hopefully perpetual), registered office and agent, purposes, powers, membership or not, the names and addresses of founding board members and ex-officio directors, dissolution process, reference to establishment of bylaws, amendment process, consent of the registered agent, and signatures of three incorporators.

When you choose a "corporate" designation, you decide if the market will be a non-profit or for-profit entity. Find an attorney to serve on your board, file your your tax status and address other legalities. Any cost is well worth it in the long run.

BUDGET

Your budget reflects many of your principles as a market organization. It demonstrates the importance of the organization in relation to farmer income, whether management is deemed professional or volunteer, and what are the priorities for sustainability in your environment. Much depends on where your market(s) is located and whom it serves.

An urban market may be part of a multi-market association with millions of dollars in sales and a several hundred thousand dollar operational budget. It may have an executive director and several staff paid salaries that would seem exorbitant to another market, yet which may be relatively low in relation to the cost of living.

A rural market may operate with twenty-five thousand dollars in annual sales and a budget of $500. The manager is likely to be a volunteer, market friend or farmer with minimal compensation.

The major difference is a few zeros. These two markets – and just about every other one in between – have a common desire for growth and a meaningful impact on their communities. Each may face severe competition, threats to their sustainability and ques-

A music stage helps make the Portland FM, OR a community builder.

tions about how to pay for promotion or staff without outside money.

In fact, start-up markets are usually funded through a state grant, the city, a chamber of commerce, the downtown business association, a mall, businesspeople, a charitable individual or fund raising. In Astoria, OR, Vance raised thousands of dollars by soliciting business and community sponsors who were listed on 500 color posters.

Lynn Bagley supplemented funding for start-up and early years of operating the Marin County Farmers' Market by purchasing baked goods from three bakeries and reselling them as a fund raiser. In every case funding starts with a dream, a plan, a budget outlining the necessities and outreach to find the financial assistance. The dynamic, founding individual or group must have a clear vision and the ability to communicate it to a funding source.

It's helpful to distinguish a start-up or development budget from a regular operating budget. The development budget can have substantial costs for personnel, phone, travel, logo development, printing, office supplies, insurance, permits, signs, advertising and promotion – all necessary development costs to get the market off and running on opening day.

The benefit of a separate operating budget is that it allows you to see the true annualized costs of running your market; in planning year two you can compare expenses and income with the first year, unhindered by all the start-up costs.

An operating budget is based primarily on vendor fees. List all your costs in operating the market and a projection of income from space fees, membership fees, sponsors, partners, fundraising and other sources.

Fundraising

Every stakeholder is a resource representing a potential source of funding. Cities have community development or other funds to assist. States have economic development funds or other sources that may be

Allen Moy, director of PCFMA project Fresh Approach, spoke at a Seasonal Supper fundraiser in September 2014.

granted through a competitive process or by staff discretion. The federal government has also been a source, through several USDA programs including transportation, forestry and marketing services.

Markets may need to look for grants from a local foundation, contributions from growers, or even loans or grants from individuals or organizations. Tie your promotional efforts to fundraising. Every time you ask for any assistance, include financial support in your request. It's a great way to gain tangible project support and if they say no, they usually are more inclined to help in other ways.

Hold a pancake breakfast and pre-sell tickets. People can make a contribution and not have to come. You aren't just raising money; you're promoting community ownership.

Fee Structure

For most markets the great bulk of the burden for financing operational costs rests on the farming vendors. Thus, it's a fair idea to give them an annual accounting of how their money is spent, although not all markets do so. There are many scenarios for gathering income. Here are some of the most common fee structures:

♦ *Annual fee:* One fee for the entire season, either equal or proportional to size. Expenses are projected and growers assessed, often with a reduction if paid in advance. Half the fee may be paid mid-season to protect farmers from one early bill of $300; the second assessment also may be adjusted up or down if the situation calls for it.

- *Annual plus daily fee:* A fee for seasonal membership plus a daily fee when they sell. This provides start-up money from funds that are equally assessed.

- *Daily fee:* Fee is usually based on total amount of space or frontal footage, regardless of sales volume. Farmers may suffer on weak days with new competition or bad weather.

- *Percentage fee:* Farmers pay 4-10% of their sales, generally on the honor system and with a minimum fee to ensure basic expenses are covered.

- *Base plus percentage fee:* Fee starts with a basic space-use fee and a percentage or step fee is added based on sales, again on the honor system.

One key issue to resolve in establishing fees is fairness. Is it fair to charge the same $150 per season to two growers, one who will gross $800 and the other $20,000? Is it fair to charge the same $12 per day of a grower selling $60 and another selling $1200? The first is paying 20% and the latter 1% of income. Some will say that it's fair because each is using the same amount of space, like rent in a mall. Others will claim it is unfair because the small farmer is just as important to overall market identity, probably gives more friendly attention to customers, and should not have to subsidize the larger farmer's true share of the operation. (Besides, malls usually charge a base plus percentage; they want a share of extra profit.)

"Why force farmers to cheat?" one will ask.

"The market doesn't make liars of truthful people," another responds.

"Doesn't a percentage fee penalize large farmers who sell more?"

"Doesn't a fixed fee penalize small growers that we most want to help?

Anyone thinking market environment doesn't make a difference hasn't been to the Friday Harbor Farmers' Market. Even a Rapid Market Assessment is pleasant amidst the surrounding waters of San Juan Sound in Washington..

"Should farmers be forced to reveal their sales?"

"In any other marketing venue someone else knows the farmers' income. The manager will keep individual incomes confidential."

You can easily see this discussion is never-ending, but you do need to make a decision. Whatever it is will be difficult to change years later because the status quo is hard to shift and you will have gained a following of farmers who believe the fee structure is fair. Markets with a straight daily fee tend to see the benefits of simplicity and avoid the fact that they don't know their sales. A market across town may operate with a percentage fee and know exactly how each holiday or week of the month affects gross sales.

Set your fees high enough to provide for adequate advertising and other expenses. Don't be surprised if personnel comprises 50% of your budget, perhaps with 35% for promotion and advertising, and 15% for insurance and office expenses. With a small, rural market and a volunteer manager, the percentages will differ drastically.

Your budget will change based on your hours and choice of vendors. A downtown evening market might have graduated fees according to vendor type: hot foods pay 10% or $40 minimum, artisans 8% or $30, value-added processors 7% or $25, and farmers 6% or $20. If you state the standards clearly in advance, you can avoid a cart vendor rolling up and taking advantage of your market. This also requires that you clearly delineate the physical area over which you have city authority.

Fees Essential to Planning

The goal is to fairly charge according to the benefit that each farmer derives from the market. We want to help small, independent, family farmers. When a farmer sells product through a shipper, broker, wholesaler, retailer or restaurant, there is a fee which relates in some way to volume. There may be discounts with greater volume but it still costs more to ship more, and many intermediaries work on a straight percentage. So, farmers are not shocked in dealing with fees that are based on their sales.

When markets charge a percentage fee, they become better at business. They learn the numbers. Knowing daily sales like any other retail business is essential for making good decisions with space fee income.

With sales figures a manager can analyze whether a marketing campaign is effective. Advertising or promotions have a cost. Farmers' anecdotal responses about sales going up are not reliable

Vermont's seal of quality states Buy Local: It's Just That Simple. Rural residents recognize the power of their food dollar more readily than urban shoppers.

in determining whether your expenditure paid off. You don't want to be wasting farmers' money. With good farmer income figures, a manager can chart sales growth resulting from different advertising strategies and continue the ones that pay off.

Daily sales also help a manager track how each farmer is doing and how they are impacted by their competition. The manager may see that a farmer's sales are level when they should be growing with overall market growth. When a farmer complains that competition is killing him, the manager may note that other farmers with the same product are doing well and additional competition has led to increased

demand and more satisfied customers. In other words, knowledge of the full sales picture gives a manager the ability to defuse an angry vendor. Without that knowledge the manager would be limited to an emotional rather than a rational response.

Membership

Membership at farmers' markets is used to build a sense of ownership, give privileges to a defined group, establish seniority, collect basic operational money and provide a base from which to elect leaders of the organization. Some markets require it as a condition for selling, others have no membership, and still others make it optional with non-members paying a higher fee to sell.

Well-run markets often use membership as a basis for building camaraderie among farmers. There may be an annual dinner, perhaps covered within the cost of membership to encourage attendance, at which board elections take place.

Membership fees vary much like space fees listed above. They may be a modest $5 or $10 a year to cover postage and low overhead for a small market. To maintain a full range of market association services in a large, urban market, fees may amount to several hundred dollars per year. In some markets selling privileges are part of the membership fees. More commonly, selling fees – daily, monthly or by the season – are separate from membership costs.

For instance, a farmers' market may charge a membership fee of $35 per season and then charge a $20 daily space fee or a 6% fee; a non-member might pay $25 or 7%. Thus, a short season farmer might choose not to join as a member while most farmers would see the financial benefit of becoming a member and having voting rights in the organization.

Some associations provide for a consumer membership, giving them a sense of market ownership as well and perhaps the right to elect board members. Other markets have a separate 501 (c)(3), nonprofit, tax-exempt Friends of the Market organization to encourage active customer participation and raise additional financial support for educational campaigns. This allows the market to solicit tax-deductible donations while keeping them separate from the market's taxable activity.

Insurance

A market should have coverage year-round to protect itself for all functions in which the market is involved. If a person attends a winter meeting and falls on a slippery step, you could get sued. A skateboarder falls or injures a customer. A dogfight occurs. A customer cuts her leg on a wire basket carrying green beans. A man says he got food poisoning from a processed item. You need protection. If someone sues one farmer, basic coverage will protect all the others. Markets generally encourage or require their individual vendors to provide proof of their own insurance. Consider directors' liability insurance for board members along with your normal liability coverage.

Make sure your comprehensive general liability policy includes product liability. Your city may have insurance that covers a farmers' market on municipal property – but you may need additional coverage. You'll need insurance if you're on private property. Do your homework. Costs vary widely from under $100 well into the thousands per year based on market size, usually vendor and patron counts.

University District FM in Seattle developed this attractive barrier to capture attention. The signs on either side are "Saturdays 9 AM – 2 PM" and "Washington Farmers."

Nationwide and State Farm have long served the agricultural industry, but regional or statewide farmers' market associations have saved markets money. The state association obtains a policy as the lead insured and provides it to markets and vendors. Generally a policy covering up to a two million dollar claim is sufficient. Call your state farmers' market association or department of agriculture. [Also see Appendix]

On-going Support

It's probably occurred to you by now that starting a market is a lot of work. And once you start it, there's the job of running it. Don't try to do all this alone. Join internet web discussion groups, go to small farm conferences, call a consultant, get some technical assistance, etc.

Join a farmers' market association and the national Farmers Market Coalition. You can get help on a steep learning curve through association conferences, online webinars and friendships. They offer many group advantages including cost reduction programs on insurance and bag purchases; educational workshops and programs; cooperative market promotion; networking opportunities; and collective government representation.

In certain areas both urban and rural you may find an existing farmers' market association that wants to host an additional market. It makes sense to combine resources and not replicate all the work done by another organization. However, if you have different goals or want to do it yourself, go ahead! Most markets are run independently by a unique collection of people in that community. ❧

Managing the Market 8

"The best manager is someone who likes constant problem solving, is a good listener and enjoys the swarm — the people coming, sellers, hearing community desires and resolving issues. It's both the fun and the tough part. It's the magic."
– Randii MacNear, Mgr., Davis FM, CA

Management is not easy, especially with dozens of independent farmer personalities. Throw in a board of directors to whom one must be responsible and you have a real job. Managing a market is like juggling seven different fruits and vegetables while surfing on 20-foot Maui waves.

You probably know that by now, and that's what you love. As some see it, that's the magic of the job, dealing with lots of personalities and issues, and learning to resolve disputes while weaving a sense of joy through all you do.

The good news is that customers are paying attention. According to a King Retail Solutions 2012 survey of equal numbers of millenials, gen x'ers and baby boomers, farmers' markets and independent grocers are ranked third among America's 15 favorite grocers, behind Walmart and Kroger, and ahead of Safeway, Trader Joe, Whole Foods and the rest. Thirteen percent of those surveyed ranked a farmers' market, co-op or small local grocer among their top three most frequently shopped groceries. We can still try harder.

 ## DAY-TO-DAY CONCERNS

Management issues can occupy considerable time but the overriding concern for any manager is the big day.

Market Day

Some managers could write a book about their activities on market day. We'll try to be more brief. The manager can become a whirling dervish, spinning from one situation to another as he/she seeks to:

- Place directional and parking signs;
- Set up blockades and signs at entrances;
- Assure restrooms are clean;
- Maintain an information center with canopy, sign, recipes, brochures, news and promotional items;
- Supervise customer parking;
- Have improperly parked vehicles towed;
- Assign vendors to their stalls;
- Handle late vendors;
- Ensure quality control;
- Interpret and enforce rules;
- Settle any disputes;
- Maintain a clean, safe and attractive market;
- Solve emergency needs with first aid/EMT training;
- Coordinate volunteers to help with various tasks;
- Handle health department and other inspections;
- Direct special events;
- Hold raffles or drawings;
- Handle consumer relations;
- Conduct surveys;
- Collect space fees, receipts and load lists for market reports;
- Oversee break-down and clean-up of market; and
- Store signs and pack up info center.

General Responsibilities

For smaller markets a big portion of the job is done on market day, but that's really just "show time." Backstage, during the rest of the week, you're doing all the tasks that make your market day(s) run smoothly. The manager is accountable to the board of directors (or steering committee or supervisor), and regularly reports to the president. Throughout the course of the week and the season, the manager frequently will be responsible for:

- Overall market administration;
- Market promotion, advertising and public relations;
- Vendor recruitment and quantity/quality control;
- Rule enforcement;
- Musician/busker scheduling;
- All information and communication including letters and newsletter;
- Food store price tracking for vendor comparison;
- Statistical information for timely reports;
- Vendor compliance with laws, codes and regulations;
- Financial planning;
- Board meeting preparation;
- Office and paperwork; and
- Other tasks, as assigned.

An enthusiastic busking musician performs in front of a sticky bun cart at the Davis FM. Irregular, surprise musicians are an important part of the dynamic chaos that all markets should strive toward.

Managers can become overwhelmed by paperwork like any office worker. A manager is hopefully a "people person" so being tied to paper or computer is about as fun as getting caught in a haybaler.

In many areas managers are using their own home phone, fax machine, computer, and are working in a cramped corner in their home. There is value to frugality; however, if the manager feels unsupported and ill-equipped to perform at maximum efficiency, it may be time for a farmer board member to ask, "Would I want to do what the manager does under those conditions?" If the board is unaware of the conditions, the manager needs to communicate.

You get what you need, generally, if you ask specifically. Start your wish list and prioritize. Ask for more better office space with a window and storage for market equipment that overflows your garage. It

may be in a local church, an empty storefront on Main Street, a community center, city hall or the Cooperative Extension office.

For computer bargains, check online with Free Geek, Ebay or other websites. Or visit a Habitat for Humanity ReStore. If you need top-of-the-line efficiency, ask your local charity with a formal letter or contact one of the major computer companies at their corporate office. Explain how you can streamline your office, gain productivity and thus save or make money. They realize that, just like the schools, once they have you hooked, you'll probably buy your next computer.

Farm out the financial paperwork to an accountant, either a volunteer, board member or professional accountant. Many are willing to handle the market ledger for around $50 per month if it's not too confusing.

"The proliferation of multiple-market organizations has professionalized management. With three year-round markets and four additional seasonal markets throughout Seattle, NFMA is typical of associations experiencing growth pains. We employ 10 FTE year-round including development and bookkeeping, and 7 PTE in high season. Scaling up has generated higher efficiency as people are hired for narrower skill sets."

– Chris Curtis, Exec. Dir., Neighborhood Farmers Market Alliance, Seattle, WA

Manage My Market

With so much paperwork overwhelming managers, it's no surprise that a solution was explored and developed in a strong market city: Portland, OR. In 2009 Manage My Market began providing a comprehensive data management service to simplify and professionalize managers' duties. It includes online vendor registration, stall assignment and date rescheduling, integrated email, license and payment tracking, accounting, invoicing and many website tools. Consumers can visit market sites for a vendor list, product search and an interactive market map.

> "Managemymarket.com is all about saving me time – eliminating the manual tracking of vendor information, making it easy to communicate with my vendors via e-mail either individually or collectively, and sorting through data to provide the market with important reports. The vendor registration process used to mean hours of stuffing envelopes, making copies, running address labels, stamping packets…now it happens in the click of a mouse. I am able to manage a lot of data in one central and secure location. It is a tool I use every day and couldn't live without."
>
> – Ginger Rapport, Market Master, Beaverton FM, OR

Some old-timers show resistance but most farmers love the fact that they can fill out one application including all their products, licenses, insurance and more. Their profile is then available for use by 3, 13 or 30 markets where they sell.

With several hundred markets on board in 38 states and 4 provinces, plus Guam and Australia, the management system is especially good for new markets that may lack a vendor base. Vendors at other area markets can see and apply to a market without the market even knowing them. The new manager can then see their product list and decide whether to accept them as a vendor.

Pay & Benefits

Generally, large markets have full-time staff, and likelihood of pay goes up with market size and sales. With most small to medium-sized markets, managers are either volunteer or part-time (year-round or seasonal). Regardless of pay, you can easily feel overworked and underpaid as a one-person operation or several people running multiple markets.

Again, if you want a change, create a plan to make it happen. Develop it with the help of one or two trusted board members – or co-staff if you're in a government position – to make sure that your request

for additional staff support or an increase in pay is reasonable and doable.

For farmers their pension is tied up in their land; when they retire, they often cash out. Managers need the greater pay now to start a pension program or a SEP/IRA. As markets gain stability and longevity, associations and cities are beginning to develop pension plans along with other benefits. More established boards have recognized the need for a reasonable pay and benefits package as managers have lengthy careers of service. It may be time for other managers to bring up this issue as markets age into maturity.

Manager burnout is, but need not be, a problem. Communicating with other managers and networking at state conferences provides a relief valve for frustrations, a sharing of common experiences and a learning experience for new ideas to implement.

Geographically isolated managers should call another manager somewhere in their state, or even around the country, and gift themselves a 20-minute call once every week or two. The payback will be enormous. Another opportunity to connect is via a farmers' market internet discussion group. [See Resources]

Managerial Stability

"It is the most stressful and difficult job I have ever had. There are so many organizations, community members, customers, vendors, etc. to maintain and keep happy. It is a very involved process to manage a farmers market.

"In need of financial support. I really thought as the market grew in popularity we would receive financial assistance from our local government.

"I believe the amount of work required of market managers is sometimes underestimated and undervalued and as a result the positions are more often than not underpaid which I think accounts for high turnover in some areas.

"Market managers need to be valued more by their organizations. Living wages need to be paid. Benefits need to be provided by the organization.

"It's an exciting time to be working in this field."

– Summary Report: Farmers Markets and the Experiences of Market Managers in Washington State, WSU, 2013

Too frequently managers are leaving their positions because of low pay or burnout. When a market board does not deal with fair pay, benefits, a regular personnel review policy, office equipment and other issues, they are abdicating their responsibility to be good stewards and overall managers of their association.

As the industry continues to mature, our markets need to do longer-term planning. Coming to grips with staff continuity and a realistic financial picture are essential. With anything but small markets, staff must be paid. This may require a review of space fees. Instead of low seasonal fees that amount to less than 2% of sales, daily fees are reasonable. Going from $8 to $10 daily, or $35 to $38, will probably not put anyone out of business. If it does, what kind of a business was it?

That minor change will give the market 25% more money to operate properly. It may mean you can raise the manager's salary or purchase equipment or create more publicity so that the market can grow and increase its income even more.

If market associations or cities fail to plan for manager retention, they plan to fail. It will cost associations much more in the long run when they lose a manager with experience, contacts and goodwill in the community. Frequent manager turnover can reflect a board that wants to maintain absolute control at the risk of making their market suffer.

The list of responsibilities is substantial. Managers know that either you are incredibly organized, your market is not too big, or you need an assistant.

Managers are big on to-do lists and mental note storage. Keep some post-its in your pocket or carry a clipboard. Wear a hat and a distinguishing vest with a nametag. If you have the same blue vest or funny hat every week, you will be clearly identifiable and memorable so vendors won't have to remember what you are wearing to refer customers to you. And just so you

Good managers must maintain healthy relationships with vendors and make consistently fair decisions based on board policy.

inspire others, wear a smile! It may be the best tool you can use.

Board-Manager Balance

How boards and managers view the issue of in-house competition (discussed later in this chapter) – favoring a free market versus a protectionist approach – is one example of the dilemmas that an organization and its manager may encounter. If a manager is put in the position of enforcing what he/she feels is an unjust policy, it may lead to termination or resignation. The organizational challenge is to provide direction and oversight, yet allow a manager to be strong. In the long run, an organization is healthy when it has both a strong manager and a strong board. Weakness in either or both leads to problems.

A manager needs to know what the role of the board is vis-à-vis the manager. Usually the board or sponsor role is one of policy development. Even if it branches into a more active involvement in market set-up, promotion development, volunteer coordination or vendor outreach, it's a good idea to have the manager as overall coordinator of all activities. There needs to be one person keeping a grip on all the market minutiae; let them manage.

One critical area is finding good board members. If they are producers, they have a self-interest in preserving and improving the organization for benefit of all vendors. They must be ready to withdraw from any vote where there is a conflict of interest and they could benefit individually.

Farmers and other board members need to know their input is valued. Sponsoring agencies may squeeze out the farmer voice and there will be few farmers willing to serve in the future. Yet, farmers are a critical voice to be represented in the management of your farmers' market, even if yours is run by a community organization. Make sure the farmers' opinions are clearly heard or you may lose them.

Market Volunteers

For many farmers' markets, volunteers are the angels-from-heaven that keep the market alive. Treat them well! Washington State markets had an average of 338 volunteer hours in 2009, or 9.5 FTE among the 56 markets using volunteers.

> "The secret in keeping good volunteers is to give them interesting jobs, rather than just using them to do the jobs you don't want to do."
> – Rose Munoz, former Mgr., Torrance FM, CA

Here are a few jobs that volunteers might perform for you:

- Design a cable TV cooking show;
- Gather farmer/consumer recipes for a cookbook;
- Coordinate musical entertainment;
- Solicit chefs for cooking demonstrations;
- Distribute posters and fliers;
- Sell promotional items;
- Direct traffic and parking;
- Provide answers at the information table;
- Coordinate special events;
- Give farmers restroom breaks;
- Maintain the restrooms;
- Collect items and hold prize drawings; and

- Assist vendors with set-up and break-ddown.

We may think that a task is above or below the dignity of a volunteer, but there are all types of people. Some people simply want to help, to be of use. Others have an idea that would challenge the most capable professional. Our management challenge is to be supportive and diplomatic about the importance of every task that needs to be done. It helps to follow up with a thank-you note, a gift basket or even a volunteer recognition dinner at the end of the season. Be sure to include your property owner, the firefighters who hang your banner and the retailer that allows use of their restroom. What goes around, comes around!

Keep a wide view as you conceive of your next volunteer. It may be an architect, a minister, an attorney, a homemaker, a senior or a Rotarian. Along with all the social contacts you make, try calling a volunteer service center, SCORE (Senior Corps of Retired Executives) and VISTA (Volunteers In Service To America) – the Peace Corps to America.

Your next volunteer may be in training to become a great board member.

Stall Fees

The larger the city, generally the higher the fees to sell. Vendors pay from nothing to $50 per day or more. When a sponsor raises fees, they would do well to explain it to their farmers much as a farmer explains a

Volunteers can help sell promotional material and encourage customers to sign up for the market's e-newsletter.

price increase to her customers. There's volume to be sold and there's a cost to making it all happen in a big way.

Markets that are not very successful in small towns, or anywhere, should consider why. If you have no stall fee, you don't value the service that you provide farmers. We all pay for products and services in society, so why expect something for nothing? It may be time for farmers create a marketing plan and figure out how much each should pay toward the active management of that plan.

Permanency

Finding a permanent location is a critical issue for any market. Markets in Washington with more than 10 years of history have moved an average of 2.2 times. One in six markets desire more space or a permanent location. It's not good to be forever moving your location, although as the first Portland, OR market found out in 1998, getting a rent increase was actually a blessing in disguise. They moved to a downtown university location and the market took off. However, it's a good idea to get your city planners thinking about where you may be able to operate more long-term as happened with the Vancouver Farmers' Market (WA) move in 2000 to a city park.

"The main thing that market organizers could do to help us is to locate good sites, even possibly year-round farmer-oriented sites. It is getting

The Lynchburg Community FM, VA, has a permanent structure which signals community commitment to a stable ongoing market.

more and more difficult to market at certain places with zoning regulations."
– *Barriers & Opportunities,* Farmers' Market Trust

If you are organizing markets in numerous places, you undoubtedly know how important it is to have each market be unique. It is not a matter of stamping out cookie-cutter markets. When Santa Barbara began a new market in Solvang, it worked to find new members from that area.

"The bureaucracy is complex, with conditional use permits, licenses, coastal development permits, weights and measures, and health permits. Santa Barbara, Carpinteria and Solvang are independent municipalities with their own regulations. Then in Goleta we deal with the county, since it's an unincorporated city. The process is getting more and more complicated. Now we must get re-approved every five years. It just gets tougher, more regulated and harder to maintain. We set aside money for project planners and lawyers."
– Mark Sheridan, former Mgr., Santa Barbara FM Assoc., CA

After a number of years of community service, especially if you have substantial growth, you should have the attention of city officials in acquiring a permanent or semi-permanent site as the Davis market has experienced. They had enough credibility after fifteen years that they were the major determinant in the style of the multi-use facility the city built as part of Central Park renovations. Since these markets should be sustainable, find locations that are viable in the long term. If you can't find more than a five-year contract for a site, search for a permanent site with city or county help.

[Market buildings are addressed in Chapter 12.]

Regulations

Any manager needs to build a good, working relationship with your health department and your city. You may have health permits, business licenses, and state code to interpret for the market and even farmers. As Jay Visser of J-N-A Produce in Manhattan, MT, explains, "The biggest problem we see is the regulations involved in all aspects of farming. The paper work has taken the fun out of it. They've passed a law in Montana stating that all products sold in polyethylene bays need to be classified as processed products. They haven't enforced the law yet, but they could at any time." A manager may get involved interfacing with a state agency on this issue much as managers were heavily involved for years in the creation of the California Uniform Retail Food Facilities Law (CURFFL) and its update by the Department of Health Services. If law is going to affect you, become an advocate.

> "About 43% of market managers mentioned obstacles to entrepreneurial development. The most frequently cited obstacle was inconsistent health department regulations – in particular, regulations about sampling and selling prepared foods."
>
> – Farmers' Markets and Rural Development Project

A Washington study found that 82% of managers said their vendors developed or expanded their farm, craft product or business outside the farmers' market within the prior three years, most commonly with a storefront, restaurant or farmstand. Other avenues included online, grocers, co-ops, restaurants, wholesale and CSA.

> "[A soup vendor] uses local ingredients and now they have two storefronts … [A] restaurant opened a second location based on popularity from the … market. Two farmers have expanded into a processing kitchen on their farm to sell longer into the season after the main growing season … A goat cheese vendor has outgrown our markets except for occasional visits. They boosted their retail sales so much they don't have enough product for the market. [One farmer] doubled their CSA business based on contacts made at the market.
>
> – Summary Report: Farmers Markets and the Experiences of Market Managers in Washington State, WSU, 2013

Various states have implemented cottage food laws allowing home-based kitchens to be used in processing goods for sale at farmers' markets. For instance, Arizona law is very friendly. For less than $20, a producer can be selling baked goods and confections nearly anywhere within one week. Oregon law is more difficult for the license, over $150, but flexible once a processor is set up.

A comprehensive overview of cottage food laws – state by state – is available at:

www.forrager.com.

It rates each state program including the types of venues where home-based food is permitted, annual sales limits, and type of food allowed. A quick web search for your state name and "cottage food law" should lead you to your state's particular legalities.

While community kitchens have been developed to facilitate cooperative processing, cottage food law may shift interest away from that trend. Established kitchens will probably continue, and others may develop in states where no cottage law or poor cottage law exists. In these cases, contact your local Small Business Development Center for assistance.

Supplemental Nutrition Assistance Program

When food stamps disappeared in 2002, SNAP debit cards replaced them. Many markets were not prepared to handle these EBT (Electronic Benefits Transfer) cards, and lost those customers. Slowly, markets have been rebuilding their lower-income customer base. By January, 2015, more than 5,000 farmers' markets were licensed by USDA Food and Nutrition Service (FNS) to accept SNAP benefits.

FNS and the National Association of Farmers Market Nutrition Programs (NAFMNP) began MarketLink in 2014 with $4 million in grants to streamline how farmers' markets and farmers get authorized as SNAP vendors and get the equipment to accept SNAP benefits. With nearly 1-in-7 Americans relying on SNAP, MarketLink is a one-stop shop enabling markets to assist your communities more easily.

> "My most persuasive argument for accepting SNAP is that you don't know which of your customers might be using EBT. They might not be using it at your market because you don't accept it. You don't know. Or maybe customers

A Washington State market flyer clarifies that customers can swipe their EBT cards and receive up to $15 match on every transaction.

A market manager instructs an EBT customer on how to process a debit from their card to receive farmers' market tokens.

who used to come to your market don't come any more because their circumstances have changed. Accepting SNAP has brought more dollars into the market. It's money that's going to our farmers instead of corporate grocery stores. I would like to see more markets accept SNAP...I think it contributes to the sense of supporting community."

– Annemarie Bruun, Mgr., Pawtuxet Village FM, RI

MarketLink allows markets to handle SNAP EBT, debit and credit transactions on one machine. A Washington State University study of 17 farmers' markets showed total EBT, debit and credit sales of $285,000 from July-October 2011, and only 6% of all transactions were in cash. The average electronic sale was $34.57. A statewide survey found that acceptance of credit/debit cards is tied to a moderate or large sales increase for a majority of markets.

You can increase your farmer and market income considerably and help low-income people learn to shop at a healthy place, where they can purchase produce with cash as well. Make sure farmers display signs stating, "We Accept EBT." If your farmers don't have individual machines, the market needs to process the requested amount from the customer's EBT card and give them market scrip, usually tokens.

Double SNAP programs

In 2005 NYC Department of Health and Mental Hygiene staff realized that they needed to incentivize people to shop for fresh fruits and vegetables at farmers' markets. With city money they provided shoppers in Harlem and the South Bronx with $4 of HealthBucks when they spent $10 of SNAP credit. Then a market in Lynn, MA, used a $500 donation for a similar food stamp-friendly effort in 2006.

By 2007, the idea mill began to work in earnest. The Crossroads Farmers' Market opened outside Washington, D.C., serving 70% customers who are Spanish-speaking. Gus Schumacher, a former top USDA official, received $5,000 from the National Watermelon Association to start the one-for-one doubling program. With chef Michel Nischan, he then started Wholesome Wave to assist doubling programs nationwide. Others followed.

Oran Hesterman created Fair Food Network to build Double Up Food Bucks with 50 partners, primarily foundations. From five Detroit markets in 2009, it expanded to 150 sites in 2014, serving 200,000 families and 1,000 farmers in 2013 alone, and giving a $5 million boost to Michigan's economy. Double Up has also been at the forefront of innovations in healthy food incentives, expanding the model

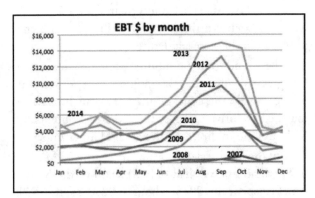

Farm Fresh Rhode Island's data reflects dramatic SNAP sales growth at farmers' markets in the first eight years since accepting SNAP in 2007.

to grocery stores and developing new mobile payment systems.

Roots of Change, with Specialty Crop Block Grant funding, conceived the California Market Match Consortium to assist growers, build consumer access and demonstrate the power of motivated community-based organizations. Within three years it aided 840 farmers and 37,000 federal benefit customers at 134 farmers' markets by linking partners in 16 counties. By 2012, they generated sales of $880,000 for 32% of all California certified producers, a 171% increase over 2010. They created a branding program for markets that allows for experimentation with varying match ratios. Even a 40% match – rather than 100% or 1-to-1 – has proven effective in attracting new EBT customers. The Market Match report is downloadable at:

www.RootsofChange.org/reports-resources/

reports-whitepapers/

When Roots of Change passed the torch, the Ecology Center led its farmers' market partners in developing the California Market Match Consortium to expand ROC's work. A $2.5 million grant from First 5 L.A., the result of Proposition 10's 50-cent cigarette tax, will allow Market Match to expand from 14 to 37 Los Angeles County markets by 2019. A Market Match Nutrition Incentive Program is being proposed in the state legislature.

These and other doubling programs impacted Congress to allocate $100 million over a five-year period to help these match programs, which must be matched by private funds; thus, there is potentially $200 million in direct consumer and farmer impact.

On the local scale, the Hub City Farmers' Market in Spartanburg, SC, had only $11,000 of the SNAP benefits spent in 2013, about 0.02% of the $61 million in SNAP money in the county. Recognizing the economic and public health need, they worked hard to connect farmers and SNAP users through a

California Market Match Consortium provides professional templates to 150 farmers' markets allowing them to promote Market Match. See www.marketmatch.org.

Double SNAP program designed with help from the United Way of the Piedmont.

In an interesting twist, on the first market visit they matched $.50 on every dollar debited, on the second visit $.75, and on the third and subsequent visits, they matched dollar for dollar up to $40 of card benefits (or $80 total).

The Department of Social Services helped create an additional program, Healthy Bucks, that gives a $5 token for fruits and vegetables when people debit $3 from their card. Together these programs increased the food buying power of SNAP families. Addressing the food deserts in their area, they also purchased and refitted a step-van in 2010. They purchase from farmers at their markets and take it to churches, schools, community centers, corporate offices and special events. In 2014 their farmers' market on wheels, know as Mobile Market, made 370 stops.

WIC Farmers' Market Nutrition Program (FMNP)

Established by Congress in 1992, FMNP serves WIC (Women, Infants and Children) recipients that meet income guidelines. In 2013 grants were awarded to 36 states, 4 territories and 6 tribal organizations. WIC coupons can be used directly with farmers to purchase fresh fruits, vegetables and edible herbs. Nutrition education is also provided through the local WIC agency along with Cooperative Extension, local chefs, farmers, markets or other nonprofits.

Agricultural Institute of Marin reinforces the program with a welcome to WIC mothers on its website at:

www.agriculturalinstitute.org/affordability/.

AIM also has posted price comparisons with local supermarkets on alternate years for both conventional and organic produce.

Senior Farmers Market Nutrition Program

The Senior FMNP similarly provides coupons between $20 and $50 to qualifying seniors through grants to states, territories and tribal governments, generally state-wide. These can be exchanged directly with farmers for fresh fruits, vegetables, honey and fresh-cut herbs.

Farmers Market Bingo became instrumental in rebuilding the Senior FMNP in Louisiana after Hurricane Katrina and it helped to develop a multi-faceted culture of incentivized public health change in the farmers' markets.

In Decorah, IA, it was initially coordinated by a dietician at a local hospital which gave "in kind" support through secretarial time, supplies, and printing of pamphlets. Public health nurses were involved in the distribution of coupons to their senior clients. Funded through United Way, farmers and seniors love it.

A participant survey indicated that 92% of the seniors increased their intake of fruits and vegetables as a result of the program, 72% used all of their coupons during the season, and 67% visited the farmers' market six or more times in the season.

[For senior nutrition resources, see Resources, Chapter 8, "Managing the Market."]

Many farmers' markets have active waste management programs; Portland even has a corporate sponsor. Santa Monica provides a clear vertical cylinder for customers to recycle their batteries.

Environmental Standards

Work with farmers to create agricultural systems that are more environmentally friendly. If your farmers are committed to certain policies, you may gain greater consumer acceptance. Find out if they have been approved by Food Alliance, Salmon Safe, Penn State Extension Friendly Farm Program or others with a rating system that acknowledges protection of natural resources, reduced chemical use, care for the welfare of workers, etc. As they build greater awareness of worker- and environmentally-friendly growing practices, including pheromone mating disruption and black lights to control codling moth, these organizations can promote our markets in educating and improving the system that feeds us all.

Those markets that allow coffee or other products produced globally are wise to encourage sourcing that encourages fair trade standards. Requiring a Fair Trade certification is a valuable statement to customers who care about a market's integrity.

Ask your farmers to provide specific, printed or visual information that will help educate consumers to the positive, environmental steps you are taking.

Washington State markets are environmentally conscious with 92% having good or excellent access for bicyclists and 65% having public transportation. Most feel they are reducing food miles and pollution, encouraging sound and organic farming practices, and educating and modeling sustainable practices. Over half do recycling, and one-in-five do composting.

The Long Beach FM (CA) has attracted bicycle consumers since 2013 with city-installed bike racks and Pedal Movement, a free private bicycle valet service that also offers free labor in doing minor maintenance and tuneup work while bicyclists are shopping.

MANAGEMENT ISSUES

As if "day-to-day" management concerns aren't enough, there are several on-going, broader issues that farmers' markets face.

Grants

There are several federal programs that are potential funding sources for markets. Most prominent is USDA's Farmers Market Promotion Program (FMPP) which supports farmers markets' and other direct producer-to-consumer activities. Awards range from $15,000 to $100,000 per proposal. With $13.3 million available, a total of 183 grants were awarded across 45 states in 2014 for market development, branding, CSA storefront, manager training, websites, marketing, EBT improvements and more

An equal amount is available under the Local Foods Promotion Program (LFPP) which supports enterprises that aggregate, store, distribute and process local and regional food. A 25% match is required. The planning grants can include market research, feasibility studies and business planning, with a range of $5,000 to $25,000. Implementation grants can include training, technical assistance, outreach, working capital and infrastructure improvements, with a range of $25,000 to $100,000.

USDA's Farm to School grants have $6 million in funding for planning, implementation, support services and training. It funded 221 projects between 2012 – 2014.

The largest portion of USDA's $97 million to expand access to healthy food and support rural economies is distributed by the states through $63.2 million in Specialty Crop Block Grants. Applications are done directly to your state department of agriculture or at:

www.ams.usda.gov/scbgp.

They usually require a large institutional partner. Review past grants awarded before considering an application.

Farmer Grown

Since the 1970s a new wave of farmers' markets has hit the country. By definition, farmers' markets are producer markets, meaning that vendors are also farmers. Yet, because they are not under corporate control, each has evolved with differing rules based on the goals of their creators. In some states regulation or law has impacted the type of vendors who may sell.

One major function is to support local farmers. Another is to provide customers with produce. These two functions sometimes can erupt as conflicting goals, leading to a philosophical and practical split within the ranks of farmers, managers and boards.

Producer-only

Those who favor a "producer-only" market see it as a means of supporting farmers by ensuring a fair and level playing field. Regulations are used to prevent or limit the selling of produce not grown by the vendor. Since resellers (peddlers, hawkers or high-stallers) may provide non-local produce or undercut the price of locally grown produce, their presence puts farmers at a competitive disadvantage. This regulatory perspective holds the high moral ground for agriculture in that:

+ Customers have greater faith in a producer-only marketplace;
+ Everyone appreciates the market's integrity and wants to tell friends;
+ Farmers analyze their own sales' techniques rather than blaming peddlers for low sales;
+ New people see product niches to fill;
+ Farmers educate the public about seasons and crop failures;
+ Farm organizations are more likely to support a program for farmers, and
+ There is a connection between farmers and consumers.

These people are likely to yell, "peddlers!" in disgust or point out that when a market has too many non-farmers, others take control and the farmer gets squeezed.

"The purpose of peddling is to increase the appeal to customers but it raises customers' expectations to unreasonable heights and creates a Safeway-like atmosphere where seasons and weather mean nothing."

– Clem Clay, Mgr., Berkeley FM, CA

They correctly show that farmers will have a tough time competing with wholesalers or peddlers who buy from any source without having to "take the good with the bad, like having a freeze or getting hailed out," according to Chris Burke, co-founder of Colorado Fresh Markets. Farmers can't compete with someone who can buy wholesale goods from areas with longer growing seasons and lower labor costs. Those people do not gamble with the unpredictability inherent in agriculture.

Peddlers Allowed

The other school of thought focuses on the primary function of farmers' markets as serving the customer with the greatest variety. Here, regulation that discourages resale is seen as protectionist, creating an artificial market that favors farmers and encourages high prices. Markets that favor deregulation believe it encourages free enterprise, allowing any type of vendor to respond with greater flexibility to customer desires and enabling the overall market to more effectively compete with other retailers. (This implies that a farmers-only market doesn't provide competition for the consumer's benefit.) The major arguments are that:

+ Peddlers are necessary because of limited, local produce supplies;
+ There is more variety when allowing re-sale;
+ Small producers are encouraged to sell products through cooperative arrangements;
+ Customers demand certain products not grown in the area; and
+ The disappearance of farms makes it difficult to maintain a base of home producers.

Markets on the extreme of this position may give a bad name to "farmers' market" by being more of a flea market with all kinds of products and sellers. Or

they may have one or two resellers who dominate the market, sourcing product nationally or even worldwide. However, most farmers' markets are not inclined to allow a free-for-all. They tend to feel pushed into allowing peddlers because of local agricultural conditions.

"The present-day realities of farming such as production and labor costs, and crop failures, etc., are putting pressures on the farmer… There might be consumer demand for a crop that requires equipment that is too costly for the farmer to purchase, for example. Rather than buy equipment, the farmer might purchase the crop from a neighboring farmer or from the wholesale market. Farmers are doing whatever they need to do to meet consumer demand and stay in business. Some markets are catering to a diversified crowd and allowing farmers to supplement what they grow, but this can destroy the markets by attracting hucksters who stop farming and only buy from the wholesale market."

– Al Smith, Mgr., D.C. Open-air FM, Washington, D.C.

It's a slippery slope. You want to help farmers so you let them buy to supplement their production. Soon you have people selling who are more hucksters than farmers.

Contrasting visions

The difference in these models is one of long-term vision versus short-term survival. Since both models have evolved worldwide for several millennia, neither school will necessarily win the debate; both will continue to discuss whether customers know or care if they're buying from the real McCoy.

The producer-only model has succeeded in major cities and small towns where organizers commit to the hard work of outreach. The consumer-oriented model has its proponents where distance, large growers, a small populace or limited local variety is the basis of vendors being allowed to buy outside products. They would like to be producer-only but can't see a way to survive with those restrictions. So, they lose the

Farmers can create immense displays of baby broccoli for $5 per pound in Santa Monica, giving many customers simultaneous access.

authenticity that gives the farmers' market its particular atmosphere and identity.

Some organizers suggest starting markets with a loose standard and reforming later. However, one might say, "once tainted, always unpure." Allowing peddlers because of "customer demand" may backfire in several ways. The standard that you set becomes familiar to your clientele. Why set the bar lower than you ultimately want it to be? You may set yourself up for a lawsuit by allowing, and then disallowing, resale vendors. If you bite the bullet and work hard doing outreach with every tool available, you may be surprised by the number of people who come forth to help build a truly local marketplace with real farmers. You also will avoid the label of being just another flea market encouraging hucksters and low quality. Reflect on your goals and the standards. The process will become clear.

Ultimately, markets often allow resellers because it is easier. Resellers can get almost anything they or the manager wants them to get. The Olympia, WA, market has had great success with good producers from a several-county local area. However, it allows two resellers to purchase produce from eastern Washington. Who knows how many more producers would be involved if outreach were done east of the mountains to replace the resellers? And would those farmers fill the voids on a consistent basis compared to the two very successful, and thus dependable, resellers? This consumer-oriented model actually protects resellers and hinders free market competition just as some argue that the farmer model protects farmers from the vagaries of a true open market.

Solutions

"Market quality seems to evolve to the level demanded by the consumer with some markets very quality conscious and others not. All markets are not the same in both product preference and product price. The most pernicious counterproductive element to damage markets is the buyer/reseller of products."

– Ron Enomoto, Enomoto Roses, Half Moon Bay, CA

Competition need not force price and quality downward if consumers in a local trade area demand quality. Your clientele are largely based on the way you position your farmers' market with a targeted advertising strategy, reflecting your values on quality and price.

To allow buying and selling opens the doors for farmers to be beaten. Yet, there is a difference of degree in allowing a farmer to buy off the wholesale market versus buy from or sell some product from neighboring farmers. In small, rural communities three or four organic growers may work together to get their products to distant farmers' markets or to maintain their presence in a small local market.

"Cooperative partnerships strengthen the community. At the market vendors cooperate to strengthen their businesses by selling each other's produce from time-to-time under a second certificate… This lets small-scale producers continue to market their produce at a certified farmers' market even when their production is too low to warrant their own direct participation. It also helps keep product diversity at the market."

– Comment from Laytonville, reported to have California's smallest farmers' market

Another option is to allow a member to buy an item to fill a product void, as in Camden, Maine. The member must have approval, must label it as bought and must wait for any other actual grower of that item to sell out. Somewhat north in the university town of

THE NEW FARMERS' MARKET

Orono, that solution was rejected in favor of a recruiting drive to fill the voids. Looking for farmers rather than re-sellers when you need a product makes sense to farmers. It encourages farmers to plan and expand their acreage or variety. It requires a manager who cares enough about the consumer to search out products in demand or encourage a farmer to grow a particular crop. It is not as easy as calling a re-seller or having a farmer buy product from afar. But it does lead to a local agriculture with greater crop diversity.

The farmer-grown model also makes it simpler to demand the same standard if you allow crafts. Conversely, if you allow peddling of produce, it is difficult to disallow peddled crafts from around the world. The market becomes an entity where the best seller wins, not the best farmer. If we want to stimulate a renaissance in all forms of local production, we need to give artisans of the soil and other materials the opportunity to present their craftwork to the public on a level economic playing field.

Enforcement

Most markets have a variety of consumer-oriented regulations. Some markets allow one farmer to sell for another while others permit a farmer to purchase a certain percentage of what they sell from another source. Some require that only the vendor sell his/her own production and others allow produce from various states and countries. Ensure that any limitation imposed on the vendor is actually followed, so that everyone knows they are playing by the same rules. This can be a major management challenge requiring a different set of rules and procedures, including inspections.

It's possible, though not easy, to change horses in mid-stream. Even with a 75%-your-own standard, the Hillsboro Farmers' Market in Oregon admittedly had a problem with enforcement. After fifteen years they were afraid of a lawsuit threat from one or two "growers" who seemed to be buying almost all their produce. Fortunately, in 1998 they began the Hillsboro Tuesday Marketplace in conjunction with the chamber and downtown business association. We pushed to establish a "producers only" standard for farmers and artisans in the new market. As a result the Satur-

day market later upgraded its standard. The threat of lawsuits never materialized.

Other markets operate under limitations of state law. Maine law requires market vendors to grow at least 75% of what they offer for sale. Individual markets can require that all products sold are grown, baked, or processed by the seller. Similarly, California law permits one farmer to sell product of another producer, but each market can require a higher standard, like 100%.

> "The farmer-grown issue is the hottest topic in our part of the world. Texas growing conditions are tough, and farmers have a hard time producing here, period. It's hard to compete with farmers' markets that are not truly farmers' markets, where the growers are reselling from the produce terminals. They call themselves farmers' markets but they're not farmers' markets at all. They mislead the public, and our state organization, the Texas Certified Farmers' Market Association, is in the process of bringing this issue to the Texas Department of Agriculture and seeing what we can do about truth in labeling."
> – Elizabeth Massey, grower, Sunset, TX

In the final analysis, the question of "producer-only" is not simply about standards, but enforcement. If a market allows farmers to bring 25% of their volume from a farmer up to three miles away or from within the same county, that standard is fair for everyone. The problem occurs when a farmer is bringing 10% his own production and buying the other 90% and management does nothing to stop it. Even a market that has a 100% grow-your-own rule is not exempt. One option is to have farmers sign an agreement saying they understand that they can lose their selling privilege, and then remove them when they break the rules. It's the only way to maintain farmer loyalty and consumer trust.

> "The producer-only image is a definite plus for the market. In Minneapolis I know there are some farmers' markets that include dealers, and we get lots of customers that drive over from Minneapolis to come to the St. Paul market

because they tell us they know that they are buying local here… One of the things managers really need to stay on top of is the rules and regulations of the market, and what the growers have signed up for in the spring that they will bring to the market, and what they're bringing to market now. We do field-checks, and people have to fill out an application every year and tell us what they're growing and how much, and when they expect to bring it to the market. So if there's any question about what they're bringing to the market, you can go and look at their application, and if it's not there, it had better be in the field. Because if you go out and check and it's not, there are major fines. The first infraction is $500, the second infraction is a year out of the market plus $500, and the third time you're gone."

– Patty Brand, Exec. Dir., Friends of the St. Paul FM, MN

Set up your rules so that violators pay for your inspection program. Listen to farmers when they complain about corn appearing at the market in May. Make some phone calls. Some markets have hired other managers to save money on long-distance inspections. State conferences and workshops on integrity are a great place to build relationships with others who share the goal of protecting farmers through an inspection-based protocol. By caring, you show respect for the vision of your governing body's standards.

Commitment follows vision. Consider your organization's purpose in promoting a regional agricultural system that serves local farms and the community. If you focus only on the consumer, you may be short-sighted and diminish your chances of truly influencing farmers' attempts at sustainability. We can all do our part to keep them on the land.

California law

Consumers across California and managers across the nation took note in 2010 when NBC-LA revealed a 3-month undercover investigation of misrepresentations by "growers" at Los Angeles farmers' markets. The Los Angeles County Agricultural Commissioner,

who could only claim four small instances of wrongdoing, became serious and within several years cited 66 cheaters with fines up to $6,600 each, as well as 16 suspensions and proposed suspensions.

Responding to farmers' market industry pressure, the legislature passed AB 1871, which provides a new level of enforcement in California with $1.35 million – more than three times the current level – of revenue as farmers pay $2 instead of $.60 daily along with their space fees. Rural markets allowing only their county's farmers can petition CDFA for a $1 fee. From 2016 onward, other food and craft vendors at farmers' markets pay as well. The additional funds are slated for new state inspectors, a market and grower database, and investigations at the county level.

"This is the single most significant change to farmers' market laws since they were established in 1977."

– Ben Feldman, Program Manager, Berkeley FM, and Chair, California Alliance of FMs

Consumers can expect to see more inspectors at farmers' markets, ensuring that growers are producing what they sell. As cheaters are caught, fined or suspended, shoppers will regain trust in the markets they have loved for local producers. No fresh whole fruit, nuts, vegetables or flowers will be allowed in adjacent non-agricultural sections where markets sometimes have added products from outside the state or country. This especially pleases flower growers competing with South American flowers.

Growers must now post a sign with their farm name, location and the key statement, "We grew what we are selling." The fraudulent use of the term "California grown," including products harvested in surface or coastal waters, is now a misdemeanor punishable by a fine up to $2,500 or imprisonment up to six months, or both. Alternately, CDFA or a county agricultural commissioner may level a civil penalty of $500 to $5,000 per violation. Markets also may contract with a county agricultural commissioner for field or storage inspections of their producers.

Markets in major cities like Los Angeles, San Diego, San Francisco and San Jose now have a viable, funded enforcement method. Agricultural commissioners in rural counties now have the funding to make timely farm visits.

Local

Whole Foods Market began defining "local." It had mini-signs, attached by velcro to larger price signs, which proclaimed that the product was grown within 150 miles or a given state. They color coded signs indicating "organic" or "conventional" production techniques. Quite adroitly, they recognized customers' desire for more information, and tried to build trust in their program.

Esther Kovari, former president of the New Mexico Farmers' Marketing Association, notes, "One advantage the markets can play up is to promote the locally grown issue, because the natural food stores aren't buying much local." As Whole Foods Market swallowed their natural foods competitors, they took on the major food chain mentality of buying from larger producers. They have tried to balance that tendency with regional specialty food buyers who are attuned to local production.

A voluminous Satsuma mandarin display is needed when sampling CCOF certified organic in Los Angeles. In most states an organic certification can be part of the market enforcement mechanism.

Your market needs a significant selling edge over supermarkets. Ask yourself how you can draw customers for whom the supermarket is an easier shopping experience. If your competition is open 24/7 and your farmers' market is open only four hours on one or two days each week, what advantages do you offer? Fresh produce can be brought in from Chile but you can promote "local" with a definition that will make shoppers into converts. Disallowing "imports" promotes local agriculture and aids the regional economy. A mileage limit on where any product can come from is even more specific for shoppers.

The Ithaca Farmers' Market limits sellers to a 35-mile radius. This guarantees "local" is queen of the market. When such measures are enacted and enforced, they can serve to:

- Promote value-added processing as farmers and others look to expand selection;
- Guard against long-distance competitors with unknown labor standards or subsidized production inputs;
- Invigorate creativity as entrepreneurs realize they can compete on a local level;
- Guarantee quality because of social pressures;
- Increase the likelihood of inspections of the farm or production facility;
- Assure consumers they are re-circulating dollars in a local economy; and
- Build stronger social ties among producers and between them and customers.

On the other hand, certain areas with a population base aren't necessarily perfect for diverse production. The Astoria Sunday Market, begun in 2000 at the mouth of the Columbia River, invited farmers and artisans from both Oregon and Washington. While 70% of the producers were local, some growers came as far as 300 miles one-way from the Yakima Valley. The commitment to "producers only" brought out many local artisans and is contributing to increased production locally as farmers realize they have a transportation advantage.

If producers come from a wider area, the market may be buffered from localized weather disruptions. However, the manager will have a greater challenge doing enforcement. No matter what the geographical range, farmers' markets can use their "local" standard as a marketing tool to attract customers well aware of the downside of our global economy.

The reason some customers support natural food stores with standards is because they want to trust a marketplace. They don't have time to review every issue. They want to come to a place where they can buy confidently, where there is a clear set of values. Some farmers' markets know this kind of consumer is the segment of the market they're shooting for. Others believe that customers don't care where the product came from; they're focused on price. If that's your market perspective, that will be the kind of customer you will get. While every market is entitled to its own values, some enthusiasts wish there were tighter, legal, "local" standards, including limitations for those using the term "farmers' market."

Supermarket Competition

"The dinosaur is turning its head around."

According to Tony Manetta, former director of New York City's Greenmarket program, farmers' markets are going to have to hustle to stay on the leading edge of supermarket competition. "Twenty years ago a ripe tomato was exotic," Manetta says. "Now the supermarkets are carrying super-sweet corn and low-priced greenhouse tomatoes from Holland, Canada and Mexico, organic lettuce mixes from Dole, and mushrooms like shiitake and oyster, and our markets have a challenge to meet in staying special. Differentiating ourselves from supermarket competition has become a major issue."

It depends on the local market area. Along the central coast of California, 30-year farmers' market administrator Peter Jankay feels that, "the supermarket can't possibly provide all the unique varieties people find at the farmers' markets, and certainly not the quality. You might find lemon grass in little packets at the supermarket but you won't find the beautiful, foot-long leaves of lemon grass that this one grower brings to the market."

That comparison epitomizes the difference between a large city and a small town. Farmers' markets have more strenuous competition in the cities with sophisticated customers demanding new varieties and superb attention to detail no matter where they shop.

"The supermarkets are getting more variety as well as produce that looks good and tastes like something, but unfortunately that has been done mostly through genetics rather than buying local.

I've recently seen some very interesting things in the supermarkets like beta-caratene enhanced carrots out of Texas A&M. It's really beautiful – it's a maroon carrot that's gorgeous, and to see this at a supermarket before I see it at the farmers' market caused me to pause.

"It's like the dinosaur got hit on its tail 20 years ago, and it's finally turned its head around. Some New York supermarkets are doing a superb job in changing the image of what supermarket produce is like. I see more good quality, more diversity, and the kind of attention to detail that I only used to see in farmers' markets."
– Tony Manetta, former Director, Greenmarket, New York, NY

Marin County Farmers' Market founder Lynn Bagley, an early pioneer and leader in Bay Area markets, sees a downward cycle:

"The farmers are stressed. The more markets there are, the more the supermarkets copy the farmers' markets. More farmers in each market also leads to increased competition, so the farmers make less money and have to go to more markets. They can't seem to find the time to do the things that bring people to the farmers' markets in the first place, like being on the leading edge of product variety and quality.

"Stores have gotten quite competitive, and in some cases they are introducing varieties that are not yet available to farmers' markets. New products almost always used to be introduced at the farmers' markets; now there is much more crossover. Products like mesclun mixes and fuji apples, and white varieties of nectarines and peaches...we had these five years in the markets before they hit the supermarkets.

"Even the flower vendors are not as creative as they used to be… You'll see unusual varieties at the supermarkets that are not even in the farmers' markets. I bought a very unusual mum at the supermarket the other day that I've never seen at the farmers' markets – a beautiful lavender mum with a yellow center – and things like that never used to happen. Excuse the pun but with flowers it's the status quo at the farmers' markets. Wreath-making should be more artistic, more interesting and more unusual at the farmers' markets than anything you could find anywhere, yet it seems that there is not the level of care with wreath-making that there used to be. When you lose that you lose everything."

– Lynn Bagley, Dir., Golden Gate FM Assoc., Novato, CA

One way Bagley suggests to arrest the downward spiral of quality and competition is to work closely with restaurants. "There's a lot of creativity going on the in the food industry with the chefs and restaurateurs. The chefs are mixing foods from different ethnic groups and preparing food in a synergistic way from lots of different styles of cooking, such as back-to-the-country cuisine. All these styles of cooking are infusing creativity and the quality is very, very high. That's how the mesclun craze got started – with a farmer working with a restaurant."

"Over-expansion nearly always kills quality," Bagley continues. "The markets are too consumed with the money and they're losing the meaning and purpose of the markets... They're cutting corners and in the end it will also downgrade the economic viability of the markets, when customers no longer feel there's any difference between the markets and the supermarkets."

Tony Manetta offers his solution:

"We've been telling growers that they have basically two cards left to play. The first is the heirloom varieties... It's the sheer novelty of what's coming into the markets that's keeping customers coming back. The supermarkets are starting to display some heirloom varieties, but the quality is often very poor – it's seems it's there strictly for show. The other aspect of the farmers' markets that the supermarkets will never have it is the farmers themselves. Farmers being on-site is a critical component of the market, yet as the markets grow, we're seeing more and more employees at the market rather than the farmers themselves. We feel there is an impact in not having the direct connection with the customer."

Superior local product and exemplary customer service by farmers are two advantages that farmers' markets must use to the fullest.

Manetta continues: "Some supermarkets are trying to get in on the locally-grown angle, and if they are really doing that, bless them... The reason they're doing this is because they understand business, and they know that this is what people are looking for. So the dinosaur has evolved; the supermarkets are responding quicker and evolving faster than they used to."

"It gets back to consumer education. Do we want local, fresh produce, or corporate-grown food heavily laden with chemicals that's been on a truck for three weeks?"

– Lynn Bagley, Dir., Golden Gate FM Assoc., Novato, CA

"I hope to beat the supermarkets on customer service. Markets need to start going the extra mile and help people park and carry their bags out. And the farmers need be on the front line of service with courtesy and customer service. The supermarket can't have 30 people behind the tables waiting on you, smiling, and saying, 'Come back next week!'"

– Mark Sheridan, former Mgr., Santa Barbara FM Assoc., CA

Competition within your market, and the resultant choices for consumers, may be your greatest advantage over supermarkets. While they offer only one or two varieties of tomatoes, you may have three or a dozen tomato sellers with 30 tomato varieties!

Design your rules to encourage other farmers' market "advantages," such as premium quality, one-day fresh, and a friendly social experience.

Price may be another advantage which markets in certain areas should emphasize. The same corn that Charlie & Vicki Hertel sell 4-for-$1 in Portland, OR, sells at 8-for-$1 in their hometown Hillsboro market less than 30 miles west. When the cannery is paying only a penny an ear, even that hometown bargain price brings the Hertels a great profit by comparison.

Not all supermarkets are competitors. Various smaller operators, usually family-owned, have allowed farmers' markets in their parking lots. Williams Brothers allowed one to operate in Morro Bay, CA, for 12 years. Customers bought strawberries at the farmers' market and their canned goods and milk in the supermarket. Then the supermarket decided to develop the property. Six months later, the store admitted that Saturday had been their busiest day and they wanted the farmers back. Spencers Market now hosts the market.

> "There are some things that the supermarkets will never be able to compete with us on, such as product freshness. Then there's the pickup trucks at the markets and the whole ambiance of the farmers being there, and the opportunity to ask the growers: 'How did you to grow this?' and 'When did you plant it?' This is impossible to do at supermarkets. People come here to talk and to see friends and to visit and there's a whole social fabric that's developed."
> – Peter Jankay, Admin., San Luis Obispo County FM Assoc., CA

All seem to agree on a few advantages where we can capitalize: market ambiance, unparalleled freshness, innovation through new varieties and unique processed goods, customer service, education and the farmers themselves. Most of our superior position relies on the degree to which farmers take pride in creating new products, providing knowledge unmatched by a stockboy, talking about their farms and giving people a direct connection to the land.

Competition Within the Market

When one farmer brings a small volume of peas or corn and sells out quickly, he may feel threatened by a competitor recruited by the manager. However, the manager needs to focus on pleasing customers so they tell their friends that the market is a reliable place for purchases. This competition factor is more powerful than many farmers, concerned about their own financial welfare, may be willing to admit. True free market competition is one of the reasons customers become loyal to farmers' markets versus the supermarket, which only has one source of lacinato kale, for example. A good manager ensures that competition exists and educates the farmer to the fact that overall market sales increase with a more competitive market. That makes for contented customers and leads to the continual development of new product opportunities in a constantly changing rather than stagnant market. This is the pre-eminent advantage of the best farmers' markets.

Do you limit the number of apple or tomato growers or do you let the market dictate? A laissez faire approach may be best. Like the manager of a wholesale produce market, you need not control product supply and demand. Let every grower have free and equal access and let the consumer enjoy the result of fair competition.

In other words:

> "Don't look at farmers' markets like clubs. Make room for new growers."
> – A farmers' market manager

Many other managers take a more protectionist tact, often due to farmer pressure. Especially with board member pressure or board policy, a manager is hard-pressed to advocate an open market. Yet the market may suffer. If the consumer is finding less competition and fewer options of variety, quality and price, they may not be as enthusiastic in their word-of-mouth encouragement of other customers.

> "Fair and healthy competition is what creates the market. The opportunity to choose between two or three tomato growers is what brings customers to the market. It's like a shopping mall – if

Who's the Competition

Focus on the bigger picture. See the forest, not just the trees. Together we are a market. We compete in a world of markets. Our main competition is with the major grocery store and discount food outlets, not with each other.

The primary competitive edge that we have over the grocery stores is that we have a number of different farmers and give a number of choices for the same product. Sure we talk about vine-ripened and tree-ripened quality, but the primary distinction we can make over our competition is that the customer has more than one choice.

Our success is built on the promotion that we are the "shopping mall of farmers," the one-stop shopping for locally grown produce. We are in competition with the grocery store for the type of customer who wants a choice.

Customers who don't care about more than one choice will always shop at the grocery store. Grocery stores are convenient and quick shopping. We are not. At our farmers' markets customers need cash, have to pay at each stand, walk around with multiple bags, take many trips to the car, shop during our time schedule, brave the weather, and on and on. The types of customers who come to our markets are not just after quick and convenient. These people are shoppers!

Again, we are a "shopping mall of farmers." A full market of farmers attracts and keeps more customers. If you have ever been to a shopping mall which is dying, you will see a couple of big stores and a lot of vacant little shops. Slowly the customer base falls down to the point that even the big stores leave. Where do they go? They move to successful malls which have no vacancies and all their little shops are full. Successful malls that are drawing the customer by providing them what they want. Many choices. A shopping experience.

We all have to promote the merits of the market for it to be successful. Let's keep the competition within the markets friendly and positive. Don't disparage each other, especially within earshot of customers. We are a market of many good choices. Where else can the customer get so many good choices? Certainly not at a grocery store.

– *Renae's Rutabaga,* April 1999, Renae Best, Sacramento Certified FMs, CA

you've got several stores selling dresses, you're going to have a lot of dress shoppers."

– Another farmers' market manager

Rules and procedures help a manager determine who is admitted. Some require on-farm site visits. Markets establish waiting lists and prioritize those with new and different crops over those who have more of the same as existing growers. One goal is to avoid too much competition within any category. "Too much" depends on the eye of the beholder. When you let growers into the market without rhyme or reason, you are being disloyal to the farmers who are there; they may react by going to another market as soon as they can. On the other hand, if you don't allow for any additions or changes, you may not be responsive to customer desires and you may lose them. Finding the right path between these extremes of farmer protection versus consumer service is where a manager shows true management finesse.

In some markets the limitation on the physical range or geography of vendors is based on the desire to serve local farm interests and limit competition from afar. This is quite valid if codified in the organization's rules and bylaws. However, this cannot happen under California law that allows any California farmer to sell at any certified farmers' market. For example, Santa Barbara cannot stop a Butte County pistachio producer from coming 400 miles to compete with a home-county grower, even the board president.

Managers may limit participation, and thus competition, based on physical limitations of the market, a waiting list, seniority or any means that guarantees fair and equal treatment. Grower challenges to poor policies or implementation will continue pushing management to higher operational standards.

In the process managers realize they are the lubricant between farmer and consumer. They must strive to represent the interests of both groups, much as a Department of Food and Agriculture, by its name, indicates its concern for both consumers and farmers.

Market Proliferation

"Too many farmers' markets everywhere. Farmers are stretched too thin."
– Dale C. Whitney (RIP), former Mgr., Harbor Area FMs, Long Beach, CA

The popularity of California's 800+ certified farmers' markets has brought problems. With more than 130 markets in Los Angeles County alone and big numbers in the nine-county Bay Area, many farmers and managers have complained for decades

How One Manager Makes Issues Look Easy

The Dane County Farmers' Market (DCFM) is the largest farmers' market in the U.S. with over 300 vendors stretching all around the two block, state capitol square in Madison, Wisconsin. About 25,000 people come to the market each Saturday in a city of 200,000, and recently-retired market manager Mary Carpenter attributes the market's phenomenal attendance to several factors. Its customer base is "middle class to affluent," and the market is close to the University of Wisconsin at Madison, one of the largest universities in the country. "It's a very health conscious city," Carpenter says. "The university was one of the most radical campuses in cities in the 60s, and I think the market has bloomed into a great farmers' market."

Another factor in the market's success is that its customers include a wide variety of ethnic groups. For example, about 10% of the market vendors at the market are Hmong. Carpenter says she feels the market's vendor base should reflect people who are growing and producing crops and reflect local agriculture.

There is a two-year waiting list for qualified persons wishing to join the market. After about ten years as "daily vendors" members may graduate to "season stall" status which allows them to have the same assigned spot each week. Only about 40% of vendors have "season stalls"; thus, more than half the vendors must arrive by 6 a.m. to line up by seniority. At 6:30 these "daily vendors" drive onto the square in an orderly manner and claim any open space, including any "season stalls" vacant that day. "We have 20 to 30 new vendors coming in each year from the waiting list," Carpenter adds.

"They help bring fresh ideas to the market."

The DCFM is strictly foods, flowers and fibers; no crafts are allowed at the market. Even flowers can be sold only as flowers, not with bows or ribbons. "Variety is what brings customers to the market," Carpenter says. "One vendor brings 200 different kinds of herbs."

The market is run on a free-market basis, rather than having a lot of rules and regulations about product quality. Carpenter feels market competition encourages and even demands that growers bring their best, what customers want. "You don't get away with bringing seconds or poor produce because so many growers have great produce at the market."

One market rule that is enforced firmly is the strict "farmer-grown" policy. Resellers

about the oversaturation of farmers' markets. The overabundance forces farmers to sell at more markets without substantially increasing their take-home income. And it isn't just in California.

> "Every community wants a farmers' market, so anyone who opens within a 100 miles of us will be competing with us for farmers."
> – Ginger Rapport, Market Master, Beaverton FM, OR

It is not surprising that competition between markets has developed in numerous areas. Yet we need to remember that we are working together to build a consciousness about buying at farmers' markets instead of other retailers. Here is what can happen:

+ A neighborhood group starts a market two or three miles from an existing market to serve a specific ethnic, low income or other population.

+ An ideological or managerial break occurs within a market leading some vendors to start another market close-by. Experience shows that the new market has more hurdles than the established one, unless the new market has deep financial pockets.

are strictly forbidden at the market; everything sold has to be raised by the vendor, and they can be booted out of the market for violations. Each vendor is required to sign a contract that allows the market to do a drop-in inspection at any time, for any reason. If the vendor refuses to allow an inspection, they are automatically expelled. "If a person is selling eggplant and they don't show me the eggplant in the field, they're out," Carpenter says. "It has been years, however, since a grower refused an on-farm inspection. In fact, they are always very proud of what they grow and are anxious to show off their operations. We've had only one or two expulsions a year of people reselling product."

When asked if such a strict to farmer-grown policy could work in a small-town, start-up market where some managers claim the need to relax the farmer-grown rules in order to diversify the market, Carpenter has an interesting answer: "Personally I wouldn't manage any other type of market. We started with 11 vendors. They would get demands and they would do whatever it took to grow it. They could not depend on bringing it in from somewhere else. And the market just grew naturally."

The DCFM has developed a unique solution to the "big vs. small farmer" issue when small growers feel outgunned by big growers renting multiple booth spaces. Each vendor is given a 16-foot maximum frontage, which levels the playing field. "It also encourages vendors to be very creative in their marketing," Carpenter says. "We don't want someone's bank account dictating how much space they have – 16 feet is the absolute limit."

Another factor that contributes to the market success, Carpenter feels, is that the organization has a board of entirely vendor members. "We're an independent, self governing, nonprofit organization. When it's a self-governing body, you listen to people. We're dealing with our own problems and we don't have to explain them to people who don't understand what we're doing. The board is very independent and responsive to vendor needs, and active people tend to attend board meetings."

Bounty from bounty, the market supplies 11 food banks every Saturday. "At 11:30 a.m. the food bank people come by with carts, and a lot of growers say 'take the table' and some even bring some extra for that purpose," Carpenter says. In addition, every fall a large charity dinner is held to support the food bank. The market donates the raw goods, top Madison chefs cook the food, food bank volunteers serve, and all the proceeds from a $14 dinner go to the food banks.

Does Carpenter have any management tips to pass along? "Only that you deal with things with a sense of humor," Carpenter laughs. "And it doesn't hurt that I was a teacher." ஐ

- A shopping mall uses substantial resources to kick start a market and lure customers from their competitors.
- A downtown business association feels business slipping away to malls, with or without a market, and commits members' contributions to start a new market, in order to boost waning customer counts.

The variety of scenarios is limitless; new markets cannot be stopped. We need to more creatively market our markets to survive the inevitable development and winnowing of markets.

Markets in close proximity are problematic for farmers who feel forced to sell at more markets to gross the same volume as they did with fewer markets. The customer base is being split, but it is also growing. Vendor sales per market may drop, but who is to play God and determine which markets are allowed? Open-air markets have the competitive edge in flexibility; they can respond quickly to demographic shifts in a city. They may move to a new site, draw more minority vendors or otherwise reflect the new local character.

> "Keep the markets worthwhile to the growers. Don't expand markets so fast and dilute them so much that the farmer has to go to seven markets a week to make a living selling at farmers' markets. Educate customers to build a customer base."
>
> – Another market manager

Most sectors of the economy are flexing in response to the competition with lightning speed. High tech firms are changing course weekly rather than annually. Farmers' markets aren't protected from these rapid changes. If there are too many markets in an area, the weakest will be sifted out as farmers become dissatisfied with low sales, or they will continue with a committed mix of farmers and customers who appreciate the charm and intimacy.

In 1989 there were claims that much of Los Angeles County had reached near saturation with two dozen markets. The number doubled in the 90s, even faster in the early 2000s. In July 2015 there were 142 listed on the L.A. Times website. The volume of total sales also grew substantially. The industry may feel a certain squeeze play is on, but it is no different than that felt among the supermarkets and their competitors, the big box stores and specialty retailers.

We have not reached the end of our expansion phase, never mind the settling-out phase. This occurs among supermarkets as well. During 2000 seven new supermarkets were built in Clark County, WA, (co-author Vance's home). Seven independents went under. With this "replacement" the largest supermarkets consolidated a greater share of the market, exacerbated by mergers. The result threatens midsize farmers and wholesalers, since produce contracts are primarily with larger farms.

By contrast, an ever increasing number of players easily enters the democratic world of farmers' markets and helps it expand, albeit with some negative consequences. We had better stop complaining about competition within the farmers' market world and begin squarely facing the challenge of finding and keeping customers that will otherwise be siphoned away by the huge retailers. We had also best realize that there will be a shaking down of our industry as we reach saturation, yet find ourselves faced with still more new farmers' market development.

One in five California market managers says that finding new vendors is one of their greatest challenges. The good news is that four in five don't think it is so critical, so perhaps the issue is how many customers you have in your market. Somehow it seems that all the strong markets have a waiting list trying to get in. If a market is weak, it may be a cop-out to put the blame on not enough farmers.

Yes, in certain areas farmer recruitment is a problem, but market after market has been able to encourage new entry farmers and other food producers because they created a demand. What producers need to see is a workable plan to increase supply and demand simultaneously.

There is no practical way to stop the creation of additional markets. The consumer clamor for easier access brings yet another market into existence. No one really knows which markets are meant to be successful over the long haul. A new one may do a better job and cause an old market to improve or slip quietly out of existence. If given areas are oversaturated with farmers' markets, we must admit that this "problem" results from the success of our own movement. Market associations in some cities are agreeing to hold back on development. While this may work, we can be sure that individual preferences and market forces – neither ever static – will bring about a balance which constantly changes over time. This reactivated farmers' market reality is relatively young.

Farmer & Public Education

Organize a Friends of the Market nonprofit group. This is a great vehicle for educating everyone in the community about the real concern of maintaining ag land in your area or keeping farmers viable on it. Elevating the knowledge level of consumers, you will create goodwill, loyalty to the market and greater understanding of farmer issues.

When legislation or regulation is being considered – an urban growth boundary, a sale of an urban farm, run-off standards, spraying practices, right-to-farm, organic statutes, purchase of development rights (PDRs), transfer of development rights (TDRs), the forced relocation of your market or any other issue – a Friends group can help raise awareness.

> "With The Friends of the Farmers' Market program, we do educational programs to train and encourage farmers, as well as help raise public awareness about the importance of farming. The existence of farm land around our towns is very critical to the quality of life here."
> – Esther Kovari, former president, New Mexico Farmers' Marketing Assoc.

Farmers or market people can lead the way. Gerald Bentryn, a Bainbridge Island, WA, farmer, decided to help protect the remaining farmland on the island and printed bumper stickers to advocate purchases of Puget Sound Fresh produce. Down in Goleta, CA, Michael Ableman created a nonprofit to purchase an urban farm, largely through educational and financial outreach efforts. A Friends group can do much the same, helping preserve urban farmland or assisting farmers in maintaining their way of life in the face of land or regulatory pressures.

Large-Scale Farmers

Admitting large-scale farmers is a volatile, underlying issue in various markets. The Los Angeles Times weighed in on the subject (Melinda Fullmer, May 7, 2000). One of California's largest fruit growers, with 232 varieties and 650 acres of fruit, used a refrigerated warehouse, a fleet of trucks, four supervisors and a small army of helpers to cover various southern California markets. In Torrance alone the operation was moving more than $10,000 worth of fruit on a Tuesday.

Farmers and organizers feel that the main purpose of farmers' markets is to help keep small farms viable. On the other hand, larger producers often provide the steady volume over a long season that is critical for the market's own survival. It is the same sustainability issue, for vendors and markets, which we face with the question of including peddlers. The challenge is to organize and involve enough small-scale producers to make your market viable for the consumer. Yet, limited to only small farms, the market may never realize its true potential for growth.

> "We feel the market needs a mix of smaller and larger growers. It's like in a mall, you have the anchors, larger growers who offer a large volume of products, and smaller growers who bring in exotics which generally aren't grown on larger acreage."
> – Jack Gerten, Pres., St. Paul FM Assoc., MN

An organic apple grower may get $80 a box for Granny Smiths instead of barely covering costs with a $30 wholesale price. Many large growers estimate their returns at 40% to 80% more for their crop, often selling higher than chain store prices.

Of the 5,000 California growers involved in farmers' markets, the great majority are small producers. As large growers become more prevalent and take home big incomes, the people who built the system are feeling the pinch.

One privately-funded farmers' market study found that 87.7% of the association's vendors were small producers under the USDA definition of $250,000 in annual sales or less. They were doing a great job of including mainly small farmers and food producers. One in every eight vendors have been successful in moving out of the "small" category, even though they still may have the same small-acreage farm or processing facility. Medium and large farmers have more product to move and can participate in more markets, so they have a larger share of total farmers' market sales. Markets can still heed a cautionary note in fulfilling their small-farm mission.

Managers need to be careful not to see their markets overwhelmed before they realize it. Large farms often can create huge displays and sell volume at lower prices, out-competing smaller growers. A grower doing $3,000 in a market may displace five or more local producers. As a manager, you don't have to give up. Limit the display space, no matter what size the grower. Any space limit is fair for everyone. Managers sometimes get lured into huge spaces for growers because they want to fill the market or they receive revenue based on footage. Find a proper balance.

Smaller growers should accentuate their small scale advantages. As Ali Edwards of Fan Tan Farm in Santa Cruz, CA, says, "I see the farmers' markets and CSAs as an alternative to industrial agriculture. The market is one place where small farms have an advantage." Managers need to teach farmers: if you are sitting on your tailgate, you have no right to complain about unfair competition from a large grower. Create colorful signage, build first-name relationships with your customers, re-arrange your display periodically to create visual interest, provide superior service with written and verbal recipes, and sample your products aggressively. Use photos of your farm on each price sign inside a plastic sleeve or enlarge one farm photo to 2x3 feet to set a tone for your display.

It seems difficult to define small farm under the USDA definition and exclude larger growers. How would you preclude someone using that standard and avoid litigation? The more successful your market, the more likely that larger growers will try to get in unless there are strong social and peer pressures for them to stay out or the customer base is substantially educated to small farm preservation and willing to purchase accordingly.

> "Some people feel that the markets are for smaller growers because larger growers have other outlets. People have different shopping tastes. I feel larger growers can add to the market if they don't come in and cut prices and go for volume over quality and uniqueness. That creates a problem in the market. Some markets work very well with large producers. Our vendors voted to have a sliding scale for all vendors rather than a flat fee for booth spaces. The bigger growers voted also to have a sliding scale fee even though they pay $90 to $140 a day, because a flat fee would bring all big growers to the market and invite fiercer competition for them."
>
> – Randii MacNear, Mgr., Davis FM, CA

Managers want farmers with quality and consistency throughout a season. Farmers in turn want assurance that managers won't let in competitors with the same crops, or at least not without warning, so they can scale back their load.

If growers are selling out of a certain product, it's natural for a manager to be concerned for the consumer. Ask if they can bring additional product; if not, let them know you may solicit other growers with that product. A manager doesn't want a grower always trying to finish the market day sold out. That can create a downward spiral as consumers at the end of the day find little product and stop coming, the grower cuts back even more on volume, and other customers get disenchanted. Instead, we need to remember that the consumer has a choice of markets to shop. If we don't offer quality, volume, selection, atmosphere and personal service, we may lose the consumer altogether.

Farmers' market managers, just like supermarket managers, should know all the products available. That means they need to know when a grower wants to bring in a new item or one that duplicates what others have. It is a great challenge to decide the total mix and competition levels that lead to the best growth for the market. Managers must be sensitive to the concerns of individual vendors, yet maintain an overall focus on their customers, with enough product even for end-of-day shoppers. Ultimately, they are governing what many would characterize as organized chaos.

> "We have a large-scale grower at our market, and in my opinion they are not a threat to the other growers. Their stuff just isn't that good! Our Association's membership recently voted for more stringent regulations regarding farmers being at the market. As it stands now, the farmer has to be there in person once every quarter and growers feel that it should be more often. This ruling might nip the corporate farmer right in the bud, because they often can't be there more than once a quarter."
> – Mark Sheridan, former Mgr., Santa Barbara FM Assoc., CA

> "We realized years ago that farmers who pay a percentage of their sales were under-reporting. We implemented periodic booth audits where we put a staffperson in their booth to track their sales. It's worked for us, so other markets in the area are now doing the same thing."
> – Laura Avery, FM Supervisor, City of Santa Monica, CA

Backyard Market Gardeners

For any grower a backyard gardener may be like a fly on the nose – a constant irritant. Worse yet, in the minds of some Davis Farmers' Market growers a few years back, was a local dentist who wanted to do something positive for the community. He brought in some tomatoes from his garden, sold them at 10 cents a pound and donated all the proceeds to his church. Local growers felt he was undercutting them unfairly.

> "It's not all pie in the sky at the farmers' markets from a larger grower's perspective. You can't compete on prices with hobby or backyard growers who don't depend on the markets for a living."
> – Rick Noffke, Collins Produce LLC, Neenah, WI

In most cases, however, it seems that tiny producers are contributing to their own income while bringing a specialty product to the market and giving it an extra dose of personality. They have much more time to spend with customers, and that's good since some customers want the attention.

> "We love backyard farmers. Growing is a hobby or a passion for them and they give us a variety at the market that is not available otherwise. At our market you can find orchids or hardy banana trees, all grown by hobbyists. If someone has what I want and if they have the proper licenses, I let them in. The commercial growers don't seem to complain because they know it's variety that brings people to the market."
> – Ginger Rapport, Market Master, Beaverton FM, OR

If your backyard gardeners step on the toes of growers making a living, establish a minimum price. Growers can barely survive selling to the wholesale market, so a figure somewhere over wholesale price seems reasonable. The Yakima Farmers' Market set that minimum price at 60% over wholesale.

> "I have no problem with the market grower, because there's people that have an eighth of an acre, and they're serious about making a living from it. But then there's the person with a lemon tree and some rhubarb and they want to sell at the market. They often have seniority from having sold at the market, and they do lend character to the market, but they can be a problem for other growers who need to make a living."
> – Mark Sheridan, former Mgr., Santa Barbara FM Assoc., CA

Most farmers' market managers realize the importance of keeping gardeners involved – for the character of the market, the customer care, the unusual varieties and to provide a way for people to test their ability and interest in starting to farm more seriously. Numerous markets include community gardening groups who share a table as in Hillsboro, OR, while others allow farmers and gardeners to drop off product and have it sold for them by the market. Down in Eugene and Corvallis a considerable quantity moves at the community table, which charges about 30%

commission. That's another way to make sure it's not too cheap.

Market Mix

As with the farmer-only proponents, there are those who believe a farmers' market should have only produce, without any processed goods, crafts or other non-agricultural items. They argue that customers only bring so much money that rightly should go to farmers. They may feel that "crafts can be a cancer" which spreads until they overrun the farmers. Especially with processed goods, what they may truly want is some assurance that any of these other products are produced with the same family labor as they put into their produce.

> "If you allow crafts in a market, it becomes a crafts market and overruns the market. Non-ag producers try to come in and get rich quick, and if they don't, then they leave and you're stuck."

A second group favoring inclusion of crafts and processed foods, if not more, argues that we need to give customers an even fuller shopping experience. The market suffers if a florist manages to prohibit the market selling cut flowers or if it doesn't have oranges that are farmed locally. By the same token, we should allow – nay, encourage – other small businesspeople who happen to work with local foods, fibers or other materials to make a living.

The same purist standard can be applied if the market requires that everything be produced by the seller. Some require that you grow the fruit or berries for your jams, others say all ingredients must be locally produced. These standards mean little without enforcement, including inspections of records. Standards vary with breads, oils, vinegar and more. Whether through dried products, processed nuts, hand lotions or floral bouquets, the key is to keep farmers in agriculture by diversifying their product line and extending their market season.

> "We don't sell T-shirts and trinkets at our market. Customers know they can find a great variety of food products here, from trees and perennials to herbs, fresh flowers and produce of

A colorful stall netting of handmade alpaca wool hats is the perfect local artisan addition to the Brattleboro Farmers Market, VT.

> every kind, as well as gourmet items like herb vinegars, fresh pasta, and excellent bakery and dairy items. Our suburban customers have yards, they have gardens, they are making meals for their family, packing lunches for their kids. They come to us looking for ways to accomplish their goals in a way that makes them feel good about how they have spent their dollars."
> – Ginger Rapport, Market Master, Beaverton FM, OR

The main problem for the above two groups is with those who favor the extreme open market where anyone can enter with any product. Carved wood from Africa and baskets from Thailand go right alongside bananas from Costa Rica and mangos from Brazil. Throw in Mary Kay Cosmetics for good measure. These advocates say, "Let the customers decide."

Solutions

> "Markets might want to consider that no more than 25% of the display area be taken by value-added products. I feel it's OK to sell value-added, where the main ingredient is raised and grown on the farm. This helps balance things if you have a crop failure."
> – Caryn Robertson, Kitsap Food & Farm Alliance, Ollala, WA

There are countless ways to treat artisans/crafters, processed items, hot foods or other vendor types:

♦ You can place them in a separate area apart from your farmers.

- Limit the percentage or number allowed, just as with socio-political groups, non-profits or downtown retailers.
- Allow any individual no more than two weeks per month or require a pre-season application for desired dates.
- Permit only one sales day per month as the Ferry Plaza market does with most hot food vendors.
- Allow them during any slow periods when crops are lighter such as the beginning/end of your season.
- Allow only hand-crafted items or home-processed foods (from a licensed kitchen or under cottage food law).
- Establish a minimum number of sales days per year to discourage hobbyists.

"Non-agricultural attractions can enhance the farmers' market if they're complementary. I like the producer-consumer philosophy. It has to be well regulated, so the image that you're presenting is a farmers' market. Crafters do add a lot of variety and expand the market, but if it goes too far can turn it into a bazaar or flea market… Put an ag theme on crafts. Jewelry, for example, or earrings and hair clips or pins, should have a farm theme such as fruit and vegetables, and you have to be the producer of the craft. This presents an image of integrity for the market. We have 65 farmers, 12 processed food sellers, and 6-8 crafters. We place a strict limit on the number of crafters and processed foods; otherwise they would dominate the market and take away from produce sales."

– Randii MacNear, Mgr., Davis FM, CA

Including crafts, processed foods, plants, dried flowers, and cut boughs will allow you to extend your market more than a month in either direction. You can gain extra income, but make sure you don't tarnish your more bountiful mid-season image.

"Since produce is the backbone of any market, we try to keep our membership with at least 80% produce and the remaining 20% comprised of plants and crafts. Produce always has priority over plants and crafts and is given first available space for new members. Our policies are: you grow/make what you sell and YOU sell what you grow/make. All items on the market must be produced and sold by the members. We do not allow bought items to be resold on our market. All craftwork must be original, handcrafted items which comply with the set of craft guidelines and are juried by a craft committee."

–Sara Pollard, *Do's and Don'ts of a Successful Farmers' Market*

Farmer Needs vs. Downtown Rejuvenation

We are experiencing the mallization of America. Whether a downtown is dying or dead, its downtown association and the city frequently are clamoring for farmers' market relief. While it's wonderful to be in the catbird seat, we in the farmers' market arena need to inject some realism into the view that we can be a panacea for downtown economic ills. Farmers' markets have brought thousands of pedestrian customers into countless downtowns, but when they are used without proper care, they can fail. We need partners in the process who will prioritize the survival of the farmers' market above all else.

It is critical that government and local business associations appreciate the bottom line for dozens of businesses within the market, because they can withdraw very quickly in favor of other markets. Every farm sees itself as an important business, equal to each downtown business. With the proper promotion program farmers can entice crowds to downtown streets; it's up to downtown businesses to draw them into their stores.

We need joint strategies to re-build downtown and the market together. If the market does good presentation and promotion, local businesses should be doing the same. Businesses in San Luis Obispo, California, have put live manikins in their windows, painted footsteps from the sidewalks into their stores, declared farmers' market day "specials," opened their doors and come outside to join the Thursday Night activities. There is a strong promotional attitude that permeates most businesses; they want to be associated with the success of market night. In this city of 70,000 population, a chain music store had its largest opening

The Capital City Public Market enlivens the Boise Cultural District with 10,000 customers on Saturday. Downtown businesses were so enamored that they lobbied to close four blocks that hold 150 vendors, breathing life into restaurants and other retailers.

day ever – that's right, on a Thursday. Truck deliveries to the region invariably happen on Thursday afternoon or Friday morning; people just love the excitement and energy of the market. Critical to its success – much like the Knott's Berry Farm empire – are weekly meetings of business and market people to resolve issues and plan strategy.

Numerous cities have invested thousands of dollars to start markets, realizing the attraction will benefit merchants. Sometimes, however, they push the market into a location that looks like a ghost town and ask the market to survive while they see if other businesses can be attracted. Many consumers do not want to enter a depressed zone. While markets can help with crisis management, they should not be left alone on a desolate battlefield. Planning is essential to ensure others are making an investment in redevelopment.

There are other cities who say they love the farmers' market but don't spend the time, staff or money to build or support it. As with any relationship without active love, the market is doomed to failure or a

less-than-stellar performance. Another corrosive impact results from a merchant view of the market as competition. Instead, when merchants see the market as a special event with a powerful draw, they give the support necessary.

The farmers' market should be seen as complementary to established and new businesses. To gain that downtown perspective, they can:

• Cooperate on various projects, including parades, street fairs, and all-important transportation and parking strategies;

• Attend chamber or downtown association meetings to share ideas and responsibilities;

• Conduct regular merchant surveys to assess impact on stores and improve customer circulation;

• Participate in cooperative advertising programs to promote a family ambiance;

• Promote a marketing plan with a spillover effect on the neighborhood, and

• Maintain the integrity of the market by following rules and agreements which show respect for other businesses.

For example, Santa Barbara's TV ads try to influence the public perception about the safety of one of its six market locations by emphasizing their markets as the "chefs' choice."

It is essential that we be good neighbors, since we cannot have a positive impact on every business. Any business counting on quick in-and-out customers dependent upon nearby parking may look disapprovingly at the farmers' market. While the market day may hurt their sales, the farmers' market can make efforts to improve the overall desirability of the local shopping district so that downtown visits are increased even on non-market days. ༀ

THE NEW FARMERS' MARKET

Promoting the Market 9

Studies show that customers come to farmers' markets for quality, freshness, locally grown food, reasonable prices and a fun social and shopping experience. And let's not discount the importance of vibrant farmer personalities!

Nothing in promotion we can do compares with the impact of each farmer's product, presentation and personality. We could eliminate all our promotional efforts if every farmer in the market were committed to great customer service. Of course, our communities still want everything else as well.

TOMA is an acronym for top of mind awareness, the concept that people generally buy from the place that first comes to mind. It's why Campbell's commands 85% of the U.S. soup market. Such dominance in a product category is unusual. Within any local or national market for a product, there are often profound shifts within a period of several years. This is good news for farmers' markets; we can change people's shopping patterns as we become first in their minds. Like Westinghouse we need to realize that, "The quality goes in before the name goes on." So first we need to develop our farmers' focus on every aspect of quality. Then the market must combine those efforts into a collective statement of what we are. This requires an advertising and promotional strategy that will allow us to lead the TOMA category for produce in our area.

"What are the consumers' expectations when buying food? A successful food seller offers cleanliness, quality, variety, and good prices. Convenience, accessibility and what the competition offers are particularly important questions when planning a market. They are also important concerns from a service feature standpoint. Although not commonly considered to be promotions, how a market or any retail food operation deals with these features influences how the consumer will respond to the market. The basic expectations that consumers have for buying food are not an optional consideration. Without meeting these fundamental demands, all additional promotional efforts will fail."
– To Market! To Market!, U. of Mass. Cooperative Extension

Capital City Public Market in Boise, ID includes a variety of high-quality, juried crafts that complement the farm products and offer something special to tourists.

Pick up any advertising or promotion book, and it will say that word-of-mouth is the most effective promotion there is. Yet the book *Word-of-Mouth Advertising* makes the telling point that word-of-mouth promotion has something even more basic underlying it: product excellence. If your product is excellent, promotion will enhance sales. If your product is poor, all the advertising and promotion in the world will only breed negative word-of-mouth, which in turn will scuttle your business. So before you promote your farmers' market, take a good look at your product – your market. The unfortunate truth behind the weakness of certain markets is their failure to be excellent in all regards.

Products

Are the freshness and quality of your vendors' products superior to that of local food stores and are prices competitive? Is there an adequate variety and supply of in-season products? Do your vendors offer a variety of purchasing options as far as quantity – bag to bushel?

An absolute guarantee of quality satisfaction will bring people back so that you can teach them why those raspberries got soft (in a 100-degree car for six hours) or the tomatoes lost their flavor (because 50 degrees will cause chill damage).

Look at expanding your product line within the market. If you have fewer than 100 products in your market, try to increase that figure by 30%. Can you add painted gourds? Processed jams? Oils, vinegar and chocolate? Fresh pasta, pesto and soup?

Markets tend to be seasonal because they seem to lack product diversity in the off-season. Yet, in reality they often close because of a lack of vision of how to be a year-round market. Even with the short, 120-day, Alberta growing season, the Old Strathcona Farmers' Market in Edmonton is open year-round. In mid-November 176 stalls are filled with squashes, greenhouse tomatoes, stored carrots from four farms, carrot juice, honey from four apiaries, pasta, bell peppers in four colors, mustards, cheeses, and a few ready-to-eat foods. Also interspersed are hand-crafted items which seem to occupy about half the space without overwhelming the pleasant food atmosphere. The colorful mix includes dresses and figurine candles, carved wooden hats and wood benches, etched stone and fine jewelry.

In the 1990s superstores came from nowhere to garner a 33% share of all retailing. Supermarket concentration continues to rise. By 2004, Bill Heffernan and Mary Hendrickson documented the CR5 of 46 for food retail; that is, the Concentration Ratio of top 5 companies controlling 46% of market share. Now Walmart, Ahold, Kroger, Albertsons and Safeway control 60% of all retail food sales. Those sales are premised on purchasing from large farms.

As corporate control of our food supply continues to grow, we lack the financial resources to fight fire with fire, but we do have a combination of resources that they can't touch. To maintain TOMA strength with a growing minority within our communities, we need to promote our special attributes.

There is much truth to: "Simply the steady supply, rain or shine, of the finest produce does it." However, most areas of the country are not like California. We have to consider whether handmade crafts can stretch our season AND set us apart. Farmers' markets have popularized organic produce, gourmet mushrooms, fresh herbs, specialty bread, heirloom tomatoes, unusual sprouts, goat cheese and more. We can't rest easy as the big chains add our product line to theirs. We need to proclaim what the stores cannot: incomparable freshness, straight from the producer, with all the personal service that infers.

Friendliness

The vendors' personalities behind the booths are your market's greatest resource. Motivate vendors to talk to customers. In larger retail settings employees perfunctorily do their jobs and many customers are left without the kind of personal exchange they desire. In a farmers' market the customer may make five purchases from different vendors and share friendly greetings with more, including customers. Do everything possible to increase hospitality and friendliness in your market so peoples' social needs are fulfilled and they're excited to tell friends about their positive experience.

You, as a manager, need to feel comfortable coaching vendors. Work

Pike Place Market recognizes the value of giving awards to farmers for excellent display or superior customer service. This farmer received a framed watercolor.

© Vance Corum

with them to improve their displays and salesmanship. If a farmer is sitting on the tailgate with a poor display and disappointing sales, you might help by suggesting an experiment: "Let me put out an idea that might work for you; I've seen it work with others." Then pull boxes off the truck, create a multi-tiered display with the products, and show the seller that marketing can be fun. Remind them that customers are more inclined to buy from a busy farmer than a resting farmer. Demonstrating enthusiasm may show the farmer the difference between the $200 and a $700 a day. Ultimately, it is often the difference between someone who gives up the market and one who becomes a consistent, healthy participant in your market.

Customer Service

Constantly examine your market from the standpoint of customer service. Do you have good signage to help customers find the market? Is it accessible on foot or via public transportation? Do you make efforts to reach special segments of the population by providing senior shuttles and accepting government food stamps? Is your market wheelchair accessible? Are there "customer care" centers in your market such as a free hot/cold cider table for fall customers? Do you provide carryout services for shoppers, especially seniors? If parking is distant, do you have a loading zone with claim checks?

Consumers also appreciate good enforcement of quality standards. Insist on clearly marked seconds. Designate canning product as such so that people don't buy it for fresh use.

Locating vendors consistently in the same spot makes them easier for consumers to find. Offer a directory of farmers and vendors with a site map and each vendor's name, address, phone number and product list. This encourages special orders and restaurant sales outside of market day.

A 1999 study of three Oregon farmers' markets suggested that carts or wagons might be helpful since 10% of respondents said they stopped shopping when they couldn't carry any more. Give local businesses exposure by painting their names on the side of a set of wagons. The same can be done with business and market logos screened on either side of a canvas bag.

> "Take care of your customers. Look at every aspect of your market, such as the traffic and parking situation. Can customers get in and out easily?"
>
> – Rose Munoz, former Mgr., Torrance FM, CA

Keep an open ear for complaints and concerns. A suggestion box will help. Markets often make it too easy for the customer to justify going elsewhere.

Market Ambiance

Be creative with an attractive market atmosphere. Decorate the entrance with flowers, vegetable displays, scarecrows or other seasonally appropriate themes. Use your logo or even a mascot to make the market a colorful, fun place to shop. Build your market into a community center by soliciting non-profit participation, organizing theme events and festivals, and allowing activities suggested by community members. Encourage farmers to create attractive displays and ensure that the market grounds are clean. If the market does professional signs and banners, farmers should follow suit. Since your market is a pleasant location for local residents and merchants, make sure the site is clean and orderly even when the market is not open.

MARKET DEMOGRAPHICS

Target your audience. Promotion and advertising strategies should be directed at the customer you want. Know your market demographics. Are your customers local regulars, tourists, transients, walkers, bus riders, bicyclists or drivers? Do you know their age, family status and preferences?

What's unique in your town? Your market should be reflective of your community. If 30% of your population is over 65, is that group similarly represented in your market? If your community is 40% Latino, are 40% of your vendors and customers Latinos? And if not, why? Your goal is to create a true community marketplace that is reflective of all elements of your community. Determine what population segments are missing and why; then create a targeted marketing plan with written goals and strategies to attract them.

The more you find out about your customers, the more you can cater to their wishes and increase sales. If you find you have a high-end community, direct your advertising to that market. Or perhaps your market has dense housing nearby where door hangers might work, if you have a church youth group to distribute them. Color code your flyer – yellow on apartment buildings, green on duplexes and blue on single family residences – with a coupon to check the response rate from each.

> "What to do about declining, white, traditional customer base (they are aging, eat out and eat like birds)? Today's young couples don't know how to cook from scratch and therefore are not volume customers. The answer is in the exploding immigrant population which comes from vegetable- and fruit-eating and cooking cultures. Develop PR materials in their languages and encourage vendor participation from these groups whenever possible."
>
> – Tony Evans, Maryland Dept. of Agriculture

Customer Research

Market research is generally divided between primary research – where you research your customers yourself – and secondary research – where you find available research that has already been done about your intended market. You will find a good deal of secondary research available through your local library, universities and colleges, Cooperative Extension in your state and elsewhere, and studies done by other markets. Be careful not to assume that all this research will reflect your local customer base. It may give you a good idea of the general characteristics and priorities of farmers' market shoppers. It will provide a number of questions for you to ask in your own primary research.

Before starting your market you may want information that will determine the market's character. You can do primary research through a phone survey, outside a food store or theater, or on paper placemats

Everyone loves a convenient place to sit – families with children, lovers, singles, tourists, seniors – amidst a market full of great food, music and pleasant environment as at the PSU market in Portland, OR.

at a local restaurant. Ask about their preference of day, hours, location, products of interest and media outlets: "What type of music do you most prefer?" "What radio station do you listen to?" "What social media do you use? How frequently?"

Market surveys. After you open you need to continue surveying to learn how to keep customers satisfied. Find how customers feel about prices, quality, presentation, friendliness, access, parking, ambiance and other particulars. Surveys are a much underused yet essential part of a promotional campaign. [See Surveys in Chapter 11 and the Appendix.]

You also need help in attracting people not coming currently. Survey residents via phone or intercept interviews at key locations, or use focus groups. Ask and listen – you'll learn what's missing that may be keeping people away from the market.

As a good manager you constantly listen to customer conversations in the market and elsewhere. You also engage customers about desired additions or changes. Through these indirect or direct casual contacts, you gain valuable insights to make market improvements. Thus, you show customers you care and want to maintain their loyalty. In periodic vendor meetings managers can hear more impressions of subtle customer desires. This feedback loop is critical in making market adaptations.

ADVERTISING

Some farmers' market managers say that advertising works for them; others report disappointing results. This is consistent with an old Madison Avenue saying, "Fifty percent of advertising works, and 50 percent doesn't. The problem lies in figuring out which 50 percent doesn't!" Evaluate results constantly, so you can avoid spending money on ineffectual ads or promotion campaigns, and use all the free publicity and promotion you can get.

Very few people react to just one ad or news story. Effective marketers use both publicity and advertising to increase the odds consumers will see or hear their message at least three times. A campaign that repeatedly places your message before your audience gets results. Remember, Campbell's dominates the soup market because of Top Of Mind Awareness. People will buy their produce somewhere – your advertising helps determine where.

Publicity and advertising are useful in introducing your market, building a reputation, announcing new products or services, and promoting specific events. If you can't count on free publicity when opening a market, you had better advertise. Don't take chances on all that work with the market's future on the line.

Ad Message

Advertising gurus advise to stress benefits. For farmers' markets that means "farm-fresh," "locally grown," "organic," "buy direct from the farmer," etc. Keep a consistent look with your logo but change the message to encourage shoppers to look for it. Farmers' markets also mean "fun" to most shoppers so don't repeat the same ad every week. Try a corny phrase like, "You'll be 'peased' at what you find."

© Vance Corum

Queen Anne Farmers Market in Seattle has a consistent stylized font, changing the background color and crop each year.

Something new in the ad catches the eye in a fresh way – a chef demonstration, a cookbook signing, free shortcake on the market's birthday, a melon for every 50-year-old, an apple for anyone's birthday. Have fun with this and get your growers involved.

Stress the availability of tree- or vine-ripened fruit, just picked vegetables, all from local farmers. Your press releases can address the average distance of your farmers compared to the 1,300 miles typical of fruits and vegetables in the traditional marketplace. Customers are learning through media about the need to keep their local food supply viable. Your ads should reinforce that message with "Support Your Local Farms and Protect Your Food Supply."

Always put "Rain or Shine" in ads and brochures. People won't assume you are open in a downpour, but once they know they can count on you, they are more likely to come out even if it means getting soaked.

Joanne Neft, developer of the Foothill markets east of Sacramento, reinforces, "Develop an ad theme and then use it in display ads throughout the year. Keep posters consistent from year to year."

Budget

When you know what you want your promotion and advertising to do and whom you want to reach with your message, decide how much you should spend.

For each project draw up an expenditure list. Advertising costs include media space or time, special help fees, copy writing, design, layout, photographs, illustrations, typesetting, artwork and printing. When figuring expenses for events or festivals, consider the time spent in meetings, planning, research and phone calls as well as the hard costs of postage, shipping, delivery charges, telephone and office supplies.

Use free promotion before spending money. For low-cost promotion strategy, read books like *Advertising Without Money* by Salli Raspberry, *StreetSmart*

Marketing by Jeff Slutsky and *Grassroots Marketing* by Shel Horowitz. Every promotion you do represents your market, so allocate enough money in your promotion budget to produce a promotion or advertisement that communicates quality. Without it you may be creating a negative image about yourself.

When defining your target audience, do not overlook your existing customers. Remember the 80/20 rule: 80% of your business comes from 20% of your customers. Once you have a base of loyal customers spending a target of $40 weekly, for example, shift your emphasis to those spending $25 to $35, or periodic shoppers who may need a frequent shopper card with an incentive.

Consider varying advertising strategies:

- Promote consistently to your best audience before addressing your second-best audience.
- Spend the bulk of your advertising dollars in areas or zip codes of current customers rather than new areas.
- Focus on certain income groups that are well represented among customers.
- Test the response rate to different direct mail pieces (or other methods) with small groups first before sending to your entire target.

A budget campaign of $50,000 a year for advertising may be appropriate for a strong market, while an ad budget of $2,500 may be right for a small market. Much depends on how much is dedicated to free publicity opportunities, including special events. If market sales are $100,000 per season and you have $7,000 to cover market operations, you may spend less than $1,000 on promotion and advertising.

That's 1% compared to many farm retailers who will spend 3-10% of gross sales.

So if your market is not growing, rethink how you can increase the budget to spread or reinforce the word or, better yet, create activities which renew excitement in coming to shop. Customers should enjoy you more than the competition.

"We feel that our market's best advertising dollars are spent in a free Madison newspaper called Isthmus, a free-thinking, progressive, alternative-spirit publication. We do a weekly advertisement with what's new with the market. The progressive type of crowd is the very type that comes to the market. Our market customers tend to be very middle-class and into healthy foods and organic food options."

– Mary Carpenter, former Mgr., Dane County FM, Madison, WI

Market Logo

One of the most essential tools for any size market is a logo. An attractive emblem builds market recognition and consumer awareness and helps promote a professional and cohesive identify for the market. A logo can be put on virtually anything from stationery to trucks.

Involve the community in developing a logo, and test various options with people. A market logo contest allows you to build interest and create publicity for the market while achieving a result. When you update your logo, get market customer input.

You can raise money as you build enthusiasm for the logo with such promotional items as hats, aprons, T-shirts and sweatshirts. You also might consider distributing free or low-cost items simply to reinforce this image. Buttons, pins, bumper stickers, and small posters are options. If your logo is a fun image, you might attend your county fair or city parade to apply water-based stickers to kids' arms and cheeks.

Your logo should be the central, unifying element within your overall publicity and advertising plan. Don't print anything without it, and make sure it talks loud even in black & white.

Banners & Signs

Let people know the market is there. Remind them of the obvious. Build anticipation. Set up A-frame sandwich board signs directing traffic to the market. Banners are cheap advertising in your market throughout the season. With your logo they announce market days and hours and a sense that this is the best place to be. Hang banners and place sandwich board signs for several blocks in every direction on each market day to notify approaching traffic. Especially effective is a huge, permanent sign that reminds all passers-by on a 24-hour, 7-day basis.

Wall Drug in South Dakota is famous because of its ability to draw tourists with signs. Think of all the places you can put them. Pasco, WA, and Ithaca, NY, have them on their open, shed structures. Phoenix, AZ, has them on bus shelters. Why not right on the buses? The rule-of-thumb is to tell a visual story and keep it to six words if you are attracting motorists. Work with a professional who knows size rules, e.g., six-inch high letters are readable at sixty feet. What about a farmer's barn with five-foot high letters?

This truck sign helped the Roslyn Sunday Market in rural Washington to pull I-90 travelers off the highway into a town of 1,000. It regularly gets 1,200 Sunday shoppers.

A caution sign reminds drivers to slow down for a market road crossing in Davis, CA.

"We arranged with the North Carolina Dept. of Transportation to erect directional signs on a nearby highway, routing customers to our site. Banners also alert drivers that there is a farmers' market down the road."
– Cathy Jones, Manager, Fearrington FM, NC

Ask your local legislator to intervene on your behalf with the state transportation department. There may be a charge, but it's well worth it. The Soulard Market in St. Louis paid less than $4,000 for a ten-year sign placement including maintenance.

Banners across Main Street give immediate credibility. Placement and removal can be major costs, especially if the city limits such space to one or two weeks at a time; thus, ask the city or signage company for a donation. While costly, freeway billboards can be well worth the investment.

Get on the local marquee with a large electronic sign. The Hillsboro Tuesday Marketplace in Oregon uses an abandoned theater for equipment storage and the marquee hosts the name of the band playing each market night. Or use reader boards with changeable letters in front of businesses and community centers.

"The local YMCA, community centers, grocery stores and churches originally helped us get the word out about the markets by letting us have the use of the reader board for a few days before the event begins. In one instance, I made a $100 donation for a week's use of the board.

"In 2015 we still do some neighborhood-centric grass roots style advertising; street pole banners, fence banners, A-Boards, yard signs. Our original canvas banners felt as though they cost a lot in 1998. They were silkscreened with the market logo, fruit images and information on both sides. We paid $150 each for them, and they have held up beautifully for more 17 years – great value.

"We worked with the City of Seattle on allowing permanent directional signs. We had to go through the city council to find advocacy and support for this. Ultimately, they allowed 12 permanent signs within 2 miles of the market location, but they had to be mounted to appropriate city poles. The cost for fabrication and installation is born by the market and they can be expensive ($300 each). They are simple institutional style signs that say the name of the neighborhood market, the day of the week, months and an arrow to point people in the right direction."

   – Chris Curtis, Exec. Dir., Neighborhood FM Alliance, Seattle, WA

Banners front two sides of a Prosser WA park, each displaying the logo and name of a different market sponsor.

Don't forget your customer base. Retailers across America spend literally billions each year on indoor signs that trigger the impulse purchase. Use your market space, not just local streets. Set up a permanent sandwich board in a highly visible part of the market, attaching laminated sheets that advertise your vendors, special events, service volunteers and promotional items. Your customers are the best market. Use signs that direct, inform and motivate. Encourage your farmers to do the same.

Flyers, Brochures & Posters

One of Seattle's pole-mounted street signs.

Many markets find that "guerrilla marketing" tactics with flyers, brochures and posters work great with farmers' markets. A flyer with a coupon for $2 off or a free item can be handed out by a trusted retailer when they make a sale. Place brochures, flyers or posters in store windows, schools, malls, churches, clubs, historical attractions, restaurants, museums, service stations, bed-and-breakfast inns, campgrounds, hotel and motel rack card displays, laundermats, convenience stores, fire stations, travel agencies and fairs. Ask farmers to take flyers to their roadside stands. Guerrilla marketers never stop considering opportunities for exposure.

"Look for places wherever people are encouraged to eat fresh fruits and vegetables and live a healthy lifestyle such as senior centers, fitness centers, hospital cardiac units and weight loss centers."

   – Rose Munoz, former Mgr., Torrance FM, CA

Ask local, civic-minded organizations to send your flyers with their mailings. Contact your chamber of commerce, visitors' centers and the state department of tourism for suggestions about where to place your printed material. If they offer to help distribute your literature, check to find out their guidelines for brochure size or weight, etc. before producing your printed pieces.

An 11x17-inch color poster can be a great investment. The Santa Monica market started in 1981 with $4,000 spent on 1,000, 4-color posters. Because the poster was professional and attractive, most were put up in local businesses and the last 400 were sold in the market to recoup over one-half the expense. This high-quality poster reinforced the city's intent to have a high-quality market. It quickly became one of the top markets in the U.S.

The same capital resources were not available in Astoria, Oregon, in 2000. Yet, when a printer offered a free ink color, the market suddenly was able to produce an eye-catching, red-on-yellow, 11x17-inch poster for only 15 cents per copy. With matching flyers next to many retail cash registers, the market's identity was established without an overblown, expensive approach. You don't need full color to have visual impact. Your goal is to attract the eye; when you want to give them loads of information, write a brochure instead.

The grassroots approach often requires people power to distribute leaflets at shopping malls or on parked cars. New Mexico Farmers' Marketing Association president Esther Kovari knows word-of-mouth is more effective because the personal touch works best. She says, "We still do radio, TV and print ads, but we're adding more direct methods like leafletting."

It simply comes down to the most cost-effective methods.

"Market managers are trying to reach the customer directly – like doing direct mailings or putting flyers, brochures and posters on community bulletin boards and literature tables at churches or other community outlets. We utilize flyers, direct mail pieces and less standard media advertising such as print ads. This seems to be most effective. Traditional advertising hasn't had the response that the managers would like for the amount of dollars spent."

– Jeff Cole, Exec. Dir., Mass. Federation of FMs

Direct Mail & Piggyback

Many markets find direct mailings effective, both for adding a personal touch and targeting a very specific audience. Mail a postcard with a free gift or coupon to key zip codes. Try dental or medical offices, or every retailer in town – you want them all to know you. Make sure to get the customer's e-mail when they turn in their coupon. Even without a high response rate, the reader will spend more time considering your advertisement because of the coupon. You become more memorable.

A visitor book is effective in building a mailing list. Computerize this list and keep updating to contact market-goers with seasonal openings or special

This Bellevue, WA poster concentrates on the product variety for their Thursday and Sunday markets at two different locations.

events. Have customers sign a pre-paid postcard that you mail to remind them of next season's opening. Create a "friends of the market" membership group and mail them periodic special offers at the market. Help promote word-of-mouth with "Tell A Friend" postcards. People fill them out, put them in a box at the market, and the market provides postage.

Newspaper inserts are inexpensive but they only reach those who read the paper and check out your insert. Colored paper may be worth the extra cost for your ad to stand out. Even more effective are front-page "ad notes" that every subscriber sees.

Utility inserts are less costly still. City-operated public service utilities and banks are required to reinvest in their communities. You pay only the cost of printing an insert with their mailing. This is the least expensive outreach to every household in your community; the downside is that utility mailings are mailed over a 60-day cycle. Find the requirements – deadline, size, paper weight, count – so it doesn't raise their postage. This may be the same vertical 3-up form (3 copies on 8 1/2 x 11, cut) that you use for hotel and visitor center rack cards.

Postcards are the least expensive way to mail first class and allow you to delete old names when returned undeliverable. Use postcards to promote special events – they stick out in the mailbox and are cheaper. The Portland, OR market has used color photos to entice people to their Summer Bread Festival, Tomato Fest, Fall Harvest Festival and other events.

The Santa Barbara Certified Farmers' Market Association uses full-color postcards to announce the opening of the market season and stocks them at info booths at all six markets. It is a great personal touch for customers and newcomers, more effective and much less expensive than brochures.

"Take-one" tear-offs. The Santa Barbara markets' postcard also makes a great "tear-off."

The Woodland FM used the Davis Enterprise newspaper to reach a wide readership. In 2015 these 3"x3" ad notes stuck on 9,000 copies cost $750, a cost-effective 8 cents per household.

"Blow-ups of our postcards also make great poster boards, displayed at each of the markets. Postcards in padded sets are placed on the poster boards so customers can read the schedules written on the poster board, and tear off a reminder postcard.

"The postcards are made to fit in tourist racks and they're as effective as a brochure. What customers are after is the 'where and when,' not market history. We have a four-color brochure as well, but we print these in a limited edition for people who want more information."

– Mark Sheridan, former Mgr., Santa Barbara FM Assoc., CA

Coupons

"What worked well was mailing coupons to each person in a mail route within a two-mile radius of the market. This was much cheaper than going door-to-door with door hangers. The block mailing required that the mail pieces be prepared, packaged and assorted in a certain way, which a mail service helped to do. Each coupon was good for a free basket of strawberries, and this at a time of season when strawberries were at their best, so customers were really getting something of value. The promotion didn't cost too much. The coupons could be redeemed with any strawberry grower. Whatever their price, that's what the market paid the individual grower."

– Peter Jankay, Exec. Dir., San Luis Obispo County FM Assoc., CA

If that sounds too costly, have your growers join in the promotion. After all, you're promoting their berries, not carrots or feijoas, so they should be willing to help cover the cost from their increased sales.

Radio

Radio is a medium that reaches people effectively in their personal space, getting ready for work, on the way to work, at work and before their heaviest shopping trips. Hispanics and African-Americans are heavier users of radio than other media. When the Yakima market started in 1999, it bought five spots a day for ten days and opened strongly. Ten daily commercials would not be too much, cutting back to three or four days per week, so listeners sense the frequency and assume they missed it the other days. Repetition is critical since people usually are doing other activities at the same time. Verbal commercials on a news, sports or talk show will get more attention than on a music format.

Because of its "act now" nature, radio is good for bringing people out to events such as festivals or grand openings. Radio stations will come out to market events; they can also be a good market sponsor. They can do market trades: advertising for sponsorship.

Radio works in an oversupply situation. Call a radio station on market day, tell them you're loaded with corn or asparagus, and see an impact within the hour. Compare the impact with social media.

"We do a market report on a local radio station each Saturday at 9 a.m. We tell people what is at the market that day."

– Karl F. Schaefer, former Mgr., Carrboro FM, NC

As with all forms of advertising and publicity, determine the impact of your ads through a customer survey. Ask how they first heard about the market and what forms of promotion have reached them.

"Radio has worked better than newspaper for us."

– Charlie Springer, Mgr., Richmond FM, IN

"The association does one radio program, called 'A Matter of Taste,' for which we are one of five sponsors. I go to the studio each week to talk about what's up and coming at the market, and other times the programmers come out to the market to interview growers live."

– Mark Sheridan, former Manager, Santa Barbara FM Assoc., CA

"Radio is the best media for special events or sales, but keep your message simple. Use the best stations available that cater to your audience. Purchase the best times available. The ads cost more but for a good reason; they are reaching more listeners. Radio can be used to advertise your niche crop. The ad might be for a specific market, Saturday morning. Don't confuse listeners by listing your entire schedule. They won't remember it anyway."

– Dan Haakenson, *The Small Commercial Gardener*

Television

Television is obviously the mammoth powerhouse of communication. It may be within your reach. It touches emotional people with friendly farmers, colorful produce and unusual items and performers. It reaches intellectual people with a logical set of benefits including fresh-from-the-farm and great values.

Remember that sound frequently goes off with remote controls, so make sure the visuals are followed by your logo, site, day and hours in case viewers are listening only with their eyes.

Mark Sheridan outlines a television strategy:

"Years ago we put together an ad campaign called 'Chef's Choice' in which Santa Barbara's leading chefs come and shop the market. This theme is tied throughout all our print, radio and television ads. Local celebrity chef Julia Child acts as the voice-over, saying: 'The finest chefs shop at the farmers' markets.'

"Most of the association's advertising dollars are going into television ads. Television just seems to have the greatest reach; it has more 'eyes.' Advertisements are placed on local stations, mainly in the news slots, such as the 6 a.m. morning news, as well as a few women-oriented programs during the day. Ads are run two weeks on, and off two weeks, to maximize

Postcard tear-off with six Santa Barbara locations.

dollars. It costs $250 a commercial for a prime time, 6 p.m. spot, but it's worth it! People watch the news, and they know our different commercials. We get feedback like: 'I like the one with Julia at the market.'

"Commercials get stale, so you need to make more than one commercial, highlighting what's happening in the market. Showing a grower shucking corn should happen only when corn is in. You can leave certain elements in the ad and change just certain parts of the commercial. The programmers can help you with this. We also try different appeals. Now we're stressing the convenience of the locations and times, and that carryout help is always available.

"You don't need to know anything about filming because the production crew handles all of this, but you do need to hire them at about $250 an hour to come to the market and film. We take lots of footage so we can go back to the studio and go through the archives and say 'Yes, that corn,' or 'Yes, cherries.' We might be using last year's cherry shot in a commercial. Because we own the footage, we can use it at any time."

The rates will vary widely depending upon your television ratings, whether the camera crew is unionized, and how the station responds to your request. You may be paying for editing, voiceovers, scripting and other costs.

You may think cable TV is the way to save on TV advertising because it's cheap, but remember that they know the value of what they're selling. Many cable viewers are channel flippers and you will have no guarantees on the numbers. Sheridan continues: "I wanted to go with what was guaranteed. Go through the ratings carefully and find out which shows people are watching. Many markets would probably balk at spending $250 for a 30-second ad, but we found it works. You can spend $250 on a newspaper ad and not see any difference at the market." For Mark Sheridan, the strategy seemed to be work. But that doesn't mean cable won't work for you if you are in a high-cost, urban media market and only want to advertise to a small, localized cable viewership.

"Television provides spectacular visual impact because of the sharp contrast between the colors of fresh vegetables. We use television to increase the customer base late in the season. Purchase the best times on your best station. It works. Cost: One 30 second spot on the 10 p.m. news cost us $95. Other decent times were about $50 each."

> – Dan Haakenson, *The Small Commercial Gardener*

The simple reminder that customers are buying direct is a positive reinforcement of the freshness that farmers offer. Quality flowers that last will make customers loyal.

Newspaper

Newspaper ads benefit from at least once a week consistency over the long haul. Given your food focus, you should advertise with the food pages on Wednesday or Thursday if your market day soon follows. If you operate early in the week, you may prefer a Sunday ad when people have more time to read. Try to place your ad on the right margin of the right-hand page above the fold. Use a distinctive border unless your logo attracts the eye and reminds people of your news in today's ad. A coupon also helps make the ad memorable even if it isn't clipped.

Place classified or display ads in local papers to alert customers of days and hours plus a list of products available. Look for "Penny Saver" type free newspapers that can exactly target your zip codes and do a half- or full-page insert – this makes a very effective low-cost newspaper advertisement. However, Sandra Zak, manager of Soulard Market in St. Louis, warns that the Penny Saver may be useless in larger markets because people receive so many throw-away pieces and it's expensive because of the number of copies. Utilize newspaper ads as posters and handouts to get the most use of the money spent on the ad. Better yet, getting your newspaper signed on as a co-sponsor of your market or a particular event gives you some free ads.

To be effective with a classified ad, use it regularly, knowing that the reader is just that, not a browser. Use bold capital letters in your headline. Speak factually as if you were telling the market's benefits to a trusted friend, using words like "fresh," "free," "fun," "you," "meet farmers," "guaranteed," and "great values." Communicate your sincere enthusiasm without overdoing it.

"We spend $160 each week on advertising in local, well-read newspapers, and 40% of our customers come because of an ad in the paper."

> – Joanne Neft, former Mgr., Foothill FM Assoc., Auburn, CA

When you are consistent with your ad placement, the customer may look for your ad to see what is special this week, so vary the content to hold their interest. Use clip art to feature a new item each week or push the special event. The more advertising you buy, the lower the rate.

Rates

You are probably working with a non-profit group and you definitely represent a genuine civic interest. Be sure to ask for non-profit advertising rates and one-paid-one-free if you are purchasing a substantial quantity. You may also get a special rate by taking out a classified ad for the entire season, changing weekly as items come into season. Your biggest concern should be frequency. If you can't afford weekly ads, keep them consistent as a reminder.

Consider the media as potential sponsors. Hipfish, a cultural monthly in Astoria, OR, provided the poster layout and a large ad for months in return for major sponsor listing on a poster. A Kelso, WA radio station became a founding sponsor by giving $10,000 in air time for only $1500. In each case the monthly and the station as well as the market gained visibility without a hard cost, and reinforced the alternative nature of the other.

Coupons

Coupons can be included in newspaper display ads, flyers or direct mailings. By offering the customer a free "bonus" or savings ("two for one") for bringing the coupon into your market, coupons act as an incentive to act. Coupons also serve as a loss leader; when customers bring in coupons for a free or discounted item, they usually purchase other items as well. Get their e-mail address. Code your coupons according to different outlets and weeks so you can track your readership redemption.

Co-op Ads & Tags

"We do very little print advertising and if we do we try to co-op with all the other markets in the city. We all have the same simple message, that farmers' markets are a shopper's best choice for local, fresh, quality, diversity and meeting the grower face to face. We try to repeat that simple message over and over again in all our outreach."
   – Chris Curtis, Exec. Dir., Neighborhood FM Alliance, Seattle, WA

Develop a group ad. The Medford Growers and Crafters Association in southern Oregon takes out a display ad stating the locations and hours of operation. Growers tack on individual ads at $20 each, 25% less than individual rates because of the organization's contract.

"We developed a 'Friends of the Market' map. It identifies libraries, schools, phone booths, parks and – for a fee – merchants' sites posted also on the map. We distributed 5,000 of the maps and had 24 ads on the first map at $35 an ad. Be sure to have the merchants proof the map to be sure their locations are correctly identified. List town events as well as the market's yearly activities on the back of the map. Since the maps can be used as restaurant placemats, they were distributed free to restaurants that were glad to put them on the tables for a captive audience!"
   – Grace Richards, Arlington FM, WA

If you were selling washing machines, you would probably ask Maytag if they had cooperative advertising funds available. In the farmers' market realm, we often fail to realize how many companies want to be associated with our fresh, positive, community focus. Look at how many companies sponsor Little League Teams. A soft drink manufacturer can easily give your market a free tag on their TV ad because it shows their support of your great community event. It might be a 7-second voiceover with your logo or a video of your market at the end of their soda ad.

Local car dealers may cover your ad costs in exchange for the right to place a car in the market periodically. In Modesto, CA, the market covers all its advertising costs through co-op ad funds. In the Midwest car dealers subsidize various markets' operational costs.

Think about what ad program you want, how much it will cost, who might like to fund it. Then start to make the calls, write the proposals and meet with the people who want to help you as they help themselves. Be flexible in responding to their interest in one specific event or aspect of your market.

Chris Curtis suggests, "Go to the business community to do a co-promotion on a chefs' series. Local businesses put their ads around our ad about what chefs are coming to the market. They also help sponsor a local radio gourmet program called 'Mauny Kaseburg's Food Bites.'"

Movie Theatre Ads

Making a movie ad can be expensive if you want to show live scenes from your market. You might approach your local film instructor or ask a student filmmaker. Otherwise, your best bet is to shoot video yourself or images at the market and create a collage of all the various facets that intrigue customers and make it a people place. Keep the ad very upbeat.

The market in Beaverton, OR, tested the movie theatre world. It had difficulty justifying the high cost given that the theatre complex served a larger area than their primary market draw and they developed no concrete evaluation methods.

Yellow Pages ads

If your competition is listed under retail grocers, retail produce or elsewhere, you can gain instant credibility as an equal with the same size ad as your biggest competitor. If others aren't advertising you probably shouldn't. You might start with a listing before experimenting with a small ad. If you really want to stand out, pay for red ink.

PUBLICITY

Most farmers' markets soon realize that expensive advertising is not the only nor the best way to bring people to the market. Effective promotions don't require big budgets.

"We don't advertise. We are fortunate that since LA is such a big restaurant town, the chefs who shop at the farmers' market do a great job of promoting our farmers on their menus and at special farm dinners. Local chefs became a big part of the market beginning in 1999, and the word has spread from there.

"As one of just a few City-operated markets, our focus is on community service. We provide free classes for food preserving and partner with a local cooking school for chef cooking classes that start with a trip to the farmers' market – at no charge to our customers. The local NPR affiliate, KCRW, has a popular weekly "Good Food" program that features a weekly "Market Report" where I interview a farmer and a chef to find out what is in season and how to prepare it. Thanks to streaming and podcasting, we have an international audience."

— Laura Avery, FM Supervisor, City of Santa Monica, CA

The Beaverton FM (OR) is on the cover of the Beaverton Business Directory with a 4-page spread that includes the market layout with vendor listings, additional individual ads and special focus articles.

Local TV stations often are searching for new program ideas or may provide community service programs concerning nutrition and food. They often need material for "shorts" at the end of newscasts. Ask if a reporter is interested in doing a news story on an event or a colorful personality at your market. They might do the weather shot with your market as a backdrop.

Cable TV. Find a volunteer willing to create a weekly cable TV show featuring market products. Other stations are responsive to 30-second, public service announcements. Many stations have lots of hours to fill. Look especially for a channel that features local activities. Give viewers an update of vendors in the market and what's new in the market that month. Do a mini-documentary on your market.

The Davis FM has felt the theater to be an effective advertising site, perhaps because it is directly in the downtown area, blocks from the market.

PSAs. Radio stations are required by law, as is television, to designate a certain amount of airtime to worthy community events. Public service announcements are the way to apply for these spots. Write a 15- and 30-second PSA on a separate sheet and attach it to your press release or a letter requesting airing of your PSA. Be sure to mention that you are a non-profit organization. Practice reading each PSA to make sure they can be read in the allotted time. Be sure to spell out any unusual words (such as names of new products) for the announcer reading the copy.

"In Lexington we have a great relationship with the local NPR affiliate, WUKY. We often air spots on their station. Writing a PSA for public radio can be tricky. You can't use many general marketing principles. In fact, call-to-actions are even prohibited. This sort of PSA has to be crafted to be engaging and informative, but cramming too much information into a limited time can be counter-productive.
– Josh England, Mgr., Lexington FM, KY

Do a google search for "How to write a PSA" and you will find lots of good advice and examples. One helpful one is "PSA Examples | WREK Atlanta, 91.1 FM" at:

https://www.wrek.org/psa/examples/

Look for free community service spots telling what's to be found or products coming on strong. Consider sponsoring a radio program. Give your local DJ a tantalizing basket of fresh produce at season's opening to tell his/her listeners how good it is.

As a festive, community-oriented group, your farmers' market has lots of things going for it when it comes to getting news items into the local media. Markets are highly visual and full of potentially newsworthy stories. Your market represents a genuine community interest. Media staff want positive local stories to fill print space or air time.

Play on your particular local history and tradition. Celebrate your growers and emphasize new products. Play up your special events at the market for what they are – fun, educational, community events.

© Vance Corum

Because of limited life expectancy, newspapers are grappling with how to maintain their customer base. They may trade advertising for visibility or sponsorship of your market.

While some people believe special events detract from market sales, you want media coverage to bring more people to the market. Strive to find new and different items that will intrigue the media and ultimately your customers.

"Marcia Halligan, manager of the Viroqua market in Wisconsin, says that the Saturday morning radio spots that list the items available at market are the most important promotion for their market."
– Sara Pollard, *Do's and Don'ts of a Successful Farmers' Market*

Media List

Compile a media list of reporters and editors who might be interested in your stories, with e-mail addresses. Target individual editors – especially food editors. Note the names of reporters or editors who write for sections of the paper like Food, Leisure, Lifestyle, Agriculture, Business, etc. Tailor your stories for their specific needs, i.e., for the business section, the features editor, etc. after studying their articles and see who you want to target. Look for different radio programs, TV shows or newspaper columns featuring topics or programs related to food, home and garden, agriculture, health.

Expand your media database to include newspaper, radio and television; horticultural, agricultural and herb organizations; co-operative extension and state agriculture department marketing staff; chefs, caterers and cooking schools; city, chamber and "friends of the market." Update your media list yearly: mail out postcards stamped with "address correction requested."

There are many sources of free publicity in every community. Don't forget senior and freebie publications, church bulletins and weekly news magazines.

Get the contact person and proper deadlines for the community calendar or events listing so you can call whenever you have a special event. For TV and radio, get the names of the news directors and the names of producers for talk programs.

> "We send a copy of 'What's Fresh at the University District Farmers' Market' regularly to about 70 food writers and specialists and to about 40 chefs as well."
> – Chris Curtis, Exec. Dir., Neighborhood Farmers Market Alliance, Seattle, WA

News Releases

One of the most effective low-cost promotional methods is publicity available through local newspapers, radio and TV stations. Send out a steady supply of press releases to inspire news articles, interviews and media exposure. The ability to write a simple release and establish rapport with the local media will often result in much better coverage and results than you can achieve through advertising.

> "The Marin market has probably gotten as much publicity as any farmers' market in the nation. It came from constantly sending out press releases and never letting up."
> – Lynn Bagley, Golden Gate FM Assoc., Novato, CA

An industry rule-of-thumb is that editorial coverage is seven times as valuable as paid coverage. Readers may not believe you when you say in a paid advertisement that the golden raspberries are incredibly tasty, but they will believe it when a reporter writes an article stating that your raspberries took her to food

heaven! A good piece of publicity can be worth hundreds or even thousands of advertising dollars. So before spending money on advertising, first utilize all the free publicity and promotion available. Publicity is a boundless opportunity. Use it every chance you get. Make sure your farmers realize the importance of high quality, good displays and fantastic customer service, because a self-respecting reporter can only do so much to make you look good.

The key to getting news releases accepted is to send information about something that is unique or new and is of real interest or usefulness to the readers. A press release must be newsworthy. Editors want news, not advertising. If you expect to be taken seriously, analyze the writing style in the section to which you are sending the release. If they have to do a total rewrite, you're not likely to get ink.

If there is no other farmers' market in your area, it may be relatively easy to attract the media initially. Later, don't count on freebies coming your way so easily. You will have to work creatively for their attention, unless you're a media darling. Either way takes time and effort, socializing or putting media releases on their desks.

Create a file of "PR story ideas." As you develop media contacts, offer several story suggestions about your market. Free or community service events, such as a food-tasting, demonstration or lecture by an expert, may be of interest for the community bulletin board slot in a small media market, but you need to get more imaginative in a larger market.

> "The main purpose is to get the press out: If we get 100 new people out to the market, OK, but if we get the press out, it means 10,000 new people. Always feed the press!"
> – Market manager

While special events which are not food related may detract from the market, one has to balance the drawing power of the event and the follow-up media coverage against whatever negative impact some people may impute to the event. A strawberry shortcake giveaway may hurt impulse sales of pies and turnovers, but it should spark strawberry sales and, more importantly, give the media a reason to cover your market. Every media story means new customers.

No matter what the media, the editor will expect you to present the "story angle" in your press release. This can be a simple announcement of a market opening, the logo contest results, the manager being hired, the site being chosen, farmers getting organized, the board being elected, or a profile of chefs that shop at the market. Continue compiling a list of "angles" available for market use as well as a list of which angles have been used and the results.

Uniqueness. Ask yourself: What is unique about our market, about our vendors and their products? Does our market offer unusual food items not normally available in grocery stores?

Human interest. There's a great human interest story behind every booth at your market! Feature a "farmer of the week" in your newsletter and encourage your community newspaper to carry it as well.

Humorous events are also great for publicity: How many pumpkins can you carry? What about the juggling contest with strawberries, cabbage and eggplant?

Recipes. Offer recipes and cooking tips to local food editors for the types of produce that are coming

---

News Releases Get Results — Free!!

A press release is one of our most useful and powerful marketing tools. The press release serves two purposes. First, it gets the information of our market before the public. Secondly, because a press release is a news story and not an advertisement, it gives the story, and therefore your market, credibility. News reporters and the public will see you and your market as important and newsworthy.

Your press release should tell how the community will benefit. Include anything going on at your market: the opening for the season, any events scheduled for the season, the number of farmers participating this year, any renovations or changes made to your market, any new products offered at the market, or anything else the public should know about. If your press release reads like an advertisement rather than as a news story, your news story won't be printed.

Include all the contact information. A reporter may want to ask you a few questions or do a more complete story.

Give your press release a clear and concise headline. Your first paragraph should include all the basic information. You can go into more details in following paragraphs. Also, send along any photographs you might have. These often make the story more interesting and more likely to be printed.

Send your press releases to specific media contacts if possible. Call the papers, radio and television stations to ask who your press release should be addressed to. These could be special interest news reporters, food editors, farm reporters, business reporters, or any reporter that you have found to be interested in farmers' markets or agriculture.

Send press releases to local daily newspapers, local free papers (i.e., Pennysavers), tourist papers, regional papers, college newspapers, organization and association newsletters, corporate or industry newsletters and newspapers, local radio stations, local television stations, and local cable stations.

Once you have sent your press releases out, follow up with a phone call. This will give you an idea of how much coverage you will get. Sometimes you can add a little more information in your phone call that might make the difference in getting your story printed.

– Diane Eggert, Exec. Dir., FM Federation of New York ∞

An intriguing press release may focus on a unique, humorous event which has human interest. Be sure to set the scene with a specific reference to the visuals that a photographer or news team can capture as at this individually oriented, all-you-can-carry pumpkin contest (Santa Monica FM) for $5.

into season in your market. Food editors, and their readers, have an insatiable appetite for recipes!

Current events. The season's first strawberries or corn are timely issues and the editors especially like to know this. Consumer concern about pesticides is big news; send the newspaper a story about the organic and pesticide-free products offered in your market.

When the Department of Motor Vehicles threatened to push the San Fernando market off their parking lot, the Southland Farmers' Market Association contacted all Los Angeles media.

Business news. Look for possible business angles about your market: expansion or relocation of your market, your market's impact on local merchants or unusual accomplishments of market growers. In Pasco, WA, there was a "business incubator" story as many market vendors graduated to permanent retail space in a building across the street.

The Portland market garnered five minutes of TV coverage prior to its 2013 opening based on several market vendors who grew into storefront operations.

Market activities also make interesting news stories: special events, contests, fund-raising events, festivals or educational events. A chef cook-off or a barbecue contest provides great copy and photo opportunities.

Often, you can find market volunteers with journalistic interests who can help you supply a steady stream of great news releases to the local media.

"Concentrate on what's fresh and what's in season and highlight interesting items that the customer won't find in Safeway, e.g., we have 45 kinds of tomatoes or 12 kinds of melons and 17 kinds of peppers this week."
– Joanne Neft, former Mgr., Foothill FM Assoc., Auburn, CA

Media Relations

Back in the 1980s the Long Beach Farmers' Market had a successful 30-minute program on Ag-USA, a nationally syndicated television program for farmers that aired early Saturday morning. Vance wrote the script so that each of six or seven farmers would be asked different questions to direct their remarks. We lined them up at the market so that when the director walked down the aisle, it would look like he was naturally interviewing every farmer. While it was a slight interruption having television cables throughout the market, everyone seemed to accept it given that we gained national visibility for farmers' markets. Sometime later they asked us to produce a similar show at the Santa Monica Farmers' Market, which helped build their national reputation.

Cultivate quality relationships with local press. Then send press releases directly to their attention. Call to make a lunch or coffee appointment with the food editor of the newspaper or the assignment editor of a local TV station or public service director of a local radio station. Get to know them.

Be selective. Earn reporters' trust by sending news releases that are timely, newsworthy and targeted to readers' capacity and receptivity. Don't become a pest.

Once you get to know a media person, you can just call them, "Hey, I have a great idea. How about a 'Women in Farming' story? Would you like me to gather some information for you?" Or call the food editor, "Would you like me to put together a list of foods not available in the supermarkets?"

Agriculture and self-promoting entrepreneurs are low on the media totem pole, so present the market as a community event with many impacts.

Press kit. Prepare your market press kit, with a fact sheet of history, the number of farmers and other vendors, locations and hours, types of products featured, number of nonprofits gaining visibility, average attendance, and any reprints of past coverage. Send an updated press kit once a year or when a new person fills a media position. You might include a list of story ideas. Be careful never to cause an editor to think his/her angle would be old news.

The Oregonian newspaper used promotion staff at the Portland FM to reach potential subscribers with a $25 incentive of market cash, or $10 for existing subscribers.

Follow up your news releases with a phone call, and call again the morning of an event because media often decide each morning where to send reporters. "I'm so-and-so from the X Farmers' Market, and we just wanted to remind you about our event today. We think your readers/listeners/viewers would be especially interested because…" Be brief and business-like. If it's a slow news day, your call may make all the difference.

Organize farm tours for media and customers and send them personal invitations to events. When you get a reporter out to an event, stay with them as a host, if they are willing. Think about what you want to emphasize – consumer economic benefits, the organic food available, freshness and quality, or the tremendous labor by local producers in getting products to market. Point out these facets as you guide the reporter through your market. You can help guide the story.

"Any time you can make a news story out of a happening at your market – festival, demonstrations, ethnic produce – you're more likely to be covered by local media. Always take the time to talk with reporters and make your market available for the press to come down. You won't be sorry."
– *Farmers' Market Forum*, FM Federation of NY

Co-op news releases. Local weekly or monthly newspapers may find having a feature on area farmers' markets more appealing if each of several local farmers' markets writes up a description of its particulars and submits them as a packet to be included alongside the feature article.

"Make sure you have lined up some vendors for media interviews. They may not speak to them all, but you have covered your bases. This also eliminates the possibility of them contacting the vendor who never has a positive thing to say or who may have an agenda of their own."
– Sandra Zak, Mgr., Soulard Market, St. Louis, MO

Editors love getting free food samples, so at the beginning of every market season take a basket of fresh market produce embellished with flowers into your local newspaper, radio and TV offices, and put one on every food editor's desk. With major city newspapers, such gifts may not be allowed; leave them at the front desk.

Articles/Columns

Send educational articles to the media about the benefits of shopping locally, eating fresh foods, in-season calendar, creating new jobs in the food sector through various new entrepreneurs, etc. Suggest an article on processed foods at the market by delivering a basket for a food writer to review.

Approach your food editor about supplying them with a regular weekly "What's new at the farmers' market" column. Include how to tell when ripe, the different kinds of varieties and how they taste. You might also write a gardening column with tips submitted by grower members.

Do a recipe of the week for the newspaper's food pages. Mention that the ingredients are in season and plentiful, along with sellers' farm names.

Offer a profile of market vendors, their product lists, business facts, location and contact info. In addition to promoting each grower, consumers learn about the people who grow their food.

"The Albuquerque Journal agreed to do a bi-weekly column called 'This Week at the Farmers' Markets' featuring different markets and what's up-and-coming at the markets. It's better than an ad!"
> – Esther Kovari, former president, New Mexico FM Assoc.

"The papers like a regular column because it's something they don't have to cover. We supply them a lot of material; we have a retired farmer who likes to write and has a degree in home economics. The key is to be consistent and give them something complete and ready to run and meet their deadlines so they don't have to call us up and ask for it."
> – Karen Durham, former Mgr., Bellingham FM, WA

"Write a news release each week and focus on a farmer. The farmer is the most interesting thing at the market, plus what's new and fresh, e.g., a woman who raises oyster mushrooms; or a woman who raises plants on land that belonged to her great grandfather; or a raspberry farmer who had increased business 2000%; or someone converting successfully to organic produce."
> – Joanne Neft, former Mgr., Foothill FM Assoc., Auburn, CA

In virtually every city there are great food writers doing their own columns and shows. Carol Golden writes a monthly Local Bounty column in *San Diego Magazine* and her weekly Local Bounty blog is on their website. Pitch your idea to someone like Carol to have a feature article written. See:

SanDiegoFoodstuff.com

Edible Communities

Carol is also the blogger at *Edible San Diego*. From San Diego to Vancouver, from Palm Beach to Coastal Maine, 80 distinct editions of Edible Communities magazine connect the North American public to farmers, restaurants, food cooperatives and more, each in their own regional foodshed. Edible Radio, also owned by Edible Communities Publications, presents similar local-food stories.

"When you shop at one of the many local farmers' markets here, or dine at a restaurant that boasts about its locally-sourced ingredients, what you're really experiencing are tangible reminders that we live in a county with a genuine agricultural presence.

"We're not talking hobby farming here, folks. San Diego is the 18th largest agricultural county in the nation. We're home to the largest number of organic farmers in the country (nearly 350 of them, producing more than 150 crops), and we account for 4% of California's ginormous farm economy – producing a whopping $1.68 billion worth of agricultural products each year."
> – *Edible San Diego,* July 2014

Markets need to include their local Edible magazine on their media list, and offer to be a distribution site. Edible frequently prints localized farmers' market directories in addition to doing farm and market stories.

Visuals

Newspapers often print a great photo rather than an article, so send them one. Build a collection of electronic images, including overhead shots, good farmer-customer interaction, crowd shots, special events, seasonal crops, kids eating strawberries or people in shorts on a fall day. Strive to be the source. When they print a photo or article, send a thank-you letter.

Send an e-news release to the local television stations highlighting the visual angle of your story. Television editors want a visual story to entertain their audience, especially weekend visual events.

Create a market video for cable TV. Better yet, get on PBS. When restauranteur and cookbook author Su-Mei Yu felt compelled in 2013 to share the bounty of local producers, she created a show for KPBS, Savor San Diego, which featured the bounty of farmers' markets and farms.

Talk Shows

Let TV and radio talk shows know you can supply them with great material for their shows, and suggest special interviews with different growers or a regular interview to review what's fresh this week. Videotape farmers even during off-season and send the tapes to a local radio or TV station. The Southland Farmers' Market Association has done regular programs with a major Los Angeles network, focusing on the nutritional value, history and growing practices of one crop, then developing a dish.

"The Central New York Regional Market in Syracuse has a weekly interview on a local noon-time television news program. The farmers' market director, Ben Vitale, talks about what's new in the market that week, and what's going on in agriculture and how it's affecting the food that's coming to the market. Right now we've had a solid month of rain, so he's talking about how that's affecting the crops. The local news anchor brings up a new topic every week, and we're on for several minutes. And that's worked very well as a promotion for the market. Luckily for the market, the TV station's news director, the local news anchor, and the news director for the station, all happen to be regular customers at the market."
– Diane Eggert, Exec. Dir., FM Federation of NY

Tourists

Capture the tourist dollar. Network with tourist entities, get listed in their directories and summer entertainment guides, and see if they will distribute market flyers. These usually are on heavy-duty card stock with good graphics at the top, easily visible while sitting in a card rack.

Contact state, county and city tourism agencies or offices. Place brochures at interstate information booths. Call visitor and convention bureaus, your state travel director, bus tour companies, state and county fairs, chambers of commerce, bed and breakfast stops, motels, hotels, restaurants and other tourist attractions such as ski resorts, historic sites, and museums. Distribute flyers at major festivals.

You may want to take your entire market directly to the tourists as at some East Coast turnpike rest stops. Or consider a tourist destination. At the least, tourist hotspots recognize the importance of numerous attractions helping to draw people back to the area, so they generally will help spread the word if your market is a colorful addition to the area.

The North (San Luis Obispo) County FM Association hosted a Melon Mania event to capture both public and press attention.

Once the tourists are in your market, make sure your farmers are ready for them. Consider what new value-added products and quantities tourists may want, what container will keep the berries from becoming a mess, and gift packs for house gifts. The Soulard Market warns about low sales with senior bus tours.

A "Where in the World Are You From?" sign & global map inviting customers to identify their hometown with a stick-pin is a great idea for tourist-heavy markets. When the map is filled with stick-pins, it will show the market's connection to the world.

Tourists can be a boon, especially since they cause vendors to think creatively about a new type of customer. Tourists want to see what's special about your area of the country, so focus on the local trade, and then consider packaging for Brazilians, Chinese and others to take home.

More Guerrilla Tactics

Freebies cost something in time, but save cash.

> "After more than 20 years of operating markets, we are now printing and distributing 'Market Bucks' at community events, speaking engagements, etc. We have had a lot of luck the past two years with our Husky Buck program; on the first Saturday of the month, University of Washington students and staff show their ID and get a $2 Market Buck to spend on anything they want at the market."
>
> – Chris Curtis, Exec. Dir., Neighborhood FM Alliance, Seattle, WA

Billboard companies may loan your market unrented space for free. Be prepared with graphics and money to cover the production cost. Perhaps a corporate sponsor can be approached to help pay for design and printing. You need to act fast on this one.

There is a story behind every artisan crafting wooden spoons, ceramic bowls or glass goblets to heighten our food enjoyment. And these Idaho products make perfect take-home gifts for tourists.

Your *answering machine* can work for you. Outline market days and hours, locations, special events, free parking, and basic vendor requirements which reassure the consumer that they are buying from producers. During the off-season, promote next year's dates and readiness to accept new applications. Provide a list of "Press 1 for market hours, 2 for directions, 3 for vendor information, …" so callers don't hang up on your long message.

Business cards carry more value with market times and a map on the back. Use a different color when your printer is doing a special color for free.

Colored *refrigerator magnets* sent to residents with the utility bill are more likely to go on the refrigerator than a flyer. They hold someone else's flyer, and the next and next.

Evening-in-the-park *concert series* are popular in some towns. You might advertise there or host a market night with the music if there is enough parking. Open the market an hour or two before the concert to piggyback on their advertising.

Parades. Years ago, markets in Los Angeles teamed up to sponsor an

Two sides of Gorge Grown Food Network's foldable business-card size pocket guide to the 13 Columbia Gorge markets in OR and WA in 2013.

THE NEW FARMERS' MARKET

entry in the Doodah Parade along with a briefcase drill team and other wacky entries. Managers passed out 40,000 fliers while pulling a cart laden with produce and tossing lemons to the crowd. Dress up for the 4th of July parade, with someone in a carrot or tomato costume wearing a sign "Come to the Farmers' Market today." Get a farmer to drive a tractor and wagon in the parade. Know your audience; if it's a drunken Mardi Gras crowd, your fruit may come back at you like softballs in an out-of-control batting cage.

Chef testimonials. If you don't ask, they can't say yes. Only Santa Barbara had a Julia Child, but Portland, OR found two restaurant chefs who take turns as market chef. Bradley Ogden helped make the Marin County markets famous. Working with your local chefs is a good way to check that you are on the cutting edge of a sustainable local agriculture.

TV weather reporter. Invite one to the market to talk about how the weather affects gardens, weather forecasting in general and how the climate is changing. Maybe she will use your market as a weather report backdrop.

Public presentations offer tremendous opportunities, including service clubs, senior centers, civic and women's groups, churches and garden clubs. Use good graphics in your Power Point to outline all the market's benefits. You may inspire support from the American Association of University Women, which sponsors a market in Fullerton, CA.

Buyers' and consumers' guides. Many states publish directories of farmers' markets. Check with your state department of agriculture or local extension agent to find out how to be included.

Welcome wagons provide newcomers with local business directories. Ask your chamber of commerce how to be listed. What about a gift and brochure for every new resident and potential customer? Soap stamped with a market or farm logo?

County fairs and home shows provide an excellent venue for flyer distribution. Make those long days fun

Saturday is market day in Davis, CA, but Wednesday evening is Picnic in the Park with music and the market in the background.

by handing out samples which gives you something to talk about, a longer period of contact. Get e-mails for your mailing list. Set up a farmers' market trade show booth at your local emporium with a little mini-tasting of different market products.

A balloon arch over the entranceway will attract attention, especially for a special event. Decorate the market perimeter with the right vendors. Internal arches and decorations add a festive element and a sense of cohesion.

Information booth. Staff a booth with volunteers. Provide educational material such as consumer buying tips, recipes, health perspectives, organic information, upcoming events, other markets and your market newsletter. Sell promotional items and solicit new vendors.

Feature vendor. Each week feature a different farm/vendor, putting them in the center in a reserved spot or placing a large ribbon on their booth. Numerous markets give various annual awards for the best display, most improved farmer, friendliest vendor and similar categories.

Malls. Move inside to the center court of a large shopping mall, perhaps for the winter season.

Weekly makeover. Customers want constant changes that we can demonstrate with new vendors, improved displays and other visual effects. A good, on-site manager continually evaluates and listens to the customer perspective and communicates valuable ideas for improvement to farmers and other vendors. Post new signs that point out the chef of the week or list new products or specials.

> "Announce vendor specials for vendors who wish to have their weekly specials announced on the PA system. Have them bring a written list of their specials to the market office after 7 a.m. on market day!"
> – Manager, Kitchener FM, Ontario

At their main Portland State University location, the Portland Farmers Market provides once-a-month space for value-added entrepreneurs that source ingredients elsewhere. These periodic vendors bring an extra level of curiosity for customers. Having a rotating group of crafters does the same. Think every week about how your market can look a little different – new products, a different musician, a juggler or clown pleasing kids, a new nonprofit, a cooking demo, a recipe contest… the possibilities are endless.

Proclamations. Since 2000, USDA has declared National Farmers Market Week to be the first full week of August, Saturday to Saturday. Approach your legislator or governor's office to issue a state proclamation.

> "Farmers' Market Week was established by the Federation in the state of New York in the first week of August primarily to enhance public awareness of the markets and their benefits. We use that time especially to educate the public about the foods that they're eating. We use a pamphlet put out by Cornell University that discusses the nutritional benefits and values of the fresh foods customers can find at the markets."
> – Diane Eggert, Exec. Dir., FM Federation of NY

Propaganda Seed Co. is "for winning the next crop of hearts, minds & stomachs in the food revolution." It is proof that small towns can be full of big ideas.

A comic message from the San Luis Obispo market (CA) could be used as a postcard reminder to customers.

This website was created by creative people in Mosier, OR, who want to share their ideas for events that are designed to highlight the different benefits of eating local. From their Fast Food Smackdown to Ingredients Spelling Bee and Map Your Tongue for Kids, you can pick up new ways to intrigue customers that are easily replicated. Check them out at:

http://propagandaseedco.com.

NEWSLETTERS

> "SpringRain Farm & Orchard is still harvesting tons of fresh greens every week! They will have bunched mizuna that has a sweet, nutty flavor and can be used like young pea shoots. Try mizuna in curries combined with peanuts and carrots for a delicious main course…Look for SpringRain outside the pavilion this week, they are moving to their summer location."
> – Port Angeles FM, WA, Issue 348, March 28, 2015 e-newsletter

Whether electronic or paper, a personalized newsletter offers a soft-sell approach that allows you to keep in touch with your customers and forge a close relationship. A newsletter make customers feel like part of the market "family." It saves postage and printing costs by compiling all your news, sales bulletins, classes offered and announcements into one mailing rather than several small mailings or numerous advertisements. With e-newsletters, it's just a question of staff time.

Newsletters also can be used for educational and recognition purposes. The more you educate people about food, agriculture and farming, the more they will understand and support you.

> "A newsletter makes people want to get involved in the market. After the initial start-up of the farmers' market, it may pay to put most or

Market Newsletters

Making Customers Feel Like Part of Your Market Family

A newsletter is an inexpensive means of communicating with your existing customer base. It provides a personal touch that makes readers feel a part of the market family and therefore encourages loyalty. This loyalty translates into regular shopping at the market and increased sales.

What makes a good newsletter? There are a few simple design elements that you should follow. First, begin with a banner. The banner should include the name of your newsletter, your market name, your logo, and date. You should also include a contact name and phone number, although it doesn't have to be a part of the banner.

Newsletters provide information, but they should also be simple and easy to read. Therefore, articles for the newsletter should be short. Sentences should not be long and the vocabulary should be simple and easy.

Your newsletter needs to grab the readers' attention and draw them into the text. You can start attracting attention by printing on colored paper. Use bold headlines to spark interest in the article. And to break up the monotony of text, intersperse graphics, charts, diagrams, and quotes pulled from the text of the article. But be careful; there is a fine line between effective use of these techniques to break up text and overkill that actually hinders readability.

Be consistent. Use the same banner each time you publish. Also, be consistent with the number of columns, the font, and the overall look of the newsletter. Also, be consistent with publishing. It doesn't matter how often you send your newsletters, just as long as you are consistent about it.

Include all the news of the market. If you have a full-scale festival, be sure to promote it to your existing customers through the newsletter. Also include the small, every-week kinds of things — demonstrations, musicians, etc.

Personal news adds to the feeling that the reader is a part of the market family. Announce any births or weddings or notify readers when one of the farmers or vendors has retired or died. Also use the newsletter to introduce new farmers and vendors. It'll help the newcomer to be more easily recognized and reduce the time it usually takes a new market vendor to build up their own customer base.

Information: Use the newsletter to educate your customers about the food they eat and the agriculture they support by shopping at a farmers' market. Feature stories on different types of produce or products offered at your market. Talk about how the product is grown, produced, or made. For example, how many of your market customers know how honey is extracted or know that tomatoes were once considered poisonous, and that the U.S. Supreme Court ruled on whether the tomato is a fruit or a vegetable?

Developing a mailing list. Where do you come up with all those names and addresses? How do you target only those with an interest in the market so that you don't waste money and resources?

One way to develop your list is to set up a table for signups at your market. Provide forms for customers to put their name and address on. You may even want to ask a few survey questions on the form. Offer a thank you, either an outright gift or as an entry into a contest. Use the signup sheets to enter them in a weekly drawing for a free prize, which you can have donated by a different vendor each week. (Be sure to give the vendor credit on the gift!)

The most important thing is just to send out a quality newsletter. By quality I mean a newsletter filled with good information and interesting news, with a personal feel to it. If people enjoy your newsletter the word will spread and the mailing list will continue to grow.

– Diane Eggert, Farmers' Market Forum, FM Federation of New York, Spring 1999 ❧

An e-newsletter can simply celebrate the pleasure of seeing friends and Mt. Adams from the Hood River FM at the high school on Thursday evening.

all of your advertising budget into the newsletter instead of paid newspaper ads."

    – Rose Munoz, former Mgr., Torrance FM, CA

Newsletters are all about keeping your best customers. If print, make it two pages and zippy, with a calendar of events and news about tastings and product festivals coming up. Include tips regarding food storage, recipes, craft projects and gift suggestions. Your Extension home economist can supply you with educational articles about food and nutrition.

Electronically, you still want to keep info pieces short, and be aware of formatting for mobile devices rather than desktop or laptop computers.

Other ideas for newsletter articles or features include:

- Farmer Profiles – where they are located, size of farm, growing practices, what they bring to market, and something personal;
- Tips on Storing and Cooking Seasonal Produce;
- Meet Our Market Volunteers;
- Editorial: e.g.: "How You Can Help Protect Farmland;"
- Have a focus with each issue, e.g., Spring Planting, Summer Recipes and Fall Preserving.

Assign different columns or spaces in the newsletter to different volunteers. Get farmers to take turns,

e.g., "How to Grow Potatoes," or "How to Cook with Herbs."

Newsletters are great, but they can be time consuming! Try to get volunteer help.

"Put up a sign at the markets looking for volunteers. Often you will find volunteers who have graphic arts, public relations or computer skills. Journalism classes are another way to find help. Students get their name in print and gain some valuable experience. A Garden Club member might write a column about gardening. Your water department or a city agency may have an article to contribute, and Cooperative Extension often has lots of informational papers they are willing to contribute. State and county agriculture newsletters often have articles or interviews that can be reprinted with permission."

    – Rose Munoz, former Mgr., Torrance FM, CA

WEBSITES

"Bill Gates meets Thomas Jefferson" is the world of our future where high technology intersects with farm culture – light speed with patient seed. In this new world of our fast-paced, convenience-oriented, "now" society, many people still find comfort in an anachronistic, slower-paced, "wow" marketplace.

Farmers' markets are places where people test thoughts and ideas with each other. Yet Bill Gates' technology is inserting itself into these farmers' markets of Jeffersonian days as a Washington farmer gives away apples at Pike Place Market in order to build his computer mail order list. Even with the introduction of this new electronic communication, we have to treat customers as friends, just as always, if we are to build and keep relationships. If we can help people touch the past even as they have stepped into the future, we will chip away the seeming barrier of an impersonal lifestyle in the new economy.

From ViridianFarms.com homepage, for example, we find this:

"We love to eat at unique, inventive restaurants. Search for heirloom seeds in southern Europe. Cook for our friends…and grow exceptional produce for creative chefs.

"With a constant eye on sustainability, we collaborate to attain gastronomic harmony, blending culinary and agricultural traditions with new farming techniques.

"We believe that food is beautiful. Complex. Expressive. It is distinct from year to year, and season to season. It communicates emotions and culture, and while it provides nourishment, it has a very short life span – enjoyed for a brief moment in what may have taken years to produce.

"We are farmers and this is our craft.

E N T E R, and come savor Oregon's seasonal ambrosia with us."

– ViridianFarms.com homepage © (reprinted with permission)

The farmers' market industry has an abundance of excellent websites, rich in diversity. Viridian Farms is one farm website that reaches for the stars, presenting an almost otherworldly offer to the viewer. Many farmers' markets do the same in a more worldly way,

tempting us with their offerings of products and programs that will revolutionize our view of the food system to come.

New York City

Greenmarket's Peers and Partners pays tribute to many organizations whose work underlies and complements their successful operation of 65 greenmarkets and 15 youthmarkets at:

www.grownyc.org/greenmarket/ourmarkets/peers partners

Their website notes *The New Greenmarket Cookbook* by Gabrielle Langholtz, editor of the James Beard Award-winning *Edible Manhattan* magazine. Having been Greenmarket's special projects manager for eight years, she beautifully presents the recipes of legendary chefs and food writers alongside profiles of farmers that she knows well.

Greenmarket's website says, "These chefs know how to shop! Many of NYC's best restaurants build their menus around the foods they buy at Greenmarket. Our farmers report that the restaurants below are regular customers during harvest season and beyond! Their food must be delicious!" It proceeds in listing 200+ restaurants, plus caterers and food trucks – each

Ideas for Your Market Webpage

- 10 reasons for shopping local
- Affordability/EBT/WIC
- Artful graphics
- Bulletin board
- Calendar (harvest/event/program)
- Community building
- Contact us
- Education
- E-newsletter
- FAQ/growing methods
- Flash page
- Food preserving

- Gift certificates
- GMO statement
- Interactive farm map
- Kids activities
- Links & resources
- Membership policies/info
- Multi-market locations and maps
- Music schedule
- Nutrition
- Other area farmers' markets
- Photo gallery
- Produce buying tips

- Radio show
- Restaurants serving local grown
- School field trips
- Seasonal eating chart
- Seasonal slide show
- Shopping tips
- Social media links
- Stories/About the farmer
- Sustainability info/greener markets
- Tours
- Videos

linked to their business website, opening us to a world of inventive food creations, New York style.

"The Greenmarket provides our restaurant and neighbors with the best variety of delicious, nutritious and beautiful ingredients; the dishes we create are often inspired by walks through the market. It is also a meeting point with the growers, the people who are the most passionate and knowledgeable about that food. It is one of our most precious resources in New York City."

– Michael Anthony, Executive Chef, Gramercy Tavern, New York, NY

If your market is not connecting with professional chefs, you may be missing out on a tremendous opportunity to have the professional food realm validate your market with the general customer, both in the market and on your website.

Des Moines

"Support local agriculture and buy direct from Iowa farmers while shopping the Downtown Farmers' Market – presented by UnityPoint Health – Des Moines. The Downtown Farmers' Market presents Iowa producers from 58 counties across Iowa, offering fresh fruit, vegetables and so much more every Saturday, May – October."

– www.desmoinesfarmersmarket.com

Because the Downtown Farmers' Market is spread over four blocks of Court Ave and three cross streets, 2nd – 4th, their homepage displays a clear map with locations of four parking places, three ATMs, four bathrooms and a bike valet (sponsored by a real estate group). Started in 1976, they know what is important and they cover it right up front to make people's visit as easy and painless as possible.

The homepage also has a fun countdown ticking away to their opening day the first Saturday in May. The menu bar at the top has a clean list of 12 topics without any dropdowns. Nine of the items are also listed at the bottom of the homepage.

St. Paul

Like various cities, the St. Paul Farmers' Market has various markets spread through the city so it does a thorough job of listing its markets, days and locations. Lowertown is most loved, open Saturdays and Sundays from late April through Thanksgiving. Like Des Moines, St. Paul reinforces the ease of parking, on the street and in several large lots. And they stake their claim on integrity: you can be sure everything you buy was grown locally.

At Easter 2015, the market website at www.stpaulfarmersmarket.com still posted a wintry scene with a manager's folksy message ("April is almost here and Easter is right around the corner. There are only two Saturdays left before the arrival of the Easter Bunny…." on their homepage, along with Facebook, Twitter and RSS Feed links.

Opened in 1853, the market's history is a valid highlight, illustrating the moves and changes that are part of its past, and those to come.

Their products page provides customer access to vendors, with phone numbers and websites. St. Paul allows vendors to protect their e-mail addresses from spambots by requiring JavaScript to view them.

Austin

At SustainableFoodCenter.org, we find a marvelous painting inspiring us with "Grow. Share. Prepare" (find this reproduced toward end of this chapter) and a photo enticing us with their Farm to Table dinner each May. There follows a menu of four options: Grow Local, Farm Direct, The Happy Kitchen/La Cocina Alegre and Farmers' Market.

SFC is strengthening the local food system with strong programs in community and school gardens; Farm to Work sites, Farm to Cafeteria and Farm to Family through bi-weekly school drop-offs; cooking and worksite nutrition education classes; and four farmers' markets and an artisan market.

Bay Area

Pacific Coast Farmers Market Association has an extensive vendor survey that gives them information

Market Website & Social Media
How they do it New Orleans

According to Emery Van Hook Sonnier of Market Umbrella, the parent organization for the Crescent City Farmers Market (CCFM),

http://www.crescentcityfarmers market.org/

the market started as a weekly market for a dozen farmers selling products to about 800 shoppers per week. The market has blossomed into a 4-day market of 75 food producing families for an average of 3,000 shoppers weekly, year-round.

Facebook, Twitter and Instagram are the "big three" of social media marketing for farmers and farmers' markets, "the most real time tools available." Use all three, but if that's too much, focus on one and do it well! Keep your initial account active and grow to include others.

CCFM sponsors workshops with the goal of every vendor handling their own social media accounts, which benefits both the grower and the market. Product listings and farm photos are critical, Emery says, "People want to see what a day in the life of a farmers looks like." It is especially important to post pictures of things people can't see at the market – how crops are grown, buildings, family, pets, life on the farm.

Use a Facebook business page for your farmers' market news; avoid your personal page.

Twitter is great to keep in touch with chefs. Follow chefs you want to sell to; what do they need; what's trending. Twitter also lets you tell customers what you'll have at market. (Tweetdeck allows you to monitor multiple accounts.)

Use Instagram to let chefs and other customers see visually what you are offering. Instagram simultaneously posts to Twitter and Facebook, i.e., once you have Facebook and Twitter running, you can keep them up to date with Instagram.

CCFM uses their website to update what's happening at the market, such as special events, product availability, recipes, Q&A, special programs for kids and seniors, and market history.

Staff carry an iPhone to post pictures. "We post what's come to the market," Emery says, "We also actively check the account to keep up with queries such as: 'Have peaches come in? Is the pie guy there today?' It's important to respond quickly to encourage them getting to market. We also post our Twitter feed on the website homepage for customer convenience."

The CCFM website gets about 1,500 hits a month and is helpful with subjects that require more space to explain. Emery advises that markets contact tourist boards about your market website, since travelers often seek out farmers' markets. Markets should also exchange links and business cards (with your website address) with local restaurants that shop at the market.

While CCFM has a weekly email newsletter, social media has become "more important for the market – it's more real time. People check Facebook more frequently now than a weekly newsletter." Nonetheless, a weekly newsletter is still useful – more space, no character limit – since some people are not on social media.

One last bit of advice from Emery: "Make your website and social media fair and inclusive for all vendors, such as the products you highlight. Make sure you include the full spectrum; change your vendor focus regularly so everyone gets included."

CCFM's parent organization, Market Umbrella, has a variety of manager and organizer tools and resources at:

www.marketumbrella.org/market share 𝓭

to create individual agricultural bio posters for their vendors.

http://pcfma.org/sites/default/files/Ag BioPosterQuestionnaire-2015.pdf

Their Cookin' the Market section posts tips and how-to videos. It also showcases their cook's recipes in such publications as the Saturday Evening Post.

PCFMA's blogs provides delightful and insightful reading, whether about the Gravenstein apple's rise to 16,000 acres in Sonoma and decline to 800 acres (July 2010); the joy of a first, tasty cucumber encounter, a rundown on varieties and a Greek dip (May 2013); or the painful assessment of the drought's impact on jobs and farm survival (August 2014). There is beauty in beets and cheers over cherimoya. The writing from staff and professional writers alike is enough to keep any consumer – or manager – quite content on a long, rainy, Sunday afternoon.

Their website is also a vehicle for announcing grant funding. When USDA announced winners of its new Food Insecurity Nutrition Incentive (FINI) program on April 1, 2015, PCFMA had it on their website immediately. Their partner Fresh Approach is one of 30 partners under the California Market Match Consortium receiving a $3.7 million grant. Fresh Approach is creating a frequent shopper program for EBT customers. When making purchases, they will receive scrip to use for fruits and vegetables from the Freshest Cargo Mobile Farmers' Market.

Seattle

The Seattle Farmers Market Association at:

www.sfmamarkets.com

provides a looped display of photographs about its three markets. Keyed on the phrase "Experience Local Flavor, Rain or Shine," the homepage offers a clean, simplified set of options: SFMA, Vendors, Recipes, SFMA Markets, Resources and Market Blogs. It is maintained by a half-time social media and content

Freshest Cargo mobile farmers' market serves mixed-to-high income sites in order to cover operating costs so they can keep prices affordable in reaching targeted food desert communities. It is a project of Fresh Approach, a partner of Pacific Coast Farmers Market Association.

manager, who also maintains individual market blogposts such as

https://ballardfarmersmarket.wordpress.com.

The focus is on the vendors.

One can find that Ballard is the exclusive outlet for saffron grown by Jim Robinson of Phocas Farm in Port Angeles, preferred by chefs for its delicacy over the Spanish-labeled Iranian alternative. A full outline of selections by Got Soup? are presented, as are the hazelnut butter and oil that Holmquist Hazelnut Orchards offers to satisfy customers with more than fresh nuts.

On their website, Seattle markets show how they seek out the unusual. They tempt customers to find contentment in Glendale Shepherd's fresh sheep's milk yogurt, and they will. But there's always something more, like Lyall Farms sweet potato chips, or Eaglemount Wine & Cider's rustic display of wooden boxes and memorable label centered on the "e."

When they introduce Soda Jerk's Raspberry Vanilla Bean Jam or Strawberry Pink Peppercorn Balsamic Jam, the site gives the reader history. Cory Clark started Soda Jerk Soda to make low sugar, great tasting drinks from the finest ingredients in an environmentally friendly way. To keep a low carbon footprint, he uses locally produced first and locally distributed next; as many organic ingredients as possible, including organic cane sugar rather than corn syrup; and 100% compostable serving materials. That's the kind of entrepreneur you feel good about promoting. (He also has a cool tiny vehicle for dispensing drinks at farmers' markets and catering gigs.) See:

www.sodajerksoda.com/schedule

With all the focus on vendors, the reader senses that the Seattle markets have a great mix of them. They would be right.

Websites are a necessity for farmers' markets. If your market is run by a city, use theirs. You can often piggyback on a community or neighborhood website. Be generous in your links since you, too, want to be cross-promoted on as many as possible.

Each website can be a thing of beauty, of curiosity, of exploration and exclamation. Tickle people's fancy, fill their visual desires, satisfy their hunger for knowledge, humor them with wit. Go explore every website you can and note what you want to avoid and what you absolutely need.

In the process, take note of one last website with an intriguing element: Coventry Regional Farmers' Market (CT) invited a team of professional photographers to document life on 20 farms through the seasons, over two years. Called the Market Roots Photo Project, customers are given a behind-the-scenes view of all that goes into the creation of the Connecticut farm products and handmade goods unique to their market.

SOCIAL MEDIA

Farmers' markets have historically been anything but high-tech, but they have gradually been coming around to the digital realm in response to their connected customers. It all started with building email lists, which led to electronic communication with customers, to e-newsletters, followed by websites and then social media.

Social media is the lifeblood of your market, meant to be exercised daily, and blogging is the heartbeat that allows you to tell your story to a larger audience. Social media forces you to become focused on your customers. Be aware of the key words and phrases that will cause search engines like Google to pick up on your content. Your sales will build as you drive traffic toward your website, so link all your social media tools to that website, validating your voice of authority.

Your blog has tremendous potential; concentrate on content and the public can take you viral. You may want to put a well-written, longer article on your blog, but remember that generally people want lists, tips, titillating stories and photographs that reinforce their urge to get to the market. Post material from your vendors that gives customers an insight into the farm or business, its history, humor and humanity. Don't avoid crop production challenges that have a healthy ending. Feature a volunteer, a longtime customer, a sponsor or a supportive business. Do it regularly.

Which social media platform will help your market the most? Facebook has the loudest impact currently (April, 2015), used most by 50% or more of every age category above 18. Facebook's Instagram was used primarily by the young but is gaining ground among those ages 30 to 44. Twitter is used mostly by the young, but is increasing among those ages 18 - 29 and those 45 - 60. Trends will continue to change.

Twitter is a mini-blogging service that allows you to send 140-character messages. Your tweets and Facebook posts attract attention and build your brand as they drive customers to your website. A unique tagline can help that branding effort. Portland, OR uses "Bringing the best of the country to the heart of the city." CUESA uses a shorter "Cultivating a healthy food system." Your posts should reinforce that tagline message as you build a stronger community by providing attention and value.

Facebook can be used to post everything from the mundane to the exciting. The Austin Farmers' Market (TX) used Facebook to host a little contest to see which vegetable was people's favorite – between eggplant and okra. When the winner was declared, they

Weeding the Social Media Garden
Social Media 101 for Farmers and Farmers' Markets

One of the clichés of social media is that it's just a bunch of narcissists talking about the sandwich they had for lunch. Critics will say, "Who cares what I ate?"

Of course social media is much more than that, but it is true that food is a hugely popular topic on platforms from Instagram to Pinterest, so market managers are lucky to have access to content with great potential to engage people.

Many market managers already have too much to do. It's essential to be strategic so you're investing your marketing time wisely.

First, clarify what your market's goals are. Do you want to attract new shoppers, or do you want your current shoppers to visit more often, or stay longer when they do visit? Do you want people to donate to your fundraising efforts? Are you advocating for local agriculture? Get clear and specific on what you are trying to accomplish.

Next, decide what actions your market will take to accomplish your goals. For example, if you want existing customers to visit more often, will you offer a punch card with incentives after 10 visits to the market? If you want new shoppers, can you give away shopping bags to first timers? What can you do to encourage people to help you meet your goals?

You can use your marketing tools to let people know about your actions, as a way to meet your goals.

Use your website as the anchor for your digital marketing. You don't own your content on Facebook or Twitter or any other social media platform, but you do own your website. Facebook has made changes to the algorithm controlling who sees your content in their news feeds and you can't control those shifts. Build your efforts around the digital marketing tool you own and keep it fresh, whether that's with a blog or regularly updating your photos and what's in season. If your website is out of date or isn't mobile optimized, you can use a template on Wordpress or Squarespace, for example, to get a more modern site pretty easily.

Email marketing remains an effective tool, in part because nearly everyone uses email on a regular basis. Social media is growing but it doesn't yet have the business effectiveness of email. For example, McKinsey reported that email is 40 times more successful for acquiring new clients than Facebook and Twitter combined, and emails prompt purchases at least three times more frequently than social media. Encourage people to sign up for your email list by keeping the focus on what's in it for them – discounts, recipes, updates on what's available.

Use social media in concert with your website and e-newsletter. Link back to your website from your social media accounts, and link to your social media accounts from your e-newsletter. Help your shoppers stay in touch with you on whatever channel they prefer.

Which social media platform you use depends in part on who you are trying to reach. More than half of young adults 18-29 use Instagram; women dominate Pinterest; Twitter's user base is largely under 50 and college educated; and Facebook remains the dominant tool, with 71 percent of all online adults using it, according to Pew Research.

Because each platform has a different user base and different rules – Twitter limits tweets to 140 characters, but you can write as long as you like on Facebook – they have different cultures and voices. While your messages should all be consistent with your strategic goals, don't post the exact same thing everywhere. That would be like speaking French in Spain. It's not that you're saying the wrong thing, you're just not using the right language for where you are.

What kinds of content should you post where?

Photos drive engagement on social media – more likes, more

comments — so you might take a picture of a vendor's display and post to Instagram with several hashtags, the keywords that help other users find content of interest to them, such as #farmersmarket or #food. If you write your caption in 140 characters or less, share directly to Twitter. Better yet, share to a Tumblr account and set up your Tumblr to automatically post to Twitter, so your picture comes through on Twitter, not just a link. Then post that same photo to Facebook but leave out the hashtags or maybe just leave one or two, and expand your text if you want to add more details.

Share photos from your vendors, especially from their farms, since shoppers can't see the fields, the barn or the baby animals at your market. Encourage your vendors to tag the market when they post something they like, to make it easier for you to retweet or share.

Post your favorite photos on your website with a "Pin It" button to make it easy for your fans to share to Pinterest, and perhaps create your own Pinterest account where you share your pictures.

Video is the hot trend, including short videos on Instagram and Vine, live videos on Meerkat and Periscope, and of course, all manner of videos on YouTube. Try shooting a quick interview with a vendor or customer, or post a short video-peek at what's happening at the market today.

Don't assume everyone knows the basics, like your hours, your location or where to park. Mix in practical details to make it easier for people to visit you. Build on that with reasons people should shop with you. What's in season? How many vendors do you have? Do they offer products only available at your market? Do you have live music or children's activities? Add in larger themes such as supporting local agriculture and the local economy. Remind your

existing shoppers why they should return and why they should encourage their friends to visit the market, too.

Write your promotional posts including clear calls to action. What do you want the person to do? Sign up for our email list. Visit the market Saturday. Bring a friend to the market with you this weekend.

Be careful not to only post promotional content. Be generous sharing content that's informative, beautiful, fun or interesting, and sprinkle in the sales messages.

Social media is social for a reason — it's a conversation, not a one-way promotional vehicle. Ask questions, from fun topics like: "What's your favorite way to use up zucchini in the summer?"

to more serious ones like "Do you prefer to buy produce labeled organic, or are there other attributes like locally-grown or no-spray that matter to you more?" Respond promptly when people ask you questions or share feedback. Listening is an essential part of social media.

On Facebook, generally you need to be friends with a person to post to his or her profile, but on other platforms, you can follow people and comment on their content without that mutual relationship. Spend some time searching for people posting about farmers' markets, local agriculture or food on Twitter, Instagram or Pinterest. Engage with them by following and commenting on their posts. Showing interest in other people is a good way to gain social media friends, just like in real life.

Watch your results and each platform's analytics, including how many fans or followers you have and how much engagement each post gets, to help gauge whether you're being effective. More importantly, watch your foot traffic at the market and talk to vendors about their sales numbers. If you do something that boosts either, that's more important than Facebook likes.

– Colleen Newvine is a marketing consultant with a special interest and experience working with farmers, farmers markets and small-scale food businesses. Find more info and other social media marketing resources at:

http://newvinegrowing.com.

shared a recipe round-up starring six favorite eggplant recipes.

The Gresham Farmers' Market (OR) announced a new farming family that had recently moved from Louisiana, and made it easy for readers to re-post on Facebook or tweet their friends. Edible Portland used Facebook to announce a free CSA Share Fair on the first day of spring in 2015, which encouraged people to "find your farmer."

> "We've used Facebook since we opened the market, and we try to post at least once a day. It really does increase interaction between your producers and customers. We're partnering with Growing Places Indy to reach out to people who think in other ways. We have a lot of dedicated customers, but we want new people and a strategic method to grow that."
>
> – Molly Trueblood, Mgr., Indy Winter FM, IN

The Burlington Farmers' Market (WI) posted a video of Simon's Gardens planting potatoes behind their tractor. The Lexington (KY) market placed a "Now Hiring" line on top of a market product photo when looking for a new assistant manager. With over 17,000 Facebook "likes," it probably got lots of people talking. Once you hire that way, announce the new assistant the same way, so you don't continue to get phone calls.

The more friends you have, the more likely any market can make a difference in sales by posting an update. Markets post anywhere from once a week to several times a day. Make every post have something significant for your community, and people will re-post so that your friends count grows quickly.

> "We utilize Facebook as much as possible. We post photos during Market day to keep it real-time. When we send our e-newsletter, we use the option to post to Facebook which lets non-subscribers access it. We also create events on Face-

Britt's Pickles of Seattle has a host of krauts, kimchi and pickles, all naturally fermented in oak barrels. Their clever label defines a new I.P.O., their Initial Pickle Offering.

book which allows our friends to spread the word so their friends can meet them at the market. Since we don't have excess staff time to post to Twitter, we set up our Facebook posts to go automatically to Twitter with a link to the post.

> "On Facebook there is also an option to promote your post; it's advertising where we basically pay according to the number of views, and we can put any limit on our spending or the number of views. I've paid to 'promote the page' which is similar to an ad that gives us a major increase in our 'likes,' and to 'boost the post' which increases our views. With a $20 boost, we might reach 14,000 views instead of just touching our 5,000 Facebook fans. We see an immediate increase in the page 'likes' and in views of posts.

> "Vendors can send me info every week, but most don't. Since we encourage them to use Facebook, I copy and post their pictures and info into our e-newsletter and repost to our page to amplify their content."
>
> – Erin Jobe, Mgr., Carrboro FM, NC

Perhaps no farmers' market uses Facebook better than the Cedar Park Farmers' Market in Austin, TX. In the first five days of April 2015 they posted 35 times with good, engaging material and, almost always, photographs. They had nearly 14,000 likes. It is no wonder that Dr. Yue Chi at Michigan State University analyzed the market's use of its Facebook page from inception. The study found that the market used Facebook to retain both customers and vendors with timely information; everyone was engaged with the page, from organizers to customers, vendor and community; and Facebook acted as "a cyber–social hub to connect and engage the local community."

> "We have abandoned most print and radio advertising and replaced it with social media. We have each manager create an individual Facebook identity for their market. We've spent time and money on a revamped, colorful, informative

and interactive website which is worth every penny. We also have about 15,000 Facebook friends, 12,000 Twitter followers and an informative and entertaining weekly fresh sheet called the 'Ripe & Ready' that goes out to about 4,000 folks via a Mail Chimp email account.

"Social media reaches all types of market shoppers but is particularly effective with millennial shoppers. They want up to-the-minute news and a good reason to head to the market – Facebook posts and tweets work well with this group."

– Chris Curtis, Exec. Dir., Neighborhood FM Alliance, Seattle, WA

"We also have developed monthly 'themes' so even an organization as diverse as SFC with three main programs can coalesce at main points coming from all the posts by the different program leads / staff. It becomes theme-based content and we can tout about what is at markets, gardens, The Happy Kitchen, but also about what is happening in the world in all the snippets of news that come across our desks."

– Suzanne Santos, Sustainable Food Center, Austin, TX

Suzanne points out the basic SFC social media strategy:

Twitter/ Facebook / Instagram/ blog / Pinterest and other social media: Capitalize on the well-followed Sustainable Food Center accounts and use them to inform followers of the market happenings.

Meet Up/Engagement: Use as a way to get people together, as well as on-line contests.

Real relationships and influencers: Outreach to organizations like Any Baby Can, Les Dames d'Escoffier, Earth Day organizers, Art Festival and

© Vance Corum

When the Memphis Farmers Market opened its 2015 season it posted a straight-forward Facebook "Let's Meet at the Market" message like whipped cream on top of strawberries.

others that organize big events so that these strong social profit organizations can advocate for the markets to their clients as "recommended."

Promotion and media relations: Keep pointing people to the website for information and dynamic changing events calendar, and "Bring a Friend to the Market" campaign, which rewards frequent shoppers who bring friends over several weeks with a free breakfast in the park.

In 2006 the Coventry market began sending e-mails via Mail Chimp. With opt ins, the list grew from five dozen to several thousand. Their open rate – the percentage of those who actually open the e-mail – has been high as is their click-through rate (CTR) – the percentage of impressions leading to clicking on a specific link. Staff recognized that using social media with a wine and art gala at the market gave customers reason be involved in spreading the word. It magnified their e-mail list, and reflected a new reality: social media is the new word-of-mouth.

QR codes also have been used by Coventry via a free code generator. Customers in line scan the code on vendor signs with their mobile device to watch a vendor video or go to the market website.

In 2011 Coventry used QR codes to win a free barn. In an awareness-building publicity move, Yankee Barn Homes joined with the Farmers Market Coalition and American Farmland Trust to hold a national contest which invited farmers' markets to share their story in trying to win a 24'x36' post-and-beam barn valued at $80,000. Entries were due in May, judges announced three finalists during National Farmers Market Week, and in early August the public was invited to vote for the winner.

With website pleas, magazine articles and QR codes on staff T-shirts, Coventry Farmers' Market encouraged 8,547 votes by customers at

www.yankeebarnhomes.com,

which was plenty to win. Yankee went into bankruptcy during the entire process, but Coventry got their barn which they use for historical demonstrations, children's activities, musical performance, art exhibits, workshops and market storage.

In 2013 the new Coventry barn was the site of Farm-to-Shaker, when the area's best bar chefs turned locally grown ingredients into cocktails, with celebrity judges, small bites by A Thyme to Cook, music and a WNPR emcee.

They weren't the only winner. The first runner-up in the contest, Hemlock Farmers' Market (MI) wanted to double the footprint of their existing 50-foot steel pavilion with the post-and-beam barn. When they didn't win the contest, they doubled down on their resolve. In early 2012 they received a Conservation Fund mini-grant based on their plan to use locally grown and harvested timber. Hemlock Semiconductor then pledged $40,000. Another $35,000 was raised through countless conversations at the farmers' market, collection bins in local businesses, Facebook donation requests and a series of creative community events, including a field-to-table dinner.

Surpassing the $60,000 needed for the barn kit, they doubled their pavilion size even before adding the barn. On September 21, 2013, they dedicated the barn at their annual Sawdust Day Festival. They turned their narrow loss of the Great Barn Giveaway contest in 2011 into a catalyst for a community building project that is the envy of many a market.

Historically, downtown marketing campaigns have often focused energy on a brochure, map or signboard listing all the participating local businesses. Today those methods have morphed into print pieces that contain QR codes, and mobile applications that allow walkers and drivers to be updated about what they are close to that they may have an interest in.

Use social media to present a simple photo of activity during your market day. Beautiful weather may inspire people to join you.

With web traffic from mobile devices growing to 50%, and computers dropping in relative usage, it made sense for the Austin Farmers' Market (TX) to work with a tourism media company, Walking Papers, to be part of a downtown-focused, mobile-optimized, interactive map in 2012. It was a vehicle that combined the conventional downtown printed map with QR codes and mobile access. People scan the QR code and immediately go to the market website. Tourists can now take notice of the market, whether they are driving through downtown, walking or eating at a nearby restaurant. The market's QR code can be printed on posters, handbags, directional signs or even packaging of vendors and supportive local businesses. Visitors then can be led to social media links as well.

Smartphone apps have reached our industry. In September 2014, iTunes announced the U.S. Farmers Market Finder app. It allows a day-based search, driving and walking directions from your current location, and identifies if credit cards are accepted by some vendors. The app has information on each market and links to websites, as available. The data is pulled from the USDA national farmers' market database. Local Harvest and Soil Mate similarly have mobile apps on a national scale.

Smartphone users can also search individual state listings with Farm/Farmers Market Finder. They may

A simple QR code in the bottom right of a poster at a vendor booth allows PCFMA to provide customers easy access to each of their farmers' market Facebook pages for regular updates. Markets can use these to provide information and videos of individual farms.

find apps such as OK Grown.com or MI Farm Market Finder. New York even has a Snap to Market site which lists markets accepting SNAP/EBT.

Markets should get on any state farmers' market listing, whether through a statewide association, state university, state department of agriculture or other. That's the best way to ensure that your market is listed on other sites, including national apps as they expand their services.

Pinterest and Flickr are both valuable vehicles for markets. The Portland Farmers Market (OR) maintains more than 1000 photos on Flickr to inspire viewers and keep them up to date. Pinterest has become the visual marketing tool for foods. As the #3 social media site in the U.S., and growing 111% in 2014, it is the best place to focus your efforts in capturing visual foodies.

It is heavily female (81%), and users spend more time browsing and sharing content than those on Facebook. Pinterest is known for real engagement and community building, and it has great images. Further-

more, it is a great way to crowdsource the upcoming food trends by searching for the high numbers of "likes" and "re-pins." It also has solid analytics for you to use, with dozens of infographics.

If you are not convinced that social media can be powerful for your market or any business, check this facebook app for Brooklyn's Phin & Phebes, that recently brushed by Ben & Jerry's as the favorite ice cream of many dedicated eaters. Be entranced by their Facebook posts and overall creative marketing.

https://www.facebook.com/phinandphebes

SPECIAL EVENTS

Special events bring out a lot of new faces! Even if it's a rainy day, growers may see their sales rise. If weather cooperates, you may witness two or three times your regular customer count. The key is to use many of the same principles used in starting a market: strong farmer volume, intense publicity, increased signage, and many elements to create a sense of fun, excitement and community spirit.

Early in its history, the San Bernardino market, CA, was small, with $2,000 in weekly sales among 12 growers. Hosting a Strawberry Festival, they did that much in berry sales alone and total sales more than doubled. That increase was sustained because new farmers were solicited for the festival and the expanded customer base had more selection to keep them pleased.

Special events done successfully are an opportunity to take your market to a new level of operation and volume. Organizers need to work constantly on getting new farmers and customers. To boost growers' sales, they must have more products with them. If they're going to risk harvesting more perishable product, it makes most sense for them to do so in conjunction with a strong promotion and advertising campaign connected to a special event.

The market should be fun and educational. Using the themes of fresh, locally grown foods and healthy lifestyle, there are numerous special events that can be created to stimulate interest in the market. Events that are part of a market's promotion create reasons for people to come and explore possibilities.

This is the case in West Palm Beach, where the City allows the Susan G. Komen Race for the Cure to take place at their Greenmarket location. It creates a mass of people who don't buy much, but hopefully it builds awareness so that they return as a customer.

"For several years, our market has promoted itself and the nutrition benefits of eating five or more servings of fruits or vegetables a day by holding seasonal 'Taste Festivals.' These are regularly anticipated events, especially amongst upscale citizens more prone to be health consciousness and apt to experiment with new foods. Patronage was increased by two to four times when the festivals were promoted heavily."

– Thomas M. Campbell, Pasquotank County FM, Elizabeth City, NC

TASTINGS

"At the 'Grill Crazy' Tasting, we take a lot of new products, show the shoppers how to grill them on the barbecue and give them out as samples. I'm not a vegetarian, but to me, eating a Japanese eggplant is like eating a New York Strip steak!"

Tastings are an excellent way not only to move a glut of products in mid-season but to introduce the public to the taste subtleties of unfamiliar varieties. Comparing the flavor and texture of 10 tomato or peach varieties gives the customer an experience unmatched in supermarkets.

Coordinate tastings with special events. A cherry or pastry tasting fit well with a Cherry Festival. Get bakers at the market to contribute examples of pastry products.

Schedule tasting events around products as they come into season. Strawberries are great for festivals – 98% of Americans like strawberries.

While it may be tempting to charge up to a dollar for a shortcake, a few hundred dollars income is far overridden by the value of community goodwill. Media coverage is also more likely if you do a give-

away or allow another nonprofit organization to benefit.

"Offer 8 or 10 different peaches and show a jillion different ways to use peaches, make peach juice, fry peaches, poach peaches."

– Joanne Neft, former Mgr., Foothill FM Assoc., Auburn, CA

In Georgia a peach cobbler may be the perfect treat. Make sure the crop is coming on time this year, and get your market bakers involved.

A Pumpkin Festival might include a carving demo and contests. Sell pumpkin or squash soup and identify varieties or make a contest of it. Have customers guess the weight of a giant pumpkin or the number of

Any Halloween event worth its salt should be full of a wicked witch or other photographic opportunities that are ready to be quickly broadcast to your social media followers to entice them to your special day. Katherine LaSusa Yeomans serves mushroom soup to complement vendor sales at the Portland FM.

seeds in a jar. Host a scarecrow contest with prize money and judging by the public and a panel.

"Tomato Day occurs on the last Saturday of July each year at the Kansas Grown! Farmers' Market in Wichita. The day is full of tomato and gardening seminars, tomato contests, diagnostic clinic, youth activities and tomato tasting. It receives free promotions from the media and draws the largest crowd of the season. Winners in the tomato growing and salsa contests receive 'Market Bucks' to spend at future markets."

– Robert I. (Bob) Neier, Extension agent, Wichita, KS

"When we have a glut of sweet corn, we get a permit from the city to have a corn feed. We hold it in conjunction with our Heritage Days celebration and everyone selling at the market dresses as in the olden days with long aprons and long dresses and skirts and gentlemen have bibbed overalls, boots and straw hats. Many of the vendors utilize containers to display items that have a link to the past like an old bushel basket with wooden handles. So often people get caught in the day-to-day business they forget to have fun at the market!"

– Bonnie Dehn, President, Central Minnesota Vegetable Growers

The Good Food Awards

The gold standard for a tasting event has to be the Good Food Awards, instituted in 2011 to honor those who produce superior flavor while respecting social and environment concerns.

Judges from across the country select winners from five regions in the categories of beer, charcuterie, cheese, chocolate, coffee, confections, honey, oils, pickles, preserves and spirits. After a Friday gala reception and awards ceremony, the winners are showcased in the Good Food Marketplace alongside the Ferry Plaza Farmers' Market at San Francisco's iconic Ferry Building. In 2015 there were 206 winners in 11 categories. All gain national media attention, introductions to local and national buyers, and a Good Foods Award Seal that can be placed on their product.

Organizing a Tasting Event

There are many forms of tastings. Generally, markets set up sampling tables in one central location. Put out samples on plates with identification signs or card tents stating the variety, farm name and farmer's location in the market. Also, have a map beside the tasting tables showing where participating farmers are located in the market. Clear your process with the health department.

If you host a tasting without a centralized location, you might have large signs and a map of tasting participants at key market entry points and encourage people to visit vendors giving samples.

In addition to slices so people can taste new products, display the whole fruit or vegetable so customers can see how it looks in the market. Have farmers contribute to a recipe sheet. Place your information booth in the sampling area where general questions can be answered, leaving the farmers more free to sell their products.

Allow the public to vote for "People's Choice" and include a short survey. Gather e-mail addresses on the voting ballot. A monthly event is a great way to build customer interest and keep volunteers excited about seasonal changes in your market. Volunteers can collect products donated by farmers, cut and display the items, answer questions, direct customers and clean up.

This product focus deserves extra advertising, a postcard mailing, signage in the market for two weeks

Winners of the Good Food Awards sample and sell products outside the Ferry Plaza Marketplace each January. They are honored for their foods that are delicious, environmentally respectful and culturally connected.

A Halloween parade led by a master pumpkin draws a large crowd of Portlanders to trick-or-treat at the market.

Chef in the Market

On-site cooking demonstrations, along with tastings, are a sure draw at many markets. Each week a different local chef comes to the market and receives product free from farmers or is given $10 or more to shop for ingredients. After cooking a dish the chef answers questions and may give tastes and recipe cards to customers. In some markets this may last less than 30 minutes while elsewhere they spend 90 minutes or more constantly cooking as long as customer interest remains high.

Local restaurants find this to be great exposure, and their food helps educate and entice customers with quality. There's no better way to teach market-goers how to prepare seasonal produce and use combinations of foods.

Send letters inviting chefs to sign up for the chef demonstration series. Point out the opportunity to introduce or remind customers of the restaurant location, distribute menus or business cards, do a drawing for discount certificates and demonstrate some signature dishes.

In Beaverton, OR, a patio and barbecue company donated the use of a barbecue cooking unit for the season. A sign and business cards demonstrated their support for the Market Chef program run for 15 weeks. In Portland two restaurants regularly share the chef demo, sponsored by a major retailer or the major newspaper which donates half the advertising.

If local regulations prohibit handing out cooked samples, ask the chefs to prepare the dishes at the restaurant and prepare a demo at the market, showing people each step as they do them. For a long time, certifications for responsible food production and awards for superior taste have remained distinct – one honors social and environmental responsibility, while the other celebrates flavor.

The Good Food Awards recognize that truly good food – the kind that brings people together and builds strong, healthy communities – contains all of these ingredients. They take a comprehensive view, honoring people who make food that is delicious, respectful of the environment, and connected to communities

in advance and as much attention as you can give. With all the increased interest in specific products, make sure the growers are stocked extra heavy. Sales should be up considerably due to the product focus and the additional tasting customers.

The Tasting of Summer Produce was originally organized by Sibella Krause as a way to connect top Bay Area restaurants and small producers in the early 1980s, and evolved into an annual one-day tasting event and farmers' market. As a major event it demonstrated the interest among the public in comparing tastes of exceptional produce and led many California farmers' markets to incorporate the concept on a smaller but more regular basis. The challenge was to find sufficient corporate funding to staff the months-long planning process; with a farmers' market you already have the ongoing venue within which to host a successful tasting of any size.

and cultural traditions. Farmers' markets do well to take the same approach.

"We do 'Farm to Fork' events every two weeks where chefs buy fresh products from farmers and cook on the premises. Farmers experience their best sales ever on those days."
– Dana Plummer, Downtown Waterloo FM, IA

"Our co-founder Ann Yonkers is also a professional chef by trade. She makes sure that the recipes submitted by the chefs are usable by everyday people and not just for restaurants in mass quantities. The idea is to get people thinking seasonally and preparing food that is grown locally."
– Bernadine Prince, Co-founder, FRESHFARM Markets, Washington, D.C.

Contests

Contests stimulate excitement and interest and bring attention to the market. They expand community spirit, involve new individuals or organizations, create memorable good times and provide media photo opportunities. It's time to sponsor a baking, gardening or music contest. When you hold a limbo contest or salsa-making contest within a Salsa Festival, you give the media the chance to focus on an average citizen within the market.

Create a contest around virtually any item, challenging your growers to see who has the best corn, melons or peaches, especially if there are several vendors of that product with different varieties. Provide small prizes, and bragging rights.

For your market anniversary offer a free trip, certificate or other prize for the best vendor display or friendliest vendor. Encourage vendors to decorate booths with flowers or ribbons. Take photographs. Consider having a theme. In Davis, California, vendors have competed in a dress-up contest, one year won by a garlic grower who wore a full headdress and necklace made of garlic.

Give pumpkin-carving classes with a free pumpkin and judge according to age categories. Involve local celebrities in teams where they compete in one-handed corn shucking, orange juggling, and "no-hands" grapefruit passes (neck-to-neck). Ask chefs to compete in a cook-off or a lunch-for-two. Hold an Easter Bonnet Contest among vendors with a celebrity judge.

"Salsa contest: We have both customers and farmers make homemade salsa, and we encourage customers to buy products at the market and to go home and make salsa and bring it back next week so they can win farmers' market bucks (1st prize $15) that they can spend at the market. The farmers redeem these and get repaid from the market."
– Mary Lou Weiss, former Mgr., Torrance FM, CA

A huge pumpkin gourd pyramid was built at a Healdsburg, CA event in 2013.

In Virginia the Staunton/Augusta Farmers' Market sponsored an art contest to showcase the work of local artists, with the market as the subject. An anonymous donor funded the $350 for first prize. The artwork was displayed at a prominent downtown Staunton location and reproduced as a print that became a great market fundraiser.

Other Events

A Farmers' Market Breakfast or Brunch is another example of using food tastings to sell food. Instead of chefs or professionals, the growers themselves donate food and serve breakfast to market-goers. And hungry customers buy more.

Try various Ethnic Days, or an April Flower Festival. Host a Cinco de Mayo celebration and send a press releases with chile ristras attached to announce a September 15 independence celebration.

Always have music at the market for ambiance. Invite local musicians to perform during market hours. Many will play if they can leave their hat or fiddle case open for contributions, others will simply volunteer for the exposure. Invite the growers to donate to a basket of produce for the musicians.

A big challenge is getting customers to the market in the winter. Your merchants' association can have a "Meet Me at the Market Week" in January and February.

A 2005 poster for Tomato Tasting Week in Maine gets market customers excited to buy the best of the season.

The Woodland Farmers Market (CA) tomato festival includes dozens of tomatoes for customers to judge on their own score sheet.

Hold a Vendor Appreciation Day with a free breakfast or lunch buffet or cater them with carts going down the aisles so farmers can eat food after they've set up for market. At the end of the season, have a potluck dinner where the market provides the main dish. The vendors really appreciate a chance to socialize outside the market atmosphere.

The Great Barrington Farmers' Market, MA, organizes a scarecrow-making booth for home gardeners. While vendors are selling seedlings, kids have a great time stuffing their old clothes with hay. This can easily be expanded into a contest or done later during fall harvest.

Go to a bookstore or ask a local newspaper food columnist if there are any local cookbook authors. Invite them to the market for a day of sales and autographing.

Here's the formula for the spectacular Zucchini 500 at Pike Place Market and other markets: Put up a 4x16-foot plywood ramp, two sheets end to end with a 1:5 slope (and a step at one end for small children) and ½"x ½" wood running down the ramp to create lanes. Give kids stickers, two pins or nails for axles and four wheels in a plastic bag for $1. Put out boxes of zucchini and invite a

DJ to be the race announcer, dressed up in official costume. Hold races and runoffs in the various age groups: "It's the 2 -year olds!" Have a checkered banner above course with your market name for all the media photos.

Still more ideas for special events include:

♦ *Opening Market Day* promoted as a Plant Day with giveaways of hundreds of plant plugs.

Even in the small town of Mosier, OR (pop. 433), 20 people gather 'round the info/consignment tables for a pie crust-making demonstration.

THE NEW FARMERS' MARKET

Portland high school students compete each year in a reusable bag design contest. At the farmers' market Arbor Day Festival, the winner receives a $1000 check from market sponsor Country Financial.

- *Soil testing day* for gardeners. Advertise free or fee for Extension to test customer soils at the market. Invite the local flower/horticulture society to co-host.

- A *Chilly Chili Contest.* If it's regularly below freezing, use a tag line like, "It's really cold but it's really hot!"

- Offer *hayrides* around the market neighborhood. In Vancouver you can take an annual wagon ride to Washington's oldest apple tree.

- *Meet the Animals Day or Farm Day* with animals for kids to see and touch, including sheep shearing and wool spinning. Focus promotion on children.

- *Flower Day.* Include dried flower wreathes and have bouquet demonstrations and classes for people to learn wreath-making for a small fee.

- *Harvest Festival.* Have a huge salad sold by the dish, a large tent filled with corn stalks, corn, baskets, and a hay or corn maze.

- *Talk with Quilters Day.* The quilters sell their items at no charge and make their own posters.

- *Corn Roast Day.* Give roasted corn away, donated by the growers. People are fascinated by corn shucking, so do a contest.

- *Customer Appreciation Day.* Give away cider, apple pie or shortcake. Ask farmers to give away some free items as random acts of kindness.

- *Market Mascot Day.* Hold a naming contest. Invite a scarecrow-costumed person to the market to talk to the kids.

- *Scarecrow making.* Have a balloon man for kids, a contest for the biggest tomato, and don't forget the home gardeners.

- *Apple Fest or Maple Fest.* Bob for apples, samples, apple/maple taste testing, posters/banners, apple pressing with hand crank, maple syrup processing equipment.

- Invite the Board of Supervisors to a *goat-milking contest.*

"We are having a multi-cultural entertainment series this summer to celebrate the diversity of the neighborhood in which the market is held."
   – Belle Rita Novak, Mgr., FM at the X, Springfield, MA

"*Herb Day.* The Kansas Grown! Farmers' Market opens each spring on the first Saturday in May with Herb Day. Extension Master Gardeners plan the event including the Herb Society of South Central Kansas. Activities include herb and environmental gardening seminars, youth planting herb containers, demonstration garden seminars, Master Gardener plant sale, herb tasting and LOTS of herbs for sale. This gets excellent free publicity and the market is kicked off with a large crowd without paid advertising."
   – Robert I. (Bob) Neier, Extension agent, Wichita, KS

"We've been experimenting in having live music or other entertainment at the market. It's unclear how many of our customers really want this – some say they are there just for the food, while others seemed drawn by the entertainment as well. It does seem to attract a different clientele."
   – Patty Brand, Exec. Dir., Friends of the St. Paul FM, MN

"We have a drawing every Saturday for a bushel basket of produce. Every grower contributes something to the basket, and the growers and the customers really love it; all during the week they sign up."
   – Connie Veselka, Mgr., Heart of Texas FM, Waco, TX

Organizing Special Events

Every event should be something of another market opening, with the chance to increase the size of your see-saw. Extra supply from your farmers is critical to meet the extra demand created by your special event publicity. If you make a quantum leap in sales, how many people do you plan for? Get the growers behind it! You need to project a certain percentage increase in customers buying their products.

Any market may find that certain ideas work while others do not. If you think a musician or clown amounts to wasted money, let them perform as buskers, earning their pay from the public rather than the market. Try a different set of activities – roasting chiles or corn – until you find a mix that feels right to

Special Events at Your Market

Events can hurt sales if they draw people who are not coming to buy. Events should promote the farmers' market concept which is to re-establish communications between rural and urban culture. Lots of people are looking for their rural roots again. We celebrate the seasons, for example, and in grocery stores there is no season.

Keep the focus on food! The purpose of special events is to promote the market. You want the attendees to come back, so before having special events, make sure your producers are providing high-quality products and services to build customer loyalty and bonding. Help keep customers coming back with constant new excitement, educational, food-related events and thematic entertainment, but don't get too far from "who you are" such that special events detract from food sales. Events that have nothing to do with food or agriculture may promote sales for that one day, but in the long

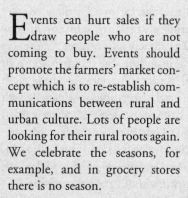

run they attract a different customer base and hurt sales.

When you have a glut of one thing (cherries, peaches, etc.) have a tasting! This turns a not-so-good-situation into a better situation. With each tasting event that you do, emphasize the quality and variety of produce to be found at the market. Studies show this is what draws the people to the farmers' markets. Whatever products you have that the supermarkets don't have, e.g., heirloom varieties of apples, a tasting helps show them off and highlights your competitive edge over the supermarkets.

In April or May flower-glut time, bring in the nurseries to talk about flower care, the local water district to talk about water-saving techniques, or chefs to do a demo on cooking with flowers.

Plan special events around what your target customer may want. Synergy begins to build and expands with diversity. With seniors, for example, you can do

a "Senior Health Fair," including a range of senior health services and nutrition counseling. Involve local businesses; get employees out at lunchtime by serving some special lunches. Each person you hook may tell 10 people.

You want your market to serve as many different types of the population as possible. Target special events to attract population segments, e.g. certain ethnic groups or a wealthy clientele. If your demographics allow it, go after the "green consumer," and you'll have a repeat customer. At the markets they can find foods grown without pesticides and a chance to help farmers preserve farmland and the greenbelt around the city. Green consumers tend to be very loyal and often have more money and tend to better educated – they are a "natural" for the farmers' markets.

One way to attract the the "green consumer" is with Earth Day and organic events. Help celebrate Earth Day with a festival and also have a year-round

your customers. Keep trying new ideas. Marketing demands innovation.

Keep a seasonal focus with the festival. If you get away from food too much, it takes away from the farmer. Use tasting or educational events – apple or cherry tastings, peach or asparagus recipe contests – that will help sell the farmers' products.

Tie special events into three-day weekends that draw tourists. Holidays often take customers elsewhere without bringing new visitors.

Plan a schedule of special events that will highlight the season and create special reasons for customers to come. Each event builds its own history, so plan event changes for future growth.

Generally, markets host events on good market days but try using an event to improve a market day

---

sign describing how farmers' markets are ecological and thus a celebration of every day as earth day. An Organic Tasting Event allows you to educate people on what is "No Spray," what is "transitional," what is actually organic, and to show people how good organic products really are.

Another way to plan great special events at your markets is to look for businesses or community groups you can network with. Look at a Calendar of Events in the newspaper for upcoming events and call the organizations to see if they'd like to come to the market to promote their organization. Read the paper and look for food, garden or agriculture-related events or experts to find people who may contribute to the market. You might find someone who can provide a gardening or cooking demo or even teach a series of classes at the market.

Take advantage of the schools. They love coming out to the markets for Farm Day. Invite teachers and classes, and invite school boards to participate in planning. Invite the Farm Bureau and Cooperative Extension. Have a

mural contest, an essay contest, a photo contest. Have a live story: "Where does lunch come from?"

Prepare a teacher packet that explains where food comes from and talks about the diversity of fruits and vegetables, etc. Have agriculture exhibits about food, where clothes come from, a recycling center, and Peter Rabbit's garden. When we get children thinking about where their food comes from, we create our future.

In conjunction with the Marin Community Food Bank around Valentine's Day, for example, the Marin County Farmers' Market held a "Have a Heart Day." A big red heart with lace around it was placed on a table, suggesting that people buy food at the market and donate for the Food Bank. To promote heart-healthy fruits and vegetables, market volunteers put little hearts on all the fruits and vegetables that are beneficial for the heart. A xeroxed list was passed out of "Heart Healthy Fruits and Vegetables."

Start out small and simple with special events, and build on it more and more. Don't plan so many events at once that you

can't do them right. Don't try to do it all yourself. Have a special event coordinator and develop volunteers, partnerships and collaborators to help. Don't call it a special event unless you're really doing something special.

Don't do the same "special events" over and over. Build on them! Build fund-raisers in conjunction with special events to promote the market in general. In the beginning when you have little or no money to spend on advertising, spend money on special events instead of large paid ads and promote these with press releases, PSAs, signs at the markets, etc.

Plan for getting maximum coverage from media. Get last year's photos to print prior to the event and shoot new photos to send the newspapers for printing after the event as well. Send out press packets early and repeat releases two weeks before the event.

– Lynn Bagley is founder of the Marin County Farmers' Market, director of the Golden Gate Farmers' Market Association and a consultant with Bagley & Associates, Novato, CA ✌

late in the month. Check the effect from year to year at different times to evaluate the cost-benefit ratio.

Set up a public bulletin board to publicize special market events with customers, and post brochures from other community organizations.

Labor can be intense with any special event. Without a paid manager, let different people play the role of coordinator for each different event to avoid burnout. Plan, pay attention to details, and have the manpower to do it right, or don't do it! A strong event committee can handle events every week, from a cookbook signing to a major festival.

Always have a Plan B. When a heavy rain hits, a great event can flop. What happens with hundreds of expectant kids when your event has to go indoors with limited space?

City Harvest: A Celebration of Local Arts and Food included the Boise Symphony, ethnic dance and water play at the Capital City Public Market.

EDUCATIONAL EVENTS

Most markets view themselves as an educational site as well as a place for produce sales. Education comes in many forms: a market information booth, literature with recipes, nutritional information, posters from product commissions, and educational pamphlets from your state agricultural department, Cooperative Extension, and health and illness prevention organizations. Invite groups to participate in market events or have an educational booth, such as master gardeners and food preservers, a nutritionist or a nurseryman.

Non-profit organizations like the American Heart Association may have a dietitian who can give people recipes and tips on how have to a "healthy heart" diet. Coordinated by the Centers for Disease Control and Prevention, there are 5 A Day Programs in every state (frequently at WIC offices), good partners with materials to encourage eating 5-9 servings of fruits and vegetables and getting 30 minutes of exercise each day. Other ideas:

♦ Hospitals and county health departments can host mini-health fairs with glaucoma screening, cholesterol or blood pressure testing at the markets.

♦ Fire departments often do safety and fire prevention awareness education workshops at the markets, bringing Sparky the Fire Dog and letting kids climb on the fire trucks.

♦ Create a photo and information exhibit showing farm locations on a map with lists of crops produced by each farm.

♦ Print seasonal availability charts listing of vegetables and fruits at your market. Many customers post these at home to remind them of what is in season throughout the year.

♦ Educators can influence in every way conceivable – kids raising gardens and becoming market sellers, a math class taught using local vs. global economics, a science class focusing on a market plant physiology, a nutrition class comparing local vs. distant products or fresh vs. frozen nutritional values. Invite local 4-H groups to educate customers about agricultural projects they've done.

"There are many educational programs you can do with the Master Food Preservers, including gauge checks for customers' pressure cookers."

"I have 200-300 school groups per year at the market, ranging from preschool to college. Teachers take the field trip for a variety of reasons: to get out of the classroom, history, math, exposure to fruits and vegetables, exposure outside their students' limited neighborhood, photography, drawing, architecture, marketing, entrepreneurship, etc. I do a 20-minute talk about the history of the market going back 200 years: how we ate with no supermarkets, prepared foods, nothing growing in winter, and a limited supply of what could actually grow in the region. I talk about transportation, refrigeration and how it changed the way we eat, ethnic foods, immigrants and refugees shopping at the market, and cultural differences."

– Sandra Zak, Mgr., Soulard Market, St. Louis, MO

How One Market Celebrated its Birthday

In Beaverton, Oregon, in 1998, the goal for the farmers' market 10th anniversary celebration was to develop an event with various elements that would capture the imagination of customers, the local community and media.

The market hired a consultant, author Vance Corum, and the result was the "10th Birthday Berry Blow-out" which had as its theme "Recreating Community: Returning to Our Roots." Every element was designed to remind Beaverton residents of the history of agriculture and community activities. The Beaverton Modular Railroad Club set up a 10x26-foot rectangular track which drew several thousand onlookers, a reminder of the key role railroads have played in carrying products to market.

The March of Dimes was invited to provide volunteers who served berry shortcake to 1800 people for an old-fashioned dime donation to the March of Dimes. All items were donated including shortcake from Franz Bakery, whipped cream from a friendly supermarket and 38 flats of straw-berries, blueberries, raspberries, blackberries, boysenberries, currants, marionberries and young-berries from (you guessed it) 10 farmers in the market. The March of Dimes was pleased to raise nearly $800.

Beaverton Bakery donated a sheet cake and a three-tier cake, both decorated with a railroad theme and marzipan fruits and vegetables which hundreds more customers enjoyed. The mayor cut the first piece for a front-page photo in the Capital Press.

Ten top area chefs took part in a "Chef Salute to the Market." Each was given a $20 bill to shop the market and then prepare a lunch for two. Five hundred people hovered around their circle of prep tables as they chopped and discussed their presentations in a non-competitive environment.

There were opportunities for fun as well as education. The Woodworkers' Store donated wheels and axles for the first 100 challengers to prepare their own Zucchini 500 racers. Heats were run down a 16-ft., five-lane, wooden raceway. Fifteeen nearby businesses gained visibility for donating prizes to winners.

The cherry pit-spitting contest drew another 150 participants, pitted against each other in seven age groups. Men, women and children took home prizes – from a bat house donated by a vendor to haircuts, music, shoe repair, travel certificates and dinners for two.

A budding, balloon-blowing clown, only 14, entertained hundreds of children in the celebration zone and collected donations as well.

The 10th birthday activities on the lawn next to the paved market space involved more than 5,000 marketgoers in one or more elements of the celebration, reinforcing the market's significant role in community-building. With three months of planning and 15 volunteers on the event day, the berry blow-out demonstrated market thanks to existing customers, while bringing in new customers and media attention to capture new ones in the future. ❧

CHILDREN'S EVENTS

Kids' events are easy to plan and promote. Kids are your future, the ones who keep the market going! Have pony rides for kids. Sponsor special market tours for children. Wait until October so families have a chance to settle into the new school schedule. Offer yourself as a classroom speaker with a slide show or provide teaching materials to show how produce is grown. When kids get excited, they will bring their parents to the market.

Set aside a booth for kids who are gardening or creating a craft. Or have a Kid's Day at the market, with kids selling in a special kid's section with spaces for kids. An annual kids' market in Vancouver, WA, adds immediacy and excitement for young shoppers to buy from other kids. They make a connection between work and income. This is also a good way to get kids into farming.

"We asked schools to give artwork done by children to display at the market. One school grew vegetables and we donated a booth for them to sell produce."

"We have a 'Dad's Day Olympics.' The father and son or daughter climb over bales, carry water together or have a watermelon seed spitting contest."

"The most successful event is the children's market, where kids sell produce or crafts that they've raised or made."
– Sara Pollard, *Do's and Don'ts of a Successful Farmers' Market*

"Flyers can be distributed through the schools if they are approved. If the kids can participate and the event is judged beneficial, the schools may even put them in the teachers' boxes."
– Rose Munoz, former Mgr., Torrance FM, CA

[See also POP Club sidebar in Chapter 7.]

On a 104-degree day a cherry pit-spitting contest is a great distraction for kids in Mosier, OR. They held their hands up high to be the next contestant.

SPECIAL PROMOTIONS

School kids' coupons. The market in Fullerton, CA has brought school classes through the market, giving a $1 coupon to every child, $1,000- $1,500 worth of coupons per year. Coupons are split in quarter pieces and farmers give at reduced prices, i.e., one farmer gives an orange for 25 cents, another some flowers, etc. They get the produce in the kids' hands, the children go home and parents show up the next week.

Promote to chefs. To increase large-order sales to restaurant chefs, mail a packet to all restaurants in the area. Include an invitation tshop at the market plus an "in-season items" flyer, and a "meet the farmers" flyer. Farmers combine trips, e.g., delivering to restaurants after the farmers' market. Elsewhere chefs call growers in advance to bring extra boxes and get paid that day. The chef can pick up from four or five growers, saving delivery costs. They're making several pickups simultaneously as they might at a wholesale produce terminal but without the middleman. Some markets allow chefs to purchase larger volumes one hour in advance of the public.

Postcards. Have customers sign a pre-paid postcard that you mail to them as a reminder of next season's opening. When trying to attract new shoppers, a flyer with real savings may make a difference.

Co-promotions. Attend a merchant meeting to present your ideas on how businesses can take advantage of the market's proximity. Be ready with specific examples of cross-promotional ideas. Encourage them to share possible strategies. Can a western wear shop put a live model in their window or have them do mime on the sidewalk? Will a shop give a discount during market hours to lure the farmers' market shopper into their store? If a local bakery doesn't want to sell in the market, will they provide discount cards for farmers to hand out to customers?

Try a *cross-promotion with businesses* in town. Connect each business with a grower. Have a strawberry grower pass out $3-off coupons for a shoe repair and have the shoe repair shop pass out $2-off coupons for strawberries from that same farmer.

> "Market dollars. This is a cross-promotion with neighboring businesses where downtown restaurants give out market dollars to customers, good for a discount at the market and possibly vice-versa."
>
> – Esther Kovari, former Pres., New Mexico Farmers' Marketing Assoc.

Drawings and raffles. Fill a weekly or monthly food basket to raffle off. Give gift certificates to be spent in the market. Raffle tickets can be used to collect names and e-mail or regular addresses of market customers. Work to build your database for future mailings.

> "An hour before closing, we have a raffle. When people win they go to the farmer's booth to pick it up and that way they get to meet the farmer. Almost every farmer donates something, so there can be many winners – both the farmers and customers like it! I give a 5-minute talk before handing out the tickets, about new items, new farmers, etc. After the raffle is over – at 12:30 – all the vendors in the market have a sale, and the market closes at 1:00. Some customers come throughout the day and some come for the raffle and the sale only. It's not the mass shoppers that come for the raffle, but the bargain hunters, so

Kids actively participate in eating at the Portland Farmers Market (OR) on Wednesday at Shemanski Park. They are likely to become long-term customers.

you get them all that way. The raffles are a success at each of our four markets. Do the raffle near closing, because after the raffle the market is dead. Lots of work, but the farmers love it!"
>
> – Nancy Caster, Mgr., Irvine Center FM, CA

> "In New Bedford, market organizer Barbara Purdy has created a weekly market contest. Every time a shopper buys something, he or she is given a ticket to drop in a glass jar. At the end of the market, the number is picked and announced. The following week, the winner gets a beautiful basket of fresh market produce. Put out a sign at your market office booth announcing, 'Last week's fresh market basket winner was…'"
>
> – *To Market! To Market!* U. of Mass. Cooperative Extension

Coupon sheet. The market in Norwalk, CA solicited its farmers and printed a flier with a dozen coupons featuring 10-25% off at each farmer stall. Have the Boy Scouts distribute these coupon sheets to customers once a month.

HOLIDAYS

Every retailer recognizes their importance. Since markets often represent the greatest ethnic diversity in a community, special holidays are an opportunity to celebrate diversity while educating and having fun at the same time.

Coordinate and plan with your farmers to prepare for each holiday. A holiday committee with vendors, community volunteers and staff can list every holiday, assign a budget figure to each and plan the marketing approach. Think of what is most appropriate for each holiday as far as music, market decorations, suggestions for farmers, gift pack ideas and even market gift baskets which include a mix of vendors' products. Your advertising should reflect your ability to celebrate every holiday in a collective way that others cannot replicate.

A 4th of July kids' bicycle parade gave community leaders an excuse to become involved as judges at the Dublin FM, CA.

◆ *Chinese New Year,* late January - early February. Giant chrysanthemums may become the "must have" gift. Get growers to hang Chinese designs celebrating Year of the Monkey in 2016, followed by Rooster, Dog, Pig, Rat, Ox, Tiger, Rabbit, Dragon, Snake, Horse and Goat in 2027. The 12-year cycle then repeats.

◆ *Groundhog Day,* February 2. Have a groundhog jump out of a farmer's pick-up and look for his shadow. Host a groundhog calling contest with prizes.

◆ *Valentine's Day,* February 14, is the perfect time for heart-shaped price signs and extra special gift packs. Apple growers can prepare by putting heart-shaped stickers on their apples just before they color on the tree. Think of how kids can buy small gifts to participate.

◆ *St. Patrick's Day,* March 17. This is the time for green everything, shamrock signs, and a best dressed farmer and customer contest.

◆ *1st day of spring /summer /fall /winter.* Celebrate the changes with color, decorations and mu-

Peter Schaner of Valley Center, CA finishes the Santa Monica market by collecting boxes of product from five farms to deliver to area restaurants before his 125-mile trip home.

sic. This is a wonderful time to experience transition by "tasting" seasonal products from new farms.

◆ *April Fool's Day* is a time for wild clothing and playful banter with customers. Make sure you have a jokester prancing around the market.

◆ *Easter.* The Glens Falls (NY) market celebrated in 2015 with a visit by the Easter Bunny, face painting, an Easter egg hunt with kids' prizes and Easter deals. This is the #3 sales week for produce departments.

◆ *Earth Day* is April 22, a great day to reinforce the "Reduce, Reuse, Recycle" conservation ethic and kick off a market zero-waste campaign. You will connect with 25% of the population that are leaders and innovators in various fields. Hold an Earth Fair. Put together the world's largest organic salad and feed 5,000.

◆*National Day of Prayer,* May. Invite various faith representatives to have a table and host an interfaith service to show thanks for the foods of our faith.

◆*Cinco de Mayo,* the 5th of May. Promote cultural awareness with a dance troupe even if you lack a strong Hispanic clientele.

- *Mother's Day,* May. Ask your farmers to help fathers and kids to find appropriate gifts for mom. Is this the time to host a special Mother's Day lunch or to kick off your market season?

- *Memorial Day.* Since everyone is barbecuing and headed on picnics, change grower signs from "sweet corn" to "barbecue corn." With barbecue on their minds, sell "barbecue garlic" as well.

- *International Children's Day,* June, is a time for celebrating diversity, acceptance and schools closing. Ask kids to dress in the native garb of their ancestors. Here's your last chance to get teachers involved this year and prepare for National Children's Day in October.

- *Father's Day,* June. Time for moms and kids to find those special "palate-pleasers" for dad.

- *July 4th.* Organize a "picnic market" where customers can get everything they need for their picnic, from corn to watermelons. Invite unusual food purveyors just for the day to complement all your regular picnic products.

- September 15. *Mexican Independence Day* to acknowledge your Hispanic vendors and customers.

- *Grandparent's Day,* September. Coordinate a cross-promotion with local businesses to give a small gift to every grandparent coming to the market, including produce and gift certificates.

- *United Nations Day,* October. Invite global groups to participate in educating about various international concerns. Celebrate your international customers or a connection to National Children's Day.

- *Halloween* is the second largest holiday for retail sales. Vendors can dress up displays and sell healthy alternative giveaways.

- *Thanksgiving* is often the biggest sales day of the year at farmers' markets, especially strong for flowers. Get your chocolate covered nuts and other delicacies ready.

- *Christmas.* As our largest holiday it causes even seasonal markets to re-open for a few weeks in December, especially if you have good artisans.

- *Kwanzaa,* an Afro-American holiday on December 26.

- Be aware of any special holidays of any ethnic or religious cultures that your market serves, and celebrate those at the market!

"It's usually a soft market the weekend after Thanksgiving, because everyone has leftovers and refrigerators are full. But the tomato guys clean up, because everyone is making sandwiches and they like big slicing tomatoes. Learn to look for these little niches around holidays."

– Mark Sheridan, former Mgr., Santa Barbara FM Assoc., CA

PROMOTION EVALUATION

Consider ways of measuring the effectiveness of your promotions, just like your ad budget. With either you are spending valuable time or money. Shortly after each promotion and at the end of the year, evaluate your campaign. Keep a promotion book in a three-ring binder, or in a report or Excel spreadsheet so that the board can have easy access. For each event describe the promotion, budget and consumer feedback. Include copies of any paid advertising or free publicity. Then ask:

- Did we reach our target audience?
- Did we achieve our goals?

Capturing quick customer input on event day can help to make adjustments in your planning for your next event or the same event next year. Use clipboards to make it easy to fill a single-sided questionnaire.

- What was our customer count? And sales?
- Could we have prepared better for the unforeseen?
- Did we stay within the budget?
- How can we improve future promotional campaigns?

"After every promotional effort, use an evaluation form to ensure that every effort contributes to future promotional efforts. Have sections for planning, promotion, description of activity, time involved in planning, costs, implementation, ease of organization, factors which influenced success, unforeseen problems, time to set up and take down, vendor response, consumer response, approximate number that responded, and any other additional comments."

– *To Market! To Market!* U. of Mass. Cooperative Extension

Coupons serve as an effective, low-cost way to test advertisements or promotions. Put a coupon on everything you print – a newspaper ad, a flier, even a brochure. Put in a $1-off, cut-out offer on strawberries, for example. Code each coupon so you will know where it came from – this allows you to test the effectiveness of that medium. As each coupon is returned, reimburse the vendors at market value or have them share the cost. Don't count on getting a lot of coupons (unless you're giving away big sums of money) but use the response level to compare results from different media so you can improve future ads and promotions.

Tracking promotion results may take the form of talking to customers, sending them a return-mail postcard or asking them to fill out a short questionnaire. [See Appendix]

Compare sales results and promotional expenses on a monthly and yearly basis – mapping seasonal and yearly trends

The Easter celebration at the West Palm Beach Greenmarket includes vendors spending extra time with appropriate decorations.

helps you figure the impact of your promotional programs.

"Every farmers' market is unique. Each market organizer must assess the promotional ideas mentioned, and judge the best ones to be implemented. In the final analysis, only experience will answer the question, 'Which methods are best for my market?'"

– *To Market! To Market!* U. of Mass. Cooperative Extension

FUNDRAISERS

There are many ways to build your budget or cover your operating costs other than space fees. Time and creativity are the major limitations. Fundraising efforts should be seen as a vital part of your promotional effort.

When another entity may want to contribute to your fundraiser or promotion effort with money or in-kind assistance, you may need to address how much visibility to give that business or organization. If a major beverage company is willing to print 2x3-foot signs in color but their logo overwhelms yours in size, you may want to avoid the image of being controlled by a large, private firm.

Consider all the fundraising ideas possible in your community. What are the resources? Who will help? Ask farmers and customers for their ideas and a pulse on what is most feasible. List them and then start with several that seem to use your time and energy well, within your financial ability. Set clear goals and know how much you will spend to make your goals.

A *market cookbook* or other publication can be sold as a fundraiser.

A *market calendar* can make money and be a reminder of market days. Other community

In 2010 Portland Farmers Market held a major raffle with numerous prizes including a Grand Prize of a $2000 shopping spree spread over 40 weeks of market.

groups may pay to have their activities or events listed. Find an artist through an art society and have them paint, draw or photograph market scenes or farmers' fields.

An *art fair* is a perfect way to involve a large number of community artists who contribute a portion of all their sales, whether the theme is the market or otherwise. They might contribute to a market calendar or a raffle in conjunction with a dinner.

Brick sponsors. Seattle's Pike Place Market was able to re-surface the market while raising money. Customers or supporters were invited to have their names inscribed in a brick for $35 or a foursome for $140. Pike Place raised $1.2 million and the floor cost them $400,000.

Promotional items. Just about any promotional item can help you raise funds, whether a T-shirt, sweatshirt, apron, mug, hat, pin or jacket. There is a wide range of quality, styles, and prices among many national and local companies that handle this business, so do comparison shopping. Be prepared to spend money to make money.

Silk-screened T-shirts are relatively inexpensive at $7-10 each, plus a one-time set-up charge, depending on the shirt color, quality, the number of imprint colors and the quantity and sizes printed. Even a small market can probably afford a minimum run of 36 shirts, one-color. If you have a popular logo and thousands of customers, you can probably do a gross (144) in four-color, instead, for a comparable price

per piece. Continue investing once you see that your initial purchase is well received. Like farmers, you have to have substantial volume to sell; sales slow when you run low.

When you are more confident of your customer desires, you might invest in stitched items. You will pay $150-300 for an initial computerization of your image, depending on the color complexity and number of stitches, plus about $10-15 depending on shirt quality and stitch count. On a hat the maximum surface area is about 2x4 inches and you might use the same image on a jacket or denim shirt, as did the Santa Monica Farmers' Market for its managing staff. Stitched hats for sale at $15-20 can be hip for a youthful, fashion-oriented marketplace. If your customers are very price conscious, you may choose to silkscreen a $5 hat so everyone can join the fun for about $7. After all, it is a fundraiser, but like most fundraisers, be conscious that you are also gaining publicity through making someone a walking advertisement for your market.

"The Warwick Valley Farmers' Market promotes itself through selling promotional items and by offering premiums for joining a 'Friends of the Market' membership, ala Public Broadcasting TV memberships. Their biggest undertaking has been developing a Warwick Valley Farmers' Market cookbook. This was financed by selling advance copies and done by professionals that volunteered a great deal of their services."
– *Farmers' Market Forum,* FM Federation of NY

"At the beginning of each summer, The Marketplace at Buffalo gives its members sweatshirts with the logo for their farmers to wear. The market pays for the sweatshirts by printing the names of the market sponsors – one a media sponsor, the other a cash sponsor. The market also requires all vendors to wear special aprons that are designed to hold cash. The aprons create a consistent image for the market and also speed up the handling of cash."
– *To Market! To Market!* U. of Mass. Cooperative Extension

"We issue 'market money' with wooden nickels, dated with expiration date at the end of the year, with a different color each year. We purchased 10,000 at the beginning of the season, and sold them to customers, 10 for $1. We redeemed 500 the first year. They've become collectible items. Word-of-mouth kicks in, people see them and ask where they got them. We made over $400 in cash the first year. We also use the wooden nickels for our Produce Race in the fall – the nickels become the 'wheels' for the produce."

  – Rick Castellano, former Mgr., Olympia FM, WA

Shopping bags come in paper, canvas, plastic or string. They serve as a reminder to come again, and are an effective advertising tool for any market. A canvas bag with your market logo is a popular investment that loyal customers are proud to use.

"One year we sold over $3,000 worth of 'Eco bags' and made $1,600. To fill up a bag with produce for display costs us $2.34 and we sell it for $5."

  – Joanne Neft, former Mgr., Foothill FM Assoc., Auburn, CA

Library bookmarks are a wonderful way to cross-pollinate ideas. Librarians in Great Barrington, MA, were happy to promote the farmers' market with every book that was lent out, using a bookmark that gave the library locations and hours along with the market logo and hours.

Dinner. With all the great produce and other foods available at your market, you probably can organize a successful dinner with less effort than a caterer, but it wouldn't be a bad idea to have the help of one. Consider other fundraising ideas once you have all those people there. Perhaps it's time for that art fair, or local businesses may contribute items to be raffled to the highest bidder and your farmers can contribute as well. What about a weekend in a swanky hotel, a cruise on the paddle wheeler, a companion airfare anywhere in the U.S., dinner for four, a year of free movies or a bed-and-breakfast stay? Businesses want to help; they provide the gift and the market provides visibility for them.

Holding an art fair is a wonderful lasting way to insert local artists into community homes. Stories will be told. The event, the goals and the artists will be remembered.

The Reading Terminal Market makes a huge amount from its annual ball when Philadelphia's finest roam through the marketplace which includes farmer day tables. It is quite a high-brow affair, but not all dinners are so.

"In 2000, Greenmarket held a dinner dance called the Vegetable Heirloom Ball, for which some 150 folks forked out 300 bucks a pop. Held at the Judson Grill, an upscale, three-star restaurant in New York, the gala evening featured heirloom vegetables on display and as a part of the dinner, a barnyard auction and a bluegrass band. At the auction, the crowd bid on items like overnight stays at the Plaza Hotel. It was a high-end affair, but we asked people to dress down in country chic. The ball was a great fund-raiser, and it also helped raise awareness about such issues as open-pollinated varieties."

  – Tony Manetta, former Dir., Greenmarket, New York, NY

"The key to fund-raising is to hold special events and turn them into fund-raisers at the same time. A special event, through media attention, draws more people to the market. Have an annual Harvest Faire, invite artists and craftsmen to rent booths, and charge customers twelve dollars each for a country brunch, inviting celebrity chefs.

THE NEW FARMERS' MARKET

Silent auctions also can be combined with special events and are one of the most effective fundraisers. You can collect contributions from the community as well as vendors."

– Lynn Bagley, Golden Gate FM Assoc., Novato, CA

"We had a shoestring budget at start-up and we developed a coupon program that we took to local merchants. They paid us $10 and we printed coupons offering 10% off or 20% off, redeemable at their store. The customers could only get these coupons at the market, and they could only use them on that market day. Most of the stores were within five blocks of the market. We had an article in the newspaper and flyers in the merchants' windows and advertised the coupon program. It was immensely helpful in increasing the traffic flow at the market and also gave us a small amount of funding."

– Grace Richards, Arlington FM, WA

Dinners – like any fundraising event – can have a more targeted purpose. Due to a highway expansion, Tierra Vegetables in Healdsburg, CA lost a portion of their land holding their farmstand. They were offered a century-old barn to serve as a new one. CUESA, operator of the Ferry Plaza Farmers' Market, helped spread the word for a benefit dinner to cover the moving cost.

COMMUNITY INVOLVEMENT

Your market should be intimately associated with the community in everyone's mind. Whenever people think of "community spirit" or "community involvement," you want people to think "farmers' market," not your local sports team!

As author and motivational speaker Wayne Dyer says, "What you really, really, really, really want, you'll get." The four "reallys" stand for what you wish, desire, intend and are passionate about. If you "really" want to make your market the center of community, you will do many things. You will be ready for opportunities to open. You will be ready to speak before various groups without worry because your inspired focus moves you!

"You have to plant the seeds and enrich the soil to build, through marketing, a community feeling."

– Kirk Lumpkin, former Mgr., Berkeley FM, CA

Becoming the Community Center

Your goal should be to make the market the focus of many community activities. Think of every possible subgroup of the local populace and determine how they can become involved. Create a win-win situation with them.

Speak at the Lions Club, the Rotary, the Optimists and every other club or organization willing to have a presentation. Invite them to do a fundraiser at your market. You want to be the center of fundraising in your community.

Tie in with local businesses. San Luis Obispo Market, CA, for instance, sponsors a "Meet with the Chamber of Commerce" at their Thursday Night market. Downtown businesses are often eager to have a farmers' market, especially as suburban malls are killing the downtown business. If you have a downtown market in a business district, encourage businesses to come out onto the street with a cart so they can join in the market spirit. The cart, in effect, says, "We are part of the market" and it encourages people to come into the shop. Some shop owners have painted little footsteps going from the cart into their stores!

Alternately, you might host a "Business Day" at the market. Send out letters inviting local business people to the market. Extend the personal touch: walk them around the market; offer free coffee and doughnuts; give them nametags; and show them how one enterprise supports the other.

Banks are required to do a certain amount of community service by law. Encourage them to promote your market and themselves through sponsorship of your musicians, the food bank collection or the market chef program.

"As part of our 2015 publicity strategy, we are working to share the stories of our farmers with the community. One of our biggest strengths is the relationships that customers can build with

Jennifer Bartos, owner of Make it Sweet, a bakery supply store that provides classes, made this amazing cake for Sustainable Food Center's (TX) inaugural Farm to Plate dinner in 2008. She continues to make amazing offerings every year for Farm to Plate using farmers' seasonal ingredients.

the farmers and artisans. We want to help foster that relationship by helping our shoppers learn more about their farmers through vendor spotlights, interviews, and even a storytelling event in partnership with a local comedy and improv club in town!"

– Erin Jobe, Mgr., Carrboro FM, NC

Work with HMOs (health maintenance organizations): talk to their clinic manager, feed them market news for their monthly newsletters, and give them handouts to place in their clinics. You can also:

- Install a community bulletin board at the market.
- Find out what's happening in the ag community and tie into local ag events.
- Inform leaders in the faith community about your market.
- Put up a display at your local library.

- Invite local cooking schools to purchase and perform student demonstrations.
- Approach elementary schools about market tours.
- Talk to the local cafeteria directors about featuring fresh, local crops on the school menu.
- Get a soapbox, and invite political candidates to speak.

"The SLO uses the markets as a place to elect the city council every year. They all give three-minute speeches at the market."

– Peter Jankay, Exec. Dir., San Luis Obispo County FM Assoc., CA

"Bring brochures about the markets to Assisted Living Facilities, which have small kitchen facilities. Let the managers know at senior centers that if they bring seniors in to the market, you will provide parking places for them as well as provide assistants and give senior discounts."

– Karen Durham, former Mgr., Bellingham FM, WA

"Get the community behind you at the earliest date in developing or reorganizing a market – civic associations, environmental groups, churches, senior citizens organizations, etc. These groups have newsletters and hold meetings and can do wonders in helping with potential customer surveys, free PR, etc."

– Tony Evans, Maryland Dept. of Agriculture

Networking

Become an active participant in civic organizations like the Rotary Club or Chamber of Commerce. Your true goal should be to participate and contribute toward the common good and highest goals of those organizations.

Good managers are involved with their communities. It is not a one-way street. They keep reaching out to see what the community has to offer and what they can offer back. They often offer to help rather than wait to be asked. They consider how the news in the paper affects the market and work to build connections with those in the news and those who will be, because they have a good community cause.

"At a local Chamber of Commerce dinner, I sat next to the head of the City of Seattle's City Engineering Department and he ended up putting up banners for me, instead of us having to rent a cherry picker."

– Chris Curtis, Exec. Dir., Neighborhood FM Alliance, Seattle

"As a board member of the American Institute of Wine and Food (AIWF), I met a food writer and that's how our market (Marin County FM) got in the New York Times."

– Lynn Bagley, Golden Gate FM Assoc., Novato, CA

Co-Promotions

While we have touched previously on co-promotions with business, be on the lookout for potential partnerships with them or service groups. Align the market with merchant associations or service organizations that already have marketing networks in place, especially those that promote healthy eating. If you can, solicit drawing or contest prizes, or any other involvement, by speaking to a downtown business meeting. Then follow up by approaching individual businesses, many of whom don't attend meetings.

Connect with groups like the American Heart Association or March of Dimes who have staff and volunteers to help set up. People from such civic groups as parks and recreation or 4H or the YMCA may also help you with events. Ask the FFA to do a petting zoo.

The Beaverton, OR, market involved a fire station in its 1998 festival called "Salsa: Some Like It Hot." Several firefighters trained a water hose on the contestants in the hot chili eating contest, casting the firefighters in a fun, friendly light.

Be ready to donate. When other organizations are having a fundraiser, a delicious basket of fresh market produce can be a welcome prize. If the perishability of donating produce is a problem, create

Adirondack Harvest displays its local products board at the Chestertown FM, NY.

market dollars which can be exchanged at the market. This will expose the market to another organization's audience and bring more people to market.

Your promotion of another entity need not have a financial aspect. You both may simply want to provide a service and improve the public perception of your organizations. This happens when a health screening organization provides blood pressure tests or a transit organization provides rides such as the Grants Pass, OR, downtown trolley shuttling people throughout the downtown.

"In cooperation with local transit, offer a free ride to and from the farmers' market on market days. Anyone wishing to take advantage of the offer may pick up tickets from the transit company or from the market office. These free transit tickets are valid on market days only."

– Kitchener FM, Ontario, Canada

"My wife Robin proposed a business sponsorship program to our local chamber of commerce. For $150, a business could become a sponsor of the month for the Chelsea Farmers' Market. In return, the business would be mentioned in all advertising for the month they sponsored and receive a complimentary stall space during their sponsored month. They could use this stall space to promote their business. Within one week, Robin had sponsors for each of the six months that our market is open. The sponsorship program has allowed the market to advertise more frequently plus helped develop relationships with other area businesses."

– Scott E. Staelgraeve, Chelsea, MI

Art & Music

Build ties with the artistic community. A glass shop might like to sponsor an opportunity for kids to set colored glass pieces into colored cement bricks that make perfect door stops or garden gifts. A tile shop may build a welcome wall at your market site, having kids reflect with their tiles on the theme of peace as was done at Jack London Square in Oakland. Ask a photo studio or a local artists' group to co-host an art exhibit called "Food for the Eyes." You provide the food and they arrange, decorate, carve, photograph and paint food scenes.

Allied Arts in Yakima was selected in 2000 as Washington's winner of the Millenium Arts Project Award. Their project, led by a Massachusetts artist, has transformed a portion of a downtown parking lot into a new plaza celebrating water as the basis of life. Customers at the farmers' market on Third Street now can park and sit in a beautiful space, watching other market-goers shop in front of the Capitol Theatre. Under its canopy musicians play each Sunday. Thus, the food and art community blend together harmoniously.

> "We partner with the Metro Arts Alliance event, Jazz in July, that uses the farmers' market site for several Saturday performances by Iowa jazz groups."
>
> – Deb Burger, Mgr., Downtown Des Moines FM, IA

There may be a blues or jazz club that promotes musicians in your area. If your market is on a weekday when musicians' fees are generally lower, their response may be better. Make it worthwhile; encourage buskers and pay them if you can. Talk to local clubs where out-of-town musicians may be playing on a weekend; they may want another gig in the morning before leaving for home.

Sponsorship

Corporations and local businesses look for opportunities to sponsor events. Hopefully, your market is a perfect site. Corporate sponsors are an excellent source of publicity and promotion for larger market festivals with substantial crowds. Look for funding of segments of the festival as well as goods in trade, i.e., advertising for festival exposure.

Co-sponsors inevitably have a different set of goals from the market; what you are seeking is overlapping interests that give them the chance to claim your market as their own. The more community segments you have owning the market in a certain sense, the more it truly reflects your community's uniqueness.

You might start with smaller events where you build experience and credibility in the eyes of the business community. For $300 a day, one corporation donates shuttle service with their sign on a trolley. A legal firm has a private lunch area for their employees for the day. A bank sponsors a major band for $1200 while a CPA firm puts their name on the music sponsor banner for $350 the following week.

The Portland Farmers' Market, OR, successfully expanded its annual "Summer Loaf: A Celebration of Bread" in mid-July with Fisher Mills as the main sponsor. In 2000 the Northwest's top bakeries gave the city a celebration in the South Park blocks very different from the normal jazz and brew festivals along the waterfront. A bread baking competition and classes plus media attention doubled the normal crowd to 10,000 and gave bakeries a novel form of recognition.

Former executive director Dianne Stefani-Ruff acknowledged, "Events have two goals – to bring new vendors and bring new customers. A normal event takes 40-60 extra hours of work, but for Summer Loaf there is an extra 400 hours of my time, 200 hours of an assistant, plus a paid director and committee meetings for a full year." The event had its own $30,000 budget, roughly half from corporate sponsors, revenue from classes at $50 per person, and income from 17 bakeries at $250 each. Fisher Mills, which owns Fisher Broadcasting, Channel 2, provides free PSAs on television. The event, started as a celebration of Portland's wonderful baking community, has taken on national significance with well-known instructors flying in to conduct the baking classes.

The Portland market has had Provista, a specialty foods company, as sponsor of its "Tomatofest" and "The Great Pumpkin Event." The company has a market booth at both major events. Typhoon restaurant has also sponsored the pumpkin event, distributing free pumpkins and hot cider and showing off their exquisite pumpkin carving skills. A major local berry grower, Columbia Empire Farms, has sponsored the

"Going to the Market" mural by artist Jeri Moore headlines the homepage of the Sustainable Food Center in Austin, TX.

berry festival, giving away thousands of free berry shortcakes in return for promotional prominence.

> "We've built a community where there was none – on a college campus. We're a destination market. People leave voice messages saying, 'Thanks for what you're doing.' We don't have an immediate base of customers but have drawn people, overcoming our parking problems and our hard-to-describe location."
>
> – Dianne Stefani-Ruff, former Exec. Dir., Portland FM, OR

Having succeeded in building numbers through special events at its premier PSU market, the Portland Farmers Market has shifted several key events to its other locations. Still, it provides visibility to three key sponsors on the website homepage.

> "Align with other groups. Don't fight 'em – join 'em! Our Chili Cook-Off Day is held at the same time as the city's Harbor Days. So we got together with our state's chili association to make our event part of the Harbor Days, and it's helped us both."
>
> – Rick Castellano, former Mgr., Olympia FM, WA

The Market as Event Location

Look at the organizations and activities in your area. Those organizations with successful fundraisers may want to use the market as a new location for their event. Let the library or the high school orchestra know that your farmers' market is available as a fundraising site. This builds community support and also brings in publicity. As your market grows in size and stature, larger organizations will be interested in using your location to host events.

Look at your Yellow Pages for organizations, social clubs and business organizations. An interfaith bake sale may give many religious bodies new visibility. If you allow them to make money through you, they automatically will bring you money as well. You have a base of customers to which they are adding. Work with them to accentuate their publicity efforts.

Other organizations may want to create their own new events at the market. The Red Cross can do a blood drive and the garden club might do a bake or plant sale. The market can become a central meeting place for local groups and causes. Put up signs at market entrances announcing these events so customers get in the habit of checking to see what's special today.

> "Even if it's not directly a food event, we try to encourage sympathetic groups to use our market locations, and of course encourage them to get the media there. Have the announcer slip in something like: 'By the way, we're at the Union Square Greenmarket, and they're here three to four days a week, but today we've taken this section to have (event).' This doesn't require any expense or much organization for the market, but we get some great exposure out of it."
>
> – Tony Manetta, former Dir., Greenmarket, New York, NY

Free Market Booths

Set aside a few free spaces for non-profit or educational organizations such as Master Gardeners, Master Composters, community gardening associations, or an organic association. Let them have a free booth in exchange for doing some educational demo for the public or an educational and fun activity for children. Include home economics and science teachers, and invite the local humane society to adopt out animals.

Habitat for Humanity, the CROP Walk, an American Heart Association chapter, and the 4-H club suddenly gain visibility, solicit new members or raise funds. Send them a photo of their volunteers to include with an article in their newsletter.

In Davis, CA, the market provides eight spaces for organizations with a social, cultural, environmental, educational, political or religious focus, although they don't permit singing by church groups. Their board policies have city approval since the market is on the city's Central Park. They do not disallow activities but can regulate the time, place and manner of them.

"Get involved in the community and have non-profit booths. They can have a booth for so many weeks in the season and in turn they are required to send out a news release saying that they will be at the farmers' market and say what they're doing. We ask that they send out a minimum of 10 news releases and we ask them to take flyers and talk about them in their organizations."
– Karen Durham, former Mgr., Bellingham FM, WA

Become a "Giver" Organization

"We encourage farmers and customers to bring canned goods or nonperishable items, or donate fresh produce. The market's donations help a local food group serve hundreds of people each week. In addition to helping others, charitable events help promote your market. When people find out what you're doing, it makes the community feel like rallying around you, that you're part of the community and you want to help."
– Rick Castellano, former Mgr., Olympia FM, WA

Encourage and arrange for farmers to donate produce to local food banks. Support other organizations by giving products or a market basket to their fundraising event. Recognize that community values do not always match market values. Be ready to flex to show support at times even when the request doesn't exactly seem to benefit your market.

Develop a reputation for being a "giver" organization, making your market a vital part of the community that everyone else wants to help succeed. Providing a scholarship to a local agricultural student gives you the basis for a press release. Give produce baskets to visiting dignitaries. When you consistently give to other efforts, make a list of your contributions for the media.

© Vance Corum

Allowing your local library or other organizations to distribute literature is a good way to generate community goodwill and word-of-mouth.

Use the market as a finish line for a 5K walk or 50K bike fundraiser for breast cancer research, multiple sclerosis, Parkinson's disease or whatever cause someone brings to you. Provide the fresh fruit and water for rest stations where your logo is visible. Keep your market name in the public eye. Work with a radio or TV station or the newspaper to co-sponsor and help promote the event. When it is covered in the media, your market gains visibility and trust among people who are watching news about events of concern to them.

You can build your community reputation even through something as unortho-

At the Davis Farmers Market a local artist crafted an art project fundraiser to show solidarity with the people of Japan following the horrific 2011 earthquake and tsunami. Market customers donated $1 to add a tile to the mosaic.

dox as buying shoes for school children as they've done in Fullerton, CA. Generally ask the beneficiary group to take an active part in a festival instead of saying "here is the check." Have them answer questions at an information booth and require them to send out news releases about their participation, as well as publicize it in their in-house newsletter. In staging nonprofit events, look for goodwill, future sales and long-term promotion rather than immediate profit. It need not always be food-related in order to meet a need. And there's always a way to make it fun and festive!

Model for Change

Your market can be a model for change among your farmers and within your community. Change is not easy, but can be fun. The old saying "If it ain't broke, don't fix it" unfortunately keeps many people stuck in the same patterns while customer demands are constantly changing. Indeed, about the only thing we can be sure of today is that change is going to come.

In promoting your market, be fearless in trying different ideas. Determine what customer problems need solving and take incremental steps so that you can modify your path if change makes things worse or simply isn't effective. Present ideas to your board and to vendors. Maybe it's time for an updated logo, a new series of special events, a different promotional strategy or a workshop on display. It's definitely time to go mobile in many communities. Become a pioneering community and health advocate – show your own motivation by outlining a plan, the rationale, the skills to be learned, the risks and the potential benefits.

"I believe that the best public health tool that we could promote is a sharp chef's knife, two cutting boards and a salad spinner."

    – Dr. Preston Maring, Associate Physician in Chief, Kaiser Permanente Medical Center, Oakland, CA

ॐ

Embracing the Community 10

> *"We seem to have lost our sense of community, opting for profits first and a survival of the fittest...I am a farmer and a good neighbor..."*
> – David Mas Masumoto, *Epitaph for a Peach*

America's demographic tapestry is constantly being rewoven with new and beautiful strands that offer complexity and opportunity. Just as has happened for centuries, each new immigrant group enriches our cultural melting pot and offers new flavors for America's gastronomic experimentation.

Nowhere is this more obvious than at farmers' markets where people from every nation come as producers and consumers, creating a more harmonious mix of food and culture than we have ever known.

Having tried bok choy and finger bananas, the consumer is now tasting kimchi and Indian or Thai eggplant. Producers are daring shoppers with samples and recipes for new products, a time-honored way to develop regular customers.

What better way to convince a hesitant customer to try a yellow beet, red carrot, burdock or fenugreek than for a farmer to include a sample in a bag with other produce. "Free gift with purchase."

America's farmers are educating consumers with samples, nutritional information, cooking tips and printed recipes even as authors complement them with a constant stream of market cookbooks.

> "The key is to educate the consumer. You need to provide recipes, cooking tips and nutritional information about the product, because it's new to them."
>
> – Rose Koenig, Haile Village FM, Gainesville, FL

Education about agriculture and nutrition is a priority for many farmers' markets. Ask farmers to talk about their challenges; ask customers what else they want to see; promote visits to the farms, and outline nutritional benefits of products. Markets are also educating consumers with tasting demonstrations, chef competitions, general nutritional information and website farm biographies.

 EDUCATING THE PUBLIC ABOUT LOCAL AGRICULTURE AND FARMERS' MARKETS

Ferry Plaza – San Francisco

In September of 1992, a one-day harvest market of farmers and local restaurants was planned on a Sunday morning. It occurred in the middle of the Embarcadero Roadway which, until just three years earlier, had been a two-level freeway separating the city from its waterfront and the historic Ferry Building. The 1989 Loma Prieta earthquake buckled a portion of the freeway, and with its removal came the opportunity to re-envision the waterfront and provide a home for a public market.

The success of the harvest market event led Sibella Kraus, who had developed the Tasting of Summer Produce for several years, to establish the Ferry Plaza Farmers Market the following spring. Every Saturday the plaza was transformed into a vibrant site of out-

On the perimeter of the Ferry Marketplace, CUESA has placed 8' x 8' photomurals in the A to Z series to introduce concepts in sustainable agriculture.

standing quality and sustainably grown produce. It quickly developed a dedicated following, enabling more farmers to participate.

In 1994, CUESA (www.cuesa.org) formed as the operational body of the Ferry Plaza Farmers Market. The name, Center for Urban Education about Sustainable Agriculture, acknowledged the founding vision of a market that educates as well as feeds its shoppers. Within a few years, CUESA offered cooking demonstrations, seasonal tastings, and other educational programs to enhance the market shopping experience and create a culture of food literacy.

Close to the downtown financial district, in 1995 CUESA started a Tuesday midday farmers' market in Justin Herman Plaza, across from the Ferry Building. This landmark but long-neglected building was slated for renovation, and a critical component in its interior renovation was the knowledge that the farmers' market would be relocated to the building's perimeter.

As the Ferry Building was being redeveloped, CUESA began sustainability education programs outside the market. Schools in San Francisco and Berkeley participated in Market Cooking for Kids, a youth cooking and nutrition program that included education about farms and seasonality. CUESA also managed Open Garden Day, a self-guided tour of Bay Area urban gardening projects, and published an urban greening resource guide.

With the completion of the Ferry Building in 2003, CUESA achieved its 10-year goal of a permanent home. Its outdoor market, office and teaching kitchen were all housed together at an iconic building, re-branded as a marketplace dedicated to showcasing small regional producers inside the ground-floor private retail shops. Farmers' market vendors were offered first crack at opening brick-and-mortar shops inside the Ferry Building Marketplace, operated by Equity Office Properties.

CUESA continued to experiment with a Thursday night market, a Sunday garden market, print materials, cookbook authors and a "Sustainable Agriculture A-Z" photomural exhibit in the arcades of the Ferry Building, highlighting sustainable farming concepts. Local chefs were happy to participate in a Shop with the Chef program since their customers were also market customers.

Tasting festivals were implemented to help move products at the height of their season, while CUESA's Meet the Producer program helped customers understand why farmers' market products are different than supermarket products. Producers or panels spoke for a half hour, frequently using photos and products to explain why they grow certain varieties and what it

The Ferry Plaza FM brand is reinforced by the iconic Ferry tower that looms over San Francisco Bay. The info booth educates and assists many customers and tourists.

takes to get their product to market. A farm tour program was developed for the public to meet the farmers on their land. Educational farmer profiles were created for display at their booths and on the website.

The work of cultivating a healthy food system continued with creation of the Sustainability Frameworks, which delineate principles and best practices for environmentally sound, humane, economically viable, and socially just food production. CUESA introduced the Waste Wise initiative, a comprehensive waste reduction program and education campaign that is a model for farmers' markets around the country.

In 2011 and 2012, CUESA launched the Schoolyard to Market and Foodwise Kids programs to serve local schools. It began its Chef Shopping program to encourage local restaurants, caterers, and artisanal food businesses to source from its market farmers. These buyers apply annually for parking permits which give them access to curbside parking, shopping carts and loading assistance. More than 200 chefs participate.

The Ferry Plaza Farmers Market operates year-round on Saturdays, Tuesdays, and Thursdays, with numerous free and low-cost educational programs to help urban dwellers of all ages learn about their food, where it comes from, and how to grow, select, and prepare it – programs highlighted in the "What We Do" section of the CUESA website. It also has given nonprofits working around food, nutrition, gardening and other issues the opportunity for exposure.

An industry leader, CUESA continues its work as a well-established, financially sound and respected organization with the support of a committed community, board, sponsors and staff. It feeds and educates 25,000 shoppers each week with a regular Culinary Market Tour, Schoolyard to Market Program, an Iron Chef Challenge, Market to Table cooking demonstrations, Farm Tours, Sustainability Talks, Discovery Stations, product festivals, seasonal celebrations and an e-letter. CUESA demonstrates that a plethora of programs are essential in fulfilling its mission.

Santa Fe Farmers Market Institute

The Institute was created in 2002 as the nonprofit arm of the Santa Fe Farmers Market. Its initial mission, according to program director Sam Baca, was a capital campaign for a market building in the city-owned railroad yard. Sarah Noss spearheaded the $4.5 million effort, shepherding along her Institute board with the farmers' market board. Both are now housed in the upstairs offices of a gold LEED-certified building. Downstairs is the 2nd Street Brewery along with shops that open on market day and 9,800 s.f. of open space for weddings, conferences, concerts and community events.

The market structure has enabled the farmers' market to operate year-round since 2008, expanding its size to accommodate 150 vendors per year, with far more farmers, value added producers and local artisans – all producing within a 15-county area of northern New Mexico.

Vendor support. The Institute provides microloans of $250 to $5000 to Santa Fe Farmers' Market vendors at 6% interest through the Sandia Area Federal Credit Union. Half goes to the credit union, and half to keep the loan fund sustainable. The loan comes with a 40-month payback period and professional assistance provided by the Institute and its partners, which ensures that farmers and ranchers can provide a constant and growing food supply to the Santa Fe region. Between 2009 and 2014, there were 150 loans totaling $500,000.

More than 30 loans have funded greenhouses that feed product into the winter market, 20 more have been irrigation loans critical to smart water use, and many more have provided farmers with essential seasonal start-up funds. After successful repayment vendors can request up to $10,000 on a second loan.

The training and professional development component enables the Institute to support all sorts of training programs on and off-site to further develop vendor skills. They send 40 people annually to the New Mexico Organic Farming Conference, and they co-sponsor the Carbon Economy series so that vendors can attend for free.

The Santa Fe market shed (left) and pavilion (right) create cover and a pleasant outdoor walkway for customers.

Educating about healthy, local food. The Santa Fe Farmers Market Institute strongly believes in a continuing education program for the public. Its film series runs for five winter months, getting average attendance of 100 community members.

A children's nutrition program works each year with a different elementary school that has at least 75% eligible for free or reduced lunch. Over several months about 300-400 children attend the farmers' market, one class at a time. After a short farmer talk, volunteer school teachers present fruit and vegetable lesson plans and let students taste the items of the day. Each child then receives $2 in tokens to make purchases at the market.

Cooking and nutritional classes for low-income families are presented in conjunction with La Familia Medical Center. Volunteer chefs do menu planning, give cooking tips and hand out recipes based on market products.

See: farmersmarketinstitute.org

The Farmers' Market Salad Bar Program

"We never thought we would see the day when kids are clamoring for kohlrabi or daikon, but after they've tasted it at the salad bar programs, they want more and more," said Laura Avery, City of Santa Monica farmers' market supervisor. The program gave local farmers' markets the chance to supply farm-fresh fruits and vegetables to school cafeterias. A fresh farmers' market salad bar was offered as an alternative to the traditional hot lunch five days a week. "I can tell you," one sixth grader exclaimed, "that we are very happy!"

The farmers' market salad bar program run by the Santa Monica Malibu Unified School District (SMMUSD) Food and Nutrition Services Department affects many children from low-income families where access to fresh produce may be limited. There was a 500% increase in kids selecting the salad bar choice once the district began buying fresh fruits and vegetables at the farmers' market rather than through wholesale produce dealers. The program evolved from a pilot program in one elementary school to a district-wide success story being implemented in all 14 schools, thanks to a strong lunchtime demand from students for fresh fruit and vegetables.

Occidental College researchers launched the pilot program in 1997 to encourage students to eat more fresh produce while simultaneously supporting local farmers. The high-fat, high-salt food school age children often eat have created a paradox: many children are overweight and/or undernourished and school food is often the only daily meal available to them. In the past, school food menus may not have emphasized sound nutrition. Food insecurity is a condition that

The Santa Monica schools saw an increase from 8% to 40% of children selecting the salad bar over hot food once the district began buying fresh fruits and vegetables at the farmers' market rather than through local produce dealers.

far too many low-income children confront daily, both inside and outside the schools.

The salad bar is a particularly compelling idea, given indications that nutritional deficiencies may have a significant impact on learning capacity. School food services often have become a political football between shrinking budgets, a reliance on low quality, commodity-based food, and the new shift toward privatized food services, which often emphasize fast-food type items.

According to Avery, "Kids pile their plates high with bright crunchy, juicy produce and often return for a second plateful. Nutritionally, the salad bar exceeds the USDA minimum requirements."

Rodney Taylor, SMMUSD food services director, says, "Serving nutritious meals that are also appealing to students encourages them to make healthy choices at an early age. Observing these good nutritional habits can help prevent a lifetime of serious health problems including obesity, diabetes, heart disease and cancer."

The items for the salad bar consist of what's in season, with many of the items picked the previous day. A typical week's menu will include two different kinds of fruit daily as well as four to six different kinds of vegetables. Since the program purchases directly from local farmers, items vary by season. There is an educational benefit as students become aware that certain foods only grow in the region during particular seasons. Students also learn about growing issues in a school garden and through farmers' market tours.

Taylor believes the salad bar program has paid for itself. It costs the district just pennies per serving as compared to the hot lunch. Because of good volume, growers give bulk discounts. The district's food budget pays for the market produce, but volunteers or others funded by federal grants bring the produce daily to the students at the salad bar.

The Santa Monica School District spent $23,400 on the salad bar program in the 1999-2000 school year. One of the 20 farmers sold $4,260 worth of produce to the district, which became a large, new customer. Sales are beneficial to the farmers even at or below wholesale price because they don't make an extra stop, don't have to make a hard sell and it's a standing order each week.

Opened in 1981, the Santa Monica Farmers Market paid $4,000 for 1,000 posters of a well-known community activist. The market is strictly limited to California farmers, and one local restaurant is allowed to sell each Wednesday on a rotational basis.

In the 2013-14 school year the program purchased $19,334 from three farmers at the Santa Monica Farmers Market on Wednesday. The volume was down slightly, proportional to the overall decrease in the number of meals served, according to Orlando Griego of SSMUSD, but "participation in the salad bar has held steady, and the salad bar is offered daily throughout virtually the entire school year. The new Healthy Hunger Free Kids Act has changed the nutritional requirements and what we serve. That information can be found on the USDA website."

Similar salad bar programs also began operating in Berkeley and Santa Barbara schools in the late 1990s. The Santa Barbara Farmers' Market approached a local school to establish a garden, applied for a grant, and the kids grew food to take to the market. They also sold to the cafeteria which met the rest of their needs at the market.

"The farmers also enjoy knowing that they are nourishing and educating a new generation of consumers. They figure that kids that start out eating good food will continue to eat good food," Laura Avery noted in 2001.

It's true. Farmers' market kids and salad bar kids around the country became the first generation of college students to demand good, healthy food. College food service has had to improve their offerings to satisfy the students, buying from local farmers and even starting college farms.

Kids notice fresh. This wave of the future may only be limited by the variety of products available locally. When highlighting the 5 A Day program or simply hosting a school tour, notify farmers to have at least one item "on special" for kids. An apple or Asian pear for a quarter starts the habit and gets an idea home. Fullerton, CA, has hosted children's tours where every student receives 50 cents of coupons to redeem with farmers. Make sure they go home with a brochure. Work with the school nutritionist to incorporate farmers' market items and education into their program.

How do you start a salad bar program?

The Santa Monica Farmers' Market was fortunate to have several supportive people to get it started: the director of Food and Nutrition Services for the district, the market manager, and SMMUSD food nutrition coordinator Tracie Thomas, who pulled it all together.

"The food services director for your school district is the first person to approach," Avery says. "In our case the director happened to have a son in the schools whom he was anxious to get on this program." Another requirement is access to a large volume and good variety of fresh produce – it takes a lot of produce to supply a salad bar daily for a school district.

With the help of grant funds, the market also sponsors a Chef in the Classroom program to partner with teachers interested in incorporating nutrition into their curriculums, even in elementary school.

National Farm to School Network

Starting with the Santa Monica program, Occidental College's Urban and Environmental Policy Institute (UEPI) has been a farm-to-school leader for more than 18 years. With $2 million of initial funding from USDA's Initiative for Future Agriculture and Food Systems, UEPI helped school districts, colleges and nonprofits develop programs in California, New York and New Jersey. Similar projects were underway in Connecticut, Florida, Kentucky and North Carolina.

Working with researchers from Cornell, UC Davis, Penn State and Rutgers as well as many others like the California Department of Education, UEPI began to address the epidemic of obesity among school children and the decline of small and medium-sized farms.

Robert Gottlieb, director of UEPI, understood the value of combining benefits under one program: creating a new sales opportunity for farmers, healthier food for school lunches, and a means of educating children about nutrition. Tapping into a $16 billion school food services budget could mean major new income for farmers, and healthy habits for a new generation of school children.

Occidental and the Community Food Security Coalition led the incubation of the National Farm to School Network until 2012, when it became an independent organization. Occidental and the Community Alliance with Family Farmers (CAFF) have partnered to create a California Farm to School Network. Recognizing that 60% of kids five and under are in childcare, and that foods liked at age four set the trend for long-term health, the network created a Farm to Preschool Initiative as another obesity prevention strategy.

School gardens have been developed as living laboratories where youth are involved in a growing experience while studying life and environmental sciences. The California School Garden Network has evolved to support school garden educators and advocates statewide.

The National Farm to School Network is "an information, advocacy and networking hub working to bring local food sourcing and food and agriculture education into school systems and preschools." It has 51 leads covering every state, and three core elements: education, procurement and school gardens. Every

Kids love to leave their mark through a mural or tile project which can be incorporated into a market building or nearby wall.

school district or university program addresses one or more of these elements. It may be as simple as buying local strawberries as a snack or corn to insert into the normal school lunch once a month. Or it may encompass a school garden, classroom curriculum and sourcing healthy, local food for a daily lunch program.

In 2012 the initial vision of farm-to-school advocates was being fulfilled in 44% of the nation's school districts, over 40,000 schools with 23.5 million engaged students. The 50-state collective impact was $385 million of local purchasing annually. The National Farm to School Network has more than 10,000 members. Learn more and search their extensive resource database of toolkits, curricula and advice at:

www.farmtoschool.org.

Under the Healthy, Hunger-Free Kids Act of 2010, Congress established $5 million in mandatory funding for farm to school competitive grants and technical assistance. The NFSN is advocating the Farm to School Act of 2015 to expand that grant program to $15 million to further address preschools, summer food service, after school programs, tribal producers and beginning, veteran and socially disadvantaged farmers and ranchers.

"Once we introduced breakfast to Detroit school children, we received feedback from teachers that kids were finally awake. One teacher said that a boy in her class quickly learned to spell after breakfast was introduced because he could stay awake for the spelling lesson that started each day. Other teachers said that kids stopped fighting and jumping around because they wanted to eat their breakfast.

"Since we don't do home economics anymore, cafeterias should be viewed as an extension of the classroom. That is where we are doing real nutrition education – on their plates."

– Betti Wiggins, Exec. Dir., Office of Food Services, Detroit Public Schools, MI

Cooking with Kids – Santa Fe

Started in 1995, Cooking with Kids (CWK) received the 2013 Culinary Youth Award from the International Association of Cooking Professionals, having involved 5,000 Pre-K to 7th grade students in 13 schools in 10 classes of food preparation and tasting, a total of 15 hours.

CWK's mission is "to motivate and empower children and youth to make healthy food choices through hands-on learning with fresh, affordable foods from diverse cultures."

It is supported by Santa Fe Public Schools and philanthropists, large and small. CWK classes provide learning in math, social studies, language arts, agriculture, art and music by studying and experiencing healthy food from cultures around the world. It is strongly based on teachers, parents and food educators as evidenced by the numbers:

- Parent volunteers: 1,444 parents and grandparents (3:1 female:male) volunteered 3,891 hours in cooking classes;
- School-day classes: 1,950 total food and nutrition education classes;
- 1,148 cooking classes taught by CWK food educators and classroom teachers;
  - Introductory class with Melon Tasting;
  - Stovetop Pizza with Green Salad;
  - Llapingachos with Red Chile;
  - Asian Noodles with Bok Choy;
  - Indian Lentils with Carrot Rice Pilaf and Chapatis; and
  - Vegetable Paella with Green Salad.

- 686 fruit and vegetable tastings taught by classroom teachers using apples, citrus and salad;
- Students at one school had five one-hour fruit and vegetable tastings, taught by classroom teachers;
- CWK re-useable grocery bags given to pre-K and K students;
- School/Community Programming included family nights at 4 schools, and Harvest Festivals in 3 schools;
- CWK school lunches served several times a month in all 19 school cafeterias; and
- Summer Programs at 3 schools with partners.

"If you're trying to convince kids to eat flavorful, healthy foods, ask them to prepare it themselves. The experience of eating and enjoying good foods, rather than just hearing the message of what's good for us, is really important. Cooking is a fun and creative process. When children eat well, they are prepared to learn. As they become educated about different foods, they are more likely to make positive food choices."

– Lynn Walters, Exec. Dir., Cooking with Kids, Inc.

Classroom teaching about healthy foods can increase awareness, appreciation and knowledge of healthy eating. Children need to be offered new food a number of times before they accept it, so CWK exposes students to a variety of positive food choices while honoring the choice and preference of each child.

As good environmental and community stewards, CWK purchases locally grown produce as much as possible. Trained food educators work with students to prepare foods that are healthy and appealing. Two decades of experience has shown that providing kids with positive, fun experiences with food increases the likelihood that they will try and enjoy those foods. In cooking classes, students work together to prepare such dishes, learning that new and culturally diverse foods can be both tasty and nutritious.

Cooking With Kids was the Edible Santa Fe 2014 Local Food Organization Hero, and CWK's founder Lynn Walters received the Olla Award as Local Food Hero.

Each cooking class begins by looking at a map or globe, reading about the history of foods in the lesson, how they grow, and how these foods support the body. Working in small groups with an adult, students learn about washing hands, working safely with foods and kitchen utensils, cooking skills and vocabulary, such as how to measure, whisk, and knead. They also learn to work together, take turns, and encourage their classmates during the process.

"Forty-five percent of the children in the Santa Fe Public Schools receive free or reduced-price meals. Studies show that school lunch is the only complete meal many children eat each day. Many children are no longer learning from their parents and grandparents how to make tamales or strudel.

"The parents of children who are in the CWK program frequently talk about how enthusiastic their children are after cooking in the classroom and that they like to cook more at home. We're encouraged about getting children excited about cooking. If they don't cook, they're definitely not going to know what to do with all of the beautiful produce at the farmers' market!"

– Lynn Walters, Exec. Dir., Cooking with Kids, Inc.

Often visible at the U District FM in Seattle are groups like Seattle Tilth and P-Patch, a community gardening program. "Giving gardens" and individual gardeners donated 20 tons of produce to food banks and meal programs in 2014.

"There is joy in my mouth now."
  – Santa Fe student during Cooking with Kids class

Grade-based curricula are available at www.CookingwithKids.net.

SNAP-Ed in Maine

In 2015 Wholesome Wave and University of New England released a new toolkit to guide nutrition educators in integrating a locally grown food and

Food Insecurity

(Part of an Essay on Food Security to Kookoolan Farms newsletter recipients on April 6, 2015)

My girlfriend Laura called me over the weekend to say that she had experienced an emotionally visceral moment of panic unlike any she had ever experienced before. Right after hearing a radio story about the drought and water rationing in California, she had gone into the produce aisle at Fred Meyer to pick up some vegetables. As she was loading her cart with bell peppers, lettuces, and carrots, all grown in California, she had an ah-ha moment when she got it: if the drought in California reduces the amount of food that California farmers can produce, well, who will feed us then?

At the beginning of the 20th century, 25% of all calories consumed in the United States were produced at the address where they were consumed. Granted, at that time more than 50% of Americans still lived on farms, and people in town all had small vegetable gardens and a few backyard chickens. Soy and corn had not overtaken the agricultural landscape; the emphasis was far more on crops grown directly for human consumption, such as wheat. At that time virtually no food was imported from other countries. Local economies were vibrant. Neighbors knew each other and relied upon each other.

There was another surge of home food production during World War Two. By the time America entered the war, much of the European countryside had been ravaged with bombings and trench warfare, and Europe could no longer feed itself, let alone its armies. America began exporting food to support the war effort, and there was rationing at home, with a strong encouragement to plant a "victory garden." Millions of Americans planted large vegetable gardens, and put up large quantities of canned foods in their pantries for winter.

Our neighbor grew up during the end of the depression and the war years, and says his family was very poor, but he never knew that they were poor because they always had plenty to eat. They grew their own.

What Eisenhower later called the Military Industrial complex emerged between the two world wars and exploded afterward: corporations exist to be profitable. When your customer is war and the war ends, you have to find new markets. The munitions industry turned to fertilizers. Remember that the Oklahoma City bombing was performed using fertilizer? Ammonium nitrate is both a high-nitrogen fertilizer and highly explosive. The need to continue selling these chemicals in order to stay in business was a big driving force in the development of large-scale "conventional" farming, largely in the last eighty years. Before that, ALL farming was organic.

When I was in school, we learned in Economics class that the poorest countries in the world were the ones that were unable to grow the food to feed themselves. Ironically, the U.S. now seems to consider itself too rich to grow its own food: that's a low-status, low-wage job that should be outsourced. I submit to you that reliance on imported food is the worst kind of food insecurity.

– Chrissie Manion Zaerpoor operates Kookoolan Farms, a diversified small farm, with her husband in Yamhill, OR. She also crafts international-award-winning meads under the label Kookoolan World Meadery. She left a well-paying job in engineering management at Intel Corporation to grow her own food because of the lack of information transparency in the modern food system. ✺

farmers' market focus into the approved SNAP-Ed curricula. This field-tested toolkit is a great resource for WIC staff to introduce class participants to local food buying. Though developed for Maine SNAP-Ed nutrition educators, it should still be useful for others nationwide. It includes a nutrition curriculum with three program models, and information about incentive programs for SNAP participants.

If your market hasn't been working with your local SNAP office, you should suggest that the SNAP office take a look at these strategies and tips at:

http://www.wholesomewave.org/wp-content/uploads/2014/07/Snap-Ed-Toolkit_FINAL.pdf

MarketLink

A new program was launched by the National Association of Farmers Market Nutrition Programs in 2013 to assist farmers' markets and farmers in serving SNAP recipients. Farms and markets can easily apply and may receive a free EBT terminal through NAF-MNP at:

www.marketlink.org.

Slow Food

Slow Food USA is part of the global good food network with more than 100,000 members in 150 countries. Local chapters are volunteer based, connecting food at our tables with a commitment to the knowledge, culture and environment that provide that food pleasure.

Their mission is good, clean and fair food for all. Many of their 175 local and campus chapters in the U.S. have a symbiotic relationship with their local farmers' market. Executive director since 2013, Richard McCarthy was co-founder of the Crescent City Farmers Market and later founder of Market Umbrella, which continues to be a rich resource for markets. See:

www.slowfoodusa.org and

www.marketumbrella.org.

COMMUNITY CONNECTIONS

Markets can address numerous social issues on a local or even international scale. Residents feel their market truly represents the community when nonprofit social groups can have a booth and talk with market-goers about the Audubon Society, Boy Scouts, PTA, Rails to Trails Conservancy, Greenpeace, American Cancer Society, Habitat for Humanity, People for the Ethical Treatment of Animals, Multiple Sclerosis Society, Rotary Club International, school programs, candidates for office or the library book drive. A free booth may be provided for groups engaged in education only, whereas a fee may be charged of those with fund-raising activities.

Markets that connect with the many interests of community members do well because the market becomes a living bulletin board for programs and activities that connect to a larger world.

A Lions Club may want to serve pancakes once a month to raise funds for eyeglasses being shipped to Africa. The Brattleboro (VT) Rotary started a water purification project in El Salvador that became its own nonprofit, Pure Water for the World. When these community-based activities grow and thrive at the farmers' market, everyone wins: nonprofit, market and the larger community.

Hunger Programs

Many markets invite a community food bank to collect unsold produce from farmers at the end of the day for distribution to low-income citizens. A market might also display donation barrels or a donation jar at the info booth so customers can join the effort. When the info booth serves as a produce donation collection point, farmers are not called upon individually and the market can document the volume collected to reinforce its tax status and include in an annual report showing your community contributions. The market can also document farmers' donations for tax purposes.

The personal connection between food bank and farmer may lead to a quick call when a future rain or hailstorm hits the farm – better to harvest for the poor than waste a crop.

Amidst the rest of its data documenting economic impacts, the Neighborhood Farmers Market Alliance reports the total weight of all products donated by vendors at each of their markets. The annual public sharing of this data gives city government and public alike greater confidence in the transparency of the organization's goals.

Homeless Adults

Where once stood Homestead Air Force Base before Hurricane Andrew, today there is Verde Gardens. It has a 3-prong program of a 22-acre farm, 145 units of housing and the Homeless Assistance Center. The program is the first of its kind in the country, helping cut Miami-Dade's homeless population dramatically.

Housing was completed in 2011 for 580 people, including 10% veterans and 315 children. Formerly homeless families work the land to help pay rent. While they work, children are cared for at the center. The fruits, vegetables and herbs from the farm are sold at their own farmers' market at Verde Gardens, and a Miami restaurant.

Verde Gardens is a $20 million partnership between the Miami-Dade County Homeless Trust and developer Carrfour Supportive Housing, with many nonprofits. It caters to families with at least one person with a disability. Residents accept random drug and alcohol testing and monthly social worker visits.

Homeless and Kids' Programs

In too many communities there are youth who live on the streets, in abandoned homes, under freeways or in hidden places. Often churches and social service agencies are working to provide them basic food, shelter and encouragement to return to school. Farmers' markets can connect with these agencies to provide

Seattle Youth Garden Works provides youth employment and empowerment in the garden and in local farmers' markets.

jobs with farmers, as market staff or becoming entrepreneurs themselves.

Seattle Youth Garden Works hires 16 to 21-year-old homeless and underserved youth to work in their gardens and to continue their education around gardening, cooking skills, nutrition education, small business training and public speaking. They also sell at two of NFMA's markets in University District and Columbia City.

"There is a separate program for homeless kids in these urban neighborhoods. At-risk kids tend and harvest large community garden plots in both neighborhoods. They sell a portion of their harvest at a nonprofit booth. Most of these kids are terribly marginalized and have truly fallen through the system's cracks. This particular program has worked beautifully for some. It has given them responsibilities in a school-like setting and something to care for and nurture. Dozens have gotten off the street and are back in school or working at real jobs. I don't think the farmers' market is the total reason but a small part of the solution."

– Chris Curtis, Exec. Dir., Neighborhood Farmers
  Market Alliance, Seattle, WA

Following the 1992 riots in Los Angeles, a teacher and students at Crenshaw High School transformed a ¼-acre abandoned lot into a fruit and vegetable garden, donating 25% to the needy and selling the rest of their organic produce as Food From the 'Hood at the Santa Monica Farmers' Market. With the help of a public relations expert, a Los Angeles Times story led to a connection with a salad dressing executive.

Initially a model for kids with a food business using farmers' markets as the test market, Food From the 'Hood soon expanded sales of three bottled salad dressings into 2,000 stores nationwide and on Amazon.com. Profits allowed each student to bank their hours for

The Uptown Farmers Market in Phoenix has partnered with Careers through Culinary Arts Program to offer a Veggie Valet. Customers buy fruits and vegetables. While they continue shopping, students prepare meals for them. Donations are accepted. C-CAP gives out 30 scholarships to Arizona H.S. students.

individual education funds, with equal points for all company tasks. More than $250,000 in scholarships were earned by 80 student managers before the business closed.

Grow Dat Youth Farm produces 10,000 pounds of produce, 60% of which is sold at their farm stand and New Orleans farmers' markets. Working with nine partner schools, each fall they hire 50 kids, ages 15-21, as crew members and leaders.

Grow Dat teaches around four curriculum pillars: leadership, agricultural skills, wellness, and food justice and food systems. Each youth receives a competitive stipend and a bonus based on work habit progress.

Markets and Health

"Obesity is the terror within," said U.S. Surgeon General Richard Carmona. "Unless we do something about it, the magnitude of the dilemma will dwarf 9-11 or any other terrorist attempt."

The Surgeon General pointed out that one of every eight deaths – more than 300,000 annually in America – are caused by an illness directly related to overweight and obesity.

"The crisis is obesity. It's the fastest-growing cause of disease and death in America. And it's completely preventable.

"While extra value meals may save us some change at the counter, they're costing us billions of dollars in health care and lost productivity. Physical inactivity and super-sized meals are leading to a nation of oversized people.

"Excess weight has also led to an increase in the number of people suffering from Type 2 diabetes. There are at least 17 million Americans with diabetes, and another 16 million have pre-diabetes… It can lead to eye diseases, cardiovascular problems, kidney failure, and early death."

– Richard Carmona, U.S. Surgeon General, July 16, 2003

In a 2008 speech Carmona noted that 9 million U.S. children are overweight or obese. See the impacts in a powerful film, Killer at Large:

http://www.snagfilms.com/films/title/killer_at_large

Nutritionists say that the problem is partly due to lack of nutrition knowledge and access to healthier foods. A 2006 urban Midwest study found that race and income seem associated with food outlet locations and the selection of healthy food. The result: lower income and blacks are less able to make healthy food choices than higher income whites.

The estimated medical cost of obesity in the U.S. was $147 billion in 2008, with $1,429 higher medical costs annually for an obese person than one of normal weight. Obesity's impact on the economy is horrendous and will worsen given the aging baby boomers.

By 2014 more than one-third (34.9% or 78.6 million) of U.S. adults were obese. The rate for black adults was 47.8% and Latino adults 42.5% while whites are 32.6%. Among youth the obesity rate was 17%, with Latinos at 22.4%, blacks at 20.2% and whites at 14.3%. According to the LA County Department of Public Health, 42% of children are obese or overweight.

The Surgeon General outlined the three key factors that we must address to reduce and eliminate childhood obesity:

- Increased physical activity,
- Healthier eating habits and
- Improved health literacy.

The Milpitas FM is very successful in serving working class Asians and Indians. Prices are competitive and fancy foods are uncommon at this site, one of the 60+ farmers' markets run by the Pacific Coast FM Association.

As poverty increases, rates of obesity rise. People trying to pay bills do not prioritize their food choices. Besides diabetes, obesity leads to diseases such as cardiovascular disease, hypertension and asthma. The African American death rate from heart disease in 2000 was 29% higher than among non-Hispanic whites, and the diabetes diagnosis rate is twice as high.

Whatever farmers can do to encourage eating right will help our nation to become healthier and address the crisis of rising health care costs that is set to overwhelm our economy.

> "The true lethal narcotic in this country, the real killer, is not crack cocaine, not tobacco or even alcohol. It is cheap, subsidized, processed sugar and enriched starch that layer with folds of blubber the rear, the belly and the thighs of the American eater."
>
> – Victor Davis Hanson, *Fields Without Dreams*

Farmers' markets can become part of a circle of hope – for farmers and city residents. With help from foundations and nutrition organizations, we can revive blighted urban areas and bring quality, fresh produce to millions of lower-income residents. There is no need to segregate the wealthy and the poor. Especially minority producers and those who appreciate every person's right to food access will attend markets in poorer communities in spite of lower prices. In part, they continue because of appreciation

shown by their customers and because they can relate to the need for good food themselves.

Market development is most feasible in areas heavily dependent upon USDA food stamps and food coupons. Farmers' markets should be ready to do aggressive advertising of their participation in those programs to attract recipients and they should link with the local food bank to provide excess food for the needy.

New markets also will appear in higher-income areas. As organizers plan in any community, they will study demographic patterns. The "traditional" family, where one spouse works and one stays at home with the children, represents less than one-fifth of American households; there are twice as many dual-income households. Consumers' lives are more busy, providing new challenges for organizers selecting market hours and new opportunities for value-added processors.

Low-Income Communities

Although some people wonder how low-income people's focus on price is going to jive with small farmers' focus on sustainability, many farmers' markets do exist in low-income communities. There are several factors for farmers and organizers to consider:

- Just because people are low-income does not mean they won't spend money on food, even organically grown.
- Poorer people have traditionally spent a disproportionate amount of money on food.
- Consumers without health insurance may realize that a healthy diet is their best insurance. The Affordable Care Act quickly reduced the 49 million uninsured and under-insured to 35 million, still leaving many to depend on food for health.
- A market serving low-income customers may well reach middle- and upper-income groups as well. If the farmers' market has good support from the local WIC office, there can be thousands of dollars of EBT and food coupons coming into a single market.
- Farmers have committed to supporting farmers' markets in low-income areas based on their desire

THE NEW FARMERS' MARKET

to contribute to the social well-being of that community and their customers' appreciative response.

+ Nutrition education is a valuable part of attracting and maintaining a younger customer base, inexperienced in preparing foods.

+ Immigrants seem especially receptive to specialty crops that farmers cannot move in other venues.

In January, 1999, the Community Food Security Coalition (which closed in 2012) released a report, Hot Peppers and Parking Lot Peaches: Evaluating Farmers' Markets in Low-Income Communities by Andy Fisher. [See Resources.]

The Villa Parke farmers' market has operated since 1980 in a small park in an African-American part of Pasadena, CA, not far from the Rose Bowl. About 25 farmers sell here every Tuesday. Market managers Betty Hamilton and Gretchen Sterling attribute the market's longevity to the broad base of neighborhood support. Betty notes, "This is their market." Betty and Gretchen have fostered this integration of the market with the community by returning the market's modest profits back to the community. They have sponsored soccer teams, bought a wheelchair for local organizations and at one point even bought 50 local kids new shoes. Another key to Villa Parke's success is that the managers subsidize its operation with fees earned managing a highly successful, middle-income market. They realize that subsidies may be the only way a low-income market can survive.

Like Villa Parke, San Francisco's Heart of the City Farmers' Market was sponsored in the early 1980s, by the American Friends Service Committee, as part of an effort to improve access to healthy foods in the nearby Tenderloin district. With about 60 growers in summer and 30 in winter, Heart of the City has a mixed-income customer base: office workers from the area's many business towers, tourists, and the Tenderloin's largely poor southeast Asian and Latino

The Portland Farmers Market has promoted health through its weekly youth cooking program, Eat Like It Matters.

populations. The middle-income customers are key to balancing market economics, providing farmers with a stable sales base. Appropriately, the market is located on United Nations Plaza. The product mix reflects the ethnicity and income levels of the clientele. While a few stands sell upscale products, most sell basic fruits and vegetables at rock-bottom prices because of the high volume. Vietnamese and Lao growers from the Central Valley predominate, selling Asian vegetables to fellow Asian consumers.

Across the country on the northern edge of Manhattan, amidst the hustle and bustle of a Dominican and Puerto Rican neighborhood, the Washington Heights Greenmarket had a fantastic business four or five months of the year. It redeemed $800,000 in FMNP coupons each year, well over half of sales. Without these vouchers, Washington Heights and a network of smaller Greenmarkets in the city's poor neighborhoods were likely to collapse. The conversion of paper food stamps to the EBT debit card system was another major threat to their existence.

As these examples illustrate, farmers' markets can be a valuable tool for improving access to affordable and healthy food for lower-income communities. However, low-income markets offer special challenges in addition to those facing all farmers' markets. Certain barriers are common among low-income markets. These include:

Fair price, low cost. There exists a fundamental tension between farmers' obtaining a fair wage and low-income consumers' desire for cheap food. Supermarkets can source produce more cheaply and undersell small-scale family farmers. Supermarkets often use produce as a loss leader, selling it at or below cost to attract customers. In addition, low-income households may have little money available for food purchases beyond staples.

Transportation. Low vehicle ownership rates in low-income communities reduce the cumulative purchasing power of the target market. Limited transportation options diminish the trade area and impede consumers' ability to get to the market and purchase large quantities.

Convenience. Low-income individuals generally have less time and fewer resources. Shopping at farmers' markets during designated hours is less convenient than other food outlets.

Given the many barriers present, the challenges of organizing a market in a low-income community are greater than in a wealthier neighborhood. Following

---

Researching & Getting Grants

It's great to educate your community about farmers' markets and local agriculture, but how do you fund the programs to do this? One answer is through grants. To finance the ambitious and far-reaching educational projects of the Friends of the Farmers' Markets, executive director Pam Roy spends an appreciable amount of time writing grant proposals, developing business sponsorships, and spearheading an annual fund-raising campaign. FFM is set up as a nonprofit 501(c)(3) and acts as an umbrella for several organizations to help fund and develop their educational outreach programs.

"You really need to research who you are applying to, what they want, and what their purposes are," Roy says. To find out who's giving grants, go to the National Foundation Center website at: www.foundationcenter.org.

On their website you can search for information about foundations that may be interested in your organization's mission and programs, doing searches under specific key words such as "sustainable agriculture," "organic," "local agriculture" or "farmers' markets." Try to let your initial search be as broad as possible. Then you can narrow your search by state or by more specific categories.

Also consider what the foundations' major interests are. Sometimes you may think they are not interested in your proposed projects when in fact they may be, and sometimes the opposite may be true. "Simply calling them will let you know for sure," Roy says. Usually their phone numbers and e-mail addresses are listed as well as their mailing addresses. Often the listings will give information about what kinds of projects they have funded in the last year and of course this is a good tip-off about their interests and potential for funding your project.

Did they fund large projects or small, locally oriented agricultural projects? How much have they given in the past and how much do they now have available to give? Be realistic about their potential to fund your project. Look at how much money they gave last year. Often they will list both the total and a minimum and maximum range of money per project. Also take a look at which regions they target. They may only donate to a city or state that doesn't include your area, so don't waste your time applying where there's no possibility.

Take a look at who their executive directors are and consider if you know anyone in that community. Check with them to see if you know any of the board members. "This research often takes a lot of time and can be grueling," Roy says. "In order to maximize your efforts, you need to be realistic not only about who to go to, but in how much you can do as an individual or an organization."

Local community foundations often provide either workshops or services on how to write grant proposals – look under "Foundations" in the yellow pages. Often City Hall will have directories of local nonprofit community foundations and services. Community colleges, farm conferences and Cooperative Extension often have courses or workshops on how to write grant proposals. &

basic market organizing and management principles and having skilled staff are just as important in low-income as in middle-income markets. Successful low-income farmers' markets have additional criteria, however. These include:

Community support. In the most successful examples, the markets are well integrated into the community with citizen board members and profits donated to local organizations. Grassroots community organizing may prove more successful than a publicity drive in building support for a new market.

Subsidies/incentives. Low-income markets may need subsidies in the form of middle-income shoppers or creative market management that allows a wealthier market to support a poorer counterpart. Market match programs to incentivize SNAP EBT participants have been critical.

Product mix and prices. Market managers should encourage a product mix of basic foods at affordable prices. Building a connection between minority consumers and growers of the same ethnicity can also help to strengthen consumers' loyalty to the market.

Health and Food Safety

Whenever there is an outbreak of concern about pesticides or chemicals in food, a surge of consumers may occur at farmers' markets because they start thinking about who is producing their food. While certain natural foods and mainline supermarkets respond with country- or state-of-origin labeling programs, farmers' markets provide the ultimate guarantee: a grower's word. This makes it all the more imperative that farmers recognize and respect their place within a cooperative-styled organization.

The saying, "An injury to one is an injury to all" holds true. A farmer lie or misrepresentation will come out eventually and hurt that farmer's sales; it also hurts the credibility of all others in the market. An aggrieved customer can cause the loss not only of other existing customers but of ones you will never meet.

Thankfully, most people do not have adverse physical reactions to food inputs. Yet, for those who do, their sensitivity to particular ingredients, additives

or chemicals used in the production of food is of critical concern. They often depend on farmers' market products for a certain level of food cleanliness or absence of toxicity. They need to depend on our word; if producers declare that a product is organic, the market should stand behind that claim. We should clarify and standardize what is meant by "no sprays" so that customers do not believe they are buying "organic."

Try to promote the concept of knowing who's producing your food and what they're putting on your food. Also, work closely with your local and state health departments to determine acceptable practices within your farmers' markets concerning food safety.

> "Consumers are concerned about where their food comes from. In the scare about sprouts that had E. coli they found that the seeds were imported, which made customers think it's important to have a local food supply. Our county is the largest raspberry producer in the nation, and customers ask: 'These berries aren't from Chile are they?' In the off season I shop at one of our local grocery stores and they've begun to label the country of origin. They sell tomatoes from British Columbia, right across the border, as well as South American tomatoes. The owner of the store told me they sell a lot more of the BC products because people feel they can trust something more local."
>
> – Karen Durham, former Mgr., Bellingham FM, WA

An awareness of food problems around the globe, including the deaths related to mad cow disease in Europe, have prompted a safety response. Health departments are increasingly focused on hygiene rules from farm to restaurant. Businesses may be required to log crucial actions under Hazard Analysis Critical Control Point standards, known as HACCP. They also may face new machinery and building requirements for processing.

Dangers are overblown and consumer fears manipulated. In protecting themselves from consumer lawsuits, government protection agencies are over-regulating artisanal production in favor of a

With the help of nutrition students from local colleges, L.A. County Health reached thousands of market customers with recipes, samples and nutrition information.

homogenized food supply which favors large companies. The net effect of this regulatory environment is that larger businesses strictly adhering to HACCP become immune to prosecution for food poisoning, quality food is replaced by clean food (which doesn't mean it's good), and small businesses are regulated out of existence.

Ask the Dietitian. Not all health departments are focused solely on regulation. In a more productive vein, the Southland Farmers' Market Association teamed up during the 2000 season with the Los Angeles County Department of Health Services Nutrition Program and California Project LEAN/LA Region to sponsor an innovative program linking registered dietitians to farmers' markets. The goal of the "Ask the Dietitian" Program was to improve fruit and vegetable consumption at eight select farmers' markets in the county. It gave shoppers the opportunity to ask nutrition questions, learn about healthy eating practices, and get tasty low-fat recipes.

The greatest concern is that people are not eating right. A 1999 study by the California Department of Health Services reported that adults are not following recommendations for healthy eating, leading to greater risk of heart disease, cancer, and diabetes. Only 30% eat the recommended five daily servings of fruits and vegetables. Almost 35,000 Californians are diagnosed each year with diet-related illness. If we increase fruit and vegetable consumption, we can reverse these trends and lead to improved wellness and reduced health care costs.

Farmers still need to follow good cleaning and handling procedures. An article in the August/September 2014 issue of Food Safety magazine reminded us that farmers' markets are not immune to food safety problems:

- Campylobacter infections affected 18 people who ate contaminated raw bagged peas from five Alaskan markets in 2008.
- Salmonella in guacamole, salsa and tamales sickened 25 people at various Iowa markets in 2010.
- Escherichia coli O157:H7 in strawberries at Oregon farmers' markets and roadside stands caused one death and sickened 16 others in 2011.
- Salmonella again led to 14 individuals affected by cashew cheese at Sacramento area farmers' markets and retail markets in three states in 2014.
- Listeria monocytogenes contamination led the California Department of Food and Agriculture to recall raw cream at several Fresno area markets in 2007.
- A similar listeria problem in cheese caused a Washington Department of Agriculture recall with farmers' markets in three counties in 2012.

Another large incident, though not related to farmers' markets, occurred in 2012 when 38 people were affected by campylobacter in organic, raw milk from a Pennsylvania dairy.

A Michigan farmers' market apple cider vendor caused four people to be sickened by E. coli O157:H7. Cited by MDA for being an unlicensed processor and failure to meet safe production standards, the vendor continued to produce and sell cider, which led to a charge of criminal negligence. Pleading guilty to willful misbranding and adulteration of food products, the vendor was convicted in February 2014.

Listeria is the third-deadliest food-borne pathogen in the U.S. as many found out when contaminated cantaloupe from a Colorado farm killed 33 people and sickened 147 others in 28 states in 2011. Although the cantaloupe came from a farm 90 miles from Rocky Ford, the farm identified its melons as Rocky Ford-grown because the area is known for quality cantaloupe. With their name tarnished, growers quickly formed the Rocky Ford Growers Association, trademarked their cantaloupe geographically and rebuilt their 125-year reputation.

In 2014 a federal judge sentenced two brothers to five years probation, six months home detention and $150,000 each in restitution fees to victims and families of the Listeria outbreak. This was one of the first cases where criminal charges sent a strong message that government prosecutors are treating deadly foodborne illness outbreaks seriously. Growers and managers should realize that there could be major impacts if such an outbreak were to occur in the farmers' market realm.

While protecting small farmer access to consumers, market management needs to remain aware of the risks and take precautionary steps to ensure proper food safety standards or risk losing their customers. They also need to remind customers of the importance of of buy-local campaigns such as Know Your Farmer, Know Your Food, because a local food culture limits the reach of any food safety outbreak.

Hospitals and Community Health

Long-established tax law allows nonprofit hospitals to avoid federal taxes by conducting a community health needs assessment (CHNA) and implementing a program to address those needs. Usually they have taken charity cases, covering the health care costs of low-income people. Those cases should decline as people gain coverage under the Affordable Care Act.

Based on public pressure, nonprofit hospitals can now claim a tax credit for programs that promote healthy food access such as lowering the cost of fruits and vegetables in farmers' markets, grocery stores and schools. At the end of 2014, IRS approved this community health improvement approach. Farm and market leaders need to ask local nonprofit hospitals to address access to proper nutrition by sponsoring their

Kaiser Permanente has been the hospital leader, hosting 57 farmers' markets in six states, and sponsoring massive education campaigns like "thrive" with its own employees and patients.

market, an incentive program, or a fruit and vegetable prescription program.

IRS' final regulations expanded a hospital's option under its CHNA to include "the need to prevent illness, to ensure adequate nutrition, or to address social, behavioral, and environmental factors that influence health in the community."

Jefferson Memorial Hospital in Martinsburg, WV committed $30,000 to a local farmers' market. Since nonprofit hospitals generally spend 7.75% of operating budgets on these community health initiatives to maintain their exemption from federal tax, such commitments could lead to millions or even billions of dollars to encourage healthier eating, according to Gus Schumacher, Farmers Market Coalition board member.

Community Food Security

All markets should be considering the relative food security needs in their own communities. There are many model initiatives and many have received grants from various sources to address their creative solutions.

Since 1996 USDA has had a Community Food Projects Competitive Grants Program (CFPCGP) which helps fight food insecurity through projects that promote low-income communities' self-sufficiency while benefiting farm producers. The projects funded must address two or more sectors of the whole food system, support entrepreneurs, develop innovative nonprofit and for-profit linkages, encourage long-term planning activities, and build long term community capacity for addressing food and agricultural problems.

The grants for eligible private nonprofits are funded one time up to $125,000 for one year and up to $400,000 for four years, and require a dollar-for-dollar resource match. With historical funding at about $5 million per year, it increased to $9 million in 2015 for only two types of grants: Community Food Projects (CFP) and Planning Projects (PP).

King-Pierce County Farm Bureau (WA) promoted this thoughtful poster reassessing what constitutes true Homeland Security.

Gleaning programs alone have helped direct tens of millions of pounds of excess food to faith-based and nonprofit organizations that feed the hungry. They provide technical assistance to anti-hunger and community food security projects. One of their partnerships brought together Hewlett-Packard and Second Harvest Food Bank to update computer technology and match companies with nonprofits.

The Community Gardening Initiative involves the American Community Gardening Association, the Garden Clubs of America and the Garden Writers of America Association. The goal is to increase the number of low-income Americans obtaining food through community gardens, school gardens and private gardens that "Plant a Row for the Hungry." A Utah 4-H program, Fresh From the Heart, has kids gleaning produce from urban gardens.

A partnership with Share Our Strength, based in Washington, D.C., seeks to recruit chef volunteers to teach nutrition education classes. Even student chefs in Rhode Island have done demonstrations at farmers' markets.

Farmers' Markets As Economic Incubators & Job Creators

Since the 1970s thousands of farmers' markets have been started in towns and cities across America. While local farmers, consumers and economies benefit, a shift in federal food policies could generate even more activity.

In 2011 the Union of Concerned Scientists (UCS) released a report, Market Forces: Creating Jobs through Public Investment in Local and Regional Food Systems, that noted the doubling of farmers' markets nationwide between 2000 and 2010 from 2,863 to 6,132. With 136,000 farms selling directly to consumers, this expansion has occurred with relatively little USDA support, less than $100 million annually for all local and regional food system programs. Meanwhile, the USDA spent $13.75 billion in commodity, crop insurance, and supplemental disaster assistance payments mostly to support large industrial farms.

"On the whole, farmers' markets have seen exceptional growth, providing local communities with fresh food direct from the farm...But our federal food policies are working against them. If the U.S. government diverted just a small amount of the massive subsidies it lavishes on industrial agriculture to support these markets and small local farmers, it would not only improve American diets, it would generate tens of thousands of new jobs."

– Jeffrey O'Hara, UCS Food and Environment Program economist

Direct agricultural product sales totaled $1.2 billion in 2007, which creates a positive multiplier effect as money recirculates locally. Local revenue stabilizes local economies, and creates jobs. Local food generates 13 farm jobs for every $1 million in sales, compared to 3 jobs with normal food distribution.

Agriculture Secretary Tom Vilsack asked Congress to set a goal in the 2012 Farm Bill of helping 100,000 Americans become farmers through entrepreneurial training, providing farmers' market support and other programs. The UCS report states that local and regional food system expansion support is central to meeting Vilsack's goal.

The report called on Congress to:

- Support new farmers' markets, farm-to-school programs and other local food system projects. The Farmers Market Promotion Program (FMPP) could stimulate up to 13,500 new jobs nationally within five years, through modest funding of 100-500 farmers' markets annually.

- Invest in infrastructure such as meat-processing or dairy-bottling facilities to give rural producers equal market access, increase consumer choice, expand food market competition and generate community jobs.

- Increase access to fresh fruits and vegetables for low-income Americans by ensuring that all farmers' markets can redeem Supplemental Nutrition Assistance Program (SNAP) benefits.

Various researchers have used their own survey data and the IMPLAN input-output model to estimate the "economic multiplier" of farmers' markets in their states, that is, the increase in economic activity resulting from direct market sales. Impact levels varied with different assumptions and survey methodology – farmers' market consumers, vendors or both.

However, they all found positive statewide economic impacts from farmers' markets:

"Hughes et al. found that 34 farmers' markets in West Virginia led to a gross increase of 119 jobs

Marin Roots Farm demonstrates the most effective way of creating the next generation of farmers.

(net increase of 82 jobs), a gross increase of $2.4 million in output (net increase of $1.1 million), and a gross increase in personal income of $0.7 million (net increase of $0.2 million).

"Henneberry, Whitacre, and Agustini found that 21 farmers' markets in Oklahoma led to a gross increase of 113 jobs, $5.9 million in output (with a multiplier of 1.78), and a $2.2 million increase in income.

"Otto found that 152 farmers' markets in Iowa led to a gross increase of 576 jobs, a $59.4 million increase in output (with a multiplier of 1.55), and a $17.8 million increase in income.

"Myles and Hood found that 26 farmers' markets in Mississippi led to a gross increase of 16 jobs, a $1.6 million increase in output (with a multiplier of 1.7), and a $0.2 million increase in income…"

– Jeffrey K. O'Hara, Market Forces, UCS, August 2011

Henneberry, Whitacre, and Agustini estimated 5.4 jobs per Oklahoma farmers' market, while Otto reported 3.8 jobs in Iowa, and Hughes et al. found 3.5 gross jobs (2.4 net jobs) per West Virginia market. All included both full-time and part-time jobs. Hughes et al. converted their estimates to full-time, finding 69 extra full-time-equivalent jobs and a net increase of 43.

"Farmers at local markets are a new variety of innovative entrepreneurs, and we need to nurture them," wrote Jeffrey O'Hara in the Market Forces report. "Supporting these farmers should be a Farm Bill priority."

O'Hara also emphasized the development of certification standards by market managers to ensure customer confidence that "vendors are involved in the production of the food they sell and are undertaking environmentally sustainable production practices.

"Vegetable/melon and fruit/nut producers," O'Hara said, "each account for 28 percent of the value of all agricultural products sold via direct consumer marketing (USDA 2009). Forty-four percent of all vegetable and melon producers sell directly to consumers, as do 17 percent of fruit and nut producers, but only 7 percent of livestock producers."

Other studies by Swanson in several Midwest states, and Connor et al. and Cantrell et al. in Michigan have found that thousands of jobs and millions of net income would be created if fruit and vegetable consumption were to be met by in-state production, and similarly if in-state fresh fruit and vegetables were to replace processed.

Jeter et al. found that if California consumers were to increase fruit and vegetable consumption to five-a-day, farmers would see an extra $460 million, and seven servings a day would amount to $1.5 billion.

These messages are important for farmers' markets to convey to city, state and federal representatives. They helped move forward the Farm Bill in 2014, which included expansion of the Farmers Market Promotion Program (FMPP) and created equal funding for the Local Foods Promotion Program (LFPP). In 1970 there were 340 farmers' markets, and today over 8,000; these funding sources should help expand the impact of these markets.

COMMUNITY OUTREACH

An essential part of farmers' markets success lies in making it a vital part of the community fabric. It's vitally important in maximiz-

Grow Portland has two community farms and five community gardens with 300 garden plots, and is expanding. They are connecting refugees to ultra local farms so that they can serve area farmers' markets.

ing a limited budget to piggyback your efforts with other organizations.

"Market managers are exploring new community connections that may become important new markets for their growers. In one community, where the market is sponsored by the local Lions Club, market stall fees contribute to community service projects and organizations such as the teen center and the food bank. These relationships create goodwill between the markets and the community, contributing to a better business environment for farmers and other market vendors. In some communities, managers have made contacts with hospitals and senior citizen centers to explore institutional food purchases from the market."

– Farmers' Markets and Rural Development Project

"Collaboration is very important for any non-profit," says Pam Roy of New Mexico. "When you work with other organizations, you get whole organizations as well as individuals involved and invested in your programs, and you also get invested in their programs. Involving the broader participation of the community is really imperative to farmers' market success."

On Seed Planting Day in Santa Fe, Friends of the Farmers' Market (FFM) works with the Master Gardeners as well as different local nurseries and landscapers. Presenters are asked to work with some of the farmers or plant producers in the market, and talk about the plants that they have found in the farmers' market, and also mention who they got it from in the market, just as chefs mention farmers by name while using their products.

Cooperative Extension Service regularly does food preservation and nutrition presentations at markets. The WIC (Women, Infants & Children) staff distribute farmers' market nutrition program checks at the farmers' markets. The idea is to build on the theme of health and nutrition and invite other groups' participation.

The FFM also works regularly with the Department of Community Services and the New Mexico

Youth at Montpelier H.S. (VT) have raised funds and traveled to Ban Sa Som, Thailand with help from farmers' market customers.

Department of Agriculture on the state and local level. "We also look for nonprofit groups that are working along similar lines or goals," Roy says. "The Children's Museum, for example, has helped us with equipment. We invite them to be part of our programs like the Kids in the Garden projects and we also go out to their activities to do presentations about food, nutrition and farmers' markets.

FFM works with a group called the Food Depot which runs a food assistance program, helping over 50 agencies in the Santa Fe Community that provide shelters, soup kitchens and cooking programs to seven counties and 30,000 people. The Food Depot has a booth at the Santa Fe markets and customers are invited to donate. At the end of the day, farmers also donate what hasn't sold. "All of the food is weighed out so that we know exactly what came from the farmers' market," Pam Roy says. Farmers receive receipts for a tax write-off.

Serving Your Community

Being a credible, major player in your community may require that the manager or board members serve on various boards, participate in other organizations' events and, in general, help others to succeed as much as your market. When a local parade is organized, get a grower to drive a tractor towing a wagon with a farmers' market display, as they've done in Pacific Beach, CA. When you are asked to provide a basket of products for a fundraising event, respond with a gift certificate to get the recipient to the market.

The Springfield Farmers' Market at the X, MA, has a community information table featuring a different nonprofit organization each week. Other markets allot two or ten spaces depending on the size of their market and the demand from the nonprofit or business community.

In Yakima, WA, the Volunteer and Career Center's director volunteered to do outreach to hundreds of nonprofit organizations and coordinate their periodic participation in the market. It gave her center greater visibility with community groups and gave the market valuable community connections while saving the manager's time for other duties.

Elsewhere, managers send letters to local restaurants encouraging them to buy direct from market vendors and to promote their market and vendors' products at other community events and locations. A grocery store has been known to sponsor an annual benefit for the local farmers' market. Community gardens are invited to join as compatible organizations.

A historically interesting social impact occurred in Long Beach, CA where a large farmers' market surrounded four sides of a downtown park. With the start of World War II, more than half of its farmers were forced into internment camps along with more than 120,000 Americans of Japanese ancestry. The Alien Land Law of 1913 had barred "Orientals" from

The Inner Sunset neighborhood has a community board at their farmers' market, a vital way to reinforce local connections with other San Francisco community interests.

© Vance Corum

The Tuesday market on a street in Manhattan Beach, CA turns an adjacent plaza into a vibrant gathering place for moms and nannies.

owning land, so first generation "Issei" could not own the land they farmed. Now, suddenly they could not even farm the land they didn't own.

After the war the market never recovered its momentum and slipped out of existence in the 1960s. The Interfaith Hunger Coalition and California Department of Food and Agriculture called their new effort in 1980 the "re-opening" of the farmers' market, though there was no organizational connection. Japanese-American and other farmers were invited to return and remind longtime residents of the wonderful bounty of the past in once again serving the community.

A Presbyterian minister, Dale Whitney, helped in the initial organizational effort. He later became manager of the Harbor Area Farmers' Markets from 1989 – 2014, expanding the association from three to six markets. His legacy is a healthy market system including one that regained center stage every Friday in the central core of downtown Long Beach.

Markets and Health Activism

With more than 400,000 new diagnoses of diabetes each year, Mexico's 32.8% adult obesity rate surpassed that of the U.S. in 2014, pushing the government to impose a soda tax nationwide. Just as every 10% increase in the cost of cigarettes caused a 4% drop in the rate of smoking, initial results showed an immediate drop in Mexican soda consumption.

On November 4, 2014 Berkeley became the first American city to pass a sugar-sweetened beverage tax (Measure D) with a 76% landslide vote, in spite of more than $2 million against it from the American

Beverage Association. The next day Time.com quoted Measure D leader Vicki Alexander saying, "Berkeley has a proud history of setting nationwide trends, such as non-smoking sections in restaurants and bars, curb cuts for wheelchairs, curbside recycling, and public school food policies."

The Ecology Center and its three farmers' markets across the city were on the front line in the "Berkeley vs. Big Soda" campaign. With grassroots organizing, volunteers, and 1-on-1 discussions, they overcame Big Soda's slick ads which cost more than $50 per voter, or $200 for every negative vote they garnered.

With 40% of kids likely to have diabetes in their lifetimes (50% for Blacks and Hispanics), our country is in crisis mode. Measure D sets up a panel of healthcare, child nutrition and education professionals to advise the City Council on how to reduce sugary drink consumption and improve children's health. It's paid for through a distributor tax of a penny per ounce of soda, energy drinks, and sugary coffee syrups.

> "Being part of the Berkeley Healthy Child Coalition was a natural decision for us since we strive to feed the healthiest food to our community and educate them about the food system. With a core of young interns, we reached thousands of market customers about the link between sugary sodas and obesity, Type 2 diabetes and other diseases."
>
> – Martin Bourque, Exec. Dir., Ecology Center, Berkeley, CA

Immediately following passage of the soda tax, the Berkeley campaign was contacted by other cities, states and countries eager to learn about the strategy that finally enabled a city to defeat Big Soda. How Berkeley implements the health panel and educates its youth may have a major impact in improving the health of youth and all its citizens.

Such community health initiatives are a crucial way that farmers' markets can show support for the concerns of people in their communities. In some cases it may start with a decision to stop selling sodas to fund the market, and keep a commitment to building healthy bodies. This is a health battle with epic economic impact. Every community ultimately will need to face the hard costs of our failure to educate kids about limiting their soda intake.

Just as markets have played a pivotal community role with health departments in expanding farmers' market access through Market Match programs, there will be many local health initiatives like the soda tax that can build strength for a national consensus through community initiatives at farmers' markets.

SURVEYS

In most communities we can only guess at the farmers' market impact on the lives and happiness of area residents. In fact, only 27.6% of managers nationwide conduct surveys, according to USDA.

Serving people with special needs starts with flat surfaces for wheelchairs and appropriate height displays.

Phone surveys can be used to survey the larger community, including market shoppers and non-shoppers, both about a potential market or an existing one. More typically, surveys of customers on market day allow us to quantify the market's impact.

In 1998 U.C. Cooperative Extension surveyed customers at 18 farmers' markets serving some of San Diego County's 6,500 farmers. They found 63% are weekly shoppers, travel four miles to market, purchase 47% of their fruits and vegetables at farmers' markets, and spend a seasonal high of $19.25 per trip from five farmers (elsewhere $10-15 per person is more common).

Customers in inland, north county markets were 75.7% white, median age in their late 50s and income above $60,000. Those in central and south county markets were 80.9% white, late 40s, and below $50,000 income. The most purchased products, in order, were vegetables, fruits, cut flowers, fresh herbs (one in two customers), organic produce (nearly half), followed by baked goods and precut vegetables (one in four).

Knowing demographic and values differences may cause your market to slant a direct mail or other ad piece, or seek out producers of distinct items. A thorough analysis may lead you to help farmers develop additional sales through value-added products. Market studies can help you find that customers want more kids' activities, regular chef demonstrations, a larger range of products, more sophisticated crafts, cleaner restrooms, and more entertainment.

Plan how you will use your research results before you choose the format or write the questions.

Survey Tools

Many markets have used various survey tools to determine the demographics and shopping habits of their customers. Some results are quite sophisticated, with extensive graphs and statistical analyses of respondents' answers. Market surveys should provide data and insight that lead to improvements in marketing and management.

As a first step into the realm of data collection, many markets have used the Rapid Market Assessment (RMA) approach developed by the Oregon State University Small Farms Program, which includes customer counts, dot survey questions and team member insights into the physical site, vendors and products, and market atmosphere.

Using four butcher paper pads to capture customer input on four different questions is admittedly a limited approach. However, the ease of participation can guarantee a high rate of consumer response if the intercept team is well trained and stays positive. RMAs are a transparent, customer-friendly vehicle that get your market involved in basic customer research. From there a market may recognize the need for more detailed surveys that allow for cross-tabulations of various questions. These allow for analysis of spending by income level, spending by age, local business spending by type of customer, etc. Any factors you desire can come into the analysis so that you see the various sub-groups of customers at your market.

Market Umbrella, a New Orleans nonprofit, has used its Crescent City Farmers Market to test numerous resources that they have used in assessing other public markets. Their website allows review of their FEED, NEED and SEED measurement tools as well as videos, green papers, resources, links and more. They encourage a national collaboration through their "marketshare" project.

Economic impact studies can lead to increased business support; funding from city, county, state or federal government; foundation support; and a greater awareness of the role of a market in building healthy partnerships for the local business community.

Examples of several types of studies above are visible on Vance's website,

www.farmersmarketsamerica.org.

Survey goals

Look outside your immediate customer base. Maybe you will find what is hampering your advertising efforts to attract new customers. An on-the-street or telephone survey of non-customers may demonstrate

Having a diverse group of men and women of varying ages soliciting customer participation led to dependable results at the Capital City FM in Montpelier, VT.

frustration over poor parking, high prices, poor quality, narrow aisleways, inconsiderate employees or lack of support for local nonprofits.

A survey in Portland, OR, showed that 28% of farmers' market customers were coming downtown on Wednesday just for the market, even though parking is an acknowledged sore point. The market is now keenly aware of its powerful pull on customers that has spin-off benefits for local merchants.

When USDA asked market managers nationwide the top three reasons why they think customers shop at farmers' markets, they answered: freshness, taste, and access to local food. Then came support of local agriculture, variety and price ranked sixth. Last was knowledge of how the food was produced. These manager assumptions should be checked at the local market level to find out if customers at your market rank their priorities similarly.

So what's most important with a survey? First determine what results you want so that the right questions are asked, and worded properly. When San Diego customers were asked what factors influenced their decision to buy at farmers' markets, the order was: freshness, quality, taste, local (7 in 10), help farmers (6 in 10), followed by nutritional value, atmosphere, best value, convenience, selection and price. Asking their "top reasons" yielded somewhat different priorities. It's important to know that food buyers in general prioritize convenient location, price, quality and parking.

Clipboards and a table to sit at make longer surveys pleasant, especially with a $2 incentive for customers' time.

When a survey tells you that 74% think quality is better than at local supermarkets, especially the tomatoes, you have the basis of your next advertising campaign. Quality was #1 in Santa Barbara markets so they had Julia Child do a "Chef's Choice" commercial to reinforce that the choosiest chefs shop at their farmers' markets. Since convenience is also a high priority there, ads and promotional materials emphasize the choice of six different market locations and the customer service assistants to carry purchases to customers' cars. [See also Appendix, "Customer Surveys and Public Opinion"]

Just ask. Every market knows improvements are possible; the question is where to direct limited resources. If we ask the right questions, there's a good chance that we'll find out how we can better attract and embrace our entire community.

Consistent Research

Your market deserves better than a one-time survey. Commit to a plan to survey your customers several times in the next year – or at least once a year for several years – so the first survey is not the only data you have, but a base point from which you measure whether you are meeting your target goals for improvement.

What did your last survey tell you?

The baseline data from a 2008 survey in Roslyn, WA showed that the Sunday Market was the key motivation for 43% of market shoppers coming to town. Exactly two years later, it rose to 56%. The customer satisfaction level also grew by 13% in that period. These are two clear indicators of improvement. Largely, those shifts resulted from the action plan to attract new vendors, which successfully grew the vendor base by 71% in that two-year period.

By scheduling customer surveys every year in the same week, your market (or even a farmer) can see that the benchmarks you set are being met. Comparing your business to past performance (or even other markets'), you can assess your progress, establish your next set of goals, implement an action plan to meet them, and then evaluate once again using your customer feedback loop.

Every set of survey results should lead you to plan, implement and evaluate a new set. Queen Anne Farmers' Market in Seattle saw that it needed to strengthen its vendor base and did so with very specific targets in each product category, inviting vendors with different price points.

Ask customers not simply "Are you satisfied?" but what improvements they would like to see. If they use a rating scale, you can quantify the relative importance of more farmers vs. more organic farmers, improved quality, more specialty products, better parking, more hot food and more crafts/artisans.

Evaluate the effectiveness of your action plan in improving customer satisfaction. Did your attempt to improve the product selection this year meet your goal of 75% satisfaction? Did your new market layout or parking arrangement gain a positive response within the first month? Did the addition of crafts or alcoholic beverages sink or swim? Did the newest market pavilion design gain a higher positive response than the last? The issue should define the time frame of your survey.

If your action plan did not fare well with customers, go back to the drawing board and to your customers, adding questions to clarify what you have learned earlier. An Idaho market asked if customers spend more or less than $20. The next time, find out how many people spent $0, $5, $10 and so on up to $100, and ask everyone what would cause them to spend more. Then listen, and create another action plan to give them what they want.

You can do this process through a survey at the market, or a quick survey sent online to your loyal customer base for whom you have email addresses. Determine if you want to get quick feedback every 3-6 months to the changes you make, or annually for larger changes.

Listening to conversations among customers will help you to know if you need to do more frequent surveys to get a regular read on your customers. Collaborate with a sister market in another town or city to compare and challenge your market to make constant improvements in your best business practices.

With the RMA format, consumers are able to see others' responses and evaluate how an issue is seen by the public. Columns of the same width help avoid bias, but a traditional survey avoids it altogether with individual response sheets.

Avoid Researcher Bias

If you are creating – or commissioning – a survey, make sure you guard against bias that can make your results unreliable. You want honest answers from your respondents, which requires that you design your survey with unbiased structure and wording. Your own bias in hoping for certain results may affect the survey. Several things to watch for are:

Right people – Avoid selection bias by knowing your target population. You don't want all 20-year-olds intercepting customers who may be largely seniors. Instruct your team to approach all customers without pre-determining that certain ones will not participate. You want even first-time market visitors because they will always make up a certain percentage of customers. Your respondents should represent the full range of customers by age, race, income, with children, etc., and check them against U.S. Census data for your community.

Right questions – Don't ask "Should we have local crafts in our market? Yes or No" when your customers probably have far more nuanced perspectives. Test the question with a small number of people, and you will see that they may want a limited number of artisans, from a certain geographical area, once a month, segregated from the food producers, only if juried by artisans, etc. Look at other markets' surveys to note their questions, wording and potential answers.

Right collection method – Don't expect to learn why residents don't shop at your market by surveying market customers. You may have better results putting the survey on paper placemats at local eateries, making it a clip-out survey for newspaper readers, or using direct mail to every (fifth) household in your community. Your goal defines whether you want a representative sample of people in your area or of market shoppers.

Right results – When the researcher has one or more hypotheses, there can be a tendency to read into the data, resulting in poor interpretation. Decide first on your plan to analyze the raw data, and write your questions to fit the plan. Know which questions will have simple responses leading to a pie chart with percentages, and which will be multiple choice with a rating scale that allows you, for example, to clearly quantify customer interest in more organic produce vs. lower prices or more processed food.

A good survey software program (such as Survey Monkey) can help prevent you from falling inadvertently into bias traps. Know the analytical tools that your survey software offers before crafting a market survey. If you carefully consider your methodology, you will be more confident of the results you present, whether to your market customers, city council or your market board of directors. ❧

Adding to the Product Mix 11

"We pay the doctor to make us better. But we should really pay the farmer to keep us healthy."
— Facebook/Thomas Organic Creamery, September 5, 2014

While farmers' markets in the late 20th century had largely a fruit and vegetable presence, that is no longer the case. Markets are expanding their product line as they hear the customers' insistence on a one-stop service of local foods and seek to gain customer share.

What is hopeful for the future is that farms are able to sustain themselves as they diversify their markets and diversify their products. They no longer need to be so dependent on the weather determining if they will send their kids to college or make their farm payment.

The 2006 USDA National Farmers Market Manager Survey collected responses from 1,292 managers. They found that various products were at U.S. farmers' markets in the following percentages: fresh fruits and vegetables 91.8%, herbs 81.4%, honey, nuts and preserves 77.7%, baked goods 72.9%, crafts or woodworking 50%, meat or poultry 45%, prepared foods 38%, processed foods 28.1%, milk or dairy 27.2%, fish or seafood 16% and other products 38%.

Most of the geography and population of the country is not hospitable to farmers' markets with a full line-up of fresh produce as seen in supermarkets. There simply isn't enough local supply and variety of fresh produce items to keep a population base satisfied, or there isn't enough population to keep the farmers satisfied, or both. As a result not every market has everything, and thus the median season for U.S. seasonal farmers' markets was 4.5 months in 2005. More than 90% operate six months or less, and make just over one-third as much monthly as markets open longer (USDA).

The beauty, and at times the struggle, of farmers' markets can be found in their ever-changing mix of products and the creative characters behind them. In every market there needs to be a range of products. When there are not enough local fruits and vegetables, someone will frequently say, "We need to get produce from outside the area or even the state." People sometimes take opposing sides, suggesting that it should be local while others say it's more important to have the products people want.

Market organizers and public are faced with a conundrum — do we operate a market with only local produce and limit our season or fail, or do we operate with produce from outside the region or crafts and succeed? The same discussion can take

Percentage of U.S. Farmers Markets with Selected Products

Product	Percentage
Fresh fruits & vegetables	91.8%
Herbs & flowers	81.4%
Honey, nuts & preserves	77.7%
Baked goods	72.9%
Crafts or woodworking	50.0%
Meat or poultry	45.0%
Prepared foods	38.0%
Processed foods	28.1%
Milk or dairy	27.2%
Fish or seafood	16.0%
Other products	38.0%

USDA National Farmers Market Managers Survey 2006. Compared with an overall response rate of 34.6%, Edward Ragland and Debra Tropp noted a low 10.3% response from managers with multiple markets, which is the case in 57% of California markets. Thus, the Far West is under-represented.

place relative to vegetarian or meat-inclusive, local cheese or worldwide, alcoholic beverages or abstinence, local seafood or imported, hot foods or none.

Where many rural markets may struggle to find interested vendors of any sort, their counterparts in heavily populated areas may need to be selective or find themselves overrun by a huge number of sellers.

In New York City – just as in Los Angeles or San Francisco – Greenmarkets attract an incredible diversity of products from farms that may be over 300 miles away. From Black Dirt Region vegetables and Hudson Valley Orchards to Finger Lakes wines and Long Island fisheries, the full view of those distances is presented at:

http://www.grownyc.org/files/u19/SeedToPlate_Map_ForProjection_V2.png

We must respectfully note that the solution to each of these questions is based on resources and values at the market level. Each must grapple with the question in a fair and inclusive manner, acknowledging the divergent views in the community. The result will vary based on local cultural traditions, the size of the target population, what other local markets are doing, the availability of a wider mix of potential products, a consensus on how the proposed new products match the values of the market, and the responsiveness of the proposed vendors.

To stay consistent with market values as you expand the range of products, you may want to involve consumers, producers and local business in discussion with management. Be aware of all viewpoints, allowing space for expression of all values, as possible. Surveys and open meetings may be helpful. After a decision over a proposed product, work to include the minority viewpoint. For example, a less than overwhelming consensus might lead to a trial period or a limitation on the product in the market. A negative decision might lead to periodic sales as a concession to the minority opinion.

When a market plentiful in produce considers adding crafts to the mix, there can be vociferous sides taken, usually by the crafters who want to gain entry and the existing produce vendors who feel that limited dollars will be "stolen" by the crafters. The decision may be to allow a certain percentage of the market vendors to be crafters or artisans, and a jurying process may be established. Another market might allot a limited number of craft booths, or only on certain days of the month. Yet other markets might allow crafts that display a "food" theme and are locally-made, such as wooden salad bowls and utensils, fruit-themed earrings or ceramic vegetables.

If not handled with respect and sensitivity for both sides, the decision can lead to a market break-up and the creation of another nearby craft or non-craft market, which may hurt the relative strength of both markets. Using nonprofit booths for the expression of minority viewpoints may lessen the likelihood of such a fracture.

The "big tent" product philosophy necessary to expand your market with new products may require an equally broad tolerance of viewpoints. Even GMO advocates, for example, could be invited to an evening discussion where listening is encouraged as the community seeks to learn, appreciate varying views and gain customers who might otherwise feel excluded.

An open discussion of ideas starts with market management educating itself about sustainable ag issues and product arguments that exist in other markets in your state or the nation.

Whatever food choices are made in your market, there is little doubt that farmers' market customers are more aware than most consumers that we are supporting a specific food system each time we eat – that we "vote with our fork." Your farmers' market is in an ideal position to help educate customers about making conscious, wise food choices. So with examples rather than endorsement, we present various product areas that reflect how markets are changing as they seek the perfect balance to meet the needs of their communities.

Certified Organic

A national survey in 1997 of nearly 1,200 organic farms (of 5,000 in the U.S.) by the Organic Farming Research Foundation (OFRF) found that 30% used farmers' markets to market 33% of their production, or 3,684 of their 11,183 acres.

By 2000 there were 6,600 certified organic farms nationally, yet OFRF director Bob Scowcroft estimated an additional 15,000 farmers had organic production that was not certified.

As consensus grew for an organic food law, USDA initially proposed the inclusion of irradiation, biotechnology and sewer-sludge fertilizer as acceptable for organic foods. When 275,000 people protested, the USDA reversed itself and banned all three methods under new organic standards implemented in 2002. These were the first standards ever imposed for the labeling and processing of organic foods, dividing products into four categories for labeling purposes:

- "100% organic" – products must contain only organic ingredients;
- "organic" – products must contain at least 95% organic ingredients;
- "made with organic ingredients" – products with at least 70% organic contents, up to three of which may be listed on the package front, and
- products with less than 70% organic – may list organic ingredients on the information panel but not mention organic on the front.

Many small producers mistakenly believe they are exempt from the organic standards if they sell under $5,000 per year – not true. They are only exempt from the requirement to be certified by an accredited certifying agency and from submitting an organic systems plan.

Managers need to ask organic farmers about their certification plans. If a producer claims "organic," he/she must be certified unless they meet the $5,000 exemption. Any organic processed products must be made using raw products from a certified source.

Gee Creek Farms of Ridgefield, WA has used unconventional pricing to attract the consumer's attention to their organic produce, grains, fermented foods and more at farmers' markets and through CSA.

"Many farmers have spent years and thousands and thousands of dollars for certification," said Scowcroft, "and it's not fair that someone else can scratch the word 'organic' on a piece of cardboard" and benefit from credibility and higher price.

The organic market continues to grow, although some farms eschew certification and thus forfeit their right to use the "O" word. Those "beyond organic" farms have confidence in their customers who are familiar with the mantra of USDA's program Know Your Farmer, Know Your Food.

By 2014, the U.S. had 19,474 certified organic farms of 27,814 globally, and organic food sales of $35.9 billion, up more than 10-fold from $3.4 billion in 1997. In those 17 years, organic food sales grew from under 1% to almost 5% of total food sales. Organic fruit and vegetable sales were $13 billion, or 12% of all produce sold in the U.S., according to the Organic Trade Association, and 36% of all organic food sales. With the biggest increase in six years, organic dairy sales rose to $5.46 billion in 2014.

The organic food industry is coming of age; every major market chain is a player in the organic realm. To maintain credibility, the farmers' market industry needs to work closely with the organic industry to reinforce the organic standards for individual producers. Market rules need to ensure that claims made to managers and consumers are valid, with definitions and enforcement protocol for "organic," "no spray," "pesticide-free," "hormone free," "antibiotic-free," "pasture-raised," "free range" and various eco-labeling terms. Farmers' market consumers want information about production practices. When producers violate the rules, there should be repercussions, even a loss of selling privileges. If there is no enforcement, customers lose trust.

A very high standard should be set for any market presenting itself to the public as an "organic farmers' market." The People's All Organic Farmers' Market in Portland, OR, requires all sellers to be organic; other markets hopefully will meet that threshold in the future.

For many years organic products were available in farmers' markets more prevalently than in most grocery stores, but no longer. Organic growers have been more likely to sell in farmers' markets than conventional growers. Certainly, in our largest cities the prevalence of organic products has been noticeable, so much so that some consumers have believed that all farmers' market vendors are organic.

According to Jasia Steinmetz, a University of Wisconsin professor of food and nutrition and the author of *Eat Local,* the major benefit of organic produce lies in reduced pesticide exposure, especially in children. Decreased pesticides also help keep our water and soil safe. Early studies either show some nutritional advantage in a few nutrients or no differences. So it's probably best for organic producers to refrain from making claims about nutritional superiority of organic foods without further conclusive studies.

The 2006 USDA manager survey showed that in farmers' markets carrying organically labeled products, the three most popular product categories are fresh fruit and vegetables (91.4%), herbs and flowers" (46.3%), and meat and poultry" (30.1%). Of all organic vendors at farmers' markets, 60.2% have fresh fruits and vegetables, 16.7% herbs and flowers, and 9.3% meat and poultry.

When organically labeled products are available, markets seem to include meat, poultry and dairy products in their mix. It seems that farmers' market customers may prefer these products organically produced.

Certified farmers are wise to make sure customers can easily find the products with growing standards they are looking for.

The 25,000 farmers, ranchers and other businesses that are organically certified encompassed more than 5.38 million acres in 2011, including 131,000 acres of fruit, 23,000 acres of nuts and 147,000 acres of vegetables. Managers can access a list of all certified organic operations in the U.S. at:

http://apps.ams.usda.gov/nop/

With $1.35 billion in 2014 organic sales overall, California leads the nation, followed by Washington, Oregon, Wisconsin, New York, Florida, Pennsylvania, Texas, Colorado and Minnesota. Solid organic farm numbers exist in Ohio, Iowa, Vermont and Idaho, but with lower gross sales. Thus, the West has the highest concentration of organic farms, with the Midwest and Northeast doing fairly well. Organic products at farmers' markets might be expected to follow those regional trends.

The Union of Concerned Scientists 2011 report, Market Forces: Creating Jobs through Public Investment in Local and Regional Food Systems, noted that farmers selling direct tend to have environmentally sustainable practices. Markets should advise their vendors to prominently display their eco-labels and be ready to explain meanings – otherwise they could be losing out on a distinct marketing edge.

Organic direct marketing growers earned 75 percent more on average than similar conventional growers. They also sold more volume than organic farmers who did no direct marketing. About 2% of national organic production was sold at farmers' markets in 2008.

Most consumers agree that organics is the ideal; they would prefer a return to pre-World War II, chemical-free production practices. However, many have become accustomed to food taking a smaller bite out of their budget, even as medical care has grown immensely. Continued education around a host of issues relative to price is critical to growth in the organic sector at farmers' markets. Market share will be gained one customer at a time through personal contact, quality samples and reasonable prices.

Baked Goods

Good bread has been the standard at many farmers' markets for years, but the temptation for some markets is to protect their one bakery rather than allow people a choice of as many different bread styles as there are fruits.

Portland's reputation as a bread city has been cemented by the PSU market which showcases bread with a range of styles from Pearl Bakery's classic levain to Gabriel's blue corn and Fressen's many brots. Dave's Killer Bread began at this market, just as Starbucks started at Pike Place Market in Seattle. Then there are macaroons from Two Tarts, which closed up its retail store at Christmas 2014 and returned to just selling at the farmers' market. Black Sheep Bakery did the same thing, holding onto its farmers' market life.

Fail Better Farm presents a variety of breadsticks, scones and cookies at the Waterville FM in Maine.

The bakery realm is so full of richness, that competition really means variety. The Hudson Farmers' Market (NY) has breads, sourdough breads, focaccia, criossants, cinnamon apple cakes, sourdough pizza crusts, pies, tarts, cupcakes, cookies and sweet and savory strudels with hand pulled dough and Hudson Valley fruits and veggies.

Fred Price and Faye Chan started out as bakers, and later became farmers. Since 1983 Fifth Floor Farm Kitchen has been considered Greenmarket's best small bakery, wowing customers with their savory and sweet treats using local and organic ingredients. Now based in Moravia, NY, they travel to their local Ithaca market, and 250 miles to Union Square with

such goods as vegetable pies and turnovers, Hungarian cakes, seaweed-wrapped rice and nut rolls, seaweed cheese bread and plum tarts. They also cultivate shiitake and blewit mushrooms, and have gathered ramps and wild onion, garlic and onion.

As with so many other bakers, Windfield Farm Bakery has experimented with new items at the Crescent City Farmers Market (LA), adding pecan ganache shortbread cookies, coconut cake and blue cheese walnut bread to their existing line of breads, granolas, breakfast pastries and dessert bars.

In most cases market bakeries are local independents. The Washington State Farmers Market Association has tried to assure that by codifying in its rules that no member market may allow a franchised bakery. In next door Oregon, that is not the case.

A recent dramatic change at farmers' markets is the prevalence of gluten-free bakeries. For example, Copia is creating gluten-free granola cookies in the Stony Brook business incubator in Calverton for sale at the Riverhead Farmers Market (NY). According to Edible East Side, "these cookies use oats sourced from GF Harvest in Wyoming, the first certified gluten free oat farm in the United States."

Were it not for the great mix of artisan bakeries in the Portland, OR market, one might almost feel over-run with gluten-free options. There are New Cascadia breads and pastry, Queen of Hearts sweet and savory pies and quiche, Enlighten Your Palate desserts, Petunia's Pies & Pastries, Happy Campers bread, aptly named Divine Pie, and Three Sisters Nixtamal with stone-ground, GMO-free, handmade masa and tortillas.

While showing that gluten-free is delectable for most everyone, they prove once again that more consumers have interest in a product line when there is choice from among several producers, rather than a monopoly.

From wooden ties and belt buckles in Boise to spoons and cutting boards in Ithaca, NY (above), wood products add richness to any market with an encouraging "Wood You Please Touch."

Crafts

If you are in Chugiak, Alaska, you don't expect to find only produce at the local market, the Peters Creek American Legion Post 33 Farmers Market and Crafts. That can be said along the Oregon coast, in the south of Florida or in most any small town in America. The relative dearth of people often sparks the creative imagination of the few.

There is strong opinion among many of the best farmers' markets in America that crafts only dilute the effort to build sustainable food markets that can help rebuild our small farm movement. Yet, we must reckon that opinion with the fact that the majority of our 8,000 plus farmers' markets do allow craft items. That fact may explain why many of those mixed markets are not among the strongest, but it also may explain why many of those same mixed markets are still in existence today.

When the Astoria Farmers Market asked for promotional help in the late 1990s, they were at the end of the rope. With seven vendors, there was not a farmer in sight. Their re-birth as the Astoria Sunday Market in a new downtown location gave local craftspeople an outlet for their creations, and the outpouring of customers gave farmers reason to follow the intrepid few growers who initially supported the new endeavor.

Astoria quickly became the second largest craft market in Oregon, and farmers have been an important part of the mix. Local agriculture benefited from having an alliance with local crafts. Local musicians are another comfortable ally, playing to an open-air audience every Sunday instead of inside bars and clubs alone. Downtown businesses are now open on Sunday throughout the summer season.

Astoria is one of the best stories of a craft community rescuing a market, with an end result benefitting farmers, local businesses and the entire community as well. It's the craft equivalent of what local food has done for the town of Hardwick, Vermont. That's the place that inspired Ben Hewitt's book, *The Town That Food Saved*, which documents the ambitious young "agripreneurs" who have rescued a town of 3,200 residents from the clutches of a dying granite industry.

Meat and Poultry

Twenty-eight states have their own meat and/or poultry inspection programs based on the Federal Meat Inspection Act of 1967 (FMIA) and the Poultry Products Inspection Act of 1968 (PPIA). These programs cover about 2,000 small or very small establishments and are run cooperatively with USDA's Food Safety and Inspection Service (FSIS), which provides up to 50% of operational funding.

The state programs must be "at least equal to" federal inspection, and there has never been a docu-

Primitive artist Bill Dodge of Long Island, NY has sold originals and puzzle copies of his paintings at the Astoria Sunday Market in Oregon.

THE NEW FARMERS' MARKET

mented food illness from state-inspected meat and poultry products. State-inspected facilities produce about 10% of red meat consumed, while imported meats constitute about 20%, meeting a similar "equal to" standard.

By 2005, U.S. consumers ate 4.5 billion pounds of meat and poultry from 38 countries, while state-inspected meats could not cross even state lines. The inherent unfairness of this free trade limitation for small businesses finally led to Congress' shift in the 2008 Farm Bill. After four decades, small business operators with state-inspected meat plants were permitted to make interstate shipment of beef, poultry, pork, lamb and goat.

Long before Upton Sinclair's 1906 book, *The Jungle,* there was a time when Americans bought meat that was raised on pasture and had the flavor of the local grasses. Gradually, the stockyards of Sinclair's day became the large Concentrated Animal Feeding Operations (CAFOs) of today, where a large animal operation is typically more than 1,000 cattle, 2,500 swine or 125,000 chickens. Animals are fattened with grains for 45 days or more before slaughter. The idea is to raise animals for market with the least amount of inputs, in the fastest time, with maximum profits.

"Grazing and growing feed for livestock now occupy 70 percent of all agricultural land and 30 percent of the ice-free terrestrial surface of the planet. If present trends continue, meat production is predicted to double between the turn of the 21st century and 2050. Yet already, the Earth is being overwhelmed by food animals that consume massive quantities of energy and resources, whose wastes foul waterways and farmlands, and when eaten excessively, degrade our health."

– CAFO: The Tragedy of Industrial Animal Factories, cafothebook.org

Confining animals in close quarters is a disease risk, as any outbreak would spread quickly and kill many other animals. Thus, antibiotics are routinely added to the feed. The over-use of antibiotics in agriculture has generated a severe human public health crisis with more than 23,000 Americans dying annually from antibiotic-resistant "superbugs" that have evolved to be impervious to antibiotics.

Kookoolan Farms promoted the national media attention being given to Oregon's proposed legislation in 2015 to ban preventive use of antibiotics in livestock that are not acutely ill. They urged people to consider the refugee camps we associate with earthquakes, hurricanes and war, where cholera and other diseases proliferate. Those are similar conditions to the cramped, unsanitary housing of animals which are daily fed more than 70% of all antibiotics used in the U.S.

Concerns about the quality of meat from large production and processing facilities, the control of the meat industry by a handful of companies and the ethical and humanitarian issues of animals raised in small spaces without access to the outdoors have led some consumers to seek meat, poultry and eggs from small-scale, local farmers who use alternative production methods. Farmers who pasture small herds of animals cite the relative environmental and nutrient benefits of raising grass-fed animals compared to large-scale animal production methods.

Through films like Food, Inc. and books like *Diet for a New America* by John Robbins, and *CAFO,* Americans are slowly shifting their view of animals, adapting to animals raised with respect, or cutting that protein source entirely.

"The majority of the world consumes a plant-based diet stemming from the intensive resources, including land and water, needed to raise animals (whether feedlot- or grass-fed), and the resulting higher price. Many local food advocates, trying to find other options besides the factory-farm meat products are generally looking at two directions: eating less meat and purchasing local, hormone-free, or reducing or eliminating meat consumption through a plant-based diet."

– Jasia Steinmetz, *Eat Local: Simple Steps to Enjoy Real, Healthy & Affordable Food*

Official U.S. government dietary recommendations advocate a predominantly plant-based diet for health reasons, since plant-based diets are typically low in fat and high in fiber. Some advocates cite: "The most important thing you can do for the environment is to become a vegetarian." John Robbins states that grass-fed as well as feedlot beef production contributes to global climate change:

http://foodrevolution.org/blog/the-truth-about-grass-fed-beef.

Grass-fed proponents, too, are educating the public about alternatives to the industrial meat system. EatWild.com, for example, displays a myriad of farmers who are raising grass-fed, grain-free, hormone-free, antibiotic-free, chemical-free, free-range, whey-fed and pastured animals.

While not all ranchers selling at farmers' markets have similar sympathies, just as not all farmers are organic, the simple presence of customers who care to ask questions directly of meat and poultry producers has led many more sustainable producers of healthy animal products to participate.

Kookoolan Farms began in Yamhill, OR in 2005. For Chrissie Manion Zaerpoor, an electrical engineer by training, the decision to farm was a personal testimonial to life. Suffering ill health and taking seven prescriptions daily, she began reading…

"… the nutrition books of Andrew Weil. In one of them he made a passing comment that our

Paleolithic ancestors ate mostly vegetables, berries, and wild grass-fed game, and if wild or grass-fed meats were available in the U.S. he would recommend that diet as a first choice, but since they're not, his second choice, the Mediterranean diet, was his official recommendation."

– Chrissie Zaerpoor, Kookoolan Farms e-newsletter essay of April 28, 2015 on Why I Became a Farmer

Chrissie followed Weil's advice; to do so, she and her husband Koorosh became farmers. Below is her body's testimony to her Intel engineering existence in 2001 compared with her farm existence in 2014:

March 2001. Chrissie is an engineering manager at Intel.	October 2014. Chrissie is a farmer and entrepreneur.
Age: 36	Age: 50
Height: 5'6"	Weight: 120
Weight: 125	Height: 5'6"
Cholesterol: 292 (should be <180)	Cholesterol: 186
Triglycerides 280 (should be <150)	Triglycerides 109
LDL:HDL ratio 7.0 (should be < 5)	LDL:HDL ratio 3.1.
Iron 25 (should be 45-160)	Iron 73
Blood pressure 120/80	Blood pressure 109/71
Diet: skim milk, grains, commodity chicken breast, fish twice a week, tofu once a week, salad every day, some fruits and vegetables, too many cookies and scones. No red meat ever.	Diet: whole milk from 100% grassfed cows, red meat from 100% grassfed beef and lamb, lots of vegetables and fruits, one glass of wine or mead every day. Dark chocolate. Dried fruits and nuts. And too much sugar!

Small ranchers are intent on survival, and on producing animals with ethics that many customers appreciate. As customers support them in large cities and small towns, they are voting for an alternative to the CAFO model.

Whether producers in your market choose to serve those seeking to reduce their meat consumption through hormone-free, local meat, or eliminate it with a plant-based diet, farmers' markets are in the forefront of serving a public that is rejecting factory farmed meat and poultry.

Processed Foods

Studies have shown that small farms selling direct often grow multiple products (Starr et al. 2003). They constitute 28% of farmers – and 49% of organic producers – with value-added goods (Martinez et al. 2009). Farmers' market vendors have expanded or developed additional product lines, processing, mailing lists, business contacts, and skills in customer

© Vance Corum

Maple Grove Farm of Putnam Station, NY sells their pastured animal products in small towns throughout the Adirondack Mountains.

THE NEW FARMERS' MARKET

relations, merchandising and pricing (Feenstra et al. 2003).

When looking at organic value-added sales, the top states in dollar volume are California and Texas with $93 million and $79 million, followed far back by Oregon, Pennsylvania, Vermont, Washington and Wisconsin. The southern states also do well in production and sale of organic value-added commodities, with Kentucky, Oklahoma, Tennessee and Virginia near the top.

Most states have cottage food laws, but the vast majority limit the foods that can be produced to non-refrigerated foods like jams and baked goods, and some states have a ceiling on profits.

For example, Michigan allows cottage producers of baked goods, jam, dried herbs, dried pasta, popcorn, vinegar and chocolate-covered foods such as pretzels or fruit. The law has a maximum limit of $15,000 gross annual sales, and a list of restricted foods.

Along with the expected salsa and candied pecans, many farmers and other entrepreneurs are stirring up local culture with probiotic foods to improve public health.

Fermented Foods

While a long-established tradition in many parts of the country, fermented foods are experiencing a renaissance. There is a palpable excitement that one senses in conversation with these producers, whether they are farmers doing fermentation with their own produce or independent start-ups purchasing raw products. Both may be carrying the fermented foods message to a larger audience than just farmers' markets.

Lactic acid bacteria (LAB) fermentation is a centuries-old natural process that preserves crops at harvest to be consumed over the winter months. These fermented foods have been shown to promote good digestion and improve overall health. Generally, they are considered a processed food that requires a commercially inspected kitchen or a licensed home kitchen, depending on state law. In Minnesota fermented foods are protected under the Pickle Bill, which covers all home-canned and home-processed food with an equilibrium pH value of 4.6 or lower. Sandor Katz has two books that cover fermentation and state regulations.

Fermenters are inspired, passionate and open. Brassica and Brine is a micro craft business that proudly promotes its five organic suppliers as readily as being named one of the LA Weekly's Top Ten Los Angeles Artisan Food Producers of 2012. Wild West views itself as a nano business in Marin County and encourages others to explore for themselves.

"We refuse to be another mass producing food company that lets quality and creativity suffer in the lust for higher profits. The magical transformation of fermentation is our passion. We hope to inspire you not just to incorporate more of these incredible health restoring foods into your diet, but also to inspire a re-evolution, and connection to ecology. To encourage wild fermentation in your own kitchen is to take local food to the microscopic level, as the microorganisms in your home and garden are different from those of your neighbor."

– www.WildWestFerments.com/products

Britt Eustis is a former Eden Foods buyer who became intrigued with small-scale, family fermenting that he observed on a buying trip in Japan in the 1980s. He has always been fascinated by the health benefits and old world wisdom contained in the process of creating and consuming sauerkraut (known as the poor man's penicillin), kimchi and other naturally-fermented products. In 2012 he realized his dream with Britt's Pickles, in his sister's basement. Today these live culture foods are handmade at their Whidbey Island facility using natural fermentation processes, proprietary recipes, and time-honored techniques. They are vegan, free of gluten and preservatives, and incorporate locally grown produce whenever possible. Their time and care attending to quality ingredients defines their product and price.

"Fermented foods are analogous to bread 25 years ago, when people woke up to what bread is. There is a whole flavor palate. Fermenting vegetables is like bread, wine and beer; they all have many elements.

"Being at farmers' markets is an education process. People are so brainwashed that things that grow on our food are bad for us. I tell people that white is yeast; it doesn't kill you. Don't eat the colors – mold. I tell them that we evolved on these foods. They help our digestion. And I listen, because they want to tell their issues, their stories, their awareness.

"If they use our Pickle-ator to make their own fermented foods, they will come tell me that the kraut doesn't smell good. I say, "Wait six weeks and it's really good for you."

– Adele Eustis, artist and sister of Britt's Pickles owner, Seattle, WA

Britt Eustis started making fermented foods because he realized that Japanese culture had something to impart, and the Puget Sound had a food culture ready to incorporate his ideas.

Brian and Connie Shaw of Oregon Brineworks make pickles, real ketchup, hot sauce, beet kvass, ginger gold kvass, pickled beets, ginger roots, saueruben and beet apple kraut at their Hood River "fermentary." They use quality, organic, lacto-fermented vegetables from local farms – 90% within 100 miles – to support the regional food shed while building customer health.

Especially popular in Russia and the former Soviet states, kvass is a fermented beverage commonly made from black or rye bread, but Oregon Brineworks uses beets, herbs and ginger.

Oregon Brineworks is only colonizing the Pacific Northwest, although their distributor, Azure Standard, could make their products available in 38 states. With the understanding that digestive dysfunction is the root of most illness, they believe: "A pickle a day keeps the doctor away!"

"People's Co-op has a long tradition of handling quality, hand-crafted food products so it feels good to sell to them and in the farmers' market outside. We use it as a way to get our products into people's mouths. Because it's a small market, we only sell about $2-300 on Wednesdays year-round, but we meet a lot of chefs there –

great people and potential customers – and I link it up with my deliveries to New Seasons, Whole Foods, Food Front and our other retailers."

– Brian Shaw, Farmer/Fermenter, Oregon Brineworks, Hood River, OR

The Shaws love beets because they are a year-round crop and "an amazing vegetable." As fermenters, they use beets in beet apple kraut, pickled beets, ginger roots and their kvass, which is the brine of their fermented products. Their ginger gold kvass is made with filtered water added to the viscous brine of the ginger roots – gold beet, carrot and ginger.

Farming organically since 2004, Brian and Connie recognized that they could better sustain their 2 ½-acre organic farmstead and lifestyle by fermenting fruits and vegetables of their own and other local organic farms. They started with a domestic processor's license at their farm in 2013, but the demand from grocery stores forced their move to a small business park.

Brian has a consciousness about sharing ideas, having hooked up over Instagram with others like Harvest Roots Farm & Ferment. Based in Falkville, Alabama, they believe in food as medicine just as Dr. Mercola who sent off his sauerkraut for a lab analysis:

THE NEW FARMERS' MARKET

"We found in a 4-6 ounce serving of the fermented vegetables there were literally ten trillion bacteria. That means 2 ounces of home fermented sauerkraut had more probiotics than a bottle of 100 count probiotic capsules. Translated this means one 16 ounce of sauerkraut is equal to 8 bottles of probiotics:

http://nourishingplot.com/.../sauerkraut-test divulges-shock.../"

– Facebook.com/Harvest Roots Farm & Ferment, December 1, 2014

"One striking observation of ethnic cuisines is that it is rare when meals are eaten without at least one fermented food. In France if one were to take away bread, cheese, wine and beer—all produced through fermentation—meals would be much impoverished. In Japan, it's not a complete meal without miso, soy sauce and pickles—all fermented foods. In India soured milk is consumed at practically every meal. In Indonesia tempeh is eaten regularly, and in Africa porridge of fermented millet, corn, cassava, and sorghum are daily staples. In Moslem countries they consume fermented-grain breads and milk products.

"Fermented foods are usually produced as a means of preserving perishable ingredients such as milk, vegetables, and fish when refrigeration is unavailable or too costly. Beyond its use as a valuable food preservation method, unique nutrient complexes are also created during fermentation. The abundant microorganisms in the fermentation process produce vitamins, enzymes, antioxidants, beta glucans, and phytonutrients."

– Robert L Lawrence M.Ed., D.C., D.A.C.B.N., at www.ancientawakenings.net

Dairy and Cheeses

With all the milk, cheese and ice cream that we consume as children, it is not surprising that people often continue that trend with their own children. When that happens, they feel

Vegetarian cheeses are made in a Swiss-style copper vat using organic milk and microbial rennet. Hawthorne Valley Farm keeps vegetarians and non-vegetarians alike happy.

especially good knowing, for instance, that the yogurt is rated high on The Cornucopia Institute's list of 114 rated brands, especially if they have read the institute's excoriating 2014 report, "Culture Wars: How the Food Giants Turned Yogurt, a Health Food, into Junk Food." Some of Cornucopia's top 10 yogurts are well known in farmers' markets, including Hawthorne Valley Farm at New York City and Strauss Family Creamery in Sonoma and Marin counties.

Among America's favorite farmers' market cheese artisans, Willi Lehner of Bleu Mont Dairy is clearly a leader, not simply because he is one of many at the Dane County Farmers Market. Rather, it is because he is a renegade, second generation, Swiss heritage artisan who acts as an open source bible of cheesemaking knowledge. He makes cheese using organic, pastured milk at four local dairies and brings the cloth-wrapped, English style cheddar wheels back to his underground, straw bale, cheese cave lined with cedar boards which help control humidity and temperature. Both the vault and his farm run on wind and solar power.

Local farms like Strauss and Bleu Mont are reclaiming yogurt, cheese and other products, reminding people of what real food can taste like and what health benefits it brings, and pointing out how agribusiness will capitalize on the well-deserved reputation of these products and adulterate them for the popular palate. The Cornucopia study noted the nutritional benefits of eating whole-milk organic yogurt and, like other peer-reviewed findings, found that organic yogurt had healthier ratios of omega-3 to omega-6 fatty acids than conventional yogurt.

As with other products, farmers' markets should encourage a wide selection of cheeses from various farms so that they can compete with the cheese selection in local stores. Some markets allow a cheesemaker to sell more than their own production.

Clint Harris recognized that glass bottles were the key to capturing new customers, as he has shown at the Saco FM just south of Portland, ME.

Chocolates

Countless books have been written about chocolate, romances have flourished under its effect, and some people can't start or finish their day without it. There is little wonder that chocolate is part of so many markets, even though purists would remind us that chocolate isn't grown here. When some things are so entrenched in the human psyche, we incorporate them into our markets because without them there would be a void. It's true for bread, coffee, chocolate and a number of other items dependent on our local food culture.

Pix Patisserie in Portland, OR used the largest Portland farmers' market as a launch pad for its retail location, as have other businesses around the country. Others like Alma Chocolate have taken its place.

Regular eating of dark chocolate is a healthy source of antioxidants that can lower the risk of heart disease. Compounds in 70-85% cocoa-rich chocolate lower blood pressure and protect against the oxidation of LDL, low-density lipoproteins, the bad cholesterol which reacts with free radicals in the body. Dark chocolate also may protect the skin against sun damage and improve brain function. These are all good reasons that may give market managers justification for including their local chocolatier, because people do love to satisfy their taste buds.

Beverages

Farmers' markets feed people and they provide drinks. For years it was often just lemonade, but usually that means a commercial, worthless drink of sugar. It's not like the real organic lemonade sold by two brothers, Ben and Steve Miller, from Carpinteria, CA at area markets back in the 1980s.

Today the closest thing might be Lori's Lovely Lemonade, also of Carpinteria, made with nothing but organic lemons and cane sugar, brewed lavender tea and filtered water. That's a drink meant for a farmers' market, without GMOs, corn syrup or concentrates. It's so good she has a Lemonade Club so customers can receive a dozen 16 oz. bottles every month.

Soda is also present in some markets. Hot Lips, a Portland pizza company, sold their berry soda for a few years in Oregon markets. That's better than most commercial sodas that a farmers' market might sell to cover its costs.

Juices are much healthier, especially when they are straight from the farm, because they are healthy for the body, and for the local economy. Growing their own veggies, The Juice Bar transforms and sells them at the Burlington Farmers Market.

On Facebook they show customers their field of beets and more, or suggest what makes your skin hydrated from the inside out. You click to find out more. They suggest what to eat if you're grumpy: calcium, chromium, folate, iron, magnesium, omega-3 fatty acids, vitamin D, B6, B12 and zinc. They also post fun things, like a new record of 110 juices served in 2.5 hours at The University of Vermont Medical Center Farmers' Market on April 2, 2015. It must have been warm that day.

Like most juicing companies, Beet Generation in the Bay Area keeps an active presence on Facebook, posting lots of happy photos of finished and raw product like green grapes from Smit Ranch, ready for their Yardbird special. Since they are not regulated under Cottage Food Law, the health department inspects them as a temporary food facility.

As with most food businesses, these entrepreneurs have a passion for the health benefits. Get Fresh – NewBo educates people in Cedar Rapids, IA just as Julia's Juices does in Arroyo Grande, CA and The Juice Joint in Charleston, SC.

So whether it's a standard apple juice or orange, kiwi, pineapple, peach or a mix, or even hibiscus, Jamaica, horchata, or organic ginger lemonade, the farmers' market is a great place to experiment with flavor combinations.

Ginger beer has flowed in cities like Austin with its Soco Ginger Beer and Seattle where Rachel's got its start at several farmers' markets in 2011.

In 2013 Rachel Marshall opened a flagship store in Pike Place Market, in place of a Seattle's Best Coffee. Her plan is to fill the 50-seat shop with some of the Pike Place's 10 million visitors. To meet the demand she bought a $75,000 juicer from Spain that processes 100 gallons of lemon juice per hour, up from eight.

By 2015 she was selling 600 gallons per week, not yet capacity. However, she is spicing up the drink world and inspiring a craft soda industry from her farmers' market digs, proving that Seattleites will pay dearly for a real soda.

A second Seattle company, Malus Ginger Beer, debuted at the Broadway Farmers Market in late January 2015, as Seattle's only fermented, non-alcoholic ginger beer, also using organic ingredients: water, ginger, honey and lemon. John Struble has additional plans: "…with healthful ingredients that epitomize Malus's herbalist tradition and stout opposition to the heavily medicated culture created by the American Medical Association." Strong words, indeed, but then these are independent thinkers who dare to challenge the primacy of fake lemonade and root beer.

Kombucha, a fizzy fermented beverage made from sweetened tea, is alive and well in Seattle thanks to

Rachel's friendly presence and use of Tonnemaker Farms' nectarines in her ginger beer makes her a popular Seattle vendor. Rather than create a shelf-stable soda using preservatives and flavorings in order to do wholesale, she geared up the volume of her fresh product to meet strong local demand at the Pike Place Market because she loves to brighten people's day.

CommuniTea Kombucha, that has been researching and experimenting since 1993. They sell at Ballard and University District farmers' markets as well as their brewery, stores, cafes and on tap. Starting with biodynamic organic green tea from Darjeeling, they craft small batches with low levels of sugar to not overpower the beneficial live cultures in every bottle and keg, and they reuse all of their bottles.

Pickle Me Too sells strawberry hibiscus kombucha, lemon ginger, cherry vanilla, root beer, apricot and star anise, blueberry lavender and much more at her North Dakota farm. Her blog is a great resource for the beginning fermenter, starting with her own road to real food when her first child was diagnosed with autism. She recommends the Kombucha DIY Guide and Kombucha Kamp among the many resources available online.

Symple Foods sells their SOMA kombucha and other fermented foods at Portland area markets including at Oregon Health Sciences University, where its lab results may get more attention. Symple has their own probiotics and supplements tested along with the competition. While other kombuchas register up to 3500 probiotics per gram, SOMA's products register between 6 and 8 million.

"People deserve to know what's in the products they're spending their money on, especially with all the health-oriented advertising happening right now, and the FTC actually encourages comparative advertising as long as claims can be backed up.

"I'm a big fan of getting creative and resourceful, and finding ways to make even bigger wins for everyone than just choosing the lesser of two evils. My homemade kimchi scored around 380,000 probiotics per gram, which is actually ten times higher than the second-place kombucha.

"Here's the real win for the consumer…find a local microbiology lab and see if they'll test your favorite kombucha or supplement for you. It should cost around $15. I'm really excited to suggest this because there's so much green washed advertising…in the natural/organic food biz…An empowered customer could change the game and push 'green' companies to be more transparent."

> – Jean-Pierre Parent, Author, *Kitchen Sink Farming*, and Owner, Symple Foods, Portland, OR

Craft Alcoholic Beverages

The explosion of the craft wine, beer and cider industries starting in the 1980s revealed keen public interest and led farmers' markets to incorporate this new alcohol sector. It has expanded the farmers' market customer base, including the new generation of millenials. Time magazine kicked off 2015 saying, "Archeological evidence dates wine made from honey to as far back as 7000 B.C. – and it's about to be more popular than ever."

"Farmers' markets that have wine vendors next to cheese and artisan breads report good cross marketing from these pairings."

> – Oregon Farmers Markets Association

Beekeepers John Hersman and Melissa Hronkin of Greenland, MI have driven an hour to sell honey at the Lake Linden Farmers Market since it opened in 2011. It's a small market with 15-20 vendors, including a bakery, coffee roaster and artisans, and about 200-300 customers in a town of 1,000 residents. Averaging $150 per market day, their honey sales barely made it worthwhile to make the 100-mile roundtrip. Their mead sales began in 2014 and gave them an extra $100 a day, making it bearable.

"Adding mead to our product line has sustained our business, and gives us revenue to reinvest in our bee yard each spring since the cold of Michigan's Upper Peninsula causes a die-off every year. Now we've been testing honey sodas to take a kegerator to market and add to our income. In sparsely populated areas like ours, producers have to be creative in expanding our product lines, for self-preservation and for market survival."

> – Melissa Hronkin, Algomah Acres Honey House & Meadery, Greenland, MI

Algomah Meadery sells mead in a 500 ml. lock-lid bottle for $14-18. Just as they have revived a rural church building as a retail location, they are rekindling interest in everything from tart cherry, choke

Algomah Meadery opened for retail in an old Catholic Church in an isolated rural area of Upper Michigan, funded by a Kickstarter campaign. Making customer contacts at a new farmers' market in 2011, they exceeded their 60-day goal of $93,000 with 170 donations to fund improvements and permits.

cherry, elderberry and thimble berry to the more common raspberry, strawberry and blackberry meads.

"On any given day the Ithaca Farmers Market has up to 10 different wineries, cideries and breweries present, starting back in the 90s. The loyal cadre of local customers are really there for the cabbage and carrots, but they still buy from us. What we really provide is a momento for the tourists and day-trippers who aren't looking for vegetables, just as the prepared food people give them a hot bite to eat.

"In a university town we have a short window to catch students and their parents. Later we see these two sets of transient customers visit our tasting room, and we know they are buying at local restaurants and retailers.

While less than 10% of our sales are at the farmers' market, that's where we build awareness that drives traffic to our farm, where we do 80% of all our sales. The market has a direct economic benefit for us, but the promotional value is huge. The farmers' market has created a community to be part of. And besides, it's a lot of fun."

– Bill Barton, Bellwether Hard Cider & Wine Cellars, Trumansburg, NY

While there are clear advantages for craft beverage producers and for farmers' markets, there are time-consuming obstacles along the way. In most states both groups will need to involve themselves in writing legislation that addresses sampling, competition, raw product sourcing and other issues. Without the right to sample, the size and growth of beverages in markets will be severely limited. If farmers' markets are to be viable outlets, there will need to be a continued push for more open laws and policies on federal, state, local and market levels.

Wine

The United States had 7,762 wineries in 2013, according to Wines and Vines. That number quadrupled in the prior decade. California is the leader with nearly half of all wineries and 88% of total U.S. wine production.

Over 77%, or 6,013 U.S. wineries, are very small, with under 5,000 cases annually. They lack legitimacy with customers and distributors, making it difficult to survive, especially in emerging regions. In trying to beat the 80 percent failure rate of all new businesses, farmers' markets can help them address the liability of newness.

While California allowed wine and cider into farmers' markets in 2001, they didn't allow sampling. Thus, few wineries bothered to get permits, and sales without samples were slow.

In 2014 California governor Jerry Brown signed wine sampling legislation. Wines must be estate grown, no winery can exceed 5,000 gallons in farmers' market sales annually, only one winery is permitted daily at any market, and market operators have the discretion to allow or prohibit wine sampling.

Obviously, the farmers' market industry does not want to see markets become wine bars. With a daily monopoly of one producer, sales in California farmers' markets will be constrained. Managers will need to wisely apportion the slots throughout the season, making sure that wineries get a Type 02 wine grape producer permit and Type 79 market wine permit from the California Department of Alcoholic Beverage Control (www.abc.ca.gov/distmap).

"The U.S. has been the largest wine consuming nation since 2010," says the Wine Institute. We are now consuming 330 million cases annually, so farmers' markets are joining the trend, with 10 states having legislation by 2014. Most states – from Washington to Vermont – do not limit their markets to only one winery.

Washington, second in wine production with 689 wineries, was just ahead of California with sampling legislation in 2013. This followed a 15-month sampling pilot in 2011-12 with 16 wineries and four breweries at 10 farmers' markets.

Paul Beveridge of Wilridge Winery, who spearheaded the legislation, had been actively selling at six Puget Sound markets that were part of the pilot. Beveridge found that customer satisfaction increased; his sales tripled; and he hired additional staff.

"We made an exception to accept a winery association as the 'vendor' and rotated qualifying vineyards through a portion of the market season in the same space. Many vineyards thought it was good marketing, but the association didn't feel there was enough association benefit to continue, at least with shared funds. One member stayed."

– Rebecca Landis, Market Director, Corvallis-Albany FM, OR

In Massachusetts, farm wineries have been permitted at certified events including farmers' markets since 2010.

"The farmers' market is a good place to introduce wines to consumers, especially for somewhat isolated farms. After three years, we've found that selling costs have been higher than projected. Several markets are now charging $50 per day. Ours is a higher quality sale since our wines sell from $20 to $35. We offer wine shares with 10-25% savings based on the volume of quarterly shipments. Our customers are likely to come back to buy.

"I thought I could predict good markets, but it's not so easy. We drop them if they don't make sense, but we still sell at 12. You need a critical mass of farmers and customer traffic, but you also need a certain demographic and good energy from a manager."

– Kip Kumler, Turtle Creek Wine, Lincoln, MA

Beer

"Our customers are extremely interested in everything Michigan-grown, which includes wineries and breweries. The demand is there. In 2014 we had our first orchard sampling and selling their wines. We inspect our farms to ensure the product source. From November to April, they can supplement their production only from the lower 48 states, but they must label it with neon pink signs."

– Shelly Mazur, Manager, Royal Oak Farmers Market, MI

Prohibition succeeded in cutting alcohol consumption in half during the 1920s, even though wine and cider could be made at home. While the 18th Amendment was repealed in 1933, it wasn't until 1978 that President Carter passed a homebrewing law, and then in 1979 deregulated the brewing industry. Grant's Brewery Pub opened in Yakima, WA in 1982, and in the late 1980s the industry took off.

Brewers Association statistics for 2013 show the greatest craftbrew strength exists in the Pacific Northwest and in the Northeast. Oregon had the highest ratio of craft breweries (181) to 21-year-old adults, followed by Vermont (29), Montana (39), Colorado (175), Maine (47), Wyoming (18), Alaska (22), Washington (201), Idaho (34) and New Hampshire (22). The South lagged behind in craft breweries per capita.

By July 2014 there were 3,040 breweries in the nation, and counting. With 98% being small and independent, we have revived a localized craft beer culture not seen since the 1870s. This new wave has overwhelmed the country with beer of quality and character, offering much desired flavor not available from the major breweries.

Brewers are differentiating from their increasing competition on a very localized level through farmers' markets. California allowed

Arcane Cellars and other wineries benefit from Portland Farmers Market customers who don't have to travel to the winery for a few tastes. They can buy their wine with dinner fixings at the market.

© Vance Corum

beer sales as of 2015. New York's farm brewery law went into effect in 2013; it requires a low percentage of New York-produced hops and other ingredients, with steps to reach 90% as of 2024. The NYS Brewery Association maintains hop and malt farm maps to encourage producers and connect them to breweries:

http://thinknydrinkny.com/farm-brewery/

Cider

Hard cider was the most common beverage in colonial America. It went out of style in the late 1800s with the industrial revolution shifting our population to cities, the arrival of German immigrants producing beers from cheap Midwest grains, and the temperance movement pushing to eradicate apple orchards.

Today it is back. U.S. hard cider sales grew five-fold from 2011 to 2014, helped by female interest equal to that of men, whereas men outnumber women 70-30 with beer.

Cider's dramatic resurrection is also riding the wave of gluten-free foods, led by snack foods, meat and meat alternatives, and bread and cereal. Only 1% of Americans are diagnosed with celiac disease, yet several times that number have gluten sensitivity, and 22% of Americans were occasional gluten-free eaters in 2014, led by millenials.

As with other fruit, artisanal cideries are using farmers' markets to distinguish themselves from corporate competitors like Anheuser-BBusch and Heineken by explaining their different cider-making and fermentation styles leading to more complex taste profiles. Alber Orchards in Manchester, MI grows 99 varieties of apples for fresh market and its cider mill.

With about a third of cideries growing their own apples, Bull Run Cider in Forest Grove, OR is living on its 8-acre orchard supplemented by apples from a 100-mile radius. While commercial farmers generally

Heirloom Orchards sells both hard and sweet ciders to keep alive their 19 antique cider varieties in Hood River, OR.

won't invest in a low-value cider apple, higher prices may cause smaller farmers to find this a good hedge against crop failure, especially on surplus land.

Like many crafters, Reverend Nat's Hard Cider started in a Portland garage in 2012 because his neighbor had apples. Soon abandoned orchards were found at the urban-rural interface, followed by local farmers in order to secure a continuous supply. Their substantial production demanded a distribution model.

"We saw farmers' markets as a visibility and marketing tool, not as a sales tool. In 2013 we started selling in 10 farmers' markets weekly, making $500 on $20,000 of cider. What we really made were 5,000 new fans, and entry into every New Seasons, Zupans and Whole Foods in the Portland metro area. Even if we sold zero, people would try our two samples at a small farmers' market and then buy at their local store. We got into four states, doubling sales every three months.

"In 2014 we selected seven farmers' markets and sold monthly or bi-weekly. We made $20,000 again, but with about $2,000 profit. We get double the money but we don't care about the profit; we're in growth mode. It absolutely worked for us. Now we're in seven states.

"In 2015 our tailored farmers' market strategy is reaching customers in new areas. We'll showcase three seasonal releases – cinco de mayo, passion fruit in July, and fresh hop Hopricot in October – with sales on three days at each of seven markets. We ask: 'Are these our customers and are there enough of them?' We're treating farmers' markets like a festival."

– Nat West, Reverend Nat's Hard Cider, Portland, OR

Nat connected with Randy Kiyokawa, a farmers' market grower who linked him to other Hood River apple growers as well. Before long Nat brought scion wood – Kingston Black, Yarlington Mill, Dabinett – for Randy to graft or bud onto acres of high density, dwarf rootstock. Kiyokawa Family Orchard will deliver cider apples for pick-up at the market. Reverend Nat's will continue creating new ciders like a rosé-style Mountain Rose from a single varietal for Valentine's Day, and a Randy Kiyokawa Heirloom Blend from 50 varieties that Randy delivers in February when he decides to turn off his cold storage and give Reverend Nat's the last 50 bins of stored fruit.

> "A revived cider culture is taking root across the country. This renaissance includes a great range of producers making cider in all manner of ways from the ancient to the innovative. A fermented apple, it turns out, can become many things depending on the variety and the method – from the sweet and sumptuous to the tart and tannic…At its best, we hope our cider offers an honorable and joyful taste of earth's good fruits and that it connects folks back to life on the land – reminding us to be grateful and to take care."
>
> – Crystie Kisler, Finnriver Farm & Cidery, Chimacum, WA, farmers' market vendor and winner of a 2015 Good Food Award in the inaugural cider category

Distilled Spirits

In some states where sales of distilled spirits are allowed at farmers' markets, they provide a market outlet for distillers to join wineries, breweries and cideries, and markets gain additional income to stabilize budgets, especially important on lighter volume winter market days. Portland charges about $40-45 per booth per market day or 10% of alcohol sales, whichever is greater. All craft beverages end up paying a percentage there, so clearly the customers are buying.

Because distillers generally out-source their ingredients, the Portland Farmers Market classifies them as product representative vendors. Like olive oil or other processed goods not locally sourced, they can only sell once a month. This allows Portlanders to experience four different distilleries every month in one 10'x10' booth space, and there's no lack of distillery interest. "People love it," says operations director Jaret Foster.

Fish and Shellfish

America's coasts have provided access to seafood, caught by a 60' trawler, by line or raised in a protected bay. Families from many Western states fish in Alaska and bring their catch to markets throughout the Pacific Northwest and farther afield. Others stay close to home.

Taylor Shellfish Farm in Shelton, WA is the largest producer of farmed shellfish in the U.S. They have been a leader in sea-to-table sales, growing clams, oysters, mussels and geoducks on the tidelands of Washington and British Columbia. They understand and help protect healthy watersheds, earning the Monterey Bay Aquarium seal of certified sustainable for all their Washington farms.

Bob Meek, a marine biologist, started his mussel company, Ecomar, in 1980 as a result of his study of Shell Oil platforms. Although people may consider oil platforms to be rather dirty, the legs of these platforms may be the healthiest source of shellfish in the U.S. given that they sit in water several miles off the California coast.

Ecomar divers go to about 50 feet and scrape mussels from the columns, and an underwater vacuum hose sucks them to the surface. Each year about 500,000 pounds of mussels go direct to farmers' markets and restaurants.

Consumers want seafood, and one-in-six farmers' markets nationwide are helping supply their needs.

Prepared Foods

For any afternoon or evening market, the debate over whether to include hot prepared foods is dead on arrival. It's obvious; people want to eat and they want to socialize. If there is a question, it would be: Is this a farmers' market? Absent a state law, any market can call itself a farmers' market, so the industry simply wants to know that farmers are part of the mix.

San Luis Obispo Thursday Night is often referred to as the SLO Farmers Market because the market is

From Brattleboro VT's Rigani Pizza to Bellevue WA's Veraci Pizza (above), trailer ovens are keeping farmers' markets full of America's favorite food.

the main portion of what happens on closed-off Higuera Street. But it is far from everything: numerous restaurants set up barbeque trailers, a volleyball net is available, politicians make speeches and local businesses spill out onto the sidewalks. It's an event any community would be proud of. It draws thousands of locals, tourists and Cal Poly students; professors have learned not to give exams on Friday.

Like the produce that farmers grow in any locale, prepared food helps define the town, city or region. Imagine the South without crawfish and po boys? We all love what we love, and when it is part of local food culture, we want it at the market. It becomes part of a comfort zone.

In a story as old as every city, prepared foods allow countless immigrants to bring their food culture talents into their newfound communities, to establish small businesses and become part of the American dream.

The dream of one Afghan woman searching for a better life is Bolani: East & West Gourmet Afghan Food. With the winning smile and ernest sampling of her eldest son Billal Sidiq, the "Ambassador of Love," Bolani has become the largest farmers' market company in the U.S., selling flatbreads and sauces in 200 farmers' markets.

Bolani is also the largest employer of Afghan refugees in the U.S. With processing

facilities in the Bay Area and Los Angeles, it buys local farmers' products to serve markets in those areas. Its popularity also has made it a fixture in many local and national stores, including Whole Foods, Safeway and Costco.

Bolani is just one example of the many companies that are serving Middle East specialties, enriching lives. Multiply that by countless ethnic and immigrant stories and one comes to recognize the vast richness that is farmers' markets in America.

And More

As you have read, there is an amazing, almost inexhaustible, diversity of products in farmers' markets. Still, what you have read only begins to undercover the full scope of products and services that markets provide.

If one stops by the Davis Farmers Market, there is three citrus, Yolo County grown, hand-cut marmalade from Good Humus. And then D. Madison & Daughters. Diane's nine-ounce jars of jam wonder include best selling fig, apricot saffron, Damson plum, Yuzu, Moro blood orange and Bearss lime along with quince vanilla bean jelly. And don't forget her husband's Taggiasca, Leccino and Mission extra virgin olive oils, or the skincare products she makes from

Since 2001, SamosaMan has given Congolese immigrant Fuad Ndibalema a way to support Vermont farmers while serving African natural foods in Montpelier and elsewhere. They are a Seven Daysies award winner for best farmers' market vendor in 2011, 2012 and 2014, voted on by all Vermonters.

Along with many produce options Fifth Crow Farm offers a line of specialty dried beans.

Prepared food vendors allow for community to be built around a common table where everyone eats what they like.

them. You could easily feel that there is no need to go further in the realm of jams.

You would be wrong. In farmers' markets in Ashland, Grants Pass and Medford, OR you will find more glorious jam from Pennington Farms in the Applegate Valley. Sam grows 90 acres of berries and Cathy turns them into scrumptious jams, conserves and butters: marionberry, tayberry, golden raspberry, strawberry/rhubarb and wild blackberry. And then there are berries in every other form: syrups, scones, turnovers, pies, cookies and more.

From Albany to small Adirondack towns, one can find nut and seed butters from Peanut Principle, started by Shannon Campagna of Latham, NY.

At the Crescent City (LA) market are fresh fruit drinks and popsicles from Amanda's Frozen Fruit Bars. Blue Ribbon Pies has award-winning apple, blueberry, peach, pecan, sweet potato, mincemeat and more. Challah At Me! Bread Company offers more than just challah; there's focaccia, rustic, bagels, tarts and pretzels. And L'Hosee Family Farm has organic satsumas, kumquats, lemons and grapefruit. Crescent City also has cheese, shiitake mushrooms and growing blocks, hummus, tabouli, stuffed grape leaves, pesto, soup and knife-sharpening.

At the other end of the world, a June 2014 visit to the Dorset Farmers Market revealed Sticks and Stones Farm selling an intriguing assortment of biscotti, granola, birdhouses and knit wear. Taking Root had teas (including iced), ciders, syrups, salves, tinctures, bug spray and bulk medicinal herbs. There were a half dozen produce farmers and an equal number of pasture raised meat producers, plus two wineries. There were cow and goat cheeses, soy candles, hot fudge sauces, fine art photography, ambrosia chocolates, soap, shampoo, maple syrup, hand-etched glassware, hand-painted clothing and handmade hats. With juices, sandwiches, spring rolls, casseroles, stews and sushi, one was almost overwhelmed by the selection.

All this and more along Route 7 south of Dorset, Vermont, population 2,000, near the first marble quarry in the U.S., opened in 1785.

It could be anywhere. When organizers allow the community to offer the full range of its creations, the market can indeed be full. They say, it takes a village to raise a market. ❧

Expanding the Vision 12

"...the care of the earth is our most ancient and most worthy and, after all, our most pleasing responsibility. To cherish what remains in it, and to foster its renewal, is our only legitimate hope."
– Wendell Berry

Farmers' markets involve more than the simple transfer of tomatoes for cash. They are about the exchange of ideas. As agriculture faces the greatest threat to the survival of family farms ever known, farmers' markets have a chance to be part of the solution. Farmers' markets can serve as a leading forum, a place for civic discussion about the issues our local agriculture and communities face in this new millennium.

To do so may require our most creative response to the issues of the day – declining consumer health, an obesity epidemic, sagging farm numbers, aging farmers, decaying cities and a host of others. Much as a farmers' market often has a nonprofit section, our book's nonprofit section is this: ideas for the future. Whether it's through the electronic medium of a constantly updated website or social media posts, or using the market as the physical location for lectures, debates or workshops about community issues, farmers' markets have every opportunity of becoming the focal point of the "vibrant agrarianism" that the book, *Fields Without Dreams*, maintains is the very basis of a vital democracy – and the survival of small farms.

> "If just 10 percent of our population lived on farms, did not move, never divorced, did not change jobs, and set the parameters of their day by dawn and dusk, the current madness could be stopped. Yet we lack that prerequisite reservoir of agrarians who might still arrest the itinerary of our present culture, of growing shiftlessness, criminality, and material banality."
>
> – Victor Davis Hanson, *Fields Without Dreams*

An exchange of ideas is the necessary basis of societal progress. Public debate in the best sense – maintaining civility and a sense of humor – can engender a spirit of openness and sharing toward the greater good of the community. Together, our general goals are to improve farm sustainability and maintain or enhance the quality and flavor of food consumed. With our 20th Century industrialization of agriculture, we lost several million farms and jeopardized the fabric of rural life along with tasty varieties possible only in a local agriculture. We face the challenge of bringing back old varieties, re-establishing the prominence of small farms, renewing consumer interest in real foods, reinvigorating a sense of mutual interdependence – in short, re-creating a local agri-culture.

Farmers' markets will continue to evolve as we invite young people to farm and older farmers to help train that generation. We must involve ourselves in outside struggles as well: concentration of the retail food trade, the food safety focus leading toward homogenization of all foods, rules and laws that will sink any self-respecting farmer, and the impacts of climate change. Educated consumers will be necessary in facing these and other issues.

The Retail Context

Admittedly, farmers' markets do not operate in a retail food vacuum. The potential expansion of markets is very much constrained by the unfair and sometimes illegal advantages of large food chains that purchase goods from the largest farms and food suppliers in the world. When chains purchase thousands of boxes of a given item per week, they limit the profit margin of the supplier. Low wages and poor working conditions globally fit into the low prices that consumers pay for food. Tax law can also feed into this model to keep prices low and profits high for the retailer, while farmers and small companies at the farmers' market level are paying their fair share.

In June 2015 Americans for Tax Fairness released a shocking report documenting a vast, undisclosed and relatively new worldwide network of 78 subsidiaries that Walmart has created in 15 tax havens where it has no retail stores. Typically, corporations use these tax havens to avoid taxes and public disclosure.

"At least 25 out of 27 (and perhaps all) of Walmart's foreign operating companies (in the U.K. Brazil, Japan, China and more) are owned by subsidiaries in tax havens. All of these companies have retail stores and many employees. Walmart owns at least $76 billion in assets through shell companies domiciled in the tax havens of Luxembourg ($64.2 billion) and the Netherlands ($12.4 billion) – that's 90 percent of the assets in Walmart's International division ($85 billion) or 37 percent of its total assets ($205 billion).

"The company has arranged for foreign operating companies to take out long-term loans from Walmart subsidiaries in tax havens and to make tax-deductible interest payments to those subsidiaries. This allows Walmart to avoid taxes in countries where it earns profits by simply paying interest to itself in places where the interest will be taxed lightly or not at all. This is known as earnings stripping."

– The Walmart Web: How the World's Biggest Corporation Secretly Uses Tax Havens to Dodge Taxes, Americans for Tax Fairness, http://www.americansfortaxfairness.org/files/TheWalmartWeb-June-2015-FINAL.pdf

With mammoth tax games being played by the largest corporation in the world, it is no wonder that consumers in America (and elsewhere) are induced to shop low prices at Walmart. It is also no surprise that farmers who pay taxes have trouble paying themselves when they must compete in an economy where such tax evasions tilt the scales of fair play. A massive education campaign will be necessary to shift customers to a just and sustainable system where farmers need and should make a living. Farmers' markets are a critical part of that social and economic cause.

Rural Development

Markets in rural areas are perhaps one of the greatest challenges facing the industry. There isn't the same glamour as in the big city, but small town relationships are at the core of American history, of hardworking families that value independence, thrift and community.

On a per-capita basis, farmers' markets are most concentrated in Vermont, North Dakota, Iowa, New Hampshire, Hawaii, Maine, Wyoming, Montana, Washington, DC and Idaho. Not only do more rural states have proportionally more farmers' markets, but rural areas of counties have greater farmers' market density than urban areas, per capita. These statistics reflect rural commitment to community-building and the close association of producers and consumers in rural areas, even though the biggest share of sales are in urban farmers' markets.

In 2009 a USDA study noted that most farmers' markets operate on a shoestring, with a median annual budget of about $2,000, and 59% rely on volunteer management, sometimes Extension Service staff. Those markets have average sales that are one-fifth those of markets with paid managers.

From Astoria, OR to Penn Yan, NY, we have seen that farmers' markets can successfully operate and serve a large geographical area with proper planning, a cooperative spirit and a vision of a scaled-up market.

Market Growth by the Numbers

The industry saw exponential growth at the start of the 21st century. From 2000 to 2010, the U.S. more than doubled its market scene from 2,863 to 6,132 farmers' markets. The most explosive period of growth included 589 new markets recorded in 2009, 858 markets in 2010, 1,043 in 2011 and 689 more in 2012.

Farmers' markets can be an important part of "aging gracefully" while maintaining one's sense of value to society.

The numbers calmed down to a more modest increase of 280 markets in 2013 and 124 in 2014. With 8,268 farmers' markets serving America, we may be approaching saturation. That happened with large cities years ago since only 285 U.S. cities have a population exceeding 100,000 as of 2012, and only 10 have in excess of one million residents.

Average customer counts dropped slightly from 1,055 in 2000 to 959 customers per week in 2005. This 9% drop in customers per market was more than offset by a 43% increase in the number of farmers' markets during that period. Thus, greater market density created stronger customer numbers.

Markets open six months or less had 25 vendors and $20,770 in monthly sales to 565 customers, on average. Markets open seven months or longer had an average of 51 vendors with $57,290 in monthly sales to 942 customers weekly. Year-round markets reported 58 vendors, sales of $69,497 and 3,578 customers weekly, less than one-third the per customer sales of markets open seven months or more, and only slightly more than half that of short-season markets.

Markets that are successful, as defined by sales, are most common in densely populated urban areas and on the coasts. With higher average customer numbers, Far West markets averaged $56,742 per month and Mid-Atlantic markets $41,452 while the remaining regions had about $23,000 a month.

Seasonal and year-round markets with organic products have larger crowds, more vendors and higher monthly sales. Seasonal markets with organic products report three times the sales of markets without organic products, and similarly year-round markets report more than double the sales of those without organic products. These figures are somewhat explained by the higher percentage of markets selling organic products being located in urban areas.

Farmers' market average sales in 2005 were $242,581 but median sales were only $40,000. This is another reflection of regional variability in market size, location and season. The Far West had nearly $477,000 in sales per market while the Rocky Mountain region was less than one-fifth that amount, $90,000.

All these numbers reflect a tremendous range in diversity of market size, products and sales depending on the region, urban or rural location, season length, management and community support.

Replacing Aging Farmers

Thirty percent of American farmers are older than 65. In 1978, the average farmer was 50; by 2007, the average farmer was 57. With 40% of those direct marketing having less than 10 years experience, we must support these new farmers if the United States is to sustain farming, even as we invite a new generation of youth, immigrants and second-career adults to join in the food system.

"As an older and established market, we are learning how to navigate farm and business transitions. This is an issue at the forefront of our minds, as we see many of our longstanding members prepare for retirement."

– Erin Jobe, Mgr., Carrboro FM, NC

While minority farmers compromise 4.8% of the general farming population, well over 11% of vendors at farmers' markets are minorities. Even this figure is low since California – where minority farmers are numerous – is severely under-represented in 2005 manager data.

Increasing Consumer Access

Farmers' markets are moving toward full access without regard for economic status. Numerous individual market studies show that customers of various income levels, age and race reflect the larger community in which the market is located.

Government programs are beneficial in creating access for all. The WIC Farmers Market Nutrition Program increased market sales by an average of $1,744 per month with 61% of markets participating, while the Senior FMNP averaged $1,004 in sales monthly at 45% of markets where the program was accepted. SNAP sales averaged $279 a month but only 7% of markets accepted the EBT cards (USDA, 2006).

By September 2014, that figure had risen to 35%, or 2,866 of the 8,268 U.S. farmers' markets authorized to accept SNAP, plus another 2,309 SNAP authorized farmers, including many at farmers' markets. Simultaneously, SNAP spending with these farmers and farmers' markets grew to $18.8 million in 2014, more than quadruple the $4.2 million benefits redeemed in 2009.

By May 2015 another 1,000 farmers and farmers' markets were SNAP-authorized, raising the total to 6,200 compared to 936 authorized in 2009. This dramatic increase has resulted from substantial outreach and financial assistance to markets through the Farmers Market Coalition and many market match or double-up programs improving market access for specific populations.

Funded by the USDA Farmers Market Promotion Program, the California Farmers Market Alliance produced a YouTube video promoting all the farmers' markets in the state:

https://www.youtube.com/watch?v=7qRIx5t31zo

The video highlights the FMFinder.org website where people can find the most convenient California market to attend, including which markets provide access to EBT, WIC and MarketMatch.

Food Safety

The Food Safety Modernization Act (FSMA) was passed by Congress in 2011. These regulations are meant to protect consumers against food-borne illnesses. FSMA was passed with the Tester-Hagen Amendment, which helps small farms to avoid extraneous regulation. See:

http://www.fda.gov/Food/GuidanceRegulation/FSMA/

Food-borne disease outbreaks are a continued likelihood; following known safety precautions will not address every eventuality. Aside from encouraging good growing and handling practices as well as traceability, farmers' markets should be prepared for the media onslaught that can occur with any outbreak.

Oregon Farmers' Markets Association (OFMA) president Rebecca Landis was struck with a flurry of calls and emails on August 7, 2011 when *E. coli* was found in strawberries. An elderly woman had died and others were seriously ill. The source farm was not a farmers' market vendor, but their tainted berries had leaked into six Oregon and two Washington farmers' markets (and many farm stands). Landis immediately helped the Oregon Department of Agriculture with contact information for markets where the berries were suspected to have landed, and contacted managers herself. The strawberries came into markets within their guidelines in some cases – even properly labeled – and in other cases without manager knowledge.

Landis quickly crafted a press release to the state's largest paper, a weekly regional agricultural newspaper, OFMA members and related groups.

To prepare for such a scenario, state farmers' market associations might best have an updated statewide media list and a draft press release with a general statement about association goals. Be prepared to quote the board president and local authorities.

To avoid such a scenario, markets may want to disallow any resale, or only under special circumstances. At the least, this strawberry outbreak should lead market boards to seriously address policy issues such as: percentage of resale to allow, conditions justifying that percentage, prior approval of the exact grower, a second farm application and/or letter, and labeling at the vendor's booth to ensure transparency and traceability. Markets might also allow limited consignment sales, where the grower maintains ownership and responsibility.

[See also: Resources, Farmers' Market Websites]

Food and Lodging

Since 2008, "Airbnb has opened up new opportunities for its hosts to meet new people and make money by renting out parts of their homes they weren't using," states Ryan Lawler in Techcrunch. "In that same vein, a startup called EatWith wants to offer up a similar opportunity for its users to use their cooking skills as a way to make cash and engage in conversation with new people."

Airbnb capitalized on the common practice in Europe and elsewhere of people earning side income by opening their homes to strangers. Within seven years, Airbnb was valued at $24 billion, having expanded to 1.5 million homes in 33,000 cities in 192 countries. Just as Airbnb does with lodging, EatWith supports hosts who open their homes with food. They create a memorable meal and social experience for guests – travelers or locals – who are open-minded about food and socializing.

Time will tell which social dining sites are able to survive. Another named Feastly reminds us of Julia Child's words, "Dining with one's friends and beloved family is certainly one of life's primal and most innocent delights, one that is both soul-satisfying and eternal."

Home-based dining is a liberating and edgy way of rebuilding the social fabric of food. These guerrilla marketers are enabling the next generation of chefs to test their skills without the expense of a restaurant, just as farmers' markets allow the next generation of farmers to demonstrate their prowess without the expense of a roadside stand. And people rave about both.

Daring farmers have joined the social dining realm with farm dinners in the guesthouse or in the field, even hosting a fundraiser for their farmers' market. They may combine dining and lodging with a website like FarmStayUS. What better way to combine production and marketing than by hosting a full farm-to-table-to-bed experience that people can treasure for life.

Farmers can promote their own website to encourage food and lodging on the farm. However, why not let EatWith or MealTango, or FarmStayUS or Airbnb do the marketing for you? The latter has a capitalized track record that has captivated millions worldwide. Farmers will adapt these sites to their farms, and inevitably adapt their farms to the websites as they experiment with them.

Chefs provide inestimable value to farmers. If you sell to them, you learn just as you teach. The timeless link between farmers and chefs has been revived by people like Sibellas Kraus, founder of the Tasting of Summer Produce, and Alice Waters, founder of Chez Panisse restaurant, in the Bay Area. Many other chefs have connected with farmers in cities and towns across the country. They then coalesced as Chefs Collaborative in 1993 to promote sustainability among restaurants and food service nationwide. Their Portland local and Ecotrust started the Farm-Chef Connection in 2001 which has become an annual event, sparking other annual gatherings from Seattle to Arizona and Vermont. These and other events feed a healthier farm-table knowledge and quality of food.

Food Hubs

Various food events also have led to more than 170 local and regional food hubs, outlined by USDA in their Regional Food Hub Resource Guide. This tool helps people build stronger supply chains and address infrastructure challenges while supporting food access, regional economic development and job creation.

On a regional scale, Ecotrust designed Food Hub.org which serves six Western states by connect-

Long food lines for this fundraising dinner at the Carrboro Farmers Market reflect the strong communal spirit that has been cultivated since 1977 and strengthened with this market building on the town commons in 1996.

ing thousands of farms with chefs, caterers, co-ops, schools and more. All basic profiles are free.

"On the face of it, any attempt to create a regional, small-farm based, decentralized, product-diverse food system seems to fly in the face of conventional business wisdom. Distribution systems, farm equipment, marketing costs, and access to shelf-space in supermarkets and restaurant coolers all favor large-scale, specialized production. Why fight so hard to get upstream? Why not let the current pull us effortlessly along?

"One answer might be a love of good food, the desire to save open space and habitat for wildlife, environmental concerns, interest in keeping a broad economic base, a love of farming, a desire to participate in community life that values relationships, and a show of gratitude for the people who grow our food. Those desires unite us in a common goal to save local agriculture and preserve the family farm."

– Mark Mulcahy, principal, Organic Options and producer/host, An Organic Conversation

Local Lunch and Dinner

Sonoma started holding an annual 'Wich Hunt in 2012, a contest for the best sandwich in Sonoma County. The winner – the first three years, at least – was Kendra Kolling. "Whenever I have the opportunity, I love to use apples to showcase that I'm an apple farmer's wife," Kendra explained to CUESA volunteer writer Reilly O'Neal, who points out that "farm to table is more than a trend; it's her family's way of life."

Market customers get to enjoy "the Farmer's Wife" sandwiches made from local farm products, usually accented by her husband's apples, whether on grilled cheese, in vinaigrettes or an apple-raisin-fig mostarda, an Italian condiment of candied fruit in a mustard-flavored syrup.

Many markets have similar wife-as-chef stories to tell. Still more markets will want to begin incorporating a good local sandwich maker into their vendor mix, and the inspiration may come from a 'Wich Hunt contest.

Lunch is a natural addition to any market, and so is dinner. The San Luis Obispo Farmers' Market is set amidst the larger downtown event known as Thursday Night which includes a dozen restaurants.

Having local food entrepreneurs involved in this way builds more positive linkages within the community. When they are actual farmers, we reinforce the food culture that is farm-based, ensuring its survival.

Kickstarter Helps Farm to Grill

One of the best Farm to Grill stories in the country begins with the story of Nash Huber who began a bare bones, little organic farm in Dungeness, WA in 1979 and soon helped start the Port Angeles Farmers' Market. Nash's Best! brand became Washington's top organic carrot, especially well-known through 11 PCC Natural Markets. By 2015, Nash had become one of Sequim's largest private employers, a leader of 25 year-round team members who had come to learn and practice with the organic master. See:

NashsOrganicProduce.com.

Simultaneously, Patty Pan Grill pioneered eating local at farmers' markets in 1997. It was the first Seattle market business to use lots of market-sourced ingredients and the first to become a worker-owned cooperative business. Their menu features tamales with homemade salsas and quesadillas with grilled vegetables from farms at markets where they sell, including Nash's.

Patty Pan Cooperative launched a Kickstarter campaign in October 2014 in order to buy tortilla-making equipment for the organic hard red wheat

Nash Huber has cultivated a loyal clientele with his signature trailer and folded-down sides. His environmentally friendly practices earned Nash the 2008 Steward of the Land award from American Farmland Trust.

flour grown and milled by Nash's. From farm flour to organic tortilla, they were made for each other. Patty Pan became the first farmers' market concessionaire to make their own tortillas from local, organic, whole wheat flour.

From blogs and articles, Patty Pan knew that most Kickstarter support comes from already established networks of family, friends and friends of friends. Yet, they decided to take their financial plea directly to the people who enjoy their quesadillas every week at 14 Seattle farmers' markets. When someone ordered, they explained their plans to make even more awesome quesadillas, and sampled their tortilla prototypes. They succeeded as 136 backers pledged $8,906 to fund the stand mixer, industrial tortilla press, tortilla grill and electrical upgrades.

In 2014 Patty Pan was one of 22,252 Kickstarter projects brought to life with more than $500 million from 3.3 million people. Of them, 1393 were food projects, the seventh highest category. See:

PattyPanGrill.com.

[Find Kickstarter and other crowdfunding programs in the online Resources section.]

New USDA Funding

In 2015 USDA began a new Food Insecurity Nutrition Incentive (FINI) program authorized by the 2014 Farm Bill, and awarded $31.5 million in organizational funding for programs that test strategies to increase fruit and vegetable purchases by Supplemental Nutrition Assistance Program participants. SNAP helps put food on the table for millions of American families facing hardship, with 60% of participants being children, elderly or those with disabilities. Many lost jobs during the Great Recession that started in 2008.

Several grantee organizations concentrated on double-up or match programs to give SNAP participants double the amount of their EBT debit for purchasing fruits and vegetables, and expanding their programs to more recipients over a wider area. Various programs in Utah and Portland, OR added up to $10 in SNAP benefits per purchase while PCFMA and The Food Trust in Philadelphia have tested a 40% increase in SNAP participants' purchasing power.

FRIENDS OF THE MARKET

Friends groups sometimes operate in conjunction with a farmers' market to provide support and assistance in various forms.

"To help pay for continuing market renovations, we asked people to buy a brick as a permanent legacy of the Royal Oak Farmers Market, estab-

Patty Pan Grill won the hearts of Seattle farmers' market customers starting in 1997. In 2014 customers showed their love by funding their Kickstarter campaign for tortilla equipment to process organic grain from Nash Huber, a rock star of Washington organic food.

lished in 1927. People created their own message commemorating a special occasion or honoring a loved one, $50 for a 4'x 8' or $90 for an 8'x 8' brick, including clipart. Proceeds pay for wall brick restoration, floor repair, PA system, lighting, etc."

– Shelly Mazur, Mgr., Royal Oak FM, MI

The St. Paul Farmers' Market opened in 1853. It has had a marvelous career with several downtown locations. When Patty Brand stepped down after 14 years as manager, she was the perfect person to lead the Friends of the St. Paul Farmers' Market from 1997 to 2010. Their goal was to help rebuild and expand the market structure. When it was completed, the Friends group dissipated.

Opening in 1907, Pike Place Market was an eyesore by the 1960s, scheduled for demolition. Friends of the Market formed in 1964, led by architect Victor Steinbrueck, to protect the market from developers and lead a Market Initiative that ended in a 1971 public vote to "Keep the Market." A Market Historical District was created and placed under public control. It continues to develop plans that reinforce 10 million visitors each year.

Operating since 1976, the Olympia Farmers' Market serves Washington's capital city of 46,000 people and visitors with over $4 million in sales from April through Christmas.

In the mid-1990s a partnership was formed between the City of Olympia, the Port of Olympia, and the market organization to build a permanent market facility. The city floated a bond to pay for the structure on Port land. The market pays a land lease to the Port, makes annual payments on the City bond and covers ongoing facility maintenance.

The membership is set up on a farmer-grown and crafter-made basis, with on-farm inspections and juried membership in admitting up to 25% crafters. Farmers come from a three-county area.

Given its considerable overhead, the market has very reasonable stall rental rates. Farmers and crafters pay 6.5% of gross sales, processors pay 8.5%, hot food trailers pay 9.5%, and two contract fruit vendors pay

The Shreveport FM has a massive wooden, clerestory building and a tent in the background to protect customers from the Louisiana sun.

10.5%. This ensures that vendors are serious and successful.

The Friends of the Olympia Farmers' Market is set up as a nonprofit, tax-exempt organization with 501(c)(3) status and the stated purpose to lessen the burden on local government. It has provided the market with brick walkways, picnic tables, benches, heaters, emergency medical equipment, a public address system, electrical upgrades, bike rack, cooking demonstrations, a security camera system and a website.

In a four-year fundraiser, 2,000 people bought bricks engraved with their names, which provided walkways to enhance the facility while raising funds for the market. Their annual Taste of the Market dinner sells out its 400 seats every year.

Since tax-exempt organizations like FOFM cannot give directly to for-profit groups such as the Olympia Farmers' Market, their activities primarily enhance market facilities and public education.

FARMERS' MARKET COALITION (FMC)

At the turn of the century two million acres of vulnerable farmland were being converted to housing subdivisions, roads and shopping malls each year. In 2000 an estimated one million Americans shopped at their local farmers' market each week. By 2012, with over 8,000 markets, that increased to 3 million weekly customers purchasing directly from 70,000 farmers with at least $1.5 billion in spending, according to USDA.

The Farmers Market Coalition was initially conceived to educate the public on the economics of urban-edge farms and the role of these farms in countering urban sprawl and protecting open space.

As a tax-exempt nonprofit, FMC is dedicated to strengthening farmers' markets across the United States so that they can serve as community assets while providing real income opportunities for farmers.

FMC has developed many programs to benefit its member markets across the country, including numerous webinars on management topics. FMC also supports many agencies and organizations that help markets to exist. It serves as a central hub to locate allies, share best practices, and positively impact public policy related to farmers' markets, including through its extensive resource library.

In February, 2015 the Farmers Market Coalition began a free SNAP EBT equipment program resulting from a partnership with USDA's Food and Nutrition Service (FNS). FMC covers the costs of purchasing or renting the EBT equipment set-up costs, monthly service fees and wireless fees for up to three years. If approved, eligible farmers and farmers' markets choose their own SNAP EBT service provider from a list, but must pay their own transaction fees for SNAP EBT, credit and debit payments.

First-come, first-serve, the program lasts until all funds have been allocated to SNAP-authorized farmers' markets and market farmers. They must have been authorized before November 18, 2011, and not currently possess functioning EBT equipment or possess equipment received before May 2, 2012.

Another program FMC began sponsoring for its member markets in 2012 is a partnership with Jarden Home Brands – makers of Ball jars – around canning education. Through the "Discover You Can Learn Make Share" program, markets host workshops and demonstrations all season, helping farmers sell produce and increasing consumer attendance, sometimes using local chefs and celebrities. Missouri's art educator of the year designed and painted, with high school

student help, a 12' mural as a canning workshop backdrop at the Springfield Farmers Market.

FMC teamed up with Chipotle in 2015 to sponsor POP Clubs at 75 FMC member markets nationwide. The Chipotle sponsorship provided the selected markets with the physical materials needed to run the program and up to $2,000 in farmers' market vouchers for participating youth.

Policy Papers and Economic Studies

Community food studies are becoming more popular. Ten Rivers Food Web, started in 2006, has led three county food assessments as it actively builds regional food connections in the Oregon's mid-Willamette Valley region. It conducts community food assessments as a way of inspiring and documenting progress toward their goal of 30% of foods consumed in each county being local foods.

TRFW has documented various projects including the Southern Willamette Valley Bean and Grain Project, a small group of farmers and advocates focused on increasing the quantity and diversity of food crops, evaluating infrastructure deficiencies, building local buyer/seller relationships, documenting local sustainable practices, and incorporating community culture into the food system fabric. All these are directed toward the central task of creating a year-round base of nutritionally dense staples.

The 2012 Lowell Community Food Assessment found that the farmers' market is the principal local food access point for residents, and 2011 was its best year. Lowell has a poverty rate of 17.6%, and the market accepts SNAP/EBT, WIC, and Senior FMNP, which explains the presence of 46% of surveyed residents at the market.

Those who don't shop at the market credited lack of awareness of the market (42%), inconvenient hours (21%), high prices (14%), lack of public transportation (10%), poor parking (9%) and bad location (3%). Focus groups reported similar accessibility and price issues.

Thus, in spite of handling the fourth greatest volume of WIC dollars of any Massachusetts market, the Lowell Farmers' Market found that some people are still unclear on the monetary value and redemption process for their WIC and senior coupons, and want the Friday evening market to switch to Saturday.

The market is in a Catch-22: it lacks the community support to fund staff positions to enhance its community presence. This is the case in thousands of markets. Collectively, markets must listen to residents and evaluate how to bring food to their communities at a price that all people can afford, or give them assistance through some sort of match program of their federal benefits. This continues to be a central issue of our time, defining the sustainability and growth of markets.

In late 2012 the Farmers Market Coalition partnered with Market Umbrella on a research project to understand the impacts of the USDA Farmers Market

50 X 60: 50% of Our Food Requirements by 2060

50 X 60–it's the newest buzzword in our community and the best news that Ag entrepreneurs have had in years (short of less regulation). Who wouldn't be excited at the thought of more farms of all sorts dotting our landscapes, preserving and protecting productive open land at no additional cost to the tax payer, and enough Ag job opportunities to satisfy the crying need of young entrepreneurs?

Consider, where Massachusetts' thinking about food has been heading recently. There is a cry for more fresh local produce, meat, fish, and forestry products. There are over 148 Agricultural Commissions in MA, of which 117 have already passed Right-to-Farm by-laws protecting farmers and backyard entrepreneurs from ill-informed (if well-intentioned) pressures. Every day earnest and capable young men and women are knocking on websites inquiring about jobs, internships, and any ag opportunity that might be available. Ag education is thriving. It is not yet too late for a comprehensive "Marshall Plan" for sustainable growth and food prosperity in MA and the Northeast.

If we have learned nothing in the previous decades, we have learned to cut waste, enhance sustainability, and better understand natural systems. We have learned (slowly) that open space has value in and of itself and that saving resources is investing in a healthy future for generations to come. Robert Lemire's *Creative Land Development* showed us how to manage growth and preserve prime agricultural lands for future use while preserving value for landowners and their heirs. Brian Donahue et al's "50 x 60: A New England Food Vision" puts a workable, well-reasoned plan on the table succinctly outlining just how to make meeting 50% of New England's food needs grown locally or regionally by 2060 a reality.

We have 45 years to develop and implement a plan that will shape our lives and those of our children in the very foreseeable future.

Agencies like American Farmland Trust, MA Food Policy Council, regional food policy working groups and others are all working toward a comprehensive, bottom-up solution to known and foreseeable issues related to production, distribution, quality, and availability issues to insure a universally affordable food resource. 50 x 60 in New England will be the best achievable solution to a very complex question, which will focus our thoughts about food justice, quality of life, environmental and economic health. &

– Farmer's Diary, Winter 2015 (Excerpt), Edible Boston, Winter 2015, reprinted with permission

John Lee is the manager of Allandale Farm (Boston's last working farm). He writes for local news outlets and is deeply involved with farming and locally grown issues in Massachusetts.

Promotion Program (FMPP), surveying and selectively interviewing FMPP grantees (2006 – 2011). Their website reveals how these grants have benefited communities and even statewide organizations. The FMC website offers the full report, Green Paper, four case studies and a slideshow highlighting the main findings.

Market programs frequently have multiple benefits. Santa Monica's school salad bar program, launched in 1995 to expand economic opportunities for farmers, has given teachers a way to present to students the issues of locally produced food, health and small business. By 2007 it had led to similar farm-to-school education programs in more than 700 school districts in 36 states.

> "This program showed me that children will choose fresh, healthy food in the school cafeteria if we make it available."
>
> – Tracie Thomas, assistant director of student nutrition services for Compton Unified School District, in Urban & Environmental Policy Institute report, Occidental College, CA

[See Resources Online for more references to policy or economic studies.]

Food Policy Councils

In September 2009, Urban & Environmental Policy Institute (UEPI) at Occidental College was instrumental in Los Angeles Mayor Antonio Villaraigosa announcing a new city Food Policy Task Force at "30 Years and Growing." The event celebrated 30 years of farmers' market development in Los Angeles, and the task force was created to help improve poor communities' access to fresh food, foster deeper connections with regional farms and encourage green farming.

The task force's work led to the creation in 2010 of the Los Angeles Food Policy Council, to bring Los Angeles in line with the emerging "good food" movement nationwide.

As of September 2014 there were 200 Food Policy Councils in the U.S., 57 in Canada and 6 in tribal nations. Only a smattering of these existed in 2000. Sixty percent are independent grassroots coalitions, 21% are independent 501(c)(3) nonprofit organiza-

tions, and 19% are government-appointed advisory bodies.

Starting in the late 1970s, some academic experts and food activists began to see how the food system was intertwined with environmental, public health, social and economic justice, and other issues. While agricultural production accounted for over $331 billion by 2009, with similar sums attributable to processing, distributing and marketing those products, there were and are tremendous health and other impacts for people eating within that system.

By 2030 U.S. obesity rates are predicted to reach a staggering 42%, up from 34% in 2012, at an estimated treatment cost of $550 billion annually. FPCs bring together community stakeholders in an effort to address food system issues that reflect their values. Each council addresses food policies in their own way, whether through farmers' market start-up, permanent sites and structures, farmland preservation, appropriate ag land taxation, food business start-up support, etc. This can also be done without a FPC through the periodic review process of city and country comprehensive plans.

> "Food policy is a set of collective decisions made by governments at all levels, businesses, and organizations that affect how food gets from the farm to your table. A food policy can be as broad as a federal regulation on food labeling or as local and specific as a zoning law that lets city dwellers raise honeybees."
>
> – Michael Burgan and Mark Winne, Doing Food Policy Councils Right: A Guide to Development and Action, 2012

Good Food Awards

Starting in 2011, the Good Food Awards were envisioned as a celebration of the tasty, authentic and responsibly produced food we all want to eat. Each January at San Francisco's Ferry Building, awards are bestowed on farmers and food producers who epitomize craftsmanship and sustainability while enhancing the agricultural landscape and building strong communities. Many of these producers got their start and are still selling at farmers' markets. Producers

Harv Singh, the Northern California specialty foods buyer for Whole Foods, tastes a sample from a Good Food Award winner outside the Ferry Plaza Marketplace after the inaugural award ceremony in 2011.

winning a Good Food Award often use it to gain access to top restaurants and gourmet markets. See:

www.goodfoodawards.org.

Good Food Jobs

From bakers to butchers, from farms to foundations, Good Food Jobs provides a valuable job listing site for all kinds of food-related entities at a nominal price. Taylor Cocalis and Dorothy Neagle started the jobs search website to connect good food businesses with people who wanted a good food job. Starting in 2010, they listed more than 20,000 jobs in their first five years. See:

http://goodfoodjobs.com/.

Good Food Jobs also hosts "the gastrognomes," a blog full of engaging food professionals who will inspire food lovers to new passion in their work.

 ## THE FARMERS' MARKET FORUM: ISSUES FOR INTERNAL DISCUSSION

We addressed integrity in the chapter on management, yet it bears repeating as an issue evoking considerable debate in the future. With farmers' markets becoming more attractive as marketing venues, other companies will want to take advantage

of their success. Sponsoring boards will debate what range of products to include and whether national brands and franchisees should be allowed. The outcome may depend upon existing competition, alternative local outlets that might be approached first and the level of commitment to development of a localized food system.

Real Farmers?

A 2006 survey of farmers' markets conducted by the U.S. Department of Agriculture found that 63% of markets stipulate that "vendors can sell only products they produced themselves." That is the first step to an authentic experience for the consumer, but not every market wants to have that rule because it might limit their product mix.

If the standard is in place, more farmers should be actively promoting a customer satisfaction guarantee that includes "if we sell it, we grow it – 100 percent." Valuing their own participation, vendors need to report suspected rule abuses to the manager, assist in inspections, support fines for infractions, and insist on adherence to the highest standards of integrity. Certain markets have already hurt themselves and tarnished the image of farmers' markets in general by having a loose or non-existent standard.

Maintaining market standards is not easy, given market seasons and local production patterns. Market managers nationally reported to USDA that a median of 81% of vendors sold only what they produced. It varied from 61% in the Rocky Mountains to 94% in the Southwest.

Managers said that 25% of vendors used their market as their sole marketing outlets, down somewhat from five years earlier. They are diversifying their marketing channels further.

Sixty percent of farmers' market managers in the USDA survey reported that all sales were directly to final consumers. Another 38.3% said that direct-to-consumer transactions were 76% to 99% of all sales.

Only 1.6% said direct sales were between 51% to 75% of total sales.

A push for reappraisal of state law, as in Maine and California, may be necessary in other states to clarify who can use the term farmers' market, and what producers should be allowed.

By the same token, we may see markets defining themselves more frequently as "local" by having a distance limit on producers, e.g., 50 miles. Others may use certain geographical boundaries, supporting producers within a watershed or "foodshed." As markets align with other organizations promoting a regional economy, these standards will evolve with individual variations.

Market Competition

As with individual farmers, managers are more aware of the need to improve when they have another farmers' market nearby. However, most markets already have nearby competition in the form of retailers who will take our customers if we are not vigilant, creative and responsive to the local populace.

Good managers and good boards are motivated to be the best, regardless of the competition. They look at other farmers' markets as friends, supporters and helpers in the overall drive to attract and hold customers as farmers' market loyalists. We share in common the goal of improving farmers' lives through educating local residents about the importance of supporting local agriculture. Without this active commitment – this partnership of those who believe in a regional food economy – our farms will continue to disappear as they have during the last century.

Strong markets do not hesitate to establish fees that reflect the real value that they provide producers. Jim O'Neill, former manager of the Old Strathcona Farmers' Market in Edmonton, Alberta, explained the pricing of a corner space at $64 per day versus $53 for a regular aisle space, "People want the corners. They recognize the value of additional display space." With good oversight of additional income, the market can implement a promotion program to continue improving their market share vis-à-vis other competitors.

Market sales data will help markets retain good managers. A governing board has solid information on which to base personnel decisions. Dianne Stefani-Ruff became the first Portland manager to receive a full-time salary plus an incentive bonus derived from gross sales and net market operations. Increasingly, markets are recognizing the high cost of manager turnover. A sign of sustainable farmers' markets is the evolution of salaries commensurate with a job done professionally. Markets unable to pay comparable wages need to provide learning opportunities, praise, recognition and a flexible work schedule if they are to keep good employees.

Farmer Competition

Many farmers are riding on the coattails of other vendors, failing to do their part in what has to be a collective effort at merchandising if they expect their marketplace to sustain itself. Seeing competition within a supermarket should give farmers reason to pause in their complaints. Encountered in a recent supermarket visit were three organic milks, five different soy milks and seven yogurts – all in six linear feet of refrigerated space.

Strong markets recognize the critical role of substantial competition within many different product categories. One individual seller reminded this author how much she appreciated a new carrot grower – the fifth one – in pushing her to a higher standard of quality, value, merchandising, friendliness, customer service and the introduction of new product line. That response shows her sophistication in marketing and her positive view of her own product and selling ability. Unfortunately, many of us become lazy or unimaginative when we are too comfortable with our position.

Celebrate a new competitor in the market who jolts you into new product development. It's better to have a good competitor in our market reminding us what we need to do than to have him/her enticing our customers outside the farmers' market. We all know we are more complacent when we aren't staring a threat directly in the face.

Like it or not, small farmers should prepare for the continued entry of mid-sized and larger farms into farmers' markets, especially urban markets with substantial product movement. As the largest growers increase exports and sign more direct supermarket contracts, those in the middle are looking to replace sales lost to wholesale markets. They are part of America's farm heritage that needs protection by personal initiative.

Often ignored is the fact that overall sales in many markets are dominated by farms well above the "small farm" definition limit of $350,000 sales annually. Certainly, that standard may not be reasonable if one expects to send kids to college, but an analysis of one urban multi-market association showed 3% of their vendors with farmers' market sales of $1 million or more. Over 11% of their vendors were selling at more than 20 farmers' markets.

Farmers' markets will satisfy the need of new farmers to enter the market realm, test new products and varieties, notice whether they are sufficiently people oriented and practice their customer relation skills.

There will be more pressure on management to be professional in dealing fairly with questions of access. Waiting lists will become more sophisticated including point systems focusing on prioritized crops and varieties, organic and specialty production, farm size, environmental impact, worker safety and other issues.

Across the United States several model programs are attempting to give farmers increased market access and higher price in the conventional marketing system. These will be used within farmers' markets as well. The Food Alliance, founded in Portland, OR in 1994, now has certification standards met by various farms and food handlers in 20 states that are committed to continual improvement, reducing chemical dependence, protecting natural resources, supporting safe working conditions and guaranteeing food integrity.

The competition, especially in good markets, will force farmers to clearly address how their products stand out from the rest. Individuals concerned about too much competition should be asked: If you were selling on your own, without any competition nearby, would people be attracted to stop at your stand?

THE FARMERS' MARKET FORUM: ISSUES FOR PUBLIC DISCUSSION

Many issues may be considered internal – for association discussion only. However, once these issues have had that discussion, it is often healthy to bring the dialogue out into the public realm. Indeed, consumers and the larger community often have a real stake in the outcome, and may help bring clarity to the issue.

Winter Markets

Increasingly, markets have been stretching their seasons as farmers build tunnels or greenhouses to lengthen their season or add new crops. When the Portland Farmers Market (OR) first did a Thanksgiving market, it set a new record for one-day sales; there was no lack of product, yet many vendors sold out in two hours; there was simply an outpouring of pent-up demand for a longer season.

From artisans to holly and Christmas tree growers, vendors may push to gain the benefit of holiday shoppers. Rightly so, given that it is the #1 buying season of the year.

A significant number of markets have grown into year-round operations, keeping vendors alive, avoiding the potential loss of customers each year, and addressing food security on a continual basis. The Hillsdale market was the first in Oregon to go year-round; they have had strong winter markets – every other Sunday – since 2006.

"We have found that this is where our microgreen production is most appreciated by consumers. Given that the local winter produce is more limited in variety and quantity, people pay a bit more attention to the smaller, more delicate items. We also sell our winter flowers, herbs and greens at our winter markets.

"The winter markets have been particularly lucrative for our farm in the months of November and December. We have been selling fresh evergreen wreaths with dried flower/pods/cones accents for two decades now via special order or at local craft shows. Now, having weekly Saturday farmers markets during the holiday season has been keeping us profitably busy in a season that used to see more money flowing out than in. We've expanded into selling loads of center-pieces, holiday bouquets, flowering narcissus, rosemary 'trees' and many assorted types of wreaths besides the traditional evergreen wreaths."

> – Linda Chapman, Harvest Moon Flower Farm, Spencer, IN in *Growing for Market,* March 2011

About 12% of farmers' markets in the U.S. operate during the winter, and the number is growing. Most markets are affected; they expand from three to four months, from six to nine months, or perhaps they have made these gradual changes and they test a monthly market through the winter.

Year-round markets vary by region. In the Far West, 35.4% of farmers' markets are year-round. (This figure is probably low given the poor response rate of managers running multiple markets.) On the other end of the spectrum, only 3.5% of markets in the Northeast are year-round, according to the 2006 USDA study of market managers.

In 2005 seasonal farmers' markets averaged 4.5 months of operation, according to USDA. The Far West, Southwest and Southeast were open longer, given their warmer climates and longer growing seasons.

Urban Agriculture

Winter markets are made easier by more urban farms. From Brooklyn Grange Farm in Queens to Rising Pheasant Farms in Detroit and Ghost Town Farm in West Oakland, numerous creative people are growing food in unusual places. While volume may be a goal, the real value is in reaching over 80% of Americans who live in urban areas. Urban agriculture is multiple

Novella Carpenter of Ghost Town Farm, and author of Farm City, is one of the urban farms profiled in the Lexicon of Sustainability.

stories that encompass empty warehouses, rooftop gardens, utility strips and vacant lots.

> "Urban agriculture's real contribution is not in the quantity of food that it grows, but in the number of people it touches who can then understand and learn about food, how we grow it and how it feeds us."
>
> – Eli Zigas, Food Systems & Urban Agriculture Program Mgr., SPUR, San Francisco, CA

People are creating businesses by growing gardens in others' backyards, because homeowners want the garden but not the work. Two guys in L.A.'s San Fernando Valley started suburban micro Winnetka Farm, where "local is my own backyard." Others like Will Allen with Growing Power in Milwaukie have developed food production systems inspiring people across the Midwest. Many of these farms are concentrating on high-value crops with quick turnover.

Among them are controlled environment agriculture (CEA) players like Farmed Here, with 25 crops per year and a million pounds of baby greens, basil and mint, all from a 90,000 s.f. warehouse outside Chicago. However, CEA is controversial because of its high energy demands with artificial lighting.

Through The Food List, more than 300 thought leaders, activists and advocates are sharing their words and ideas in a weekly cross-media format to move us toward a sustainable food future. These new farmers add a vibrancy, intensity and curiosity that can be appealing to the next generation of market shoppers.

The Lexicon of Sustainability™ is based on a simple premise: people will live more sustainably if they understand the most basic terms and principles that will define the next economy. See:

http://lexiconofsustainability.com/

Sponsors

Just as car dealers have sponsored farmers' markets in the past, new food alliances are being created to support markets. Dave's Killer Bread began its story at the Portland Farmers Market, and after several years it gave up its place to new bakers. However, they didn't want to let go of their roots, so they continue to sell on a once a month basis as a major market sponsor.

The Bellingham market has Friends donation levels from "Cabbage" at $25 to the Heirloom Tomato level with a $1,000 donation. The mayor tosses out a cabbage to open the market in early April.

Connecting with artist organizations is one of many avenues for profitable linkages. In Woodland,

The International Culinary School at The Art Institute of Portland (OR) has been a major market sponsor. It gains new students by its association with a premier market, and then builds the farmer-chef connection into its program so new chefs continue to buy from local farms wherever they go.

© City of Lexington

Fifth Third Bank Pavilion in Lexington, KY is event space, performing arts venue and farmers' market. It has huge fans below the skylights that generate cooling breezes. It also hosts the 5/3 Thursday Night Live music series, weekly from April through October.

CA the Market on Main developed a series for all of May, 2015 leading up to a May 30th Chalk on the Block. Modeled after Chalk it Up in Sacramento and Pastels on the Plaza in Humboldt County, the event invited all levels of artists to chalk up a square in Heritage Plaza with a farmers' market theme. Events like these can be fun fundraisers, with each square sponsored by businesses and community members who want more art in town.

There are numerous potential sponsors awaiting a market's creative planning. Start small, yet respect the value inherent in your weekly reminder to consumers of the value of sponsors who help keep your market alive.

Premier Sites and Buildings

In 2014 USDA pointed out that many unique locations have been part of our expansion to 8,268 farmers' markets. They include ferry terminals, train depots, grain mills and shipping containers.

In Knoxville, TN, the Southern Railways Station architecture has justified its repurposing into office spaces and a banquet hall where a monthly winter farmers' market takes place.

In Chester Springs, PA, a water-powered mill was restored in 2004, the millstones once again mill flour after a 70-year rest, and a weekly farmers' market attracts traffic to add to the mill's history buffs.

Markets often demonstrate significant growth in sales when they erect a building. With the right site, the City and other funders may come forward in helping pay for construction. Many factors come into play.

Seasonal markets nationwide averaged $135,500 in 2005, while year-round markets hit six times that amount, or $833,958 each. Even analyzing on a monthly basis to avoid the bias created by a longer season, year-round market sales were $70,292 per month versus $28,836 per month for seasonal markets. [USDA]

In Brooklyn, NY, the DeKalb Market operates in several colorful shipping containers, amidst artists, craftsmen and chefs. Similar shipping container farmers' markets are operating on undeveloped lots in Boston and Raleigh.

The Bellingham Farmers Market in the far northwest corner of Washington was opened in 1993. It existed on a shoestring with a loyal but small customer base for a full decade, never going over $0.5 million in gross vendor sales, as seen in the graph starting with its second decade of operation.

When the board made a commitment to establishing a market structure that would also be available for community use, they embarked on a fundraising effort which ultimately raised $2.7 million including city, county, state and federal help. A local Rotarian, Brian Griffith, committed to raising $50,000 from customers at the market which would be matched by his Rotary.

Beginning in 2004, all the fundraising efforts created some consternation among area nonprofits that depended on limited local resources as well. The fundraising friction made newspaper headlines for several years as the building was being developed. All the media attention served to build public awareness of the market, and sales jumped by about $200,000 during both 2004 and 2005.

With a longer season and the opening of the Market Depot pavilion in 2006, sales went up another $250,000 and by $350,000 in 2007, when sales were triple those of the market only four years earlier.

Having expanded to an April-to-Christmas season with the new building, the market directors felt confident of public support about a winter market. After surveying enough farmers who were ready with season extenders like hoophouses, in 2012 they launched their once-a-month winter market from January to March.

From 2009 to 2014 sales consistently exceeded $1.8 million. With the extra winter sales, it is nearly a $2 million market.

There is room for more than 100 vendors in the 5,200 s.f. pavilion and three 125' sheds, built on a rectangular layout on a city parking lot. Winter market days are split in thirds among farmers, artisans, and prepared food and concessionaires.

Much of the steel for the pavilion came from the Skagit River bridge which was torn down during the lengthy fundraising process including federal, state, city and private sources.

For its first decade the Bellingham Farmers Market sales never exceeded $500,000. While raising $2.7 million dollars to construct a market building, public awareness and attendance grew. The market building allowed for more vendors and year-round operation, leading to nearly quadrupled annual sales.

The Bellingham Farmers Market is proof of what a community can build, even with a short season agriculture. With the city's population growing in the first 20 years of the market from 56,000 to 82,000, the market is poised to help Bellingham continue to grow as a great city for locals and tourists alike.

Every market does not need a structure, although rising sales prove the benefit. Every market, however, does deserve an attractive, consistent location which customers can depend on. In spite of tight funding, markets are increasingly trying to stabilize their future by ensuring a permanent location. A market with good customer rapport over a lengthy period should qualify for consideration by the city, a foundation or service club to assist in this goal. For many the goal of permanence will be helped by a market building. Several new buildings are finding high demand from other users when the market is not open.

The Carrboro FM (NC) building on the Town Commons protects product and people and has helped the market go year-round on Saturday.

"Since our farmers' market is in a heated and cooled building owned by the City, we are year-round. The market runs Saturdays 7 a.m. to 1 p.m. Our staff then flips it for rental at 3 p.m. We do a lot of pairings with nonprofits, and 40 weddings per year. Some annual events have space booked four years ahead. Every Saturday and 80% of our Fridays are booked over a year out. Every event held at our 22,000 s.f. market building makes people aware of the farmers' market, so having a permanent building has been a real boon to market growth."

– Shelly Mazur, Mgr., Royal Oak Farmers Market, MI

As markets are constructed, the quality of produce, displays and the overall character of markets will improve with the result that more farmers' markets will be asked to set up in premier locations. These sponsoring locations will seek higher standards to complement downtown Main Street programs, malls, parks and other retail experiences. Larger businesses will look to sponsor a farmers' market or elements within it, such as cooking demonstrations, entertainment and special events.

As they come to the fore, downtown business people will become better customers, their interest and involvement accelerated by market basket CSAs run by the market. Travel companies, hotels, leisure resorts and other businesses will seek face-to-face contacts with high-end customers through more tie-in promotions. Banks, restaurants, car sales outlets, hardware stores and other retailers will continue to be good partners in communities at all socio-economic levels.

Professional architects will more frequently incorporate design elements for comfort, functionality and attractiveness, including public seating, heating, electricity, shade, public art, restrooms, telephones and color.

Where markets have existed for at least a decade, cities will seek to validate their importance by building or converting buildings for market use. Multi-use facilities with primary market use such as in Davis, CA, and re-use facilities such as Edmonton, Alberta's converted bus barn will become more prevalent.

These market buildings may be simple steel shed structures like the Cartwright Pavilion in Marshalltown, IA, or they may include a clerestory element allowing heat to escape the city parking lot in Pasco, WA.

Based on a city bond, Olympia constructed a double row shed with a center pavilion and sliding, barn-like doors that allow airflow or close to keep the space warmer. Ithaca's open, clerestory, wood structure is T-shaped and, like Olympia, includes rest-

During a rainstorm, this Edmonton, AB market moved into an abandoned City bus barn, and never left. Ten years later the City wrote a lease.

THE NEW FARMERS' MARKET

rooms and an office. It was built largely through donations and vendors' sweat equity.

Ithaca also garnered state funds available through a farmers' market expansion program created by the legislature in the 1980s, inspired by Bob Lewis of the New York State Department of Agriculture and Markets.

Philip and Judith Chute were visionaries who started a Wisconsin market in 1994. Philip also doggedly attended city council meetings for years in order to secure a covered home for the market in 2006. The site is a city park at the confluence of two rivers. The market website declares that "in years to come we will tell about the man who founded and managed the Eau Claire Downtown Farmers' Market. The man who changed the very fortunes of families and farms in the Chippewa Valley."

When a market building is erected, each effort needs a leader – manager, farmer or citizen – and the active imagination and involvement of market vendors and community members ready to create an environment more conducive to a lengthened season and a more secure future.

> "The Santa Fe Farmers' Market Pavilion is the heart of the City's Railyard development plan. It is not only a permanent, year-round home for the market, but has become a gathering place and an important resource for community and nonprofit events."
>
> – Kierstan Pickens, Executive Director, Santa Fe FM Pavilion, NM

The Olympia FM has an open, airy feeling due to its high ceilings, skylights and visible wood trusses.

Supporting the Local Farm Economy

Labeling programs are being recognized for their value in promoting a local region as with the Puget Sound Fresh program (WA), a countywide program such as the Sonoma Select campaign (CA) or a statewide program such as Pick Tennessee. Farmers' markets can connect to these programs through mutual advertising and membership. Reinforce the local label at your market.

The Massachusetts Department of Food and Agriculture has done consumer focus groups and phone surveys, discovering that customers want to buy local but they don't know much about local agriculture. "Most people in the survey said if the quality was good and the price was fair they would buy local," says market bureau chief Susan Allan. "Most farmers could do a better job labeling their locally grown produce. Customers don't often know what's in season and they don't know whether or not produce in supermarkets is locally grown. A few counties are looking into the labeling of regional products, and our office offers the 'Massachusetts Grown and Fresher' logo, as well as signs and stickers and artwork for farmers to use in their advertisements or put on their trucks. A lot of farmers' markets, roadside stands and an increasing number of supermarkets use our logo."

Diane Green of Sandpoint, ID, says that, "The strength of a farmers' market lies in promoting 'locally grown.'" In many communities the increasing diversity of farmers and farm products is making the local marketplace reflect how interconnected the peoples of the world have become. With an incredible variety of ethnic foods and faces, the global village has become local.

Immigrants are providing a new generation of active farmers reinvigorating markets. Often they are at a disadvantage selling through wholesale markets – linguistically and otherwise – so farmers' markets offer a wonderful chance to make cash and learn English quickly. The immigrant farmers help spread the word through their informal networks to increase the participation of more minority customers as well.

Markets should be building close associations with local agricultural organizations. As managers become

The Farmers' Market Pavilion at Phoenix Park in Eau Claire, WI is a U-shaped building 216' long with 96' sides.

more professional and have more time, farmers' markets will seek periodic visits from 4-H programs, petting zoos, pony rides, Master Gardeners, Master Food Preservers, Master Composters and those able to educate about agriculture in general. Managers need to engage organizations in conversation, suggesting programs in which they are interested, looking for sponsorship of special ag awareness days, and asking how they are most interested in connecting to market customers.

Farm Loss

"For one final moment in our evolution as a nation we still have a community memory of the family farm. Many still carry the personal baggage from our rural past, a history of family members who sustained the land, and the legacy of a community that worked the earth for generations. But this is the final generation holding an affinity with the American family farm. This is the generation that will control the destiny not only of my Sun Crest peaches but also of my way of life."

– David Mas Masumoto, *Epitaph for a Peach*

Among the many reasons for farm loss in this century are the industrialization of agriculture, processor and middlemen control, competition from imports, government policies and population changes.

In 1900, for every $1 spent on food in the United States, 20 cents went for marketing and 15 cents went to input costs such as land, equipment and fertilizer. The farmer received 65 cents of every dollar.

By 1990, marketing had tripled to 60 cents and inputs had increased by two-thirds to 25 cents. The farmer was left with a fraction of what he had ninety years earlier, 15 cents on the dollar.

Much of the agricultural establishment and press has emphasized the need for producers to cut costs, but no matter how much they do, as other farmers do the same, they will be pinched even further. Like the corporate food barons, farmers need to vertically integrate; they do so as they take back control over marketing their products. They can't survive getting 15 cents of each dollar. They need to take that other 60 cents now eaten up by processors and marketers.

"Educating customers about produce comes naturally at the farmers' markets with the everyday banter with customers. If someone says my prices are too high, I explain that the price of food is too cheap. A lot of farmers are going out of business because food is too cheap. The USDA for years has had a cheap food policy, 'Get big or get out.' We explain about the centralization of the food industry, and how produce is used by supermarkets as a loss-leader to battle each other for customers. Food is also cheap because it's grown by low-paid workers in Mexico and Chile with pesticides, or with federally subsidized water in California where they couldn't grow it otherwise. We also talk about buying local food and what it means for the local economy."

– Tom Roberts, Snakeroot Organic Farm, Pittsfield, ME

U.S. Secretary of Agriculture Dan Glickman acknowledged in 1998: "I'm not afraid of running out of wheat or corn. I'm afraid of running out of farmers." The USDA considers farmers' markets and organic agriculture to be important economic vehicles for keeping folks on the farm. With six hundred family farmers going out of business each week, these alternatives need to be consistently re-thought. We need constant improvement to increase sustainability.

America has shifted from being 75% rural to being 80% urban. That urbanization has concentrated retail power as independent grocers have been consumed by larger and larger entities, leaving people with farther to travel. The impact of the automobile cannot be denied; as people travel farther to go to big box stores for cheaper food, farmers' markets must compete on a different basis – quality and service.

The 2010 U.S. census revealed continued shifts among our 309 million population, impacting the South and West, making farmland loss a big story. Development threatens valuable farms along almost the entire West Coast, from Canada to Mexico. It is much the same in the South as people flood to the coasts. The Northeast long ago faced the pressure of overpopulation and struggles to maintain farms close to its cities. Once surrounded by rich farmland, Philadelphia new receives 70% of its food from out of state. Distant farms can easily compete since real transportation costs are subsidized. Thus, farmers' markets become essential in providing higher returns to cover the costs of farming close to cities.

> "People should be educated to see the choice: support local farms and keep a balanced landscape or the land will sprout houses instead."
>
> – Dean Bruschi, Martin County, FL

The farmers' market "movement," so-called given the dedication and enthusiasm of its foremost activists, has succeeded in slowing, and in certain areas reversing, the decline in the number of farms and of local, small and micro enterprises. We have provided an entry point into the world of commerce for many new businesses, including those owned by youth, minorities, immigrants and second-attempt farmers.

As various pressures force farmers and others out of business, many will re-tool their minds and re-invest in agriculture and other food enterprises with an entirely new focus. Unnoticed by statisticians, one business dies and a stronger one emerges – a process increasingly seen in farmers' markets.

Food Selection

Food business start-ups include the predictable to the novel – Grandma's molasses cookies to vegetarian sushi rolls. More delicacies are appearing as food connoisseurs recognize the opportunity to start micro-enterprises around their favorite old recipes or newest creations. Dessert cakes, cookies, fruit chutneys, teriyaki sauce, pad thai, pickled products, fudge, cheesecake, bagels, pestos, smoothies and salsas.

In warmer climates entrepreneurs will consider opening juice bars. More hot and prepared food businesses will open within markets and nearby to take advantage of market pedestrian traffic. Markets will have "food courts" much as the Old Oakland Farmers' Market, CA, as businesses offer tastes of the familiar and the boutique to ethnically diverse consumers. Our food experiences and tastes will expand.

We will see an expanded array of products within farmers' markets. The challenge is to introduce new tastes to people. Tastings will continue to surge in popularity with new and old varieties of peaches, tomatoes and melons competing for customers' loyalty. The most progressive markets will attempt to lure people across ethnic lines by combining the familiar with the bold. Along with a fall tomato tasting where one can compare fresh tomatoes and tomato soup, they will offer bittermelon soup and bittermelon leaves braised in oil. These advances will be triggered in part by chefs who are constantly experimenting with cross-cultural innovations.

As a greater number of local, non-farm businesses take part, personal and political connections abound. The support and dependence of urban, non-farm businesses on farmers' markets heightens city interest in downtown markets. As a local market economy builds, a physical structure to house the farmers' market for an extended season becomes more realistic.

Corporate Control

With most of the producers in farmers' markets being organic and/or small farmers, there is considerable concern about large farmers. Thus, it is understandable that there would be real apprehension about the danger to our communities of a corporate agriculture that concentrates too much power in too few hands.

California has some of the best examples. Surplus water from the California Water Project began arriving in 1973, delivered to growers on the backs of many urban water districts' taxpayers. Kern County has regularly taken the majority of project water. In the first nine years, they received 1.8 million acre-feet of water, according to the Marc Reisner's book *Cadillac Desert,* for about $6 million; the rest of the $170 million cost was paid by Metropolitan Water District customers in Los Angeles for water they never received.

Two-thirds of the Kern district acreage – or 227,545 acres – receiving this subsidized water was owned by eight companies: Chevron, Tejon Ranch, Getty and Shell (each with over 30,000 acres), Prudential Insurance's McCarthy Ranch, Blackwell Land Company (foreign investors), Tenneco and Southern Pacific Railroad (which owns more than 800,000 acres across the state).

On land whose value increased from $50 to $2,000 per acre as a result of the Water Project, Prudential's 5,000 acres of olives near Bakersfield matured in 1978. Immediately, California's olive production expanded by 46%, and prices plummeted. Prudential gave a sweetheart deal to the state's largest independent olive processor to take all their olives for less than the harvesting cost alone. Hundreds of small producers were devastated; a few found salvation in farmers' markets but most went under.

As Prudential was to olives, Tenneco was to almonds, the largest producer in the U.S. In 1981 Tenneco made a similar power play to control the almond market.

"They pay a severance tax to California on oil they pump off Long Beach, which is immediately put into a fund that makes annual interest-free 'loans' of 25 million a year to the State Water Project, which delivers doubly subsidized irrigation water to their formerly worthless land," notes Reisner.

When Congress allowed farmers to deduct all expenses on crops, principally fruits and nuts, while they were maturing and bearing no fruit, it gave farmers encouragement to invest. Unfortunately, corporations took advantage, investing their millions from oil, banking and railroad profits. With the help of 1960s tax law and 1970s Water Project, these corporate "farmers" threaten and dispose of countless small specialty growers.

At the Food and Agriculture Day in Seattle on December 2, 1999, farmers from more than 30 countries participated in a church breakfast followed by panel discussions, press briefings, workshops and a noon rally at the Pike Place Market. The topics included genetic engineering, food security in a globalized economy, and food safety.

Food and Ag Day finally brought the voices of small farmers and their supporters into the decades-old discussions about the world's food supply. Size, national rights and sustainability were at the core.

> "In 1998 in Canada, farm income was $29 billion…Cargill's revenues that same year were $75 billion. We are the model the world is supposed to follow…and we're dying of it…It is not the levelness of the playing field, but the size of the player. If the rules are in favor of the big players and the field is level, they will roll over us."
>
> – Nettie Wiebe, Canadian National Farmers Union

Farmers and consumers realize that farming as a way of life is threatened with extinction in many places. If free trade is a "rising tide that lifts all boats," one may ask why real wages are falling and 475 billionaires control assets equal to the annual income of 3 billion people, according to Jerry Mander of the International Forum on Globalization. While the level of corporate control is nearly absolute in many industries, everyone has an interest in assuring a safe and secure food supply based on a diversified delivery system. Farmers' markets are part of the solution in keeping tens of thousands of farmers on the land and connected to consumers.

Genetically engineered crops. Genetic engineering involves a set of very powerful tools that can change any life form on earth. Genetic traits that affect such factors as yield, hormone production, and cold or pesticide resistance can be moved across kingdoms –

from plants to animals, humans to plants, animals to bacteria. In Edinburgh scientists have inserted a fluorescent jellyfish gene into a potato so that it glows green when it needs water. Unfortunately, genes used to modify crops can jump the species barrier and cause bacteria to mutate. A German researcher found that the gene used to confer Roundup resistance was found in the genome of yeast and bacteria in the guts of bees.

Doreen Stabinsky, of the Council of Responsible Genetics, contrasted the general European approach to genetically engineered foods using the precautionary principle with the U.S. approach of regulating only where sound science indicates proof of actual harm. "As a scientist, I resent this misappropriation of the word 'science.'" She reinforced the right of nations to determine their own environmental protection standards without fearing World Trade Organization (WTO) sanctions.

Scientific and public skepticism about the unknown risks of gene splicing has led companies like Frito-Lay, Gerber, Heinz and Nestle to go GE-free with some or all of their products. About nine of every ten North Americans want GE foods to be labeled, but it is currently optional. A strong majority see GE foods as a safety issue; they do not break down in the gut as previously thought. Genetic drift, now known to be up to 12 km. (7 miles), threatens virtually all organic producers since the definition of organic excludes any genetically modified organism.

A statewide campaign to label GMO foods was tested in California in 2012, where Proposition 37 failed by less than 3% after a $45 million NO campaign was funded by Monsanto and other industry members. In 2013 Washington's Initiative 522 narrowly failed by 51%-49% – 38,000 votes of 1.7 million cast – after the Washington No campaign spent a record $22 million. In 2014 Oregon's Measure 92 failed by 809 votes of the more than 1.5 million votes cast.

In 2015 the Federal District Court upheld a GMO labeling bill passed by Vermont's legislature in 2014. As of July 2016 food for retail sale produced with any genetic engineering must be labeled.

Cars in Tacoma, WA promoted a "yes" vote on a ballot initiative that would have required genetically engineered foods to be labeled. A similar guerrilla marketing approach might be effective in grabbing the attention of potential farmers' market shoppers.

The Trans-Pacific Partnership threatens to derail Vermont and other state law that may follow. TPP not only will open the world to more free trade to take advantage of low-cost labor, but it also will make GMO labeling illegal. That puts farmers' markets in an advantageous position vis-a-vis ensuring that the American public has the right to know what they are eating. Surely, the government would not crack down on individual farmers proclaiming that they are not selling genetically modified crops. These farmers have been telling customers this since GMO crops were approved for human consumption in 1995.

In 2000, Genetically Engineered Food Alert discovered StarLink, a corn variety intended for animal feed, in taco shells intended for human consumption. The Taco Bell crisis sounded a consumer alert leading to the first ever recall of a genetically modified food. Aventis created a program to buy back corn that had been mixed with StarLink, which cost between $100 million and a billion. In 2003, farmers who had suffered economic losses from depressed corn prices after the recalls settled a class-action lawsuit for $100 million.

Bioengineered animal feed corn and regular corn for human consumption were not segregated at most grain elevators. Proper testing and government oversight were not in place. The FDA and the EPA lost consumer confidence in their oversight of GMO crops.

StarLink contains a pest-repelling protein, Cry9C, that may be hard for humans to digest. StarLink corn was found again contaminating foods in Saudi Arabia in 2013.

This is only the tip of the iceberg when we look at the unknowns of inserting genes across species. Research is forging ahead with government approval, without heed for the precautionary principle in protecting human health and the environment.

Some leading farmers' markets have concentrated on having a majority of organic farmers. As the debate over genetically engineered foods continues, markets are likely to declare themselves GE-free. They will be seen more prominently as the place to get straight answers from farmers about genetically engineered crops if actual GMO labels are prohibited outright.

Terminator and Traitor

Seeing the potential loss of seed as a right is one more reason for farmers and consumers to come together. Farmers need to maintain small seed companies and resist the temptation to purchase seed with Terminator and Traitor technology. According to a 2000 report by the Rural Advancement Foundation International (RAFI), both are on a fast track to commercialization.

Terminator technology, the genetic engineering of plants to produce sterile seeds, is universally considered the most morally offensive application of agricultural biotechnology, since over 1.4 billion people depend on farm-saved seeds. Traitor technology, also known as genetic use restriction technology (GURTs), refers to the use of an external chemical to switch on or off a plant's genetic traits. According to RAFI, the goal of genetic trait control is industry-wide and the multinational agrochemical firms dominating biotechnology hold more than 30 patents.

The Director General of the United Nations Food and Agriculture Organization (FAO) Jacques Diouf has declared his opposition to Terminator technology, defending the right of one-quarter of the world's population to save their seed for survival. It seems unbelievable that farmers could be forced to pay for seeds to which they have had free access for millenia.

Oddly, terminator technology now may become acceptable as organic farmers consider how to protect their fields from GE contamination. Food-safety groups are also concerned about food crop contamination by crops engineered to produce chemicals or pharmaceuticals. If genetically modified plants survive only one planting, the technology's threat seems to dissipate.

Massive political pressure on national governments and at key international fora will influence the debate just as boycotts will pressure elusive corporate decision-makers.

For an update, see Dr. Vandana Shiva's article, "The Seeds of Suicide: How Monsanto Destroys Farming," on the Centre for Research on Globalization (CRG) website at:

www.globalresearch.ca.

Water

With the Reclamation Law of 1902, Congress hoped to populate arid Western lands by subsidizing water for small, resident farms up to 160 acres. As farm size has increased with mechanization, the challenges to the 160-acre limit and residency requirements have continued. Larger corporations have controlled the political process, the water continues to be subsidized without regard for the acreage limits and the federal goal of helping small farmers has never been realized. It is generally small farmers without subsidized water who need and are selling at farmers' markets and in niche markets to get a higher price for their crops, while subsidized operations with larger economies of scale ship product around the world competing with other, more local farms.

There is a dangerous trend toward privatization of water resources, which will result in a bidding war among the large corporations and ultimately affect small farmers. Trade rules may precipitate a global water crisis. "Wars of the next century will be about water," said Maude Barlow of the Council of Canadians and author of Blue Gold: The Global Water Crisis and the Commodification of the World's Water Supply. Access to drinking water will be determined by wealth.

Indian physicist and food activist Vandana Shiva agrees, seeing the contest as one of drinking water for the poor versus swimming pools for the rich. People don't understand how a natural resource like water, anymore than seed, can be owned. This is why Shiva, author of *Biopiracy* and *Stolen Harvest,* is leading a "five freedoms movement" to declare freedom for water, seed, food, earth and the village forests and pastures.

NEW RELATIONSHIPS WITH HOPE

With articulate care farmers sample products, intermix flowers with vegetables, write 3x5 cards with recipes, laminate a Johnny's Seeds catalog description, remove yellow leaves, and protect the tendrils on mini-pumpkins. A curious question is met with an offer of a stem of mizuna or an entire crisp Asian pear; suddenly the customer feels befriended as an individual.

In displaying product and personality, farmers show themselves to be the characters they are. Through farming and interacting with farmers' market shoppers, each farmer serves as an exemplar for responsible citizenship.

Farms give our culture stability. Farmers' markets give farmers hope by providing an environment for meaningful experiences. In selling their crops, farmers notice customers' lives fulfilled, oddly enough, by some sense of connection to their labor. Just as in every other marketing channel, they need to build relationships, this time with many individual buyers. The person who does this will survive, because relationships mean you are listening and responding to the other. No one is guaranteed or owed a future

because of the past. Each day presents an opportunity to build trust through communication and a focus on value.

If we listen, communicate and develop relationships, we will travel to new places never imagined. An olive crop freezes and the grower starts making an olive oil soap with organic mint leaves. A farmer is trimming apricot and fig trees and the prunings go to Berkeley restaurant Chez Panisse for flavorful grilling.

Farmers should be doing periodic demonstrations at farmers' markets and constantly improving their presentations. Inviting customers for a farm tour each year – spring or fall – will spark a newfound loyalty and level of interest in their farms.

When you know your customers, you are more likely to treat your produce with greater respect. Show the best face of the food, stack less high, fill displays more often, avoid packing pint baskets too tight, leave it easier for customers to pick out their choice, and ask, "Does it hurt the food?"

Past and Present: Relationships in Community

For thousands of years markets have existed as caravans met on various trade routes. Cities sprang from these fountainheads as commerce and culture inextricably intertwined and evolved. Even as goods were exchanged, ideas were carried from one people to another. Democracy flourished with the healthy exchanges of an economy based on agrarian values. The two have been intertwined in the history of our national development as well. Our democracy has suffered in direct correlation with our shift from an agrarian to a corporate culture. It can be revived.

Today we still recognize the open dissemination of thought inherent in the exchanges among people from various backgrounds: rural and urban, local and

Chris Mezak of gC Farms in Greene, RI, proposed to Gwen Stokes by planting beans in a newly cleared field. When the green letters began to be legible, he asked her to go check the beans. She accepted. Such love will hopefully inspire another century of agriculture, a community of culture that loves the soil.

© Chris Mezak & Gwen Stokes

tourist, established and immigrant. Food is an essential connector. It is a vibrant vehicle for sharing and celebration, holding within it the power to shatter barriers and build relationships.

Just as bards and troubadours passed through the markets of yore, we need to stay receptive to the unexpected – the artist or juggler drifting through town, the Andean band or the mime troupe performing at the local junior college the evening before market day. Music and other art forms give a sense of community; they are integral to bringing people closer together. Cultural activities are drawn to good markets, and good markets are a barometer of local culture.

Markets also reflect the temperature of the local economy. As farmers go out of business, we recognize the heat of corporate control and shrinking competition. With each farm loss we further risk the very structure of our local economics and, ultimately, our localized culture. As new food entrepreneurs heat up our markets, we feel revitalized by the growing food culture in cities and countryside alike.

More communities will use farmers' markets as a tool to maintain or revive their local economy. New farmers' markets will express the goals of a new generation of young visionaries, market founders and farmers, who want personal, local relationships rather than an impersonal, world marketplace. Without becoming political in a larger global sense, people feel good about the politics of local food – taking a stand for maintaining small businesses in their own hometown. On that basis they increasingly will feel it appropriate to use the farmers' market as a vehicle for a public discussion about the issues of the day – how to determine water use policy, where to locate a new city hall, what to do about the homeless and underemployed, how to address the obesity epidemic, and how to creatively support the farms that beautify our local landscape.

Jim Tamai of Oxnard, here with his granddaughter, grew strawberries for decades. A son led the farm diversification into numerous vegetables. One daughter started a bakery to join the farm at L.A. markets. Another daughter moved 300 miles north to sell at Bay Area markets.

Aspiring to be the community center will become a broad goal, not something achievable only by markets in Madison, Davis or New York City. It is within the reach of virtually every market that plans and works toward that goal. Farmers' markets will be a focal point for public debate and community action, where people easily socialize with neighbors and new friends, building connections through our common love for food.

Farmers' markets are sustained through numerous positive relationships. While egos cause separation, farmers' markets have the transformative potential of connecting people. If we collectively envision our highest goals for true community and economic sustainability, our farmers' markets will become the centerpiece of community activity and pride even as they sustain the farms that form the true basis of a democratic society.

"Farmers' markets are the most democratic institution in America."

– Jim Hightower, Hightower Radio and former two-term elected Texas Commissioner of Agriculture ❧

Index

Sustainable Agriculture
Research & Education

SARE Resources

SARE's print and online resources cover a range of topics, from tillage tool selection to interpreting a soil test for your conditions to conducting effective market research. Resources include books, bulletins, fact sheets, webinars, videos and more. Most resources can be viewed in their entirety at www.SARE.org/Learning-Center.

BOOKS (www.SARE.org/Books)

Building a Sustainable Business (280 pp., $17)

Building Soils for Better Crops (294 pp., $20.95)

Crop Rotation on Organic Farms: A Planning Manual (154 pp., $24)

How to Direct Market Your Beef (96 pp., $14.95)

Manage Insects on Your Farm: A Guide to Ecological Strategies (136 pp., $15.95)

Managing Alternative Pollinators (158 pp., $23.50)

Managing Cover Crops Profitably (244 pp., $19)

The New American Farmer, 2nd Edition (200 pp., $16.95)

Organic Transition: A Business Planner for Farmers, Ranchers and Food Entrepreneurs (180 pp., $16.00)

Steel in the Field (128 pp., online only)

Youth Renewing the Countryside (171 pp., $24.95)

BULLETINS (For complete list, visit: www.SARE.org/Bulletins)

To Order: Visit www.SARE.org/WebStore or call (301) 779-1007. Please allow 10 days for delivery. Books: Shipping and handling fees apply. Prices are subject to change and bulk discounts are available. Bulletins: Bulletins are free (including standard shipping) and available in quantity to educators.

LOCAL AND REGIONAL FOOD SYSTEMS (www.SARE.org/Local-Food)

Discover a wealth of multi-media educational resources in SARE's Farm to Table: Building Local and Regional Food Systems topic room, including materials on business planning, marketing, distribution and aggregation, food safety, food processing and community development.

For other in-depth topic rooms visit: www.sare.org/Learning-Center/Topic-Rooms

GRANTS AND RESEARCH

To learn more about SARE grant opportunities, visit www.SARE.org/Grants. To explore sustainable agriculture topics on your own, search SARE's database of more than 5,000 funded research projects at www.SARE.org/Project-Reports.

Vance Corum

- Farmers' Markets America has more than 30 years of experience, starting the first farmers' markets in southern California and working with new and existing markets across North and South America.

- Experience in market research, site selection, branding, vendor outreach, organizational development, publicity, major tasting events, television, magazines, manager tours and seminars, consumer research, and economic development workshops – every aspect of market development in small towns and large cities.

- Speaker at national and regional conferences – across U.S., Canada, Cuba and India.

- Conference coordinator – national and regional conferences.

- Market tours based on hundreds of markets visited in North America, Eastern and Western Europe, Central and South America, and Asia.

- Consultation in person or by phone.

"The structure of the direct marketing industry in California is an ongoing tribute to Vance's creativity and foresight."

– Les Portello, Ex-Mgr., Direct Marketing Prog., Calif. Dept. of Food and Agriculture

"Vance …developed a set of recommendations which helped the market scale and improve its vibrancy."

– Scott Smith, Queen Anne FM, Seattle, WA

"Your keynote address…your images of farmers' markets around the world perfectly illustrated creative approaches to marketing in highly diverse communities…perfect tone for our conference."

– Mark Musick, Pike Place Market Farmer Coordinator, Seattle, WA

"We hired Vance to conduct a survey of our market shoppers. Vance is quick, efficient, and the results are terrific."

– Ben Feldman, Ecology Center, Berkeley FMs, CA

"Vance Corum offers the most diversified breadth of experience and exposure to all areas of direct marketing, including firsthand working knowledge of sites, organization, community development, marketing, and evaluation."

– Randii MacNear, Mgr., Davis FM (32 years)

- **Farmers' Market Development, Expansion, Rehab**
- **Conference & Seminar Speaker**
- **Special Events**
- **Board Training**
- **Market Research & Development**

Call Vance to learn how you can grow your market:

Farmers' Markets America
Vancouver, WA
(360) 693-5500
vcorum@gmail.com
www.farmersmarketsamerica.org

Marcie Rosenzweig

At the time of working on the first edition of *The New Farmers' Market,* I had stopped farming due to health issues and had started working on curriculum designed to help family scale producers with business planning and management skills. 2015 finds me living in the beautiful Willamette Valley in Oregon. Though semi-retired, I still consult with individual growers as well as non-profit organizations when asked.

Market Farm Forms is still available on the web in both new and used versions. Google will help you find it. I can be reached at:

marciearosenzweig@gmail.com.

"It worked!!! Thanks so much. I really appreciate it. I have already recommended it to lots of people. The templates are terrific. If you keep adding to them, I would love to purchase whatever you do - your work is top quality ...I can just imagine how great your veggies taste!"

– Blessings, Cheri

"Since purchasing this from Marcie earlier this year for a conference session I gave on small farming I've incorporated it into my record keeping and can't begin to say enough how well thought out this resource is. I've had my own haphazard record keeping and other methods, but this is so VERY organized. It's worth every penny."

– Michaele Blakely, *Growing Things,* Carnation WA

ATTRA's Steve Diver:

"Since it came to our attention here at ATTRA, some co-workers in vegetable production and agricultural economics have really been impressed at this genuinely useful and farmer-friendly book and spreadsheet combination. While a number of farm management spreadsheets exist, Market Farm Forms is the best one I've seen to help organize and calculate a mix of vegetables and related crops raised by market gardeners, truck farmers, and CSAs. On top of that, it supports the needs of certified organic growers with special features."